NOW YOU KNOW

BIG
BOOK OF
SPORTS

Featuring a special section of
OLYMPICS facts, legends, and lore!

NOW YOU KNOW

BIG
BOOK OF
SPORTS

Featuring a special section of
OLYMPICS facts, legends, and lore!

Doug Lennox

DUNDURN PRESS
TORONTO

Project Editor: Michael Carroll
Contributing Editor: Shaun Smith
Copy Editor: Jennifer McKnight
Design: Erin Mallory
Printer: Trancontinental

Library and Archives Canada Cataloguing in Publication

Lennox, Doug
    Now you know big book of sports / by Doug Lennox.

ISBN 978-1-55488-454-4

    1. Sports--Miscellanea. 2. Olympics--Miscellanea. I. Title.

GV707.L46 2009   796   C2009-902997-9

1   2   3   4   5   13   12   11   10   09

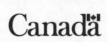

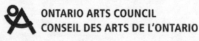

Conseil des Arts   Canada Council
du Canada   for the Arts

ONTARIO ARTS COUNCIL
CONSEIL DES ARTS DE L'ONTARIO

We acknowledge the support of **The Canada Council for the Arts** and the **Ontario Arts Council** for our publishing program. We also acknowledge the financial support of the **Government of Canada** through the **Book Publishing Industry Development Program** and **The Association for the Export of Canadian Books**, and the **Government of Ontario** through the **Ontario Book Publishers Tax Credit** program, and the **Ontario Media Development Corporation**.

Care has been taken to trace the ownership of copyright material used in this book. The author and the publisher welcome any information enabling them to rectify any references or credits in subsequent editions.

J. Kirk Howard, President

Printed and bound in Canada.
Printed on recycled paper.

www.dundurn.com

Dundurn Press   Gazelle Book Services Limited   Dundurn Press
3 Church Street, Suite 500   White Cross Mills   2250 Military Road
Toronto, Ontario, Canada   High Town, Lancaster, England   Tonawanda, NY
M5E 1M2   LA1 4XS   U.S.A. 14150

contents

preface

The vast collection of human activity called sports provides a fascinating portrait of humanity at both its best and worst. Courage, endurance, skill, tenacity, invention, cowardice, greed, pain, luck, weakness, and strength — these are just some of the qualities of human endeavour that run through the history of athleticism. They are the subject of this book.

Through questions, answers, lists, statistics, charts, and sidebars, I have tried here to assemble as detailed a collection of the most unusual, puzzling, revealing, and downright fascinating facts about sports as possible.

Who gained a winning edge with drugs, who disgraced themselves with rage, who defied the odds, and who won the love of the world? Who died on the ski slopes, who cheated at golf, who fought to win another day? What's inside a bowling ball? Where was rugby born? Why do the Japanese buy hole-in-one insurance? Where is the world's oldest curling pond? Who owns the all-time record for the most career stage wins in the Tour de France? (It's probably not who you think it is.)

All and more is here. From the power of F1 to the finesse of fencing. From the statistics of baseball to the brutality of boxing. From the speed of ice hockey to the strategy of football. A special section on the Olympics — Summer and Winter — offering material on every current official Olympic sport (plus a few extras) rounds out the collection just in time for the Vancouver 2010 Winter Games.

Let the games begin!

hockey

Where and when did hockey originate?

The location and the approximate date of ice hockey's origins, as with many sports, are much-debated and conjectured issues. Stick-and-ball games have deep roots and various types can be traced back to ancient Egypt, Persia, Greece, and Rome. Hockey appears to have evolved from a number of older sporting endeavours that employed some sort of stick (usually short and curved) and a ball: Irish hurling or hurley, Scottish shinty, English field hockey and bandy (the latter becoming popular in Scandinavia and Russia), Canadian/American shinny, and American ice polo. North American First Nations also likely influenced the development of stick games on ice and were probably inspired in turn by European games. *Gughawat,* or Indian shinny, and *baggataway,* or lacrosse, were certainly played by First Nations people when the first Europeans arrived on the scene. Both games utilized short, curved sticks, numerous competitors per team, and fierce competition (practically an all-out battle) for possession of a ball.

What is the origin of the word *hockey*?

The origins of the word *hockey* are almost as contentious as the question of who invented the game. One of the more popular derivations is the Old French *hoquet,* or "shepherd's crook," possibly a reference to the stick used in early forms of the game. Some think *hoquet* can be traced farther back to the Germanic root word *hok* or *hak*, which refers to a curved or bent piece of wood or metal. Likely, this is also the root of the English word *hook*. Nobody can say for sure, though. Hockey might just as easily owe its origin as a word to Scandinavia or Holland. One thing most people agree on, however, is that the word once signified the instrument of play rather than the game itself.

Quickies
Did you know ...
that just before British soldiers fled New York City in 1783 at the end of the Revolutionary War, they reportedly played a game of Irish hurling on skates, and that a version of hockey was played in Stoney Brook (today's Princeton), New Jersey, in the winter of 1786?

Why is street hockey called "shinny"?

Although shins take a beating during a game of shinny, the name comes from the Celtic game of *shinty*. A pick-up game of hockey, either on the street or on ice, shinny has no formal rules, and the goals are marked by whatever is handy. The puck can be anything from a ball to a tin can. There's no hoisting, bodychecking, or lifting the puck because no one wears pads. *Shinny* is a uniquely Canadian expression.

The first professional shin pads were hand-stitched leather-covered strips of bamboo, wrapped around the lower leg outside knee-high stockings.

For many Canadian kids during the 1930s and 1940s, copies of the Eaton's catalogue shoved into their socks were their first shin pads.

Who made the first hockey sticks?

The First Nations connection to the very first hockey sticks got a boost in early 2008 when the son of a Quebec City antique dealer acquired what he claims is a 350-year-old curved Mi'kmaq stick that he says proves Natives played hockey in Canada as early as the late seventeenth century. The man's assertion hasn't been met with much support among experts, but one thing is certain: the Mi'kmaq of Nova Scotia were carving single-piece hockey sticks at least as early as the 1870s and probably earlier. They utilized a wood known as hornbeam (also called ironwood) because of its strength. Later they turned to yellow birch when they exhausted the available hornbeam. These early sticks curved up like field hockey sticks and were much shorter and heavier than the kind used in modern ice hockey. The Starr Manufacturing Company in Dartmouth, Nova Scotia, started producing hockey sticks in the late nineteenth century under the brand names Mic-Mac and Rex. The company's sticks were immensely popular well into the 1930s. Starr was also famous for its skates, which it began manufacturing in the 1860s.

Quickies

Did you know ...

that the world's largest hockey stick is in Duncan, British Columbia, on Vancouver Island? The 207 foot, 32 ton wooden stick once adorned the entrance to Vancouver's Expo 86. Duncan has been home to the colossal stick since 1988 and has been trying for the past 20 years to get it recognized officially in The Guinness Book of World Records as the planet's largest. Recently, the town succeeded in its quest, though perhaps that has something to do with the fact that British Columbia billionaire Jimmy Pattison now owns the Guinness World Book Company, publisher of the famous record tome.

Who drew up the first recorded rules for organized hockey?

James George Aylwin Creighton, a McGill University student, a Halifax native, and the captain of one of the teams that played the first indoor hockey game in Montreal, has the distinction of drawing up the first recorded rules for organized hockey. He accomplished this feat in 1873, and the rules were published in the *Montreal Gazette* on February 27, 1877, after a series of four games between Creighton's Metropolitan Club and the rival St. James Club held in Montreal's Victoria Skating Rink. Creighton's rules, now called the Montreal Rules, likely derived from the earlier Halifax Rules. They are, in many respects, quite similar to the rules of field hockey.

When was the first organized hockey team founded?

On January 31, 1877, McGill University students started the first organized ice hockey club. Employing codified rules, hockey officials, and team uniforms, the McGill University Hockey Club played a challenge match against a loose collection of lacrosse and football players. McGill beat its opponents 2–1.

> **Quickies**
> *Did you know ...*
> that Montreal's Victoria Skating Rink, which opened for business in 1862, was the first building in Canada to be electrified, and was the scene of the first Stanley Cup playoff game in 1894? The arena closed for good in 1937. Today its site features a parking garage.

Why is Toronto's hockey team called the Maple Leafs?

In 1927, after having just been fired by the Rangers, Conn Smythe took the winnings from a horse race and bought the Toronto St. Pats hockey team, renaming them the Maple Leafs. Impressed with how brilliantly Canadians had fought in the First World War, Smythe named his new team after the soldiers' maple leaf insignia. Smythe is the man who said of hockey, "If you can't beat them in the alley, you can't beat them on the ice."

What was the first arena built especially for ice hockey?

There are two claimants to this distinction. Dey's Skating Rink in Ottawa was opened in December 1896 and was torn down in 1920. Ottawa, represented by the Ottawa Hockey Club (also known as the Silver Seven and the Senators), won its first Stanley Cup in 1903 at Dey's. The Montreal Arena, also called the Westmount Arena, began operations on December 31, 1898, and became home to a variety of teams, including Montreal's Shamrocks, Victorias, AAAs, Wanderers, and Canadiens. The rink burned down on January 2, 1918, causing the Wanderers to fold. The Canadiens moved back to the Jubilee Arena where they had played before taking up residence at the Montreal Arena.

> **Quickies**
> *Did you know ...*
> that the second organized hockey team in history was the Montreal Victorias, which debuted in 1881 and later went on to win the Stanley Cup in 1895, holding it from that year until 1899 (except for a challenge loss to the Winnipeg Victorias in 1896) when they lost it for good to the Montreal Shamrocks?

In the summer of 1919 the Jubilee also burned down, forcing the Canadiens to build and move to the Mount Royal Arena, the Habs' last rink before relocating to the Montreal Forum in 1926. The Mount Royal Arena, strangely enough, also burned down, but not until February 2000.

When was the first game in the National Hockey League played?

The first *two* games in the spanking new National Hockey League were played on December 19, 1917. The Montreal Wanderers edged the Toronto Arenas 10–9 and the Montreal Canadiens defeated the Ottawa Senators 7–4. The Wanderers' match only attracted 700 fans. Unfortunately for the Wanderers, once one of the greatest hockey teams and winners of the Stanley Cup four times, their arena burned down two weeks later and the franchise folded.

What was the first hockey book?

Montrealer and Hockey Hall of Famer Arthur Farrell was a star forward with the Montreal Shamrocks, winners of the Stanley Cup in 1899 and 1900. Farrell published the first known hockey book in 1899. It was called *Hockey: Canada's Royal Winter Game* and was more of a manual for the sport than a meditation about it, but at least it was a start. Farrell subsequently produced two other hockey publications. The third outlined the origins of the game, detailed the rules in Canada and the United States, and featured comments by Canadian hockey stars on the art of playing various positions. You might say Farrell was an early precursor of the likes of superstar goalie Ken Dryden and the celebrated hockey journalist Roy MacGregor, but combined in one person.

What is the legend of the New Jersey Devil?

The New Jersey Devils began their NHL life as the Kansas City Scouts. Their tenure in Kansas City lasted only till 1978, when the NHL approved the team's move to Denver as the Colorado Rockies. In 1982 the Rockies relocated once again, this time to New Jersey. After a fan vote, the new team was christened the New Jersey Devils.

Most tellers of the legend of the Jersey Devil trace the tale back to Deborah Leeds, a New Jersey woman who was about to give birth to her 13th child. The story goes that Mrs. Leeds invoked the Devil during a very difficult and painful labour, and when the baby was born, it grew into a full-grown devil and escaped from the house. People

Five Hockey Books to Take to an Iceberg

- *The Game: A Thoughtful and Provocative Look at a Life in Hockey* by Ken Dryden (1983).
- *Net Worth: Exploding the Myths of Pro Hockey* by David Cruise and Alison Griffiths (1991).
- *Hockey Dreams: Memories of a Man Who Couldn't Play* by David Adams Richards (1996).
- *Tropic of Hockey: My Search for the Game in Unlikely Places* by Dave Bidini (2000).
- *Putting a Roof on Winter: Hockey's Rise from Sport to Spectacle* by Michael McKinley (2000).

in the 1700s still believed in witchcraft, and many felt a deformed child was a child of the Devil or that the deformity was a sign that the child had been cursed by God. It may be that Mrs. Leeds gave birth to a child with a birth defect and, given the superstitions of the period, the legend of the Jersey Devil was born.

What was the first hockey movie?

The Edison Manufacturing Company made two very short films depicting hockey players in action — *Hockey Match on the Ice* (1898) and *Hockey Match on the Ice at Montreal, Canada* (1901) — so, in effect, these are the first two movies about ice hockey. The second of the two shows a couple of hundred kids playing what might well be shinny rather than organized hockey. However, the first known feature movie about hockey is the abysmal *King of Hockey*, a low-budget flick made by Warner Brothers in 1936. It stars Dick Purcell as Gabby Dugan, a college hockey player who makes his way into professional hockey, meets up with a nasty gambler, and gets involved with a socialite played by Anne Nagel. The movie is pretty hokey and terribly melodramatic, but it does feature hockey players from the University of California at Los Angeles and the University of Southern California. Still, the American writer obviously wasn't familiar with the game, since the script makes references to "fouls" and "the penalty cage." If nothing else, *King of Hockey* is a harbinger of the hockey celluloid mediocrity that was to come.

Top Five Hockey Movies

- *Slap Shot* (1977): Directed by George Roy Hill and starring Paul Newman.
- *Mystery, Alaska* (1999): Directed by Jay Roach and starring Russell Crowe.
- *The Rhino Brothers* (2001): Directed by Dwayne Beaver and starring Curtis Bechdholt.
- *Miracle* (2004): Directed by Gavin O'Connor and starring Kurt Russell.
- *The Rocket* (2005): Directed by Charles Binamé and starring Roy Dupuis.

Who wrote the original theme song for CBC-TV's *Hockey Night in Canada*?

Vancouver-born Dolores Claman wrote the theme song for *Hockey Night in Canada* (with an arrangement by Howard Cable), a ditty called "The Hockey Theme," which has become one of the most recognizable tunes ever composed in Canada. In 1968, when Claman was asked to write an anthem for the show, she supposedly had never seen a hockey game and claims she didn't actually see one in person until 30 years after the introduction of her song. The theme was first played on *Hockey Night in Canada* during the 1968–69 season. Previously, the television

Five Worst Hockey Movies

- *Youngblood* (1986): Directed by Peter Markle and starring Rob Lowe.
- *The Mighty Ducks* (1992): Directed by Stephen Herek and starring Emilio Estevez.
- *MVP: Most Valuable Primate* (2000): Directed by Robert Vince and starring various chimpanzees playing Jack.
- *National Lampoon's Pucked* (2006): Directed by Arthur Hiller and starring Jon Bon Jovi.
- *The Love Guru* (2008): Directed by Marco Schnabel and starring Mike Myers.

show's themes had been "Saturday's Game," a march by Howard Cable, and "Esso Happy Motoring Song." In 2008, after a long-standing dispute over financial compensation with CBC-TV, Claman broke with the network and signed a deal with CTV that allowed "The Hockey Theme" to be featured on the private company's televised hockey games beginning in 2008–09.

Who invented tabletop hockey?

In 1932 Torontonian Don Munro built a model for a tabletop hockey game in his basement using scrap metal and carving hockey figures out of wood. Shortly after, he sold the concept to Eaton's Department Store in Toronto, and the new game was a huge hit. Munro's largely wooden game was replaced in the mid-1950s by the Eagle Toy Company's version, which boasted painted tin figures and metal rods that allowed players to whip their hockey pieces around 360 degrees.

Top Five Hockey Songs

- "Fifty Mission Cap" by The Tragically Hip
- "Hockey" by Jane Siberry
- "The Hockey Song" by Stompin' Tom Connors
- "Hit Somebody" by Warren Zevon
- "Gordie and My Old Man" by Grievous Angels

What NHL team staged a contest between live bears and its players?

It's hard to believe, but in December 1998 the once-mighty Edmonton Oilers in a bid to boost fading fan interest actually had three of their Russian players — Mikhail Shtalenkov, Andrei Kovalenko, and Boris Mironov — hit the ice against a trio of bears borrowed from a Russian circus. The much-diminished Oilers, as represented by the aforementioned Russians, were at least able to drub the bears, which were pretty hapless on skates and in helmets.

How did the Boston hockey team get the name "Bruins"?

In the 1920s, Charles Adams held a city-wide contest to name his new Boston hockey team. Because the colours of his Brookside Department Stores were brown and yellow, he insisted that the team wear those same colours. He also wanted the team to be named after an animal known for its strength, agility, ferocity, and cunning. The public contest came up with the Bruins, meaning a large, ferocious bear.

Who are the Hanson brothers?

The Hanson brothers — Jeff and Steve Carlson and Dave Hanson — first found celebrity in 1977 in the Paul Newman film *Slap Shot* as hard-hitting, rabble-rousing hockey enforcers, the kind of players much beloved by broadcaster Don Cherry. In *Slap Shot* the trio play the fictional Hanson siblings (Jeff, Steve, and Jack). The two Carlsons and Hanson were actual hockey players in the minor leagues (and in the case of Steve Carlson and Dave Hanson, the NHL, too). In fact, Jack Carlson, another brother, had to bow out of the film because he was called up to play for the Edmonton Oilers (then in the World Hockey Association). Dave Hanson took his place. Interestingly, there is another character in the movie called Dave "Killer" Carlson, played by Jerry Houser, who is somewhat based on the real Jack Carlson and Dave Hanson, both of whom had the nickname "Killer" as players. The Carlsons hailed from Virginia, Minnesota, and first played for the Marquette Iron Rangers in Michigan. The real Dave Hanson was born in Cumberland, Wisconsin. Steve and Jeff Carlson and Dave Hanson made two wretched sequels to *Slap Shot* and continue to make public appearances as their fictional alter egos.

When did "Coach's Corner" first appear on *Hockey Night in Canada*?

The bombastic, flamboyantly dressed Don Cherry made his debut on *Hockey Night in Canada* in the "Coach's Corner" segment in 1980 with Dave Hodge as his sidekick. In 1987 Hodge was replaced by Ron MacLean, who has been Cherry's foil ever since. Always controversial, Cherry toiled in minor-league hockey as a defenceman from the 1950s to the early 1970s, finishing his playing career with the American Hockey League's Rochester Americans, a team he also coached for three seasons. He parlayed the minor-league coaching stint into a chance in the big time as head coach of the Boston Bruins, a job he held for five seasons (1974–75 to 1978–79). During the seventh game of the Stanley Cup semifinal with the Montreal Canadiens in 1979, Cherry made the mistake of allowing too many Bruins on the ice, earning a penalty for the team. The Canadiens capitalized on the error during the subsequent power play when Guy Lafleur scored the tying goal. The match went into overtime and the Canadiens' Yvon Lambert scored again, winning the game and eliminating Boston. The Habs went on to play the New York Rangers in the final and ended up winning the Cup. Cherry was fired. He bounced back briefly, though, in 1979–80 as head coach of the wretched Colorado Rockies but was fired after one season.

Six Top All-Time Hockey Broadcasters

- Foster Hewitt (1902–1985)
- Danny Gallivan (1917–1993)
- René Lecavalier (1918–1999)
- Howie Meeker (1923–)
- Bill Hewitt (1928–1996)
- Dick Irvin, Jr. (1932–)

When was hockey first broadcast on television?

Amazingly, the very first television broadcast of hockey occurred on October 29, 1938. The British Broadcasting Corporation aired the second and third periods of a game between the Harringay Racers and Streatham at London's Harringay Arena. Perhaps equally surprising, the very first telecast of hockey in North America didn't happen in Canada but in the United States. On an experimental station set up by NBC at Madison Square Garden, the network broadcast a game between the New York Rangers and the Montreal Canadiens on February 15, 1940. Not many people got to see the telecast, since there were fewer than 300 television sets in New York City. The first televised NHL game in Canada finally transpired on October 11, 1952, when *Hockey Night in Canada* debuted on the tube in French with a game between the Chicago Black Hawks and the Montreal Canadiens called by René Lecavalier at the Montreal Forum. The Habs lost to the Hawks 3–2. Three weeks later, on November 1, *Hockey Night in Canada* aired its initial English-language broadcast as Foster Hewitt provided the play-by-the-play for a game between the Toronto Maple Leafs and the Boston Bruins at Maple Leaf Gardens. The Leafs beat the Bruins 2–1. Just the last half of the game was broadcast, a policy that continued until 1968 for regular-season matches.

When did Foster Hewitt first say "he shoots, he scores"?

On March 22, 1923, Foster Hewitt uttered his signature "he shoots, he scores" in his first radio broadcast, a playoff game between intermediate hockey clubs from Toronto and Kitchener at the former's Mutual Street Arena. The broadcast was done for CFCA in a glassed-in booth near the penalty box. A month before Hewitt's CFCA broadcast, on February 18, Norm Albert, an editor at the *Toronto Star*, made the very first radio broadcast of a hockey game. The senior-league match between clubs from North Toronto and Midland, Ontario, turned out to be a 16–4 blowout in favour of Toronto. On January 7, 1933, Hewitt was heard for the first time coast-to-coast on radio when he welcomed listeners with "Hello Canada and hockey fans in the United States and Newfoundland" for a game between the Maple Leafs and the Detroit Red Wings, which the former won 7–6.

When were the first hockey cards issued?

In 1910–11 Imperial Tobacco released the inaugural set of catalogued hockey cards in a 36-card collection. The cards showcased coloured pictures of the superstars of the era such as Georges Vézina, Cyclone Taylor, and Lester Patrick and were placed in packages of cigarettes. A complete mint set of these cards is now worth thousands of dollars.

What famous explorer played hockey in the Arctic?

A recent discovery in a letter from British Arctic explorer Sir John Franklin to Roderick Murchison, dated November 6, 1825, records: "Till the snow fell the game of hockey played on the ice was the morning's sport." Franklin's men were wintering during his second Arctic expedition at Fort Franklin (now called Deline) in Canada's Northwest Territories on the shore of Great Bear Lake in October 1825. However, it isn't clear if the people participating in this activity were wearing skates. More likely, they were playing field hockey. Still, that doesn't stop Deline today from laying claim to hosting the very first "hockey" game in North America. As for Franklin, on his final expedition in 1845 to locate the Northwest Passage to Asia, he and his men disappeared in Canada's Far North. They were last seen by Europeans on July 26, 1845. It appears Franklin perished on June 11, 1847, off King William Island in the Arctic Ocean.

What teams were involved in the world's first hockey championship?

In 1883 at Montreal's inaugural Winter Carnival, the world's first hockey championship was held, pitting three teams against one another: the Montreal Victorias, the McGill University Hockey Club, and a team from Quebec City. The three teams vied for the sterling silver Carnival Cup. McGill University won the series. The championship was restaged at the carnival in 1884 and 1885.

What was the first NHL team to relocate?

Today it is all too common for sports franchises to pull up stakes and move to seemingly greener pastures. Hockey is no stranger to the pain of fans losing their beloved club. Think Quebec Nordiques (now Colorado Avalanche), Winnipeg Jets (now Phoenix Coyotes), the old Ottawa Senators (briefly St. Louis Eagles, then defunct, then revived as the new Senators in 1992–93), Minnesota North Stars (now Dallas Stars), and Hartford Whalers (now Carolina Hurricanes). The first team to leave its original city in the NHL was the Quebec Bulldogs, which headed for Hamilton, Ontario, with its superstar Joe Malone, to become the Tigers in 1920–21 after only one season in the big league. The Tigers didn't last long in Hamilton, either. Despite having a pretty good team, the club's players ended up in New York City to become the Americans in 1925–26. The Amerks, as they were nicknamed, finally gave up the ghost in 1941–42, leaving Madison Square Garden to the New York Rangers. Hamilton is still waiting for another NHL team; so is Quebec City.

Short Shelf of Fine Hockey Fiction

Boxing has *Fat City* (Leonard Gardner) and *The Harder They Fall* (Budd Schulberg), football has *North Dallas Forty* (Peter Gent), and baseball has *The Natural* (Bernard Malamud) and *Shoeless Joe* (W.P. Kinsella), but hockey is still waiting for its truly great lyric writer. There have been a few pretty good novels and one play, though.

- *Les Canadiens* by Rick Salutin and Ken Dryden (1977).
- *The Last Season* by Roy MacGregor (1983).
- *Hockey Night in the Dominion of Canada* by Eric Zweig (1992).
- *King Leary* by Paul Quarrington (1994).
- *Salvage King, Ya! A Herky-Jerky Picaresque* by Mark Anthony Jarman (1997).
- *Understanding Ken* by Pete McCormack (1998).
- *Finnie Walsh* by Steven Galloway (2000).

What is the best children's story ever written about hockey?

In 1979 noted Quebec novelist and playwright Roch Carrier first published the short story "Une abominable feuille d'érable sur la glace" ("An Abominable Maple Leaf on the Ice"), now better known as "The Hockey Sweater" in English and "Le chandail de hockey" in French. Carrier based the story on his own experiences as a child. The narrative is simple but superb in the way it gets to the heart of the mystique of hockey for Canadians, particularly children. In the 1940s a boy's hockey sweater wears out and his mother orders a new one from the Eaton's catalogue. The boy is a rabid fan of the Montreal Canadiens and their star forward Maurice "Rocket" Richard. However, when the new sweater finally arrives, to the boy's horror it's a Toronto Maple Leafs sweater, not a Habs one. The boy tries to get his mother to return the sweater, but she feels that Mr. Eaton, obviously a Leafs fan, might be offended, so she insists he wear the despicable Leafs garment to his hockey game. As expected, the boy is the only one not wearing a Canadiens jersey. "The Hockey Sweater" is often thought to be an allegory for French and English tensions in Canada. It has been published in many forms, including a picture book for younger children. In 1980 an animated version, *The Sweater*, was released by Canada's National Film Board to much acclaim.

Six Top All-Time Hockey Journalists

- Elmer Ferguson (1885–1972)
- Milt Dunnell (1905–2008)
- Jim Coleman (1911–2000)
- Scott Young (1918–2005)
- Trent Frayne (1918–)
- Red Fisher (1926–)

Where did the word *puck* come from?

A hockey puck is a hard, vulcanized black rubber disk three inches in diameter, one inch thick and weighing between five and a half to six ounces. To reduce the tendency of pucks to bounce, they are frozen before use. The origins of the word *puck* are the subject of much debate. The first verifiable reference in print to the word in relation to hockey was in an 1876 game account in the *Montreal Gazette*. Some think the word derives from the Scottish and Gaelic word *puc*. In 1910 a book entitled *English as We Speak It in Ireland* defined the word as follows: "Puck: a blow. 'He gave him a puck of a stick on the head.' More commonly applied to a punch or blow of the horns of a cow or goat! 'The cow gave him a puck (or pucked him) with her horns and knocked him down.' The blow given by a hurler to the ball with his caman or hurley is always called a puck. Irish poc, same sound and meaning."

Why is Calgary's hockey team called the "Flames"?

The "Flames" have not always been a Calgary hockey team. They started out in Atlanta during the second wave of NHL expansion in 1972, where the name "Flames" was chosen to remember the torching of the city in 1864 by Union troops, led by General William Tecumseh Sherman, during their long march through the South near the end of the Civil War. When the team moved to Calgary in 1980, the name was kept in honour of Calgary's ties to oil.

What are Black Aces?

Black Aces is the collective name for the group of players who practise with the whole team but rarely play in games. This term originated with hard-nosed Eddie Shore's Springfield (Massachusetts) Indians teams in the American Hockey League from the 1940s to the 1960s. Shore demanded that his Black Aces perform non-hockey tasks such as selling programs and popcorn during the games they didn't play.

What is a hat trick in hockey?

When a player scores three goals in one game, it's called a hat trick. The term originated in cricket where usually reserved fans toss their hats to celebrate the knocking down of three consecutive wickets. Not surprisingly, Wayne Gretzky holds the National Hockey League record for the most career three-or-more-goal games (50, with 37 three-goalers, nine four-goalers, and four five-goalers) as well as top marks for the most three-or-more-goal games in one season (10 twice, in 1981–82 and 1983–84). However, the Great One doesn't hold the record for the most goals ever scored in one game; the Quebec Bulldogs' Joe Malone does, with seven in a 1920 match. A number of players — Newsy Lalonde, Cy and Corb Denneny, Malone, Syd Howe, Red Berenson, and Darryl Sittler — have potted six in a single game. The Toronto Maple Leafs' Sittler holds the record for most points in one contest (10 on February 7, 1976, against the Boston Bruins). Gretzky *is* tied with 10 other players (including Mario Lemieux, Bryan Trottier, and Berenson) for most goals in a single period — four. A pure hat trick is when one player scores three consecutive, uninterrupted goals in a single game.

Quickies
Did you know …
that a Gordie Howe hat trick is a goal, an assist, and a fight in the same game? The NHL's second all-time leading scorer, Howe was also an able pugilist who racked up 2,109 regular-season penalty minutes.

How did the expression "hanging from the rafters" originate?

The Detroit Red Wings' old arena, the Olympia, is said to be the place where the expression "hanging from the rafters" originated. The rink was infamously steep-sided so that fans in the standing-room-only section literally hung from the rafters to see the game better. The Red Wings played their last game in the Old Red Barn on the Grand River on December 15, 1979, against the Quebec Nordiques, tying the match 4–4. Detroit moved into the brand-new Joe Louis Arena that season. The last hockey game played at the Olympia was a Red Wings Old-Timers game on February 21, 1980. The Olympia was demolished in 1986.

Quickies
Did you know …
that the Montreal Canadiens' nickname "Habs" comes from *les habitants,* a term that was once used to describe the early settlers of seventeenth- and eighteenth-century New France, the predecessor of what eventually became the province of Quebec? In fact, the Canadiens were specifically established in December 1909 in the National Hockey Association (precursor of the NHL) as a French-Canadian alternative to the many predominantly English hockey clubs in Montreal, teams such as the Shamrocks, the Wanderers, and the Victorias.

Where did the term *firewagon hockey* come from?

In the 1950s the Montreal Canadiens won five Stanley Cups (1953, 1956–59) and became known for the kind of high-speed, explosive rushes usually led by superstars such as Maurice Richard and Jean Béliveau. Sportswriters called this kind of playing style "firewagon hockey," and the Canadiens were associated with it right into the 1970s. By 1979 they added another 11 Stanley Cups (1960, 1965–66, 1968–69, 1971, 1973, 1976–79) to the five they won in the 1950s. Since 1979 the Habs have only won two Cups (1986, 1993).

What is the five hole?

In hockey goaltending there are five areas in the net where goalies are vulnerable. The holes are above the shoulders, the lower corners of the goal, and between the legs of the netminder. The last is the five hole, which becomes vulnerable when a goalie has to move from side to side quickly (for example, when he or she is deked) or when a butterfly-style netminder drops to his or her knees.

What is the slot?

The slot is the area directly in front of the net and is considered prime scoring territory. Centreman Phil Esposito, during his great years with the Boston Bruins, set up shop in the slot and got down to rewriting the record book in the late 1960s and 1970s. In 1968–69 he amassed 126 points and in 1970–71 he bagged 152 points, with 100 or more points in four subsequent seasons. His 76 goals in 1970–71 was tops in the league until Wayne Gretzky surpassed it with 92 in 1981–82 (still the record).

> **Quickies**
> *Did you know …*
> that Gretzky's office refers to the area behind a team's net? When Wayne Gretzky was on the ice, he spent a lot of time in possession of the puck behind the opposition goal, waiting for teammates to get open in front of the net. As the Great One once commented, "When I get back there, I prefer to use a backhand pass to get the puck out front. I like to use the net as a sort of screen, to buy time from the opposing defencemen who may be trying to get me.… I try to keep the puck away from them as long as possible so I can hopefully make a play."

What is a wraparound?

A wraparound occurs when an attacking player controls the puck behind the opposition's net and attempts to score by reaching around the side of the goal and jamming the puck in.

Who was the first NHL player to use a slap shot?

A slap shot is a forehand shot in which the shooter draws the stick back above the waist (the back swing) before swinging the stick quickly forward and slapping the puck. It is not unusual for slap shots to travel more than 100 miles per hour. The advantage of the slap shot is its velocity; the disadvantages include a lack of accuracy, the long time it takes to release the shot (slap shots are commonly blocked by doughty defenders), and the opportunity given to defenders to take the puck during the back swing. As to who in the NHL first employed the slap shot, like many things in hockey, that's shrouded in controversy and speculation. Early practitioners of the slap shot in the 1950s were Bernard "Boom

Boom" Geoffrion and Andy Bathgate. Geoffrion, who played most of his career with the Montreal Canadiens, says he got his colourful nickname "Boom Boom" because of that very shot: "One day I was practising at the Forum and shooting the puck hard against the boards and it was making a pretty big noise. A newspaper guy, Charlie Borie, asked me if it would be okay if he started calling me 'Boom Boom.' Since that day, the name stayed."

What is a neutral-zone trap?

The neutral-zone trap is a dreadfully dull defensive strategy that's popular with many hockey coaches because of its effectiveness. Although variations of the trap have existed for decades, it gained prominence when the 1995 New Jersey Devils used it to win the Stanley Cup. The goal of the trap is to clog the neutral zone with defenders so the offensive team has little momentum when crossing its own blueline. If successfully executed, the trap forces the attacking team to lose the puck before crossing the central redline, or to shoot it in. The Florida Panthers once frequently employed a twist on the trap by attempting to stop opponents before they reached the neutral zone, provoking a turnover near the opposition's blueline.

Six Curious Terms in Hockey

- **Baffle Play**: A former term, now archaic, for a fast deke.
- **Cookie Shelf**: The top of the net where flashy players like to shoot the puck.
- **Eggbeater**: A player adept with his stick close up, usually in the corner to stick-check an opponent and claim the puck.
- **Slewfooting**: A dangerous, and dirty, act of tripping another player from behind. A player committing this foul stands behind an opponent and uses his or her foot to sweep the feet out from under the other player, causing the player to fall backward. The offending player is assessed a minor penalty for tripping. Such fouls most commonly occur in traffic in front of the net or following a faceoff.
- **Snowplow**: To hook a player, usually between the bluelines.
- **Spinnerama**: A deft manoeuvre in which the puck carrier turns 360 degrees in an attempt to evade defenders.

Who was the last goaltender to play without a mask in the NHL?

The Pittsburgh Penguins' Andy Brown was the last NHL goalie to bare his face to slap shots and other on-ice hazards. Brown played his last NHL game with the Penguins in a 6–3 loss to the Atlanta Flames on April 7, 1974. The plucky, or crazy, netminder continued his professional career in the World Hockey Association with the Indianapolis Racers, and he didn't wear a mask there, either. Brown, like the Philadelphia Flyers' Ron Hextall, had something of a mean streak. In 1973–74 with the Penguins he achieved the then single-season NHL penalty-minute record for goalies, notching 60. He continued his warring ways in the WHA the next season, leading all goalies in that league that year with

75 penalty minutes. Incidentally, the current NHL record holder for penalty minutes for a goalie in one season is Hextall, who earned himself 113 in 1988–89 while playing for the Flyers. Hextall also has the career record for penalty minutes — 584.

Which NHL player was the last to play without a helmet?

The days of seeing an NHL player's hair or lack of it on the ice started to be numbered in the 1970s, especially after the league made it mandatory in 1979 for all players entering the NHL to don one. Anyone already in the league at that time could still go helmetless if they so desired. Centreman Craig MacTavish, once an integral part of the Edmonton Oilers in the late 1980s and the early 1990s, continued to display his greying locks until his final game with the St. Louis Blues during the 1997 Stanley Cup playoffs.

Which player in the NHL invented the curved hockey stick?

The Chicago Black Hawks' Bobby Hull and Stan Mikita are often credited with first using hockey sticks with curved blades. According to the game's lore, in the early 1960s Mikita noticed that his broken stick blade, which formed a curve, allowed him to shoot higher and harder. Soon after, Mikita and his teammate Hull were terrifying opposing goalies with shots propelled by huge "banana blade" curves. So dangerous were these shots that the stick blade's curve is now limited to a half inch. Many hockey historians currently believe, however, that right winger Andy Bathgate, one of the first NHL players to employ the slap shot, was the first to tinker with curving his sticks even before

Top Five Soviet Players Who Never Played in the NHL

- **Vsevolod Bobrov**: A forward, he played hockey in the Soviet Union from 1946 through 1957, then coached the Soviet national team, including its games in the 1972 Summit Series. Also a soccer star, Bobrov was one of his country's first genuine hockey heroes and was often compared to Maurice Richard. He was part of two World Championships and one Olympic-gold effort.
- **Anatoli Firsov**: One of the Soviet Union's earliest superstars, Firsov played left wing and centre from 1958 through 1974. He was part of eight World Championships and three gold-medal Olympic teams. Firsov boycotted the 1972 Summit Series in support of ousted national team coach Anatoli Tarasov. It's often thought that his absence on the Soviets' Summit Series team was the equivalent of Canada's inability to put Bobby Hull on the ice.
- **Valeri Kharlamov**: An eight-time World Champion and three-time Olympic gold-medal winner, Kharlamov, a forward, made his Canadian debut during the 1972 Summit Series and astonished the North American hockey world with his prodigious talent. Kharlamov played for the Soviet national team from 1967 through 1981, his career cut short when he was killed in a car accident.
- **Vladislav Tretiak**: A 10-time world champion and three-time Olympic gold-medal winner, Tretiak was the Soviet Union's greatest ever goaltender during his career from 1968 through 1984. He played brilliantly in the 1972 Summit Series and later went on to stymie many North American teams in international competitions. He was the first Soviet-trained player to be inducted into the Hockey Hall of Fame.
- **Valeri Vasiliev:** A nine-time world champion and two-time Olympic gold-medal winner, Vasiliev, the Soviet Union's greatest defenceman, played from 1967 through 1982.

he got to the big league. Bathgate, who played many of his best years with the New York Rangers in the 1950s and early 1960s, told a reporter once: "I would heat up the blades with hot water, then I would bend them. I would put them in the toilet-stall door jamb and leave them overnight. The next day they would have a hook in them." To prevent his sticks from straightening out, Bathgate added fibreglass to his blades, likely the first player to do so.

Where did the word *deke* come from?

A deke is an action that involves the puck carrier faking a move in one direction and then taking the puck in another direction. Dekes are commonly used to move the puck past defenders or to score on goalies. *Deke* is a short form of *decoy*.

Quickies

Did you know ...

that the New York Rangers' Andy Bathgate was the right winger who drilled a puck into Montreal Canadiens goalie Jacques Plante's face on November 1, 1959, causing the superstar netminder to don a face mask, an action that changed forever the way goalies played the game?

What is a power play in hockey?

A power play occurs in hockey when a team, because of penalties to the opposition, has more players on the ice than the other team. The numerical advantage enjoyed by the team on the power play affords it a good opportunity to score. Most teams dedicate much time to practising their power plays. The secret of a good power play is the ability to control the puck in the attacking zone until it can be moved into position for a shot. In the NHL, power plays are successful about 15 to 18 percent of the time.

How does an offside occur in hockey?

An offside infraction occurs when an attacking player crosses the opponent's blueline ahead of the puck. The offside is hockey's most commonly called infraction and is intended to prevent a player from camping out in the attacking zone without the puck. The position of the player's skates, not the stick, determines an offside. For the player to be offside, both skates must be completely over the blueline when the puck fully crosses it. After an offside is called, a faceoff occurs outside the blueline where the infraction took place. Until the 2005–06 season a two-line pass (crossing the centre redline and the opponent's blueline) to a teammate was also considered an offside. However, the NHL legalized such passes, hoping they would open up the game, create more breakaways, and lead to more frequent scoring chances. Critics of the rule change, though, feel that the opposite has occurred and that the lack of a viable redline promotes greater use of the neutral-zone trap and more defensive hockey. A delayed offside occurs when an attacking player has preceded the puck across his opponent's blueline and is offside but the defensive team takes possession of the puck at or near the blueline. Play is allowed to continue as the defensive team moves the puck out of its zone (and, therefore, nullifies the offside), or if an attacking player touches the puck inside the blueline.

When does icing happen in hockey?

Icing is an infraction that occurs when a player shoots the puck from his or her side of the centre redline across the opponent's goal line. This infraction is whistled down when the non-offending team touches the puck after it has crossed the goal line. If a defender can reasonably play the puck and chooses not to, or if the shooter's team is shorthanded, icing isn't called. When icing is indicated, the puck is faced-off in the offending team's defensive zone and play resumes.

When was the first Zamboni used in an NHL arena?

The Zamboni is a tractorlike machine employed to resurface the ice in a rink. The Zamboni scrapes off a thin layer of ice and then applies a thin coat of hot water, which melts small imperfections in the ice before freezing to form a smooth surface. The Zamboni was invented in the 1940s by Frank J. Zamboni, who owned one of the first skating rinks in Southern California. It was first used in an NHL game at the Montreal Forum on March 10, 1955. Prior to the invention of the Zamboni, NHL arenas were cleaned and flooded between periods by workers using shovels and barrels of water.

Who holds the most records in the NHL?

With 60 NHL records in regular-season, playoff, and All-Star games, Wayne Gretzky, of course, holds the individual record of records. Upon his retirement in 1999, the Great One actually had 61 records, but two of his records were eclipsed and he got one back. Gretzky's record of 15 overtime assists has now been passed by Nicklas Lidstrom, Adam Oates, and Mark Messier, while his record of 12 All-Star Game assists has been beaten by Mark Messier, Ray Bourque, and Joe Sakic. When Mario Lemieux came out of retirement and played more games, he lost his points-per-game-average record, which now belongs to Gretzky again at 1.921 points per game. Some of Gretzky's loftier records, ones that will likely never be surpassed, are most regular-season goals (894), most regular-season assists (1,963), most regular-season points (2,857), most playoff goals (122), most goals in one season (92), and most assists in one season (163).

Who holds the NHL record for scoring the most goals in one game?

Joe Malone of the Quebec Bulldogs scored seven goals in one game against the Toronto St. Patricks on January 31, 1920, powering his club to a 10–6 victory. Malone, born in Quebec City, was one of the NHL's first superstars. He won the scoring title twice, the first time being in the league's inaugural season in 1917–18 when he racked up 44 goals in a mere 20 games for the Montreal Canadiens. His other scoring title came in 1919–20 with the Bulldogs. Malone won three Stanley Cups, two with Quebec (1912, 1913) and one with the Canadiens (1924). Perhaps not too surprising, he was also one of the first men to score a goal in the NHL, sharing that distinction with the Montreal Wanderers' Dave Ritchie. Both Malone and Ritchie potted goals early in their respective games on December 19, 1917. Starting times for games for the era aren't known, but Malone, a Canadien, got his goal against the Ottawa Senators early in the first period en route to beating the Sens 7–4.

What was the highest-scoring game in NHL history?

This record turns out to be a tie. On January 10, 1920, the Montreal Canadiens trounced the Toronto St. Pats 14–7. Sixty-five years later, on December 11, 1985, the Edmonton Oilers slipped by the Chicago Black Hawks 12–9. The record for most goals by one team in a single game is also held by the Canadiens, who netted 16 against the Quebec Bulldogs' three on March 3, 1920.

Which NHL player has won the most scoring titles?

Wayne Gretzky, not too surprisingly, won 10 Art Ross Trophies (1981–87, 1990–91, 1994), the award the NHL has given for the league's regular-season scoring leader since 1947–48. Prior to that season, a number of players such as Joe Malone, Newsy Lalonde, Bill Cook, and Charlie Conacher won the scoring title twice, but no single person earned it more times than that. The runners-up to Gretzky for Art Ross Trophies are Gordie Howe and Mario Lemieux, each with six. The Great One has also won the most Hart Trophies — nine — for most valuable player in the NHL during the regular season.

Number 99 accomplished that feat eight seasons in a row from 1980 to 1987, then added a ninth Hart in 1989 after he was dealt to the Los Angeles Kings.

Who holds the NHL record for the most points in one game?

On February 7, 1976, the Toronto Maple Leafs' Darryl Sittler racked up an incredible six goals and four assists for 10 points in an 11–4 plastering of the Boston Bruins at Maple Leaf Gardens. That record for points still stands. Centreman Sittler was the first Maple Leaf ever to hit 100 points in a season, achieving that plateau in 1975–76, then did it again in 1977–78 when he got 117.

Who is the only NHL player to win the Art Ross, Hart, and Lady Byng trophies in consecutive seasons?

Czechoslovakia-born Stanislaus Gvoth, better known as Stan Mikita, achieved this distinction in 1967 (the first to do so) and then again in 1968. Mikita played for the Chicago Black Hawks from 1958–59 to 1979–80 and won the Art Ross as scoring leader two other times (1964 and 1965). The scrappy forward had a notorious bad temper, got into numerous fights, and racked up significant penalty minutes in his career, which makes it all the more incredible that he somehow managed to win the Lady Byng twice, an award given out for sportsmanship and gentlemanly play!

What NHL player holds the record for the most 50-goal seasons?

Even when single-season scoring tallies started escalating after NHL expansion in 1967–68, scoring 50 goals in a single season still meant something as a personal plateau, and it continues to. The Montreal Canadiens' Maurice "Rocket" Richard was the first to do it in 1944–45, and achieved it in 50 games. Teammate "Boom Boom" Geoffrion was the second to hit the mark in 1960–61. The first player to pot more than 50 was the Chicago Black Hawks' Bobby Hull, who got 54 in 1965–66 (Hull had earlier joined the 50-goal club in 1961–62). As to who's recorded the most 50-goal seasons in a career, that's a tie between Mike Bossy and Wayne Gretzky. Both did it nine times. However, Bossy only played 10 seasons in his career (all with the New York Islanders), while the Great One got his nine in 20 seasons with the Edmonton Oilers, Los Angeles Kings, St. Louis Blues, and New York Rangers. What's more, Bossy nabbed his nine in consecutive seasons from 1977–78 to 1985–86, which is also a record, one he doesn't share with anybody.

Who was the first NHL player to score 100 points in a regular season?

The Detroit Red Wings' Gordie Howe almost hit 100 points in 1952–53 when he got 95, but it took more than another decade and a half before the Boston Bruins' Phil Esposito broke the 100 barrier in 1968–69 on his way to ending up with 126 points. Of course, Wayne Gretzky blew everybody away with his remarkable feats in the 1980s, topping 200 points four times, with a record 215 in 1985–86. The Great One is still the only NHL player to score more than 200 points in one season. The Pittsburgh Penguins' Mario Lemieux came close in 1988–89 when he managed 199 points. Incidentally, Number 99 has the most 100-point seasons (15) and the most consecutive 100-pointers (13).

Quickies

Did you know ...

that Gordie Howe was 41 and in his 23rd year with the Detroit Red Wings in 1968–69 when he achieved his only 100-point season? Howe is the sole 40-year-old in the NHL to achieve this plateau. That season he ended up with 103 points. Of course, Howe went on to retire from the Red Wings in the early 1970s, then came out of retirement to play through most of that decade in the World Hockey Association, and finally returned to the NHL with the Hartford Whalers when he was 51! He retired at last in 1980 at age 52.

Who was the first NHL player to score more than 500 goals in a career?

Few players dominated his era the way Maurice "Rocket" Richard dominated his. On October 19, 1957, at the Montreal Forum he scaled another plateau when he scored goal number 500, the first to do so in the NHL. The Rocket was playing in his 863rd game. Strangely enough, Richard never won a scoring championship. In fact, he holds the record for being the runner-up, accomplishing that unfortunate mark five times in 1945, 1947, 1951, 1954, and 1955. To date only two NHL players have scored more than 800 regular-season career goals: Wayne Gretzky (894) and Gordie Howe (801).

Who is the only rookie to win the NHL scoring championship?

Scrappy, surly Nels Stewart was already 23 when he joined the NHL as a Montreal Maroon in 1925–26. Previously, "Old Poison," as he was nicknamed, had played for five years with the Cleveland Indians in the USA Hockey Association. Born in Montreal, Stewart scored 34 goals and eight assists for 42 points in 36 games in his inaugural season. That year he also won the Hart Trophy as most valuable player and helped the Maroons to win the Stanley Cup. Old Poison won a second Hart in 1929–30 and scored 39 goals and 16 assists for 55 points in only 44 games. The next season, on January 3, 1931, he potted two goals in four seconds, an NHL record that still stands, though it was equalled by the Winnipeg Jets' Deron Quint in 1995. The record for most goals scored by a rookie in the NHL belongs to Teemu Selanne, who got 76 in 1992–93 while playing for the Winnipeg Jets. That same year Selanne racked up 132 points, which is also a record for a rookie.

How long was the longest undefeated streak in NHL annals?

With Pat Quinn behind the bench as coach and top-notch, feisty players such as Bobby Clarke, Bill Barber, and Reggie Leach headmanning the attack on the ice, the Philadelphia Flyers put together an amazing streak of wins and ties that began on October 14, 1979, when they edged the Toronto Maple Leafs 4–3 and continued unbeaten until they were defeated by the Minnesota North Stars 7–1 on January 7, 1980. All told the Broad Street Bullies won 25 games and tied 10 during their streak.

Who was the first black player in the NHL?

Black players and managers have been noticeably absent from the NHL for much of its existence. Whether this had more to do with the fact that almost all big-league players before 1970 hailed from Canada and in those days the country had, relatively speaking, a small black population, or with the fact that there was an active colour barrier in place, is open to debate. But one thing isn't subject to conjecture: Fredericton, New Brunswick–born Willie O'Ree was the first player of African descent to play in the NHL. The right winger's stint in the major league was brief — he played two games for the Boston Bruins in January 1958 and 43 matches for the same team in 1960–61 — but his place in hockey history is significant. The New Brunswicker experienced much racial abuse at the hands of opposing players as well as fans, the latter insulting him by throwing black hats onto the ice. O'Ree may not have had a lengthy career in the NHL and only recorded 14 points in the big league, but he was a legend in the minors, playing in various leagues such as the American Hockey League and the Western Hockey League (largely for the San Diego Gulls) well into the 1970s. He did all this even though he was legally blind in one eye, due to an errant puck during a game when he was 18.

Quickies

Did you know …

that Sidney Crosby is the youngest NHL player and the only teenager ever to win the Art Ross Trophy as scoring champion? He achieved that in his second season in 2006–07 with the Pittsburgh Penguins when he scored 36 goals and 84 assists for 120 points. That year Crosby also won the Hart Trophy as most valuable player (chosen by the Professional Hockey Writers' Association) and the Lester B. Pearson Award (picked by the NHL Players' Association).

Who was the first full-blooded aboriginal player in the NHL?

A Saskatchewan Cree named Fred Saskamoose from the Sandy Lake Reserve appeared in 11 games with the Chicago Black Hawks in 1953–54, making him the first full-blooded aboriginal player to make it to the NHL. Saskamoose recorded no points and notched six penalty minutes in his short NHL dalliance. Later, though, he was the playing coach of the Kamloops Chiefs. During his time in British Columbia, the Shushwap and Chilcotin Bands of the province's interior awarded him the name Chief Thunder Stick, a title he assumed when he was elected chief of the Sandy Lake Cree.

> **Quickies**
>
> **Did you know …**
>
> that Jarome Iginla was the first black player to win the Art Ross Trophy? In 2001–02 the ace right winger of the Calgary Flames scored 52 goals and 44 assists for 96 points to win the Art Ross as scoring champion. Iginla also won the Lester B. Pearson Award as the NHL Players' Association pick for most valuable player and the Maurice Richard Trophy for most goals. He won the Richard Trophy again in 2003–04 when he potted 41 goals.

Who is the only NHL player ever to receive permanent possession of a trophy?

Between 1927–28 and 1934–35, Frank Boucher of the New York Rangers won the Lady Byng Trophy for gentlemanly play seven times. During that period, Boucher played 364 games and only incurred 87 penalty minutes. When the Ottawa-born centreman received his seventh Lady Byng in 1935, the NHL decided to give him the trophy for good. A new piece of hardware was then donated to the league by Lady Byng herself. Incidentally, as a player, Boucher helped the Rangers win Stanley Cups in 1928 and 1933. As coach of New York, he steered them to another Cup in 1940, their last until 1994 when they finally won it again.

> **Quickies**
>
> **Did you know …**
>
> that the first NHL player of Asiatic descent was Larry Kwong? The son of a Chinese grocer in British Columbia, Kwong was pretty much only in the NHL for a cup of coffee when he played a single shift for the New York Rangers in a game on March 13, 1948.

What kind of car was Tim Horton driving when he was killed?

Cochrane, Ontario-born Tim Horton is now better known as the franchise name of a colossal doughnut-and-coffee empire, but for 24 seasons he was one of the NHL's most durable, dependable defencemen. After a couple of brief stints with the Toronto Maple Leafs in the late 1940s and early 1950s, Horton came to stay in 1952–53. He was a fixture on the Leafs' defence until he was traded to the New York Rangers in 1969–70. During the 1960s, he and a crackerjack blueline squad that included Allan Stanley, Bob Baun, and Carl Brewer helped Toronto win four Stanley Cups (1962–64, 1967). Horton's 16 points in 13 playoff games in 1962 set a record for defencemen (long since outstripped), and he was capable of rushing up ice in a burst of speed to deliver a pretty hard slap shot to an opponent's net. The brawny defender played briefly for the Pittsburgh Penguins after his time with the Rangers, then ended up with the Buffalo Sabres and back with his old Leafs coach George "Punch" Imlach in 1972–73. Horton, now in his forties, wanted to retire the next season, but Imlach persuaded him otherwise. On February 21, 1974, Horton was killed in a car accident near St. Catharines, Ontario, after a game in Toronto. A notorious speeder, he was headed back to Buffalo in the new Ford Pantera sports car that Imlach had given him as a signing bonus to play one last season. During his long NHL career, he played 1,446 regular-season games and scored 115 goals and 403 assists for 518 points, adding another 11 goals and 39 assists in the playoffs. Today the doughnut company Horton founded in Hamilton, Ontario, in 1964 (later taking on former Hamilton policeman Ron Joyce as partner) has nothing to do with his survivors except in name, but it has mushroomed into a billion-dollar corporation that employs more than 70,000 people in Canada and the United States.

What NHL superstar was offered the position of governor general of Canada?

After Jean Béliveau retired from the front office of the Montreal Canadiens in 1993, he was offered the post of governor general the next year. However, he declined the honour, citing family obligations. Although never idolized the way his Canadiens teammate Maurice Richard was, Béliveau was one of the greatest hockey players ever to lace on a pair of skates. Born in Trois-Rivières, Quebec, the gentlemanly centre played 20 seasons (18 full) for the Canadiens and scored 507 goals and 712 assists for 1,219 points. In the Stanley Cup playoffs he added another 79 goals and 97 assists in 17 competitions, helping the Habs win 10 Cups. Béliveau won the Art Ross Trophy in 1956, the Conn Smythe Trophy in 1965, and the Hart Trophy in 1956 and 1964. *Le Gros Bill*, as he was nicknamed, retired as a player in 1971 and was employed by Montreal as vice-president of corporate affairs for 22 years.

> **Quickies**
>
> *Did you know …*
>
> that the first NHL shutout was recorded by the Montreal Canadiens' great goaltender Georges Vézina? Appropriately, given the teams' latter-day rivalry, he achieved this milestone on February 18, 1918, in a game against the Toronto Arenas (later to change their name to the St. Patricks, then to the Maple Leafs). Vézina and the Habs won the match 9–0 in the league's 29th game in its first season.

When and where was the first official NHL All-Star Game played?

Great hockey isn't something usually associated with an NHL All-Star Game, but fans do get to see the year's best players assembled in one spot, the players selected get to have a bit of fun (and grab some more money), and players who aren't picked get a rest. The league began choosing All-Star teams in 1930–31 and staged a few All-Star benefit games for the survivors of dead players (Ace Bailey in 1933, Howie Morenz in 1937, and Babe Siebert in 1939). However, the first *official* All-Star Game was played on October 13, 1947, at Maple Leaf Gardens. The initial format had the Stanley Cup champions from the previous season play a team of All-Stars picked from the league's other five clubs. In 1947 the All-Stars beat the Cup-winning Toronto Maple Leafs 4–3. Since that first official match, the All-Star Game has been moved from the beginning of the season to the middle and now the Eastern Conference All-Stars play the Western Conference All-Stars.

Why is Kingston, Ontario, thought by many to be the birthplace of hockey?

The first recorded games of shinny on ice were played in Kingston, Upper Canada, in 1839. A British Army officer, Arthur Freeling, said he and fellow soldiers played "hockey on the ice" in January 1843 in Kingston. Edward Horsey, in his diary, noted that shinny was played on the ice of Kingston's harbour in the 1860s by soldiers. However, an organized game with some rules wasn't played in Kingston until 1886. That match pitted Queen's College students against Royal Military College cadets and occurred 11 years after the first recorded indoor game in Montreal.

What is the Frozen Four?

Since 1948 the U.S. National Collegiate Athletic Association (NCAA) has crowned the Men's Division I champion in American college hockey. Today, through an extremely complex system, college teams across the country are winnowed down to 12 clubs that play one another in the annual NCAA Tournament. The quartet of semi-finalists that comes out on top is called the Frozen Four (so-called to differentiate it from basketball's Final Four), and from the playoffs in this group the year's best college team is determined. The Frozen Four playoffs are held in a different city each year, usually one associated with college hockey (such as Detroit, St. Paul, Minnesota, or Albany, New York), but not always. In 2008 the Boston College Eagles were crowned Men's Division I champions after defeating the Fighting Irish of Notre Dame 4–1 in Denver, Colorado. The NCAA started a Women's Frozen Four in 2001. The women's champion in 2008 was the University of Minnesota at Duluth.

Five Outstanding NHL Head Coaches

- **Scotty Bowman:** There's no argument that Bowman is the best NHL coach of all time. He's the all-time victory champ with 1,244 regular-season and 223 playoff wins as head coach of the St. Louis Blues, Montreal Canadiens, Buffalo Sabres, Pittsburgh Penguins, and Detroit Red Wings from 1967–68 to 2001–02. During that time, he won a record nine Stanley Cups.
- **Al Arbour**: A solid defenceman in the 1950s and 1960s for various NHL teams, including the Detroit Red Wings, Toronto Maple Leafs, and St. Louis Blues, Arbour turned to coaching with the Blues in 1970–71 and became a huge success. His most famous coaching stint was with the New York Islanders, who he backbenched from 1973–74 to 1993–94. In order to give him his 1,500th Islanders game coached, New York had him helm one game in 2007–08. Naturally, Arbour won, bringing his total coaching victories to 782, second only to Bowman. He also became the oldest man, at 75, ever to coach an NHL game. And let's not forget the four Stanley Cups he won in a row during the Islanders' salad days in the early 1980s.
- **James Dickinson "Dick" Irvin**: Few coaches can boast the longevity that Hamilton, Ontario-born Dick Irvin could. The plucky backbencher began his life in hockey as a player, breaking into the professional game with the Pacific Coast Hockey Association's Portland Rosebuds in 1916–17, but turned amateur again the following season. After the Second World War, he resumed his pro career with leagues other than the NHL until finally playing for the Chicago Black Hawks briefly in the late 1920s. He began his coaching career with the Hawks in 1928–29 but only stayed there for a couple of seasons, eventually moving to the Toronto Maple Leafs as coach in 1931–32 and winning his first Stanley Cup there in 1932. By 1940–41 he was backbenching the Montreal Canadiens, winning three more Cups with the Habs (1944, 1946, 1953) before leaving to coach his final season (1955–56) in Chicago, where he had started. Irvin won 692 regular-season NHL games, lost 527, and tied 230, winning 100 games and losing 88 in the playoffs.
- **Hector "Toe" Blake**: Few hockey personalities have excelled as both player and coach and become legends, as well. Blake did all of that with only one team — the Montreal Canadiens. During the 1930s and 1940s, Blake, a left winger, was part of the explosive Punch Line with Maurice Richard and Elmer Lach, scoring the winning goals that gave the Habs Stanley Cups in 1944 and 1946. Earlier, in his rookie season with the Montreal Maroons, Blake won his first Cup in 1935. After breaking his ankle in 1948, he left the Canadiens and played some minor-league hockey for a few seasons until retiring from the game as a player in 1951. Blake debuted as a coach with the Habs in 1955–56 and went on to lead Montreal to eight Stanley Cups, five of them in a row from 1956 to 1960. His other three were in 1965, 1966, and 1968. As a coach, he won 500 regular-season games and 82 playoff matches.
- **Glen Sather**: Some might say the formidable Edmonton Oilers of the 1980s didn't need a coach, but credit should be given to Sather as their backbencher. As a player in the 1960s and 1970s, he was a journeyman left winger, but he found his true calling as a coach, debuting behind the bench with the Oilers (when they were in the World Hockey Association) in 1977–78. He helmed Edmonton for four Stanley Cups in the 1980s and added a fifth as general manager in 1990. In his coaching career he won 497 regular-season games and 89 playoff contests.

When were the fastest three goals in NHL history scored?

In 1951–52 the Chicago Black Hawks were bottom feeders in the NHL. The club had the worst record in the league, and scores of empty seats in Chicago Stadium attested to the contempt even their own fans held them in. Long before March 1952 it was pretty obvious the Hawks weren't going to make the playoffs, but on March 23 something magical happened, one of the greatest feats ever accomplished by an NHL player. On that day the

Hawks and the New York Rangers played their last game of the regular season (both were out of the playoffs) at Madison Square Garden in Manhattan. By the end of the second period, in what was a pointless match attended by fewer than 4,000 fans, the Rangers had a commanding 6–2 lead over the hapless Hawks. In the third period, though, at 6:09, Chicago right winger Bill Mosienko scored. A few seconds later he put a second puck into the net behind Rangers goalie Lorne Anderson. Then, at the 6:30 mark, Mosienko scored a third time. The Chicago sniper had scored a hat trick in 21 seconds, a record that has stood for more than a half-century. Only the Montreal Canadiens' Jean Béliveau, who scored three power-play goals in 44 seconds in 1955, has come close to breaking this record. As for that seemingly nothing game in March 1952, the Hawks eventually won it 7–6. Winnipeg-born Mosienko, who had been a pretty good but not exceptional forward with Max and Doug Bentley on the Pony Line in the 1940s, played another couple of seasons and retired in 1954–55 with a record that may well be his for many more decades to come.

Quickies
Did you know …

that Bill Clinton was the first U.S. president still in office to attend an NHL game? On May 25, 1998, Clinton showed up at the second game of the Eastern Conference finals between the Washington Capitals and the Buffalo Sabres at the American capital's MCI Center. The president took in the game from Capitals owner Abe Poulin's personal suite and said at the time that he was impressed with the game's speed and intensity.

How did the Detroit Red Wings and the New York Rangers get their names?

In 1932 James Norris purchased the Detroit Falcons hockey team and renamed them the Red Wings. Norris had played for a Montreal team named the Winged Wheelers, which inspired the name and the winged wheel logo on the NHL's motor city franchise. After Madison Square Garden president "Tex" Rickard bought the New York team in 1926, people began calling them after their owner — Tex's Rangers.

When did the NHL's first expansion occur?

Everyone associates NHL expansion, at least the first one, with 1967–68 when the league added six new U.S. teams (Philadelphia Flyers, St. Louis Blues, Minnesota North Stars, Los Angeles Kings, Pittsburgh Penguins, and Oakland Seals, now defunct). However, the league had contracted and expanded a number of times before the days of the fabled but misnamed Original Six (Montreal Canadiens, Toronto Maple Leafs, Detroit Red Wings, Chicago Black Hawks, New York Rangers, and Boston Bruins). At the NHL's inception in 1917 there were only four clubs — Toronto Arenas (later Maple Leafs), Montreal Canadiens, Ottawa Senators (the originals), and Montreal Wanderers. The last were gone within a couple of weeks when their arena burned down. The Quebec Bulldogs (later the Hamilton Tigers, and still later part of the New York Americans) came onboard in 1919. However, the first actual expansion occurred in 1924–25 when the Montreal Maroons and the Boston Bruins signed up. The next season the Pittsburgh Pirates and the Americans, both now long expired, started playing. Then, in 1926–27, things really began cooking when the Chicago Black Hawks, New York Rangers, and Detroit Cougars (now the Red Wings) joined the party, bringing league membership to a height of 10 clubs. It wouldn't be that numerous again until 1967–68. Today the NHL has 30 teams (24 in the United States, six in Canada).

What NHL goalie nearly bled to death on the ice?

On March 22, 1989, in a game between the Buffalo Sabres and the St. Louis Blues, the latter's Steve Tuttle crashed into a Sabres defenceman and went hurtling through the air at Clint Malarchuk, Buffalo's goaltender. Tuttle's skate blade pierced Malarchuk's neck, severing his jugular vein. The goalie would have likely died on the spot if not for trainer Jim Pizzutelli, who stanched the gusher of blood until doctors could operate. Malarchuk ended up with 300 stitches to close a six-inch wound, but he returned to the Sabres' net 11 days later.

When was the first NHL game played outdoors?

Outdoor NHL games have been a big hit with the fans, the media, and the players lately. The first regular-season match held outdoors was dubbed the Heritage Classic and took place on November 22, 2003, in Edmonton, Alberta. It pitted the Edmonton Oilers against the Montreal Canadiens and was staged in Edmonton's Commonwealth Stadium. More than 57,000 spectators braved a bone-chilling -18 degrees Celsius temperature to watch the Habs edge the Oilers 4–3. Less than five years later, on January 1, 2008, a second regular-season NHL match, called the AMP Energy NHL Winter Classic, was played in Orchard Park, New York, between the Buffalo Sabres and the Pittsburgh Penguins. An NHL-record-setting 71,217 fans turned out to see the Penguins beat the Sabres 2–1 after a shootout in which Pittsburgh's young superstar Sidney Crosby got the final goal. For the first NHL game presented outdoors, though, one has to go back to September 27, 1991, to an exhibition match played in Las Vegas, of all places. The Los Angeles Kings and the New York Rangers

> **Quickies**
> *Did you know ...*
> that baseball titan Babe Ruth dropped in on an NHL game on November 15, 1927? Swarmed by fans, the Bambino swept into the Boston Garden to watch the Bruins play the Chicago Black Hawks in a bruising donnybrook of a game that prompted Ruth to comment, after witnessing his very first hockey spectacle, "Never saw anything like it. Those fellows wanted to kill one another. Thank God I'm in baseball. It's so peaceful and quiet."

took part in an odd promotional affair in the pre-season in an outdoor rink constructed in the parking lot of Caesar's Palace. No one froze at this game — the desert temperature was about 29 degrees Celsius. But the players had to put up with melting ice and a plague of grasshoppers!

What incredible feat did Mario Lemieux accomplish on New Year's Eve 1988?

During his career, the Pittsburgh Penguins' Mario Lemieux accomplished incredible feats and provided hockey fans with some of the game's most memorable moments, but on December 31, 1988, he did something even pretty extraordinary for him. In a game against the New Jersey Devils the Magnificent One became the first and thus far only NHL player to score goals in five different ways. Lemieux put the puck into the Devils' net at even strength, on the power play, shorthanded, on a penalty shot, and into an empty net in an 8–6 Penguins victory.

What happened to the World Hockey Association?

First taking to the ice in 1972–73 as a rival to the National Hockey League, the World Hockey Association had a rollicking roller coaster of a ride through professional hockey until it finally went off the rails at the conclusion of the 1978–79 season. While it existed, the WHA harried the staid NHL and forced that venerable league to boost players' salaries, consider European and U.S. talent more seriously, and generally run a better ship. Before the WHA was finished it had had 32 different franchises at one or another time in 24 cities, most of which bit the dust ignominiously. The WHA's founders were two enterprising Californians named Gary Davidson and Dennis Murphy, but if it hadn't been for the involvement of two of hockey's greatest superstars — Bobby Hull with the Winnipeg Jets and Gordie Howe with the Houston Aeros, then the New England Whalers — the rogue league would have gone belly up a lot sooner. Enticed by lavish salaries, other major NHLers, including Gerry Cheevers, Frank Mahovlich, J.C. Tremblay, and Dave Keon, jumped to the WHA. In the league's inaugural season it actually got teams onto the ice in Cleveland; Philadelphia; Ottawa; Quebec City; New York; Winnipeg; Houston; Los Angeles; Edmonton; Chicago; St. Paul, Minnesota, and Hartford, Connecticut. When the adventure was over, the WHA had just six clubs: the Edmonton

> **Quickies**
> *Did you know …*
> that the largest attendance ever for a hockey game was 74,554 for a match between the University of Michigan and Michigan State University on October 6, 2001, at Spartan Stadium in East Lansing, Michigan? The college rivals had to settle for a 3–3 tie in a hockey battle that was dubbed "The Cold War."

Oilers, Quebec Nordiques, Winnipeg Jets, New England Whalers, Cincinnati Stingers, and Birmingham Bulls. The first four teams made the transition from the WHA into the NHL. Ironically, two of those clubs, the Whalers and the Jets, have since relocated to Raleigh, North Carolina (Hurricanes), and Phoenix, Arizona (Coyotes), respectively. The WHA's championship award was the Avco Cup or World Trophy, named after a finance company. That's also something of an irony, since the league was seriously underfinanced and fiscally mismanaged throughout its entire life. What was the upstart league's legacy? Without doubt it forced the NHL to become a more globally minded sporting endeavour, propelled it into a much greater presence in the United States, and for better or worse kickstarted it into the realm of big business. Was the WHA a pale, inferior stepchild of the NHL, as many critics would have it? Let's not forget that the careers of future stars Wayne Gretzky, Mark Messier, Mike Gartner, Rick Vaive, Michel Goulet, Rod Langway, and many others began in the WHA. And let's not forget, too, that in the 67 exhibition games played between the two leagues the WHA won 33, lost 27, and tied seven.

When did the longest shootout in NHL history take place?

For three periods, on November 26, 2005, the Washington Capitals and the New York Rangers battled it out at Madison Square Garden, ending the game's regulation time with a 2–2 tie. After five minutes of overtime, the score was still tied. Under the NHL's new rule, the next step to break the tie was a shootout in which each team had a chance to score with one of its players in alone on the opponent's goaltender. The Capitals' goalie, Olaf Kolzig, and the Rangers netminder, Henrik Lundqvist, got ready for the barrage of "breakaways" they would have to face. Neither had any idea just how long the shootout would take. In the first three rounds each team scored twice but couldn't break the deadlock. After Washington's 15th shooter failed to score, it was the Rangers' turn. Coach Tom Renney had to choose defenceman Marek Malik after running out of every other available possibility. Malik hadn't scored a goal in 21 months, but he gamely skated in on Kolzig, passed the puck behind himself, and fired it from between his own legs over the startled Washington goalie, just under the crossbar, to finally end the game in a 3–2 victory for New York.

What NHL player scored a goal on his back?

The two newest NHL players to energize the game and electrify the fans are Nova Scotian Sidney Crosby, playing for the Pittsburgh Penguins, and Russian Alexander Ovechkin, skating for the Washington Capitals. Ovechkin, a left winger, debuted with the Capitals in 2005–06, the same season that Crosby, a centreman, joined the NHL. Crosby, who is barely into his 20s, has already done some incredible things such as winning the Art Ross Trophy in 2006–07 as the league's top scorer with 120 points (36 goals, 84 assists). The Penguins' captain is the youngest player ever to win the Art Ross, but he also added the Hart Trophy (most valuable player as picked by the league) and the Lester B. Pearson Award (most outstanding player as selected by the NHL Players' Association). However, Alexander Ovechkin is no slouch when it comes to matching Crosby's amazing brand of hockey. In his first year the Capitals' sniper beat out Crosby for the Calder Trophy as best rookie, scoring 52 goals and 54 assists. Then, in 2007–08, his third campaign, the Russian really broke out, scoring 65 goals and 47 assists for 112 points and winning the Art Ross. That year he also won the Hart and the Lester B. Pearson, not to mention the Maurice Richard Trophy for most goals. No doubt hockey fans have more heroics in store for them from Ovechkin, but one single action already stands out in his blossoming career. On January 16, 2006, the Capitals had built a commanding 5–1 lead over the Phoenix Coyotes when Ovechkin potted a goal that many hockey pundits have dubbed one of the greatest scoring feats of all time. Knocked down by Coyotes defenceman Paul Mara as he was surging toward Phoenix's net, Ovechkin slid on his back, facing away from the goal. Somehow he was able to hook the puck with one hand on his stick and slip it into the net past goalie Brian Boucher for his second goal of the evening.

> **Quickies**
>
> *Did you know …*
>
> that the first Finnish-born player in the National Hockey League was Albert Pudas, who played one season (1926–27) for the Toronto St. Patricks (now the Maple Leafs)? Actually, Pudas, who was born in Siikajoki, Finland, but grew up and played hockey in Port Arthur, Ontario, only got into four games in his entire NHL career. The second Finn to make the NHL was Pentti Lund, also from Port Arthur, who was awarded the Calder Trophy as best rookie in 1948–49 with the New York Rangers. The reason there were so many Finns playing hockey in and around what is now Thunder Bay is that the area attracted a lot of Finnish immigrants, as well as a fair number of other Scandinavians.

What were the first NHL teams to play exhibition matches in Europe?

If you're thinking the answer to this question lies in the 1970s onward, you would be wrong. After the 1937–38 season, the Detroit Red Wings and the Montreal Canadiens sailed for Europe by ship to take part in a nine-game exhibition tour in Britain and France. The first match was staged in London before an audience of 8,000 people. The Habs beat the Red Wings in that game 5–4 with an overtime goal by Toe Blake. The Canadiens went on to win the entire series, with five victories, three losses, and one tie. More than 20 years later, in 1959, the New York Rangers and the Boston Bruins did the Canadiens and Red Wings one better by participating in a 23-game exhibition tour through Europe, battling each other in 10 cities, including London, Paris, Geneva, Berlin, and Vienna. The Rangers added the Chicago Black Hawks' Bobby Hull to their team for the series, and in a weird twist, the Toronto Maple Leafs' resident clown Eddie Shack was paired with the Golden Jet on a line!

Which country won the first World Hockey Championship?

The answer to this question is a bit complicated. Prior to 1920, European Hockey Championships were held without North American participation, with the first European competition being held in Les Avants, Switzerland, in 1910. Great Britain won that event. In 1920 North Americans competed in international hockey for the first time at the Summer Olympics in Antwerp, Belgium. Canada, the winner of the gold medal there, was also deemed the World Champion, as was the case in the first two Winter Olympics in 1924 and 1928. The first World Championship sanctioned outside the Olympics by the International Ice Hockey Federation took place in Chamonix, France, Berlin, and Vienna in 1930, with Canada as the gold medallist. Until 1972, the first time the World Championship and the Olympic hockey tournament were played separately in the same year, Olympic and World Championship medals were handed out for the same results. In the Olympic years of 1980, 1984, and 1988 there were no World Championships played. Beginning in 1992, the Olympic hockey competition and the World Championship were once more held as separate events in an Olympic year. So the answer to the question of who won the first World Championship would be Canada, whether one uses 1920 as the first year or 1930.

Who scored the first goal and assisted on the last goal of the 1972 Canada–Soviet Union Summit Series?

The most important single tournament in the history of hockey was an eight-game series played in September 1972 between a team of Canada's National Hockey League professionals and the Soviet Union's national team. The event ushered in the modern era of international hockey, the breakdown of all professional-amateur barriers, and the emergence of the multicultural makeup of the NHL. The series evolved out of Canada's withdrawal from international competition and the Soviets' desire to play best against best, with four games in Canada (Montreal, Toronto, Winnipeg, Vancouver) and four games in the Soviet Union (all in Moscow).

Thirty seconds into the first match in Montreal, the Boston Bruins' Phil Esposito scored the very first goal in the series, and Canadians sat back, figuring the tournament would be a cakewalk. However, the Soviets stormed back in the game and embarrassed Canada by whipping it 7–3. Things improved marginally in the second match in Toronto when Canada fought back and won 2–1. After that Canadian nerves began to fray when the Soviets tied Canada 4–4 in Winnipeg and clobbered their hosts 5–3 in Vancouver. The West Coast fans booed Team Canada as it skated off the ice when the game was finished, and an emotional Esposito pleaded for respect on national television. After two violent exhibition games in Sweden to adapt to the larger ice surface, Canada entered the Soviet Union in a desperate situation, especially after the team lost the fifth game 5–4 in Moscow. As it turned out, and as every Canadian now knows, Canada went on to win the next three games 3–2, 4–3, and 6–5. The winning goal in all three matches was scored by Paul Henderson. That final game was watched by more people in Canada — something like 16 million — than any other televised show before or since. Certainly, the country as a whole breathed a collective sigh of relief at the final tally: four wins for Canada, three losses, and one tie. As to who assisted Paul Henderson on that last score against the Soviets' netminder Vladislav Tretiak, the goal heard across Canada if not the world, it was Phil Esposito, natch. Espo also ended up being the scoring leader for the series, with seven goals and six assists.

How long have women been playing ice hockey?

Women have been playing hockey for at least as long as men have. Certainly, as the nineteenth century gave way to the twentieth, women's amateur teams and leagues were sprouting up all over Canada, from the Maritimes to Dawson City, Yukon. During the Boer War, the first moneymaking women's game was staged in Montreal in a bid to raise cash to aid the wives of Canadian soldiers fighting in the conflict in South Africa. The first documented women's league began life in 1900 when teams from Montreal, Trois-Rivières, and Quebec City joined forces to compete against one another. In those days women had to wear long skirts that they bunched around their ankles and used tactically to block shots. Needless to say, the men of the era fulminated against this "unseemly" female behaviour, frequently suggesting that women weren't strong enough for the rigours of the sport or complaining about the ever-possible danger that they might fall and expose themselves. Judging by newspaper accounts in the early part of the twentieth century, women hockey players

Quickies

Did you know …

that Phil Esposito, who displayed an aggressive, almost xenophobic dislike of Soviet players during the 1972 Canada–Soviet Union Summit Series, walked his daughter, Connie, down the aisle in 1996 as she married a Russian hockey player named Alexander Selinanov? At the time Selinanov was a member of the NHL's Tampa Bay Lightning, which Esposito was president and general manager of.

could take care of themselves, and sometimes fights as vicious as those common in men's matches broke out on the ice. American women, too, embraced the new sport enthusiastically, and there is a newspaper account as early as 1899 of a game on artificial ice between two teams in Philadelphia. Early women's clubs had colourful names such as the Arena Icebergs, the Civil Service Snowflakes, the Dundurn Amazons, the Saskatchewan Prairie Lilies, and the Meadow Lake Golden Girls. Very occasionally, women would play men, and in 1900 a female squad from Brandon, Manitoba, beat a men's club representing a town bank. The first Ontario championship was played in 1914, and soon after, teams were competing for the Ladies' Ontario Hockey Association's trophy.

What was the most successful women's hockey team ever?

Although women's hockey in North America has a long history dating back to the nineteenth century, one team before the modern era stands head and shoulders above all the others. The amateur Preston Rivulettes hailed from a small town in southern Ontario. Women's hockey took a beating in the 1930s and many clubs folded during the Great Depression, but the Rivulettes thrived. Led by forwards Hilda Ranscombe and Marm Schmuck and goalie Nellie Ranscombe, the team notched 348 victories, three ties, and two losses in the decade. Along the way, the Rivs won the annual women's championships in Ontario every year and in 1933 were the first to win the Lady Bessborough Trophy, presented annually to the Dominion Women's Hockey Association national championship. The Rivulettes continued to have a lock on the Dominion trophy until the Second World War forced the club to disband in 1941. The team was inducted into the Hockey Hall of Fame in 1963.

> **Quickies**
>
> *Did you know …*
> that Lord Stanley, Canada's governor general from 1888 to 1893 and the man who donated hockey's most prestigious championship trophy, got his entire family to play the game? His daughter, Isobel, played for a Government House hockey team that skirmished with a local female squad. It is said that even Lord Stanley's wife took a twirl or two in a match.

When was the first Women's World Hockey Championship held?

Informally begun in 1987 in Toronto as an invitational tournament, the Women's World Hockey Championship has become the pre-eminent event in women's hockey, with the exception of the Winter Olympics. Not surprisingly, Canada won that first event. At the first six championships (1990, 1992, 1994, 1997, 1999, 2000) under the auspices of the International Ice Hockey Federation the results were the same: Canada gold, the United States silver, Finland bronze. In 2001 Canada and the United States once again took gold and silver respectively, but Russia nabbed bronze. The 2003 championship was cancelled

Five Top Canadian Women's Hockey Players

- **Hayley Wickenheiser**: Gold medals at 2002 and 2006 Olympics. Gold medals at Women's World Hockey Championship in 1994, 1997, 1999, 2000, 2001, 2003, and 2007.
- **Angela James**: Gold medals at Women's World Hockey Championship in 1990, 1992, 1994, and 1997.
- **Cassie Campbell**: Gold medals at 2002 and 2006 Olympics. Gold medals at Women's World Hockey Championship in 1994, 1997, 1999, 2000, 2001, and 2004.
- **Danielle Goyette**: Gold medals at 2002 and 2006 Olympics. Gold medals at Women's World Hockey Championship in 1992, 1994, 1997, 1999, 2000, 2001, 2004, and 2007.
- **Geraldine Heaney**: Gold medal at 2002 Olympics. Gold medals at Women's World Hockey Championship in 1992, 1994, 1997, 1999, 2000, and 2001.

due to the outbreak of SARS, and since then both Canada and the United States have won gold twice (Canada in 2004, 2007, the United States in 2005, 2008). The Women's World Hockey Championship isn't held in years when there's a Winter Olympics. Canada's premier women's hockey players over the past decade and a half have been national heroes such as Angela James, Danielle Goyette, Geraldine Heaney, Nancy Drolet, and the incomparable Hayley Wickenheiser.

Who were the first two women to play professional hockey in men's leagues?

Arguably the most famous female hockey player in the world in the early 1990s, Manon Rhéaume, born in Lac Beauport, Quebec, was the first woman to suit up with a National Hockey League team when she played goal in a 1992 pre-season match for the Tampa Bay Lightning against the St. Louis Blues. The next year she played another exhibition game for the Lightning against the Boston Bruins. After that she tended goal for a number of men's minor-league clubs. In 1992 Rhéaume made her first appearance with Canada's national team, and she helped it win gold medals at the Women's World Championship in 1992 and 1994. Prior to the 1997 World Championship, she was cut from Team Canada, but she made a comeback at the 1998 Olympics in Nagano, Japan. She played well, but Canada lost the gold to the U.S. team and had to settle for silver. Rhéaume announced her retirement from hockey in the summer of 2000. The second woman to play for a men's professional team was Glens Falls, New York–born Erin Whitten, who was also a goalie. In 1993–94 she debuted with the Toledo Storm, a men's club in the minor-league East Coast Hockey League. On October 30, 1993, Whitten became the first female netminder to achieve a victory in a men's professional match. She played four seasons of women's

Five Top U.S. Women's Hockey Players

- **Cammi Granato**: Gold medal at 1998 Olympics. Gold medal at 2005 Women's World Hockey Championship. Played for Team USA from 1990 to 2005.
- **Karen Bye**: Gold medal at 1998 Olympics. Silver medals at six Women's World Hockey Championships.
- **Katie King**: Gold medal at 1998 Olympics. Gold medal at 2005 Women's World Hockey Championship.
- **Angela Ruggiero**: Gold medal at the 1998 Olympics. Gold medals at the Women's World Hockey Championship in 2005 and 2008.
- **Krissy Wendell**: Gold medal at 1998 Olympics. Gold medal at the Women's World Hockey Championship in 2005.

university hockey at the University of New Hampshire and was the top goaltender on the U.S. women's national team. Whitten made appearances in 1992, 1994, 1997, and 1999 at the Women's World Championship, but the U.S. team finished second to Canada every time.

Stanley Cup Playoff Hat Trick Magic

- **Wayne Gretzky**: Most three-or-more-goal games in playoffs in a career (10).
- **Jari Kurri**: Most three-or-more-goal games in one playoff year: (4).
- **Jari Kurri**: Most three-or-more-goal games in one playoff series: (3).

Three Biggest NHL Scoundrels

- **Harold Ballard**: In 1972 the Toronto Maple Leafs' worst owner ever was sentenced to three concurrent three-year jail sentences for tax evasion. However, the miserly, mercurial Leafs autocrat spent only one year in jail. When he got out, he continued his erratic ways as Leafs owner for another two decades, easily one of the worst periods in the franchise's storied history. Obviously, being a jailbird only made him worse.
- **Bruce McNall**: In 1992 McNall, the owner of the Los Angeles Kings, was elected chairman of the NHL's Board of Governors. However, he didn't get to enjoy his lofty status for long. In March 1997 he went to prison to serve five and a half years for swindling banks and investors out of $250 million.
- **Alan Eagleson**: The impresario behind the 1972 Canada–Soviet Union Summit Series and the Canada Cup, one of the architects (and, as it turned out, exploiters) of the National Hockey League Players' Association, and the most powerful agent hockey has ever seen, Eagleson was someone you didn't dare cross in the stuffy, closed world of the NHL. That all changed, though, when the uber-agent was fined $1 million and sentenced to 18 months in jail for bilking players and purloining disability-insurance cash and profits from various Canada Cup events, money that was supposedly earmarked for the NHL players' pension fund. Ensconced in prison, the 64-year-old Eagleson worked as a cleaner and fetched coffee. How the mighty fall! He was also stripped of his Order of Canada and forced out of the Hockey Hall of Fame.

Top Five Penalty Kings in the NHL

Here, with their combined career regular-season and playoff penalties, are five of the orneriest blokes ever to lace on skates.

- **Dave "Tiger" Williams**: 4,421 penalty minutes in 14 seasons, 962 regular-season games, 83 playoff matches. Toronto Maple Leafs, Vancouver Canucks, Los Angeles Kings, and Hartford Whalers.
- **Dale Hunter**: 4,294 penalty minutes in 19 seasons, 1,407 regular-season games, 186 playoff matches. Quebec Nordiques, Washington Capitals, and Colorado Avalanche.
- **Marty McSorley**: 3,755 penalty minutes in 961 regular-season games, 115 playoff matches. Pittsburgh Penguins, Edmonton Oilers, Los Angeles Kings, New York Rangers, San Jose Sharks, and Boston Bruins.
- **Tie Domi**: 3,753 penalty minutes in 1,020 regular-season games, 98 playoff matches. Toronto Maple Leafs, New York Rangers, and Winnipeg Jets.
- **Chris Nilan**: 3,584 penalty minutes in 688 regular-season games, 111 playoff matches. Montreal Canadiens, New York Rangers, and Boston Red Sox.

soccer

What is the origin of soccer?

Soccer-like games that involved the kicking of a ball across a playing pitch have existed for eons in regions from China to Meso-America to the Arctic tundra. But modern soccer, as it evolved in Great Britain, has its roots in a medieval European game called "mob football," which was played between rival villages at times of celebration and festivity, especially on Shrove Tuesday. Played in England, Normandy, Brittany, Picardy, Cornwall, Wales, Scotland, and Ireland, mob football saw teams of unlimited size trying to force a ball (often an inflated pig's bladder) into an opponent village's main square or onto its church's steps. The rules were vague and play was often extremely violent, leading to broken limbs, internal injuries, and even the occasional death.

Why did both Edward II and Edward III prohibit soccer?

In 1314 King Edward II issued a prohibition against so called "mob football" because of the chaotic impact that "this hustling over large balls" had on the city life in London. Edward III also prohibited "futeball" in 1349 because it distracted able-bodied men from archery practice.

Who owned the first pair of football boots?

Quickies
Did you know …
that the first recorded soccer death was in 1280 when in a game of mob football at Ulgham, near Ashington in Northumberland, a player was killed as a result of running against an opposing player's sheathed dagger?

King Henry VIII's soccer shoes — called football boots — were listed within the Great Wardrobe of 1526, a shopping list of the day. They were made by his personal shoemaker, Cornelius Johnson, in 1525, at a cost of four shillings, the modern equivalent of $160 CDN. Little is known about them, as there is no surviving example, but the royal football boots are known to have been made of strong leather, ankle-high, and heavier than the normal shoe of the day.

What British king was first to give soccer royal approval?

Charles II of England gave the game of soccer royal approval in 1681 when he attended a match between the Royal Household and the Duke of Albemarle's servants.

What was *tsu chu*?

As far back as 2,500 B.C., a game of kicking a ball called *tsu chu* (also spelled as *cuju*) was played in China. *Tsu* means "to kick the ball with feet" and *chu* means "a ball made of leather and stuffed." Matches were often staged in celebration of the emperor's birthday. The objective was for players to kick a ball through a round opening into a small net attached to bamboo poles. The opening was about one foot (30–40 centimetres) wide and elevated about 30 feet (nine metres) from the ground. During the Ts'in Dynasty (255 B.C.–206 B.C.) a form of *tsu chu* was used for training by soldiers, and from the Han Dynasty (206 B.C.–220 A.D.) there survives a war manual featuring physical exercises called *tsu chu*. These exercises involved a leather ball filled with feathers and hair. With the exception of the hands, all other body parts could be used while trying to "score."

> **Quickies**
> *Did you know ...*
> that the first instance of the modern spelling of football appeared in 1608, in act 1 scene 4 of Shakespeare's *King Lear:* "Nor tripped neither, you base football player"?

What was *episkyros*?

Around 2000 B.C., the Greeks played *episkyros* (also known as *phaininda*), a kicking and throwing game played primarily by men, usually in the nude. Early balls were made of linen and hair wrapped in string and sewn together, though it is believed inflated balls — inflated pig bladders wrapped in pigskin or deerskin — were used by later practitioners of the game.

> **Quickies**
> *Did you know ...*
> that an ancient Greek marble relief housed in the National Museum of Archeology in Athens shows an athlete balancing a ball on his thigh as a young boy looks on? This very same image is featured on the European Cup trophy.

Who was Richard Mulcaster?

Richard Mulcaster, who lived from 1531 to 1611, was headmaster of the Merchant Taylors' School and St. Paul's School in London. Not only was he a prominent educator of his time, he was also one of the greatest sixteenth-century advocates of soccer. In his 1581 publication titled "Positions Wherein Those Primitive Circumstances Be Examined, Which Are Necessarie for the Training up of Children," he argued that "Footeball" was beneficial "both to health and strength" of students, and he advocated for, organized, and refereed matches to counteract the craze of mob football.

What is the world's oldest soccer club?

The Sheffield Football Club was founded in 1857 in Sheffield by Nathaniel Creswick and William Prest, and is now recognized as the world's oldest club. The club initially played its own code of football: the Sheffield rules. Players were allowed to push or hit the ball with their hands, and there was no offside rule at all, so that players known as "kick throughs" could be permanently positioned near the opponents' goal.

> **Quickies**
> *Did you know …*
> that the Inuit played a game called *asqaqtuk*, which involved booting a heavy ball stuffed with grass, caribou hair, and moss across the arctic tundra between goals as much as 10 miles (16 kilometres) apart?

What is the oldest national soccer team in the world?

That would be a tie. Both Scotland and England were the first countries to put forward national teams, in 1872. In fact, they did so for a match against each other, which also allows them to share the credit of holding the first international match. The game was held at Hamilton Crescent in Partick, Scotland, on November 30 that year, and, appropriately enough, it ended in a goalless tie.

Who drew up the first set of soccer rules?

During the eighteenth century, the game of mob football evolved into a codified sport at England's public schools like Eton, Westminster, Rugby, Charterhouse, and Harrow. The first-ever set of formal soccer rules were written at Eton College in 1815, though each school tended to have their own set of rules.

What are the Cambridge Rules?

In 1848, representatives from Eton, Harrow, Rugby, Winchester, and Shrewsbury schools gathered at Trinity College, at Cambridge University, for a meeting to codify the rules of soccer. These were the first set of rules to be used collectively by multiple school teams. When the country's leading clubs and schools got together to form the Football Association in 1863, they used the Cambridge Rules as the basis for a new set of FA rules.

When did soccer and rugby become separate sports?

When England's Football Association was established in 1863 they published the first set of rules, which expressly forbade carrying, passing, or otherwise handling the ball. Prior to this, the various codes of soccer used by clubs allowed players to use their hands to move the ball, often in a manner that resembled today's rugby. It is felt that the establishment of the first FA rules marked the break between soccer and rugby.

When did the FA Cup begin?

In 1871, Charles W. Alcock, then FA secretary, announced the introduction of the Football Association Challenge Cup. It was the first knockout competition of its type in the world. Only 15 clubs took part in the first staging of the tournament. It included two clubs based in Scotland: Donington School and Queen's Park. In the 1872 final, the Wanderers beat the Royal Engineers 1–0 at the Kennington Oval. The FA Cup is the oldest association football competition in the world.

The 12 Founding Clubs of England's Football Association

- Barnes
- Blackheath
- Forest of Leytonstone
- Perceval House
- Kensington School
- The War Office
- Crystal Palace
- Epping Forest
- Crusaders
- Surbiton
- No Names of Kilburn
- Blackheath Proprietary School

When was the Scottish Football Association founded?

On March 13, 1873, representatives of seven Scottish soccer teams gathered at a meeting in Glasgow in response to an advertisement in the newspaper. The purpose of the gathering was to form the Scottish Football Association. At the meeting it was resolved that, "The clubs here represented form themselves into an association for the promotion of football according to the rules of The Football Association and that the clubs connected with this association subscribe for a challenge cup to be played for annually, the committee to propose the laws of the competition." An eighth club, Kilmarnock, did not attend the meeting, but expressed its wish to join by letter.

When was the Scottish Cup first played?

The Scottish Football Association Challenge Cup, usually known as the Scottish Cup, started in the 1873–74 season, when it was contested by 16 teams. The trophy is the oldest national trophy in the world. The Scottish Cup was first awarded to Queen's Park when they beat Clydesdale 2–0 in the final in front of a crowd of 3,000 people.

Chronology of the Formation of the United Kingdom's Football Associations

- **England**: "The Football Association" (FA) — 1863
- **Scotland**: "The Scottish Football Association" (SFA) — 1873
- **Wales**: "The Football Association of Wales" (FAW) —1876
- **Northern Ireland**: "Irish Football Association" (IFA) — 1880

What is the Old Firm?

The Scottish soccer teams Celtic FC, founded in 1888, and Rangers FC, founded in 1873, both based in Glasgow, are collectively referred to as the Old Firm. It is not clear how this term came about. Some say it is because of camaraderie shown between the two clubs in their early days, while others surmise it is an ironic take on the arch rivalry that eventually developed between them. Whichever it is, the two clubs are indisputably the most successful in Scotland, having won between them 66 Scottish Cups and 93 Scottish Premier League championships as of 2008.

What 1882 game gave opposite records to Ireland and England?

Quickies
Did you know …
that in September 1884 the *Glasgow Evening News* produced the first-ever football edition of a newspaper giving match scores from earlier that afternoon?

On February 18, 1882, two years after the founding of the Irish FA, Ireland made their international debut against England, losing 13–0 in a friendly game played at Bloomfield Park in Belfast. This remains the record win for England and the record defeat for the Northern Ireland team.

Quickies
Did you know …
that the Scottish club Queen's Park FC, established in 1867, is the world's oldest soccer club outside of England?

What is the oldest Irish soccer club?

Quickies
Did you know …
that the Football Association of Wales, founded in 1876, is the third-oldest national soccer association in the world?

Cliftonville Football and Athletic Club, known as The Reds, is a Northern Irish football team playing in the IFA Premiership. Founded on September 20, 1879, in the north Belfast district of Cliftonville, they are the oldest football club in Ireland and celebrated their 125th anniversary in 2004.

When was the Irish league founded?

The Irish League is the second-oldest national league in the world, being formed a week earlier than the Scottish Football League. Only the Football League in England is older. Four clubs — Cliftonville, Glentoran, Linfield, and Lisburn Distillery — have retained membership of the Irish League since its inception in 1890.

What is the difference between the Irish Football Association (IFA) and the Football Association of Ireland (FAI)?

Ireland has two FAs because Ireland itself is divided into two nations, Northern Ireland, which is part of the United Kingdom, and the Republic of Ireland, which is a sovereign state formed in 1921. Beginning with the formation of the Irish Football Association (IFA) in 1879, all of Ireland was represented under that one association. But with the partition of Ireland in 1921, the Football Association of Ireland (FAI) was formed to represent the Republic of Ireland, due to bitter disputes between Dublin-area teams and Belfast teams.

When was the first international game between non-UK teams?

The first international soccer game played without involving a British side was between the United States and Canada, played in Newark, New Jersey, on November 28, 1885. The Canadians won 1–0.

What was the largest crowd to ever attend a soccer match?

The largest crowd ever to attend a soccer match was 199,854 spectators at the World Cup final in Rio de Janeiro, Brazil, on July 16, 1950. The game pitted Brazil against Uruguay. Uruguay won the match, 2–1.

Who sets the official rules for soccer?

The official rules of soccer are called the Laws of the Game and they are maintained by two governing bodies: the International Football Association Board (IFAB) and the *Fédération Internationale de Football Association* (FIFA).

What is FIFA?

FIFA is an acronym for *Fédération Internationale de Football Association*. It is the international governing body of association football, headquartered in Zurich, Switzerland. FIFA is responsible for the organization and governance of soccer's major international tournaments, most notably the FIFA World Cup, held since 1930. The Laws of the Game are not solely the responsibility of FIFA; they are maintained by a body called the International Football Association Board (IFAB). FIFA has members on its board (four representatives); the other four are provided by the football associations of the United Kingdom: England, Scotland, Wales, and Northern Ireland, in recognition of their contribution to the creation and history of the game. Changes to the Laws of the Game must be agreed by at least six of the eight delegates.

> **Quickies**
> *Did you know ...*
> that FIFA has 208 football association members?

What is IFAB?

IFAB is an acronym for the International Football Association Board. Established in England in 1886, the board was originally made up of the United Kingdom's four pioneering football associations: England's Football Association (The FA), the Scottish Football Association (SFA), the Football Association of Wales (FAW), and Northern Ireland's Irish Football Association (IFA). Its aim was to create a unified set of rules for the game in Great Britain and function as a governing body. Each of the four founding FAs had equal voting rights on the board. Beginning in 1913, the *Fédération Internationale de Football Association* (FIFA), which governs world association soccer, became a voting board member. Today, each UK association has one vote on the board and FIFA has four. IFAB deliberations must be approved by at least six votes. Thus, FIFA's approval is necessary for any IFAB decision, but FIFA alone cannot change the Laws of the Game; they need to be agreed by at least two of the UK members.

How many referees are there in a regulation soccer match?

There are three. One referee (sometimes called the centre referee), and two assistant referees (formerly called linesmen) who patrol the perimeter of the field and carry flags to signal to the referee. The referee, who is the only one of the three who conducts his duties in bounds on the pitch, is the ruling authority for any given soccer match. His word is law on the pitch.

Who was Ken Aston?

The red and yellow card system was invented by English referee Ken Aston, whose innovation was inspired one day in the late 1960s by the yellow "caution" and red "stop" lights in the streets of London. Aston sat on FIFA's Referee's Committee from 1970 to 1972. His card system was first used at the 1970 World Cup. Aston died on October 23, 2001 at the age of 86.

What does a yellow card mean?

The yellow card is a caution issued to a player by the referee. The yellow card may be shown to a player who is guilty of unsporting behaviour, shows dissent by word or action, persistently infringes the Laws of the Game, delays the restart of play, fails to respect the required distance when play is restarted with a corner kick or a free kick, enters or re-enters the field of play without the referee's permission, or deliberately leaves the field of play without the referee's permission. Any time a yellow or red card is shown, a "direct" or "indirect kick" will also be awarded.

What does a red card mean?

When a player is shown a red card, it means ejection from the game. By the Laws of the Game, a player must be shown a red card for serious foul play, violent conduct, spitting at an opponent or any other person, deliberately handling the ball in an attempt to prevent an obvious scoring opportunity, denying an obvious goal-scoring opportunity to an opponent moving toward the player's goal by an offence punishable by a free kick or a penalty kick, and for using offensive, insulting, or abusive language. A player will also be shown a red card and ejected immediately after receiving a second yellow card caution in the same match.

How many players are allowed to play for a team in a soccer match?

Soccer teams may consist of a maximum of 11 on-field players (and a minimum of seven) with three substitutes allowed per game. If, due to injuries or other reasons, a team cannot field seven players, the match is cancelled.

The Seven Ways a Ball Can Be Put into Play

- Kickoff
- Throw-in
- Goal kick
- Corner kick
- Free kick
- Penalty kick
- Drop ball

Who wore the first shin guards?

Shin guards, which are now required kit under the Laws of the Game, were first introduced in 1874 by Sam Widdowson, a player for Nottingham Forest. Widdowson cut down a pair of cricket shin pads and strapped them to the outside of his stockings. He was initially ridiculed, but the protective value of the pads could not be denied and they eventually caught on.

Quickies

Did you know ...

that a professional soccer player runs an average of 6.2 miles in a game and burns 1,000 to 1,500 calories?

What is the "Acme Thunderer"?

Through the 1860s and 1870s, Joseph Hudson, an English toolmaker from Birmingham, was using his home bathroom as a whistle-making workshop, but it wasn't until 1884 that he invented the Acme Thunderer, which is credited as the world's first reliable pea whistle and quickly became the whistle of choice for British soccer referees.

What does it mean when the referee holds his arms straight out?

This is called "advantage" and it means that the referee has seen a foul but has decided not to call it yet because the fouled team is

Fouls That Will Lead to an Indirect Free Kick

By a goalkeeper inside his own penalty area:

- holding the ball in hands for longer than six seconds;
- handling the ball after it has been released from his possession but has not yet touched another player;
- handling the ball after it has been deliberately kicked to him by a teammate; or
- handling the ball after he has received it directly from a throw-in taken by a teammate.

By any player:

- playing in a dangerous manner;
- impeding the progress of an opponent;
- preventing the goalkeeper from releasing the ball from his hands; or
- at the discretion of the referee, offences not covered under the Fouls and Conduct section (Law 12) of the Laws of the Game, for which play is stopped to caution or dismiss a player.

in an advantageous position and might possibly score. Advantage generally only lasts three to five seconds before the referee will blow his whistle and stop play.

What does it mean when the referee blows his whistle and points at a goal?

The referee has seen a foul and is awarding a direct free kick against the goal he is pointing to.

How do players know when a penalty kick is awarded?

When a referee points directly at the 18 yard (16.5 metre) area, he is awarding a penalty kick. The referee will usually run to the penalty spot, stop beside it and point straight down at it with his hand.

Why do games that are not tied at the end of regulation time often go longer?

One of the unique things about soccer is that during a match no one on or off the pitch knows exactly how long the match will go. That's because the referee is the official time-keeper, and while regulations state that a match consists of two halves of 45 minutes each, with a mandatory break at halftime, they also state that the referee has discretion to add time to the end of each half for any stoppage of play. While the rules for games like hockey, basketball, and American football include provisions for stopping the clock (such as after a goal, or for out of bounds), the clock for a soccer game never stops, except for the during the halftime break. The referee is under no obligation to tell anyone how much additional time will be added to each half. The clock runs out only when the referee says so.

Assistant Referee Flag Signals Decoded

- Flag straight up: indicating to the referee to stop play because assistant referee needs to talk to referee. Can also mean offside or be a signal for the referee to look at the other linesman.
- Flag straight up with hand held over his chest badge: indicating to referee that a player needs to be shown a yellow or red card.
- Flag out sideways at 45 degrees horizontally along the touchline: indicating for a throw-in. The team attacking in the direction they are pointing takes the throw.
- Flag pointing at the goal: indicating a goal kick.
- Flag pointing at the corner flag: indicating a corner kick.
- Flag held straight out in front of assistant referee after an offside call:
    - Up at a 45-degree angle: indicating an offside on the far side of the field.
    - Straight horizontally: indicating an offside in the middle of the field.
    - Down at a 45-degree angle: indicating an offside on the near side of the field.
- Flag held straight up suspended between both hands: substitution in progress.
- Flag held horizontally across chest: calling for penalty kick.
- Flag held behind back while standing at corner flag: calling for penalty kick.
- Flag held up after a goal: assistant referee wishes to dispute the goal

Why does the referee point at the centre of the field and not the goal to indicate a goal?

The regulation restart method after either team scores a goal is a kickoff by the other team from the centre of the field. That is why the referee points at the centre of the field after a goal. The referee is not indicating a goal, but rather calling for a restart from the centre of the field.

Four Reasons Why the Referee Can Add Time to the Game Clock

According to the Laws of the Game, time can be added if:

- time is lost attending to injuries on the field;
- time is lost completing player substitutions;
- time is lost due to delays in putting the ball back into active play after it goes out; or
- any other cause for interruption to active play the referee deems sufficient.

What is the penalty for faking an injury?

Not that this ever, ever happens (ahem!), but any simulating action that is intended to deceive the referee — anywhere on the field — must be sanctioned as unsporting behaviour. This includes Oscar-worthy performances for fake injuries. The penalty is not a golden statue, but a yellow card.

Quickies

Did you know ...
that aside from during the regulation halftime beak, the Laws of the Game do not permit the referee to ever stop the clock once play has begun?

Quickies

Did you know ...
that a ball rolling along outside the touchline remains in play as long as part of the ball is over the touchline?

When is a soccer player offside?

Provided that he is not in his own half of the field, a player is offside when he is not in possession of the ball and he is nearer to his opponents' goal line than both the ball and the second last opponent (including the goalkeeper). If an offside infraction is called, the opponent is awarded an indirect free kick (IFK). There is no offside offence if a player receives the ball directly from a goal kick, a throw-in, or a corner kick.

When is offside position determined?

Offside position is not determined at the time the ball is received by an attacker, but rather it is determined at the moment the ball was last played by one of the attacker's teammates. If, for example, an attacker kicks the ball high in the air toward the opponent's goal while none of his teammates are in offside position, but then a second speedy attacker penetrates the defence and receives the kick behind the second-last opponent, the speedy one is not offside.

Fouls That Will Lead to a Direct Free Kick

- Kicking or attempting to kick an opponent;
- tripping or attempting to trip an opponent;
- jumping at an opponent in a careless or reckless manner, or with excessive force;
- charging an opponent in a careless or reckless manner, or with excessive force;
- striking or attempting to strike an opponent;
- pushing an opponent;
- making contact with the opponent before the ball when tackling;
- holding an opponent;
- spitting at an opponent; or
- handling the ball deliberately (except for the goalkeeper within his own penalty area).

Note: If any of these are committed by a player inside his own penalty area, a penalty kick is awarded.

What is the difference between a "handball" and "handling" a ball?

A "handball" is when the ball strikes a player (other than the goalkeeper) on the hand or arm and there is no intent on the part of the player struck to control the ball with either hand or arm. As such, a "handball" is not illegal. If the player attempts in any way to control the ball with hand or arm it is called "handling" the ball, and is an illegal play.

When were the first goalposts used in soccer?

That would be way back in 1681 when a match was played between servants of the King, and those of the Duke of Albemarle. The doorways of two forts were used as goals, and players attempted to score by driving the ball through one of the doorways.

When was the size of the goal determined?

In 1863 the English Football Association decreed that the goal posts should be eight yards (7.32 metres) apart. In 1866, they further decreed that posts should be eight feet (2.44 metres) high. Both measurements stand today.

What happens if the crossbar of the goal becomes dislodged or damaged during a match?

FIFA, the world governing body of soccer, makes special mention of this in the Laws of the Game. "If the crossbar becomes displaced or broken, play is stopped until it has been repaired or replaced in position. If a repair is not possible, the match is abandoned. The use of a rope to replace the crossbar is not permitted. If the crossbar is repaired, the match is restarted with a dropped ball at the place where the ball was located when the play was stopped."

Quickies
Did you know ...
that there is no law on the books requiring the use of goal nets?

What is a striker?

A striker is a scoring forward, usually a centre-forward who is highly skilled at putting the ball in the net. The striker often plays "pushed up" into a offensive position leading the formation, while much of the rest of the team works the wings, feeding the striker or defence. Many great strikers have poor defensive skills, and are called "pure strikers." The striker traditionally wears the number 10 jersey.

Quickies
Did you know ...
that the first wooden crossbars did not appear until 1875? Prior to that, tape was used between the tops of goalposts.

What is a "sweeper"?

"Sweeper" is the name for a versatile fullback player who "sweeps up" the ball if the opponent manages to breach the defensive line. Unlike other defenders, the sweeper does not mark, or cover, one particular opponent, but covers the centre of defence. The *verrou* system in Switzerland and the *catenaccio* system in Italy were both notable for employing sweepers.

What does *verrou* mean?

The *verrou*, or "chain," is a system of play invented by Karl Rappan while coach of Switzerland in the 1930s and 1940s. It was the first system to use four players on defence, employing a sweeper called the *verrouilleur* — a highly defensive fullback who patrolled the centre of defence ahead of the goalkeeper. The *verrou* system also required players to switch positions and duties depending on the game's pattern. It was used by the Swiss national team in the 1938 World Cup to knock out Nazi Germany in the first round. The *catenaccio* system of Italy evolved out of the *verrou* system.

What does *catenaccio* mean?

Catenaccio is Italian for "bolt," as in a door bolt, and in soccer it refers to a tactical formation made famous in Italy during the 1960s by coach Helenio Herrera and FC *Internazionale Milano* (Inter Milan). It uses a strong defensive formation, such as 1-3-3-3 or 1-4-4-1, which implements a fullback called a "sweeper," who stands in front of the goalkeeper and patrols the centre of defence. From the 1970s to the 1990s, *catenaccio* became a trademark playing style of the Italian national team. The system, often criticized for its lack of offensive creativity, was nonetheless effective, employing sudden strikes to score early in a game and then relying on defence to protect the lead.

What is the WM system?

The WM system was created in the mid-1920s by manager Herbert Chapman (of Arsenal) to counter a change in the offside law in 1925. The change had reduced the number of opposition players that attackers needed between themselves and the goal line from three to two. This led to the introduction of a centre-back to stop the opposing centre-forward, and tried to balance defensive and offensive playing. The WM system employs three backs, four midfielders, and three forwards, and is so called because in a formation diagram the groupings look like an M under a W, with one player at each point of each letter.

What is Total Football?

Total Football is the term used to describe an influential theory of tactical soccer in which any of a team's players on the field can take over the role of any teammate. The foundations for Total Football were laid by Jack Reynolds, who was the manager of Ajax

Amsterdam from 1915–25, 1928–40, and 1945–47. Rinus Michels, who played under Reynolds, later went on to become manager of Ajax himself and refined the concept into what is known today as "Total Football" (*Totaalvoetbal* in Dutch). In Total Football, a player who moves out of his position is replaced by another from his team, thus retaining the team's intended organizational structure. In this fluid system, no player is fixed in his nominal role; anyone can be successively an attacker, a midfielder, and a defender.

> **Specifications For Soccer Balls**
>
> An International Football Association–approved ball must be:
>
> - spherical;
> - made of leather or other suitable material;
> - of a circumference of not more than 28 inches (70 centimetres) and not less than 27 inches (68 centimetres);
> - not more than 16 ounces (450 grams) in weight and not less than 14 ounces (410 grams) at the start of the match; and
> - of a pressure equal to 0.6–1.1 atmospheres (8.5–5.6 pounds per square inch or 600–1100 grams per centimetres square) at sea level.

What was the Jules Rimet trophy?

The original World Cup trophy was called "Victory." Designed by French sculptor Abel Lafleur, it stood 13.7 inches (35 centimetres) high and weighed approximately 8.4 pounds (3.8 kilograms). The statuette depicted Nike of Samothrace and was made of sterling silver and gold plate, with a blue base made of lapis lazuli. There was a gold plate on each of the four sides of the base, on which were engraved the name of the trophy as well as the names of the nine winners between 1930 and 1970. In 1946, it was renamed the Jules Rimet trophy in honour of the founder of the World Cup tournament.

> **World Cup Firsts**
>
> - **First goal**: Lucien Laurent (France) against Mexico, July 13, 1930.
> - **First penalty goal**: Manuel Rocquetas Rosas (Mexico) against Argentina, July 19, 1930.
> - **First hat trick**: Guillermo Stabile (Argentina) against Mexico, July 19, 1930.
> - **First player sent off**: Mario de Las Casas (Peru) against Romania, July 14, 1930.
> - **First own goal**: Ernst Loertscher (Switzerland) against West Germany, June 9, 1938.

Who was Pickles?

In 1966, the Jules Rimet Cup disappeared while on display at London's Westminster Central Hall, just a few months before the World Cup was due to take place in England. It was later found by a dog named Pickles, owned by a Thames river-barge worker named David Corbett, wrapped in newspaper under a garden hedge in south London. Pickles and Corbett received £3,000 reward and England went on to win the cup.

What was the first tied match in World Cup history?

That was when Italy and Spain came out 1–1 during the quarter-finals in Florence, Italy on May 31, 1934. The game was replayed on June 1 to a score of 1-0 for Italy, who eventually won the cup that year.

What was the first World Cup match with extra time?

The first World Cup match with extra time was played in Turin between Austria and France on May 27, 1934, to settle a 2–2 tie. Austria advanced to the quarter-finals.

What was the first World Cup final with extra time?

On June 10, 1934, Italy and Czechoslovakia played to a 1–1 tie in the World Cup final in Rome. Italy scored in extra time to win the cup.

Quickies

Did you know ...
that Hector Castro, who scored Uruguay's winning goal in the 1930 World Cup final, had only one hand?

By what unusual method did Chile qualify for the 1973 World Cup finals in a match against the USSR?

Quite simply, by kicking the ball into an undefended net. Earlier in the year, after a *coup d'état* by General Augusto Pinochet, thousands of supporters of Marxist Chilean President Allende had been executed in the National Stadium in Santiago. Out of protest, the USSR refused to play in the stadium and the match was held without Soviet players present. The Chilean players kicked off the game and scored into the empty Soviet net. Then the game was abandoned and awarded to Chile. As a result, Chile automatically qualified for the 1974 finals but were eliminated in the first round.

Why was Chilean goalkeeper Roberto Rojas banned for life by FIFA?

On September 3, 1989, Brazil was leading 1–0 with 23 minutes left in a decisive World Cup qualifier against Chile at the Estádio do Maracanã in Rio de Janeiro. In an attempt to disqualify the match, the Chilean goalkeeper Roberto Rojas pretended to have been hit and seriously injured by a flare thrown from the Brazilian crowd. The whole Chilean team walked off in protest, and the match was abandoned. Investigations by the Chilean Soccer Federation and FIFA concluded that he had faked the injury. FIFA awarded Brazil a 2–0 victory, banned Rojas from international play for life and banned Chile from the 1994 World Cup.

> **Quickies**
> *Did you know ...*
> that Mexico was banned from participating in the 1990 World Cup because they had deliberately fielded three over-age players in a FIFA international youth tournament?

What happened to the original Jules Rimet Cup?

If anyone knows, they aren't telling. In 1983, the original Jules Rimet Cup was stolen from a display at the Brazilian Football Confederation headquarters in Rio de Janeiro, and it is believed that it was melted down by the thieves. The Brazilian Football Association, who had earned the right to keep the trophy in 1970 after having won it three times, ordered a replica from Eastman Kodak, who commissioned Wilhelm Geist and Son in Hanau, Germany, to recreate the trophy. Three Brazilians and an Argentine were arrested for the theft but released. Eventually they were tried and convicted in absentia.

Which teams competed in the first World Cup match?

France beat Mexico 4–1 in that match held in Montevideo, Uruguay, on July 13, 1930.

> **The Four Countries That Have Hosted the World Cup Twice**
>
> - Mexico: 1938 and 1986
> - Italy: 1934 and 1990
> - France: 1938 and 1998
> - Germany: 1974 (West Germany) and 2006 (unified Germany)

Why was Leonidas left out of the Brazilian team for the 1938 semifinal against Italy?

The Brazilian coach wanted to save Leonidas for the final. The decision not to field Leonidas in the semifinal was obviously wrong because Brazil unexpectedly lost 2–1 to Italy in the match. Ironically, in the third-place match two days later, Leonidas scored two goals and helped Brazil achieve a 4–2 victory over Sweden.

> **Quickies**
> *Did you know ...*
> that thirty-two teams qualify for the World Cup from six regions — Africa, Asia, Europe, North America, Oceania, and South America — but only European and South American teams have ever won?

Why did England not play in the World Cup until 1950?

The four British FAs resigned from FIFA in February 1928 after a disagreement with how FIFA proposed to administer what are called "broken time payments" to amateur players in the Amsterdam Olympics that were being held that year. "Broken time payments" is the practice of a promoter or organizer compensating amateur players for lost income from their regular jobs. The British FAs had their own system in place and did not like FIFA's interference. They eventually rejoined FIFA in 1946, and participated in the World Cup for the first time in 1950.

Why did India once withdraw from the World Cup?

The team from India withdrew from the 1950 World Cup finals because FIFA would not permit them to play barefoot, as was their custom.

What was the highest attendance for a World Cup final?

There's agreement on the match, but not on the number. The BBC reports that 199,854 spectators attended the World Cup final between Brazil and Uruguay at Estádio do Maracanã, in Rio de Janeiro on July 16, 1950. But FIFA officially records the number at 174,000. Either way, it stands as a record attendance.

Who was the youngest player to score in the World Cup finals?

That would be none other than Pelé, who was 17 years and 239 days old when he scored for Brazil against Wales to win a quarter-final match 1–0 on June 19, 1958. Brazil went on to win the tournament and Pelé still holds the record for youngest player to have played for a World Cup champion team.

What was "The Soccer War"?

The Soccer War, also known as the 100-Hours War, was a five-day war between El Salvador and Honduras in 1969. It was caused by political conflicts between the two nations, namely issues concerning immigration from El Salvador to Honduras. Tensions boiled over into rioting at two qualifying matches between the nations for the 1970 World Cup, on June 8 and 15. Many people erroneously believe the war was a result of these soccer riots, but the truth was the opposite. The riots resulted from earlier tensions; indeed, by July 14, the Salvadoran air force had begun launching attacks into Honduras. The conflict lasted until a ceasefire was arranged on July 18, leaving 6,000 dead and 12,000 wounded.

Which was the first sub-Saharan African nation to play in a World Cup finals?

When Zaire qualified for the 1974 finals, they became the first sub-Saharan African nation to advance beyond the qualifying stage into the finals. The Zairean president promised each player a house, a car, and free holidays. All of these offers were withdrawn when Zaire lost all three matches, scored no goals, and gave up 14 goals.

Which country has participated in every World Cup qualifying competition but never made it through to the finals?

From 1934 to 2005, Luxembourg played 104 qualifying matches and lost 100, scoring 50 goals and giving up 356. The only two teams that Luxembourg has defeated in qualifiers are Portugal (4–2 on October 8, 1961) and Turkey (2–0 on October 22, 1972) — not quite good enough to get them in.

Why was Prince Fahid, the Kuwaiti FA president, fined $14,000 U.S. after a 1982 World Cup finals match against France?

After France scored, one of the Kuwaiti players complained to Soviet referee Miroslav Stupar that prior to the goal he'd heard a play-stopping whistle. When Prince Fahid

Quickies

Did you know ...

that Colombian player Andreas Escobar was shot dead by an angry fan after he scored an own goal that was part of his team's collapse that saw them eliminated in the first round of the 1994 World Cup?

walked out onto the field to argue the point with the referee and threatened to pull out his team, Stupar reversed his goal decision. France ended up winning the match anyway, 4–1. For their actions, Stupar was suspended and Fahid fined.

What did Brazilian player Ronaldino donate to charity during World Cup 2006?

Two locks of his hair. They were donated for an auction organized by a Swiss newspaper to raise funds for a cancer charity. The hair was collected by a team of Swiss barbers in the Brazilian camp in Switzerland before the start of the finals.

Who were "The Elephants"?

Ivory Coast's team — nicknamed "The Elephants" — created their own "elephant dance" and practised the steps in training sessions before each match of the 2006 World Cup, hoping to dance before cheering fans to celebrate a winning goal. They lost their first two group matches, but the world had the chance to watch them dance on June 21, 2006, when they defeated Serbia and Montenegro 3–2.

World Cup First Cards

- **First yellow card**: Lovchev (USSR) against Mexico, May 31, 1970.
- **First red card**: Carlos Caszely (Chile) against West Germany, June 14, 1974.
- **First coach sent off**: Cayetano Re (Paraguay) against Belgium, June 11, 1986.
- **First goalkeeper sent off**: Gianluca Pagliuca (Italy) against Norway, June 23, 1994.

What country holds the record for the longest winless streak in the World Cup?

That would be Bulgaria, with six ties and 11 losses in 17 consecutive matches from 1962 to 1994.

What country holds the record for the longest goalless streak in the World Cup?

That would be Bolivia, with a five-match goal drought from 1930 to 1994.

What country holds the record for the longest winning streak in the World Cup?

That would be Brazil, with seven matches in 2002 and four in 2006 for a record total of 11 straight wins.

What country holds the record for the longest losing streak in the World Cup?

That would be Mexico, with nine consecutive losses from 1930 to 1958.

What was the first tournament played between all four national teams of the United Kingdom?

In the early 1880s, the football associations of England, Scotland, Wales, and Ireland each had slightly different rules for the game. When friendly matches were played, the rules of the hosting team were used. On December 6, 1882, the four associations met in Manchester and agreed on one uniform set of rules. This meeting not only marked the founding of the International Football Association Board (IFAB), but also gave birth to the British Home Championship, which would see the four national "Home Teams" — England, Scotland, Wales, and Ireland — compete in a formal tournament played out over the 1883–84 season. The winner was Scotland.

What was the Ibrox Disaster of 1902?

For the final of the 1902 British Home Championship, over 68,000 fans gathered at Ibrox Park in Glasgow on April 5 to watch Scotland face England. In the first half, shortly before 4:00 p.m., a section of terrace in the stadium's West Stand collapsed, killing 25 and injuring over 500. Play was stopped, but was restarted after 20 minutes. The match played out to a 1–1 draw, but was later declared void and replayed on May 2 at Villa Park, Birmingham, to a 2–2 draw.

British Home Championship Winners

Country:	England	Scotland	Wales	Ireland/North Ireland
Outright Wins:	34	24	7	3
Shared Two-way:	14	11	3	2
Shared Three-ways:	5	5	1	2
Shared Four-ways:	1	1	1	1
Total:	54	41	12	8

What is the oldest trophy in soccer?

The Scottish Cup was made in Glasgow by George Edwards and Sons of Buchanan Street and, having been minted in 1885, is the oldest national trophy in world soccer.

What is the record attendance for a Scottish Cup final?

The record attendance for a Scottish Cup final was set April 24, 1937, when, by official counts, 146,433 spectators saw Celtic beat Aberdeen 2–1 at Glasgow's Hampden Park.

Have any teams outside the Irish Football League ever won the Irish Cup?

Since the inception of the Irish Football League in 1890–91, the Irish Cup has been won by Irish League teams on every occasion except three famous "giant-killing" occasions when junior teams beat senior opponents in the final: In 1928, Willowfield beat Larne 1–0; in 1955, Dundela beat Glenavon 3–0; and in 1976, Carrick Rangers beat Linfield 2–1.

Quickies

Did you know ...

that the first Old Firm final in the Scottish Cup was played in 1894 and saw Rangers defeat Celtic 3–1?

What team holds the record for consecutive wins of the Irish Cup?

Glentoran FC, which was founded in 1882 and plays in the IFA Premiership at The Oval in Belfast, holds the record for the most consecutive wins of the Irish Cup, with four victories from 1985 to 1988. Glentoran was also the first Irish team to win a European trophy, taking the Vienna Cup in 1914.

Who won the first Welsh Cup?

The first Welsh Cup was played in 1878, with Wrexham FC defeating Ruabon Druids in the final 1–0. Founded in 1872, Wrexham is the oldest professional club in Wales and holds the record for most Welsh Cup wins, with 23.

Quickies
Did you know …
that the record for consecutive Irish League championship titles is six, held jointly by Belfast Celtic FC (1935–40 and 1947–48) and Linfield FC (1981–87)?

Why are Wales' three historically strongest teams now barred from competing for the Welsh Cup?

Wrexham, Cardiff City, and Swansea City are teams in a kind of limbo. Professional teams from northern Wales, all three have been playing within the English Football League since before the formation in 1992 of the League of Wales by the Football Association of Wales. Prior to 1992, any FAW member team could compete for the Welsh Cup, and Wrexham, Cardiff, and Swansea had collectively garnered 55 championships since the cup's founding in 1878. But with the formation of the new Welsh league, English-league teams were excluded from Welsh Cup competition, leaving Wrexham, Cardiff City, and Swansea City out in the cold.

What is the League Cup?

The League Cup is an annual knockout competition open to the 20 clubs of England's FA Premier League, and the 72 clubs of England's Football League, which organizes the competition. It was first played in the 1961, seeing Aston Villa emerge victorious over Rotherham United in a two-leg final. Since 1982, the competition has taken its name from a sponsor and is currently called the Carling Cup.

Quickies
Did you know …
that in 1993, when Arsenal won the first-ever League Cup/FA Cup double, they faced Sheffield Wednesday FC in the final at both tournaments?

Which teams played in the first FA Cup final?

The first FA Cup final took place at Kennington Oval, London, on Saturday, March 16, 1872, before a crowd of 2,000. At the time, soccer matches were played without crossbars or goalnets. There were also no free kicks or penalties and the pitch markings did not include a centre-circle or a halfway line. The Wanderers defeated the Royal Engineers 1–0 on a goal from A.H. Chequer.

Why was the 1920 Irish Cup awarded without a final being played?

In the 1920 Irish Cup competition, Shelbourne FC, who had beaten Glenavon FC in one semifinal, were awarded the cup without playing the final, when the two other semifinalists, Glentoran FC and Belfast Celtic FC, were both disqualified — Glentoran for fielding an unlisted player, Belfast Celtic after one of their supporters fired gunshots at the Glentoran fans.

FA Cup Final Captains Courageous

- **Dave Beasant** (Wimbledon): first goalkeeper to captain a winning FA Cup side, and first to stop a penalty kick in an FA Cup final, 1988.
- **Viv Anderson** (Sheffield Wednesday): first black player to captain an FA Cup final side, 1993.
- **Danny Blanchflower** (Tottenham Hotsupr): first player to captain a team to successive FA Cup final wins, 1961 and 1962.
- **Eric Cantona** (Manchester United): first non-British player to captain an winning FA Cup final side, 1996.

How many fans came out to see David Beckham's first start in a regulation MLS soccer match?

David Beckham's first start in a regulation match as a member of Major League Soccer's Los Angeles Galaxy team was played on Aug 18, 2007, against the New York Red Bulls. Held at Giants Stadium, in East Rutherford, New Jersey, the game drew a crowd of 66,237 fans, up considerably from the Red Bulls' average draw of 11,573 fans. The Red Bulls won 5–4.

Has any player ever won the World Cup as a player and later as a coach?

Regarded by many as the greatest German footballer of all time, sweeper Franz Beckenbauer won the 1974 World Cup as a player, and the 1990 World Cup as a coach, both times with West Germany.

Who was the first Chinese player to appear for England?

Frank Soo was the first player of Chinese extraction to play for England. He was born in Buxton, Derbyshire, in 1914 and was the son of a Chinese father and an English mother.

One of the best inside forwards of the immediate pre-war era, he formed part of a legendary team that included players such as Sir Stanley Matthews and Neil Franklin.

Who holds the record for most goals in a career?

Josef "Pepi" Bican was a Czech-Austrian football forward. Records are not entirely complete, but it has been estimated by soccer statisticians that Bican scored 800 goals in all of his competitive matches, not including friendly games. For this, the International Federation of Football Historians and Statisticians awarded Bican the "Golden Ball" as the greatest goal scorer of the last century.

Players Noted For Their Noticeable Locks

Player	Worst Hairstyle
Christian Wilhelmsson	Cockatiel faux-hawk mullet
Ronaldo	The forehead wedge
Roberto Baggio	Businessman with a ponytail
Taribo West	Green cornrows
Sir Bobby Charlton	The comb-over
Carlos Valderrama	Frizzy plug-socket afro
Alexi Lalas	Billy-goatee
Rodrigo Palacio	Rat-tail braid
Djibril Cisse	Peroxide gone wrong
David Beckham	You name it, he's done it

What embarrassed Italian player Peppino Meazza during the 1938 World Cup semifinal?

As Meazza scored on a penalty kick, his shorts, torn earlier in the game, fell down. His celebrating teammates surrounded him until a new pair were produced. Italy went on to win the game, and the tournament.

Has anyone scored a hat trick in an FA Cup final?

Appropriately enough, three people have done so. Billy Townley did it for Blackburn Rovers in 1890, Jimmy Logan did it for Notts County in 1894, and Stan Mortensen scored three for Blackpool in 1953. No one has done it since.

Who scored the first goal in FA Cup competition history?

The first official FA Cup competition goal was scored by Jarvis Kenrick for Clapham Rovers in a 3–0 victory over Upton Park on November 11, 1871. It was the first of two goals for Kenrick in the match. He later won the FA Cup three years running with Wanderers.

Quickies

Did you know …

that the first televised F.A. Cup Final was April 30, 1938, with Preston North End FC defeating Huddersfield Town FC 1–0 at Wembley Stadium?

What was the "Little Tin Idol"?

The original FA Cup trophy, awarded from 1872 to 1895, was made by Martin, Hall and Co. and looked nothing like the one played for today. Made of silver, it was less than 18 inches (45 centimetres) high and cost £20 to make. It had a figure of a footballer on the top and was popularly known as the "Little Tin Idol." In 1895, it was stolen from the William Shillcock football outfitters shop in Newtown Row, Birmingham, and never recovered.

Who was Harry Burge?

In 1958, 83-year-old Harry Burge, who lived in a Birmingham hostel for the homeless, confessed to a reporter from a British newspaper that he was the thief who stole the original FA Cup trophy, the "Little Tin Idol." He claimed to have melted it down to make counterfeit half-crown coins.

Top Ten FA Cup Winners

- Manchester United: 11 wins in 18 appearance
- Arsenal: 10 wins in 17 appearances
- Tottenham Hotspur: 8 wins in 9 appearances
- Aston Villa: 7 wins in 10 appearances
- Liverpool: 7 wins in 13 appearances
- Blackburn Rovers: 6 wins in 8 appearances
- Newcastle United: 6 wins in 13 appearances
- Everton: 5 wins in 12 appearances
- The Wanderers: 5 wins in 5 appearance
- West Bromwich Albion: 5 wins in 10 appearances

What was the first non-English team in the FA Cup final?

In 1884, Glasgow's Queen's Park FC became the first club from outside England to reach the FA Cup Final. They lost to Blackburn Rovers, 2–1. They did it again in 1885, and lost it again to Blackburn Rovers, 2–0.

What was the Inter-Cities Fairs Cup?

A forerunner to the UEFA Cup, the Inter-Cities Fairs Cup was an annual soccer competition held between 1955 and 1971. It was set up to promote international trade fairs in European cities and featured teams from those cities playing in matches timed to coincide with such fairs. The first Fairs Cup involved teams from Barcelona, Basle, Birmingham, Copenhagen, Frankfurt, Lausanne, Leipzig, London, Milan, and Zagreb. Barcelona beat a London 8–2 on aggregate in a two-leg final.

How was the UEFA Cup started?

The UEFA Cup grew out of the Inter-Cities Fairs Cup after the *Union des Associations Européennes de Football* took over the competition in 1971, at which time UEFA disassociated the cup from trade fairs. The competition was traditionally open to the runners-up of domestic leagues, but it was merged with UEFA's previous second-tier European competition, the UEFA Cup Winners' Cup, in 1999. Since then, the winners of domestic cup competitions have also entered the UEFA Cup.

Why was South Africa disqualified from the inaugural African Cup of Nations?

The Confederation of African Football (CAF) was founded on February 8, 1957, in Khartoum, Sudan, by the Football Associations of Egypt, Ethiopia, South Africa, and Sudan. The same four nations were to compete in the CAF's inaugural African Cup of Nations in Sudan later that month. But no sooner had South Africa signed on than they were disqualified, having failed to field a multiracial team due to their government's policy of apartheid. Over two games, Egypt defeated both Sudan and Ethiopia to take the cup in what might be the shortest international cup competition on record.

Who was Carlos Padrós?

Carlos Padrós Rubio was a founding member of Real Madrid and later served as club president between 1904 and 1908. He was the driving force behind the creation of the Copa del Rey, which was first played in 1902 to celebrate the coronation of Alfonso XIII. Carlos Padrós refereed the first-ever Copa del Rey final, in which Club Vizcaya defeated FC Barcelona 2–1.

What is a *scudetto*?

Scudetto in Itlalian means "little shield," and in soccer it refers to a badge in the colours of the Italian flag, awarded annually to the championship club in the Lega Calcio Serie A, located at the top echelon of the Italian soccer league system. The winning team will wear the badge on their jersey in the following season. The first time *scudetto* were used was in 1924 when Genoa CFC won its eighth championship title. They have not won it since.

What is the *Trophée des Champions*?

Le Trophée des Champions, or the Champions Trophy, is a cup organized by the French Football Federation, a match between the winners of the French Championship and the winners of the French Cup.

What is the Triple Crown of Brazilian Football?

The Triple Crown of Brazilian Football is an unofficial title given to the club that wins the three most important competitions in Brazilian soccer in the same year: the Brazilian Football State Championship, the *Copa do Brasil*, and the *Campeonato Brasileiro Série A* (Brazilian Championship First Level). Cruzeiro Esporte Clube, from the city of Belo Horizonte, is the only team to have done so (in 2003).

Six French Teams With Multiple *Trophée des Champions* Wins

- **Olympique Lyonnais**: 7 wins (1973, 2002, 2003, 2004, 2005, 2006, 2007)
- **Stade Reims**: 5 wins (1949, 1955, 1958, 1960, 1966)
- **AS Saint-Étienne**: 5 wins (1957, 1962, 1967, 1968, 1969)
- **AS Monaco FC**: 4 wins (1961, 1985, 1997, 2000)
- **FC Nantes**: 3 wins (1965, 1999, 2001)
- **FC Girondins de Bordeaux**: 2 wins (1986, 2008)
- **Paris Saint-Germain FC**: 2 wins (1995, 1998)

Who was Lamar Hunt?

The man who gives his name to North America's Major League Soccer (MLS) championship — the Lamar Hunt U.S. Open Cup — was a sportsman and essential promoter of soccer in the United States. He was one of the founders of MLS as well as its predecessor, the North American Soccer League (NASL). At his death in 2006 he owned two MLS teams, Columbus Crew and FC Dallas.

What is the Voyageurs Cup?

The Voyageurs Cup is the only trophy for top-level professional soccer in Canada. From 2002 to 2007, the cup was awarded annually to the Canadian United Soccer Leagues division team finishing with the best record from regular season matches against other Canadian teams in the USL. From 2008 until at least 2010, the trophy will be awarded to the winner of the Canadian Championship. Montreal Impact has won the cup every year so far.

Has Canada ever won a major international tournament?

Thrice, actually. The first time was at the 1904 Summer Olympic Games, in St. Louis. Canada sent Galt FC as their representative team and they defeated the only two other teams entered without being scored on. The second instance was more challenging as Canada competed in a field of nine national teams from the Confederation of North, Central American and Caribbean Association Football to win the 1985 CONCACAF Championship. Then in 2000 they emerged victorious from a field of eight teams to take the CONCACAF Gold Cup.

Animalistic Player Nicknames

- Lionel Andrés Messi — Atomic Flea
- Iker Casillas — El Gato (The Cat)
- Claudio Lopez — El Piojo (The Louse)
- Gennaro Gattuso — The Pit Bull
- Eusebio — The Black Panther
- Kevin Keegan — Mighty Mouse
- Jack Charlton — The Giraffe
- Marco Van Basten — The Swan of Utrecht
- Arthur Friedenreich — The Tiger

Who was the "Little Bird"?

When he was an infant, Brazilian player Manuel Francisco dos Santos suffered from severe physical disabilities: his spine was deformed, his right leg bent inwards, and his left leg was 2.4 inches (six centimetres) shorter and curved outwards. An operation that

World's Top Ten Richest Teams According to Forbes

1. Manchester United	$1,800 million U.S. (€1,333 million/£897 million)
2. Real Madrid	$1,285 million (€951 million/£640 million)
3. Arsenal	$1,200 million (€888 million/£598 million)
4. Liverpool	$1,050 million (€777 million/£523 million)
5. Bayern Munich	$ 917 million (€679 million/£457 million)
6. AC Milan	$ 798 million (€591 million/£398 million)
7. Barcelona	$ 784 million (€580 million/£391 million)
8. Chelsea	$ 764 million (€566 million/£381 million)
9. Juventus	$ 510 million (€378 million/£254 million)
10. Schalke 04	$ 470 million (€348 million/£234 million)

enabled him to walk left him with a distorted leg. He nonetheless grew up to become a speedy winger with the nickname *Garrincha*, which means "little bird." He won the World Cup in 1958 and 1962. He died of alcohol poisoning in 1983 at the age of 49.

Why did David Beckham turn down an appearance on *The Simpsons*?

In a 2004 episode of *The Simpsons*, Marge Simpson makes a Christmas speech mocking David Beckham for an alleged extramarital affair. Apparently Boy Spice didn't laugh, and when an offer came for him to do a cameo in Springfield, he turned them down.

What creative endeavours has Pelé engaged in since retiring?

Pelé has published several autobiographies, starred in documentary and semi-documentary films, and composed various musical pieces, including the entire soundtrack for the film *Pelé* in 1977. He has acted in fictional TV shows and films, most notably appearing alongside other footballers of the 1960s and 1970s, Michael Caine, and Sylvester Stallone, in the 1981 film *Escape to Victory*, about an attempted escape from a Second World War Nazi POW Camp. Pelé was also the first sports figure featured in a video game with the Atari 2600 game "Pelé's Soccer."

What is the most lucrative contract ever awarded to a professional soccer player?

In January 2007 it was announced that midfielder David Beckham was leaving the Real Madrid squad to join the Los Angeles Galaxy, part of Major League Soccer (MLS), the North American men's pro league. The contract included a $6.5 million annual salary, sponsorship deals estimated at $25 million per year, merchandise sales worth approximately $10 million per year, and a $10 million per year share of club profits.

Quickies

Did you know ...
that David Beckham's agent is none other than Simon Fuller, creator of *American Idol*?

In total, the five-year contract would award him in the range of $250 million, putting him third at the time on the list of the world's highest-paid athletes, behind only Tiger Woods and Michael Schumacher.

Why did spies kill Lutz Eigendorf?

On March 20, 1979, after a friendly match between the East German team Berliner FC Dynamo and West German club 1. FC Kaiserslautern, East German midfielder Lutz Eigendorf defected to the West. It might not have been the wisest move, given that FC Dynamo was under the patronage of the Stasi, East Germany's secret police. After German reunification in 1990 and the subsequent opening of Stasi files it was revealed that the traffic accident on March 5, 1983, that led to Eigendorf's death two days later had been staged as an assassination by the Stasi.

> **Quickies**
> *Did you know ...*
> that when a schoolmate of Pelé's came up with his nickname, Pelé punched the boy and received a two-day suspension?

What does "Pelé" mean?

> **Quickies**
> *Did you know ...*
> that Sir Stanley Matthews, who played over 80 international games for England, played in a major contest on his 50th birthday?

The name "Pelé" has no meaning in Portuguese, the language of Pelé's homeland, Brazil. The nickname was given to him as a taunt by a schoolmate when Pelé was young. In Hebrew, it means "miracle." It is also the name of a Hawaiian volcano goddess. It also resembles the Irish language word *peile*, meaning football.

What is the FIFA World Player of the Year award?

The FIFA World Player of the Year is an Association Football award given annually to the player thought to be the best in the world, based on votes by coaches and captains of international teams.

> **Quickies**
> *Did you know ...*
> that Alex Villaplane, France's captain in the first World Cup match, was shot dead by French resistance fighters in July 1945 for alleged collaboration with the Nazis?

Why are there 125 players on the FIFA 100 list?

The FIFA 100 is Pelé's list of the "greatest living footballers." He chose 125 players to be on the list, which seems incongruous with the list's name until you understand that the list was unveiled on March 4, 2004, at a gala ceremony in London, marking part of the celebrations of the 100th anniversary of the *Fédération Internationale de Football Association* (FIFA). The "100" of the list name refers to the anniversary, not the number of players Pelé chose.

Who was "The Great Dane"?

Peter Schmeichel has been called the greatest goaltender to have ever played the game. Nicknamed "The Great Dane," he was born in Gladsaxe, Denmark, and played in his home nation until 1992, when the Danish team took the UEFA European Championship. He then joined Manchester United and was captain of their 1999 squad that won an unprecedented Treble (to win a country's top division and two cup competitions in the same season), taking the English Premiership, FA Cup, and UEFA Champions League all in the same season.

Who holds the record for longest professional playing career?

Sir Stanley Matthews, the only English player to have been knighted before retirement, was born in 1915 and started his soccer career in 1932, playing for Stoke City FC at the age of 17. He stayed with them until 1947, then moved to Blackpool FC until 1961, at which point he returned to Stoke City FC. He played his final game with Stoke on February 6, 1965, just after his 50th birthday, achieving the record of longest professional career at 33 years. Considered to have been one of the greatest players ever, Matthews died in February 2000.

Who were the Bubsy Babes?

Recruited and trained in the 1950s, the Busby Babes were a group of young Manchester United players who progressed from the club's youth team into the first team under coach Matt Busby. The nickname for the group, said to have been coined by *Manchester Evening News* journalist Tom Jackson, refers to the players who won the league championship in seasons 1955–56 and 1956–57 with an average age of 21 and 22 respectively. In 1958, eight of the Busby Babes were killed while returning from a European Cup match in Belgrade. After making a refuelling stop, the airplane they were in crashed while trying to take off from a slushy Munich airfield.

What was the "Hand of God"?

The "Hand of God" was the hand of Argentine player Diego Maradona — his left hand to be precise. In the quarter-finals of the 1986 World Cup, as Argentina faced England,

Maradona scored in the 51st minute on what appeared — at least to referee Ali Benna-ceur — to be a header. However, virtually everyone else in attendance knew, or at least suspected, that, as Maradona and England goalkeeper Peter Shilton jumped for a ball that was coming down into the goal area off a high kick, Maradona had punched the ball in with his raised left hand. At the post-game press conference, Maradona claimed that the goal was scored "*un poco con la cabeza de Maradona y otro poco con la mano de Dios*" ("a little with the head of Maradona and a little with the hand of God"). It turned out it was *a lot* with the hand of Maradona, as press photos appeared over the ensuing days clearly showing him punching the ball. Argentina defeated England 2–1 and went on to win the tournament. Maradona later admitted on TV that he'd hit the goal in with his hand.

The Munich Air Disaster of 1958

Fatalities	Survivors
Geoff Bent	Johnny Berry
Roger Byrne	Jackie Blanchflower
Eddie Colman	Bobby Charlton
Duncan Edwards (survived, but died in hospital 15 days later)	Bill Foulkes
Mark Jones	Harry Gregg
David Pegg	Kenny Morgans
Tommy Taylor	Albert Scanlon
Liam "Billy" Whelan	Dennis Viollet
Walter Crickmer (club secretary)	Ray Wood
Tom Curry (trainer)	Matt Busby (manager)
Bert Whalley (chief coach)	

What is the George Best Egg?

George Best, who died of illness related to alcoholism on October 3, 2005, was one of the greatest players ever to have come out of Northern Ireland. In June 2006, Sarah Fab-ergé — great-granddaughter of Russian Imperial Jeweller Carl Fabergé — was commissioned to create the George Best Egg as a tribute. A limited edition of 68 eggs — which feature the figure of a soccer player inside — were produced, with all profits from the sale of the eggs going to the George Best Foundation, which raises money for local football and research into liver disease and alcoholism. The first egg from the collection is now on permanent public display at the Belfast Airport, which was renamed the George Best Airport in May 2006.

Quickies

Did you know ...
that for the first anniversary of George Best's death, Ulster Bank issued one million commemorative five-pound notes?

Why did French captain Zinedine Zidane head-butt Italian player Marco Materazzi during extra time in the 2006 World Cup final?

In one of the most infamous moments in modern international soccer, French player Zinedine Zidane ended his international career and destroyed any hopes his team might have had to win the 2006 World Cup by head-butting Italian player Marco Materazzi in the chest at the 1:10 minute mark of the tournament final. The attack saw Materazzi crumple to the ground in agony and garnered Zidane a red card. Materazzi later said that after he had grabbed Zidane's jersey, Zidane offered it to him sarcastically. Materazzi then replied, "I prefer the whore that is your sister," which resulted in the head-butt. Italy went on to win the match 5–3 in a shootout. Zidane retired from professional play after the incident.

Quickies

Did you know ...

that because it competed for attention with the men's game, England's FA banned women's soccer teams in 1921?

Who were the Dick, Kerr Ladies?

The Dick, Kerr Ladies was the most famous early women's football team. Founded in Preston, Lancashire, England, during the First World War, it was a works' team for the munitions manufacturer Dick, Kerr & Co., owned by W.B. Dick and John Kerr. They played friendly matches with other women's teams during the war to raise money for charity.

Quickies

Did you know ...

that England's FA did not recognize women's soccer until 1971?

What was the English Ladies' Football Association?

In reaction to the FA's banning of women's football, the English Ladies' Football Association (ELFA) was formed. The first meeting of the ELFA took place at Blackburn on December 10, 1921. At that time there were approximately 150 women's football clubs in England. The representatives of 25 clubs attended the initial meeting. Sixty attended the second, held in Grimsby. ELFA existed for about two years, and held one challenge cup tournament with 24 teams entered in competition. The winners were Stoke Ladies, who defeated Doncaster and Bentley Ladies 3–1, on June 24, 1922.

Who is Ann Kristin Aarønes?

Ann Kristin "Anka" Aarønes is a retired Norwegian soccer player. She first played for Spjelkavik IL, then for Trondheims-Ørn, and the Norwegian national team. Later she played for the WUSA's New York Power, during the first season. She was top scorer at the 1995 FIFA Women's World Cup.

Who is Delma Gonçalves?

Quickies
Did you know ...
that in 2004, when Pelé selected his list of the 125 "greatest living footballers" to celebrate the centenary of FIFA, only two women made the cut: Americans Michelle Akers and Mia Hamm?

Born May 19, 1975, in Rio de Janeiro, Delma Gonçalves is a Brazilian women's soccer player who currently plays as a striker for Japan's INAC Leonessa. She has been a long-time member of the Brazilian National Team for which she debuted in 1991. Her nickname is *Pretinha* ("little black girl").

Who is Birgit Prinz?

Birgit Prinz is a German soccer player and the Women's World Cup all-time leading scorer with 14 goals. Born in Frankfurt am Main, Prinz has been with 1FFC Frankfurt since July 1994. She was elected FIFA Women's World Player of the Year in 2003, 2004, and 2005 and was named German "Women's Footballer of the Year" each year from 2001 to 2007.

When was the first Women's World Cup?

The first Women's World Cup was held in China from November 16–30, 1991. The American team, led by a dominating forward line dubbed "The Triple-Edged Sword" by the Chinese media, cut through the tournament to win the first-ever world championship

Women's World Cup Finals Results			
Year	Winner	Runners-Up	Result
1991	United States	Norway	2–1
1995	Norway	United States	1–0
1999	United States	China	0–0 aet (5–4 penalty shootout)
2003	Germany	Sweden	2–1
2007	Germany	Brazil	2–0

for women's soccer. The final, in which the United States defeated Norway 2–1, was played in front of 65,000 fans at Guangzhou's Tianhe Stadium.

Which player has appeared in the most Women's World Cups?

At the 2007 World Cup in China, U.S. captain Kristine Lilly competed in her fifth World Cup, making her the only woman — and one of three players in history — to have appeared in five World Cups.

Who holds the international scoring record for women's soccer?

Mia Hamm is considered by many to be the greatest woman to have ever played soccer. In 275 appearances with the American national team, she logged a record 158 goals.

Who is Marta?

Like so many other great Brazilian players, Marta Vieira Da Silva needs only one name. To Brazilians, she is simply Marta, one of the best women soccer players ever. Thrice voted FIFA World Player of the year (2006, 2007, 2008), she was a member of the Brazilian National Teams that won the silver at the Olympics in 2004 and 2008. In the 2007 Women's World Cup, she won both the Golden Ball award as the best player and the Golden Boot award as the top scorer.

Wins by Country for the Women's World Cup

Country	Wins
Germany	2
United States	2
Norway	1

Why did Maribel Dominguez's childhood friends call her Mario?

Growing up in Mexico city, Maribel Dominguez was surrounded by streets filled with boys playing soccer. Wanting to join in, she pretended to be a boy herself. She had the thin physique to pass, and kept her hair short. It wasn't until her friends saw in the newspaper that their chum "Mario" had made it onto the Mexican sub-national *women's* team that the penny dropped. She went on to eventually captain the senior Mexican women's team and was top goal scorer for them at the 2004 Olympics.

Who is called Sissi?

Here is another one-name Brazillian soccer star. Sisleide do Amor Lima is best known by her nickname, Sissi. Now retired, she was a star member of the Brazil women's national football team. She won the golden boot award in the 1999 Women's World Cup in which she scored seven goals, sharing the award with China's Sun Wen. A veteran of three World Cup finals and two Olympic campaigns, she was pegged in 2008 as the new assistant coach FC Gold Pride, a professional soccer club based in Santa Clara, California, that will begin play in 2009 in the inaugural season of Women's Professional Soccer (WPS).

What two records did Kara Lang set at just 15 years old?

Canadian Kara Lang holds the women's football world record for youngest player to score a full international goal. She scored against Wales at the Algarve Cup on March 3, 2002, at age 15 years, 132 days. She must have been on a roll, because her senior debut, two days earlier, had been a Canadian record for youngest senior women's cap.

Why does Valencia FC have a bat on their crest?

Valencia and the Balearic Islands were conquered by King James I of Aragon during the first half of the thirteenth century. In that period, the sight of a bat was considered to be an omen of good luck. On October 9, 1238, when James I was about to enter the city of Valencia, re-conquering it from the Moors, it is said that a bat landed on the top of his flag. He interpreted it as a good sign. When he conquered the city, the bat was added to its coat of arms. Valencia FC has adopted it for their crest.

What is *El Clásico*?

El Clásico is any football match between rivals Real Madrid and FC Barcelona. The rivalry comes about as Madrid and Barcelona are the two largest cities in Spain, and they are often identified with "Spanishness" and Catalanism, respectively.

What team holds the record for most consecutive championships in the French league's premier division?

Olympique Lyonnais, based in Lyon, won the premier league title seven years straight, from 2002–08, a record that no other club in France has matched.

What is the origin of Manchester United FC?

Manchester United began life being called Newton Heath L&YR in 1878 when a group of workers from the Lancashire and Yorkshire Railways formed a soccer team. The club entered the Football League in 1892 and began to sever its links with the rail depot, becoming an independent company, appointing a club secretary and dropping the "L&YR" from their name to become simply Newton Heath FC. In 1902, a sizeable donation from J.H. Davies, the managing director of Manchester Breweries, saved the club from bankruptcy. The club required a change of name to reflect the fresh start and Manchester United was officially adopted on April 26, 1902.

What is the Merseyside Derby?

The Merseyside Derby is the name given to any match between the English teams Everton FC and Liverpool FC, the two most successful clubs from the city of Liverpool. Traditionally, the Merseyside Derby was referred to as The Friendly Derby because of the large number of families with supporters of both teams. It is one of the few local English soccer rivalries that does not enforce fan segregation at games.

How did Arsenal get their strange name?

Arsenal FC were founded as Dial Square in 1886 by workers at the Royal Arsenal in Woolwich, west of London, but they were renamed Royal Arsenal shortly afterwards. They changed their name to Woolwich Arsenal after turning professional in 1891. The club joined the English Football League in 1893, but low attendance led to financial problems leaving them effectively bankrupt by 1910, when they were taken over by Henry Norris. In 1913 Norris moved the team to the new Arsenal Stadium in Highbury, North London, and they dropped "Woolwich" from their name the following year.

Why do Tottenham Hotspur FC have a bird on their crest?

That bird is a cockerel, a fighting cock with a spur on its leg. In 1882 the Hotspur Football Club was formed by grammar schoolboys from the Bible class at All Hallows Church. They were also members of Hotspur Cricket Club and it is thought that the name Hotspur was associated with Sir Henry Percy, who was "Harry Hotspur" of Shakespeare's *Henry IV, Part I*, and who lived locally during in the fourteenth century. Harry Hotspur was famous for his riding spurs and fighting cocks. In 1884 the club was renamed Tottenham Hotspur Football and Athletic Club to distinguish itself from another team called London Hotspur.

Why Sheffield Wednesday and not Thursday or Monday?

Sheffield Wednesday was a cricket club when it originally formed in 1820 as The Wednesday Cricket Club — named after the day of the week when they played their matches. The cricketers formed the soccer branch of their club in 1867. The cricket branch eventually expired, but the name survived.

Who founded Rangers FC?

Two brothers, Peter and Moses McNeil, with the help of two friends, Peter Campbell and William McBeath, founded Rangers Football Club in 1872. The original name for the club was Argyle and possibly relates to the large numbers of Highlanders who moved to Glasgow during the Victorian era. The club moved to Ibrox in 1887.

Who founded Celtic FC?

Celtic were founded at a meeting in St. Mary's Church Hall on East Rose Street (now Forbes Street), Calton, Glasgow, by Brother Walfrid, an Irish Marist brother, on November 6, 1887. The purpose stated in the official club records was stated as "being to alleviate poverty in Glasgow's East End parishes." Walfrid's move to establish the club was a means of fundraising for his charity, The Poor Children's Dinner Table.

When did Rangers FC and Celtic FC first meet on the pitch?

On May 28, 1888, Celtic played their first official match, and it was against none other than Rangers — a club that had existed since 1872. Celtic won 5–2, fielding eight guest players from Hibernian FC.

What was the first non-U.S. Major League Soccer (MLS) team?

That would be the Toronto FC, which was formed in 2006 and plays at BMO Field on the grounds of the Canadian National Exhibition. The team set an MLS record in season ticket sales, selling 14,000 before they'd even appeared in a game.

What does "bend it like Beckham" mean?

The phrase "bend it like Beckham" was popularized as the title of a British movie from 2002, starring Parminder Nagra and Keira Knightley. The title refers to David Beckham's ability to put spin on a ball from a free kick, causing it to curve — or "bend" — in trajectory around the defence and into the net. Nagra's character in the film, Jess Bhamra, shows a similar aptitude for bending free kicks.

What does "bank it like Beckham" mean?

The term "to bend" a soccer ball means to put spin on a ball from a free kick to give it a curving trajectory around defenders. The phrase "bank it like Beckham" is a joke on this phrase, playing on the title of the feature film *Bend it like Beckham*, and referring to Beckham's ability to land copious amounts of money in the bank upon signing a $250 million U.S. deal with the Los Angeles Galaxy.

What term did N.L. Jackson, founder of Corinthians F.C., give to soccer?

On May 10, 1886, N.L. Jackson, founder of Corinthians F.C. and assistant secretary of England's Football Association, proposed that all players taking part for England in international matches should be "presented with a white silk cap with red rose embroidered on the front." Caps are no longer given today, but the term has lived on, so that if a player has participated in 10 international matches, it is said he has 10 caps.

What is a friendly?

This is a non-competition game, the results of which do not count for standings in a league or tournament. The two sides are just having a friendly game.

Why is it said that soccer players dribble?

The word dribble dates back to the sixteenth century when it was used, as it is now, to describe a flow of drips or drops — though back then drips and drops were called "dribs." It was first used in relation to soccer in 1863 by British journalist A.G. Guillemard, who described an Eton player "dribbling the ball slowly forward before his feet" in the October issue of *The Sporting Gazette*. The term describes skillful movement of the ball upfield in short, small kicks.

What is a tackle?

Unlike American football, bringing another player to the ground is a no-no in soccer. To tackle another player means to take the ball from him with your feet. In soccer, you tackle the ball, not the player.

What is a square ball?

No, it is not a cube. Such a ball shape would not work well for soccer — or any other game! A square ball is one passed on the ground in a line parallel to the touchlines on the pitch.

What does it mean to say the ball has gone into touch?

It means it is dead, because it has crossed the touchlines. When the ball goes into the area outside of the field of play, beyond the touchlines, it may be legally touched by a player's hands, so the term means that the ball has gone into that area.

What is a banana kick?

This is a type of kick that gives the ball a curved trajectory — a bend like a banana — used to get the ball around a goaltender or defender.

What is a bicycle kick?

This is a highly entertaining acrobatic shot. A player kicks the ball in mid-air backwards and over his own head, usually making contact above waist level. It is so named because the player's legs spin as though on a bicycle. It is also called the scissors kick.

Who called soccer "the beautiful game"?

The phrase "The Beautiful Game" as a synonym for soccer was first coined by Didi (Waldyr Pereira), a Brazilian superstar soccer player. The Brazilian Portuguese expression *Joga Bonito* (to "play beautifully") parallels this phrase. In 1977 Pelé, one of soccer's greatest superstars, named his autobiography *My Life and the Beautiful Game*.

Quickies
Did you know ...
that because of its regulation depth of six yards, the goal area is sometimes simply called "the six"?

When was the first radio broadcast of a soccer game?

On January 22, 1927, Arsenal played Sheffield United to a 1–1 draw in a Division One match at Highbury. It was the first match ever covered by radio, as the BBC called the game from pitch-side.

When was the first television transmission of a soccer game?

In 1937 the BBC was on hand to televise, for the first time, portions of the FA Cup final between Preston North End and Sunderland from Wembley Stadium in London. The following year, the BBC televised the entire match.

Top Ten Soccer Movies

- *Escape to Victory* (1981)
- *Bend It Like Beckham* (2002)
- *Das Wunder von Bern* (The Miracle of Bern) (2003)
- *My Name is Joe* (1998)
- *Mean Machine* (2001)
- *The Match* (1999)
- *Ladybugs* (1992)
- *When Saturday Comes* (1996)
- *A Shot at Glory* (2000)
- *Phörpa* (The Cup)

Who were Mitchell & Kenyon?

The Mitchell & Kenyon film company was a pioneer of early commercial movies. Based in Blackburn in Lancashire, England, at the start of the twentieth century, they were best known for minor fictional narrative films. In 1994, a hoard of 800 Mitchell & Kenyon film negatives were discovered and restored. Amongst this collection are numerous films documenting soccer matches between English FA teams just after the turn of the century. The films are in storage at the British Film Institute, but can be viewed on YouTube.com

What are WAGs?

WAGs is an acronym created by the British tabloid press to mean Soccer "wives and girl-friends." The acronym has been in use since 1994, but became extremely popular during the 2006 World Cup, in Germany, when the press gave increasing gossip coverage to the socializing and shopping activities of the English WAGs, who were based in the German town of Baden Baden.

What is *Panini*?

These are not something you eat at an Italian soccer game. *Panini* is the brand name of an Italian firm that produces collectable stickers. The company is based in Modena and named after the Panini brothers, who founded it in 1961. It became famous in the 1960s for its soccer collections, which can now sometimes reach very high prices on the collectors' market. The slogan "Stick with Panini" could once be heard in a jingle following the television advertisements that Panini aired during children's programming.

Top Ten Soccer Books

- *Fever Pitch* by Nick Hornby
- *Among the Thugs* by Bill Buford
- *Brilliant Orange: The Neurotic Genius of Dutch Soccer* by David Winner
- *Soccer in Sun and Shadow* by Edward Galeano
- *How Soccer Explains the World* by Franklin Foer
- *The Soccer War* by Ryszard Kapuscinski
- *Foul! The Secret World of FIFA* by Andrew Jennings
- *Congratulations, You Have Just Met the ICF* by Cass Pennant
- *Futebol, the Brazillian Way of Life* by Alex Bellos
- *Now You Know Soccer* by Doug Lennox

What are ultras?

Ultras are a sanctioned form of team supporters renowned for their fanatical and elaborate displays. They are predominantly European and South American followers of soccer teams. Ultras frequently display their support through choreographed performances called *tifos* and also through "terrace chants," which are sung en masse, often to well-known tunes, but with the words changed.

What are *tifos*?

Tifo was originally the Italian word for the phenomenon of supporting a sport team, but it is now mainly used as the name for the sort of spectacular, choreographed display staged by large groups of fans called "ultras" on the balconies or terraces of arenas or stadiums during sporting events, most often soccer matches. For example, *tifos* can consist of large sections of the crowd holding and turning colour placards, to create larger "tiled" banners. Other materials that have been used include coloured plastic sheeting, flags, balloons, confetti, paper rolls, flares, fireworks, dolls, and mascots.

What is a firm?

A football firm, also known as a hooligan firm, is a gang formed to fight with the supporters of other teams. Their violent activity ranges from shouts and fist fights, to riots in which opposing firms clash with weaponry such as bats, bottles, rocks, or even knives and guns. In some cases, stadium brawls have caused fans to flee in panic, and fans have been killed when fences or walls have collapsed. In the most extreme cases, firm members, police, and bystanders have been killed in the violence, and riot police have intervened with tear gas, armoured vehicles, and water cannons.

What are casuals?

Casuals are a subculture of football culture that developed in the late 1970s and early 1980s in the United Kingdom, and is typified by hooliganism and the wearing of expensive European clothing by some hooligan firms. The subculture originated when many hooligans started wearing designer labels and expensive sportswear to avoid the attention of police. They didn't wear team colours, so it was easier to infiltrate rival groups and to enter pubs.

What is a pitch invasion?

Called "rushing the field" in North America, a pitch invasion occurs when the fans at a soccer match spill onto the pitch, usually compelled by feelings of joy after their team has won a major match, or feelings of rage after their team has lost. They used to be much more common than they are now at top-level soccer games, due to the fact that security was not as tight in the past as it is now.

Why does "back to square one" mean starting over?

During the 1930s, the BBC broadcast soccer games on the radio. As an aid to listeners they published a map of the playing field, which was divided into numbered squares. The commentators would mention the square number of the action after each description of the play. Square one was near the goaltender, so that to score you needed to carry the play the full length of the field.

> **Quickies**
> **Did you know ...**
> that in 1905, several Preston North End fans were tried for hooliganism, including a "drunk and disorderly" 70-year-old woman?

football

Who was the Super Bowl trophy named after?

While the game itself is known as the Super Bowl, the NFL's championship trophy is called the Vince Lombardi Trophy.

Vince Lombardi was the legendary coach of the Green Bay Packers from 1959 to 1967. He coached the Packers to five NFL Championships, and two Super Bowls. His career playoff record was 9–1, while his regular season record was 96–34–6.

Vince Lombardi later joined the Washington Redskins in 1969, but after one season was diagnosed with colon cancer, and passed away in September 1970 at the age of 57.

A week later, the NFL changed the name of its ultimate prize from the "World Championship Game Trophy" to the "Vince Lombardi Trophy."

How many American cities have fielded teams in the CFL?

In total, seven American cities have been part of the CFL.

In the 1990s, the CFL embarked on a grand experiment to expand into the United States. The first U.S.-based team, the Sacramento Gold Miners, took the field in 1993. The following season, they were joined by teams in Baltimore, Las Vegas, and Shreveport, Louisiana. By 1995, the expansion was struggling, and the Las Vegas team folded, while the Sacramento team moved to San Antonio. Other teams were added in Memphis and Birmingham, Alabama, with little success.

After two seasons of American expansion, all but the Baltimore Stallions and San Antonio Texans had called it quits. The Stallions — upon learning that the NFL's Cleveland Browns were moving to Baltimore — relocated to Montreal, becoming the latest incarnation of the Alouettes. The Texans, unenthused at the prospects of playing the lone American team in a league based in a country more than 1,500 miles away, ceased operations.

> **Quickies**
> *Did you know ...*
> that several American states have more than one NFL team, but only two states have three teams? Those states are California (Oakland, San Diego, and San Francisco) and Florida (Jacksonville, Miami, and Tampa).

How many times have NFL and CFL teams squared off?

During the 1950s and 1960s, there were several attempts to pit NFL/AFL teams against CFL teams in exhibition games north of the border. The games were played with mixed rules — one half would be played under American rules, the other under Canadian rules.

The first games were played in 1950 and 1951, when the New York Giants travelled to Ottawa to play the Rough Riders.

Results of Games Between CFL and NFL/AFL Teams

1950:   New York Giants (NFL) 20, Ottawa Rough Riders 6
1951:   New York Giants (NFL) 38, Ottawa Rough Riders 6
1959:   Chicago Cardinals (NFL) 55, Toronto Argonauts 26
1960:   Pittsburgh Steelers (NFL) 43, Toronto Argonauts 26
1961:   St. Louis Cardinals (NFL) 36, Toronto Argonauts 7
1961:   Chicago Bears (NFL) 34, Montreal Alouetts 16
1961:   Hamilton Tiger-Cats 38, Buffalo Bills (AFL) 21

Later in the decade, the exhibition games were revived, with single games in 1959 and 1960, and three games in 1961.

American teams won all but one of the games — the exception being the 1961 tilt that saw the Hamilton Tiger-Cats defeat the AFL's Buffalo Bills 38–21.

How did the Super Bowl get its name?

When the AFL and NFL merged, they agreed to meet in a championship game every season. Lamar Hunt — owner of the Kansas City Chiefs and founder of the AFL — jokingly referred to the game as the "Super Bowl." Hunt was playing on the name of a popular toy at the time — the extra-bouncy Super Ball.

Fans and media, preferring the ad-libbed name to the cumbersome official title — the AFL-NFL World Championship Game — used the shortened version instead. By the time the third championship rolled around in 1969, the name had been made official. The first two games were retroactively renamed Super Bowls I and II.

Who was the Grey Cup named after?

Albert Henry George Grey, fourth Earl Grey, was governor general of Canada from 1904 to 1911. In 1909 he sought to cement his legacy by donating a sports trophy.

Originally, the plan was to award the Grey Cup to the champion amateur senior hockey team in the country. However, Sir H. Allan Montagu got in the way by donating the Allan Cup — a trophy still awarded to this day. The Grey Cup was then designated for the amateur rugby football champion.

Unfortunately, Earl Grey was a little slow about getting the trophy ready. When the University of Toronto won the first Grey Cup game that December, no trophy was present. The championship team was not awarded the Grey Cup until March 1910.

When was the first night football game played?

Mansfield, Pennsylvania, was abuzz with excitement over the 1892 Great Mansfield Fair. The excitement was not about the planned game between the Mansfield Normal School football team and the visiting Wyoming Seminary. Rather, people were eager to see the area's first-ever demonstration of electric lighting. The Mansfield team had arranged to play the first-ever night game. Football itself was something of a novelty for the Mansfield squad — this would be only their fifth game, day or night.

Unfortunately, the first attempt to illuminate a football game was a resounding failure. Because lighting in the 1890s was not as powerful as it would later become, the field was poorly lit. To make matters worse, some of the lights were mounted on a pole at midfield.

At the end of the first half, with limited visibility, teams failing to attain first downs, and players unable to determine which team had the ball, the game was halted and declared a 0–0 tie.

Did Deion Sanders play in an NFL game and a Major League Baseball game on the same day?

In the 1990s Deion Sanders managed to play both football and baseball professionally, but was confronted with the same problem every season: the end of the Major League Baseball season overlaps with the beginning of the NFL season. In 1992, Sanders was a member of both the Atlanta Braves and the Atlanta Falcons. The Braves were headed for the playoffs, and Sanders elected to stick with his baseball team. The Falcons fined him $68,000 for missing the first games of the season. So, in a desire to appease his football team and make history at the same time, Sanders attempted to play two games on one day.

It would have been easier had both teams been playing in Atlanta that day. Instead, he travelled to Miami for an afternoon game between the Falcons and Dolphins, then flew to Pittsburgh for a National League Championship Series game between the Braves and Pirates in the evening.

Urban legend has it that Sanders played in both games that day. Unfortunately for the legend, and for Deion, Braves manager Bobby Cox did not play Sanders that night.

What were the four traditional New Year's Day bowl games?

Before the days of the Bowl Championship Series, New Year's Day was college football's biggest day, often with multiple games that had National Championship implications.

College bowl games in the United States have a tradition dating back to the

The 1985 Chicago Bears

As improbable as it may seem, the Bears' 15–1 record does not do justice to the dominance of the team. With Walter Payton on offence and Mike Singletary on defence, the team thrashed virtually every opponent they faced in the regular season, but truly showed their dominance in the playoffs, winning 21–0 and then 24–0, finally winning the Super Bowl with a 46–10 clobbering of the New England Patriots.

original bowl game, 1902's Rose Bowl. For many years, the Rose Bowl was the only major college bowl game. In the mid-1930s, it was joined by the Sugar Bowl, the Orange Bowl, and the Cotton Bowl.

For many years these games were played almost exclusively on New Year's Day, until BCS scheduling made it necessary to break up the tradition.

Who are the only two charter-member teams still in the NFL?

In 1920 the brand new American Professional Football Association — later renamed the NFL — took to the field for the first time. While most of the teams in the league failed to last the entire history of the league, two charter members are still playing today.

The first is recognizable because of its name: the Chicago Cardinals would later move to St. Louis and then Phoenix. The other team was the Decatur Staleys. The Staleys moved to Chicago in 1921, and later changed their name to the Bears.

While not a charter member, the Green Bay Packers are the oldest team in the NFL that has never moved from its original home. They joined the NFL in 1921.

Why are footballs shaped the way they are?

The football used in modern times is derived from the oval-shaped ball used in rugby, the game from which football evolved. A common belief is that the rugby ball became oval shaped because the original balls (before the invention of rubber) had pigs' bladders for inserts, and that these were oval-shaped. Another belief is that the old pig's-bladder inserts with leather outer shells were prone to becoming misshapen during play, and eventually people decided to stick with the unusual shape.

> **Quickies**
> *Did you know ...*
> that one of Bob Marley's sons was a professional football player? Rohan Marley was a linebacker for the University of Miami, and went on to play for the Ottawa Rough Riders of the CFL.

None of these theories holds much water when it is considered that the soccer ball, which was also made with a pig's-bladder insert, always maintained a round shape.

In fact, the rugby ball became oval-shaped because the game required players to carry and handle the ball, and an oblong ball was far more suitable for this purpose than a large, round one.

Whatever became of the real-life *Rudy*?

The 1993 film *Rudy* is the inspirational story of young man's efforts to become a member of the Notre Dame Fighting Irish football team. Despite dyslexia and a small frame unsuited to football, Rudy manages to get accepted to Notre Dame after many attempts, and is able to make the Irish's practice squad. He finally gets onto the field in the last minute of the last game for which he is eligible.

Seven NFL Teams **That Don't Have Cheerleaders**
• Chicago Bears • Cleveland Browns • Detroit Lions • Green Bay Packers • New York Giants • New York Jets • Pittsburgh Steelers

The movie is based on the real-life story of Daniel "Rudy" Ruettiger. In 1989, convinced his story would make a great film, Ruettiger met with screenwriter Angelo Pizzo, who was the writer behind another inspirational sports film, *Hoosiers*. Initially, Pizzo was uninterested. But Ruettiger persisted, Pizzo talked about the project with studio executives, and the Rudy story made another improbable journey, this time to the big screen.

Today, Ruettiger is an inspirational speaker, using his life story as an example of how determination can beat the odds.

When was the first football game televised?

Football made its television debut on September 30, 1939, when NBC's experimental non-commercial station, W2XBS, carried the game between Fordham University and Waynesburg College. Fordham prevailed, 34–7.

Professional football hit the airwaves for the first time three weeks later, on October 22, when the football edition of the Brooklyn Dodgers defeated the Philadelphia Eagles, 23–14.

What football team was named after a Burt Reynolds character?

In the early 1980s, the name "Burt Reynolds" was box-office gold. So, when Reynolds became a minority owner of John Bassett's Tampa Bay entry into the new USFL, the team tried to capitalize on the star's involvement. Taking their cue from the name of one of Reynold's most famous movie franchises — the *Smokey and the Bandit* series — the team became known as the Tampa Bay Bandits.

Top Ten Super Bowl Commercials

10. **FedEx** — "Carrier Pigeons": An office worker decides to have packages delivered by carrier pigeons instead of using FedEx.
9. **Pepsi** — "Cindy Crawford": A couple of kids watching Cindy Crawford drink a Pepsi out of one of the newly designed cans.
8. **McDonald's** — "Big Mac Song": Introduced us to the jingle that simply listed the parts of a Big Mac. "Two all beef patties, special sauce, lettuce, cheese, pickles, onions on a sesame seed bun."
7. **E-Trade** — "Trading Baby": The first in a series of commercials intended to show that using E-Trade is so easy, even a baby can do it. A simple face-on shot of a baby working at a computer, CG lip movements making it appear the baby is speaking.
6. **McDonald's** — "Showdown": Larry Bird vs. Michael Jordan taking free throws from impossible locations, catching "nothing but net."
5. **Reebok** — "Terry Tate: Office Linebacker": Unpretentious, and pure comedy. A linebacker is hired to improve efficiency and productivity through physical and verbal intimidation. A hit ad at a time when workplace shows, such as The Office, were huge.
4. **Electronic Data Systems** — "Herding Cats": Few knew what the commercial was advertising, or really understood the message it was trying to deliver, but they got a kick out of watching cowboys herding cats.
3. **Wendy's** — "Where's the Beef?": Entirely catchphrase driven, but that catchphrase took off and became engrained in popular culture. Three elderly ladies study the "nice, big, fluffy bun" on their hamburger, while one asks, "Where's the beef?"
2. **Apple** — "1984": Said to be the big Super Bowl preview that started the craze of big-money, overblown ads.
1. **Coca-Cola** — "Mean Joe Greene": A surprisingly heartwarming ad where mean old Joe turns softie and tosses a kid his jersey after the kid gives him a Coke. The best of the bunch, because it actually produced the sentimental response it was aiming for.

How did the word *sack* come to be used to describe the tackle of a passer behind the line of scrimmage?

Sack only entered the football lexicon in the late sixties and early seventies — previously, the play was known as a tackle behind the line of scrimmage.

Future hall of famer Deacon Jones specialized in the tackle, but thought a shorter term was in order. He coined the word *sack*, likening the devastation caused by tackling a quarterback to the sacking of a city in war. As an added bonus, according to Jones, "the word is so short you can even get 'Deacon' in front of 'Jones' in some headlines."

Quickies

Did you know ...
that in China, the Mandarin word for American football is *gan lan qui*, which loosely translates to *olive ball*? The name comes from the football's shape.

Why is a play referred to as a "down"?

An old rugby rule allowed a player to voluntary halt the play when held by opponents, providing the opponents agreed to the stoppage. The player would call "held," and the opponents would grant consent by responding "have it down."

Early football games allowed for a similar voluntary stoppage (without the consent of the opponent) by shouting "down." The word eventually became used to denote a play itself, and not just the completion of the play.

Though the option is rarely used, some football leagues, including the NFL, still allow for a ball carrier to voluntarily end a play by shouting, "down."

The 1962 Green Bay Packers

Having Vince Lombardi as head coach is always a good way to start; throw in the versatile halfback Paul Hornung, fullback John Taylor, and Hall of Fame quarterback Bart Starr and you've got the makings of one of the all-time great teams. The Packers were so dominant that in one game they compiled 628 yards on offence while holding their opponents to a mere 54 yards. And in the NFL Championship, Ray Nitschke proved that the team did not just have great offensive players, as the defensive linebacker shut down the New York Giants and was named the game's MVP.

If a punter misses the ball with his kick, is the ball live? And what happens if someone hits the kicker?

According to the rules, if a punter misses the ball with his foot, it is not considered a "kick." It is considered a live ball — a fumble — and can be recovered. The opposing team is free to hit the would-be kicker without fear of a "roughing the kicker" penalty, because without a kick, there is no kicker to rough.

Why is a football called a "pigskin"?

Prior to the invention of vulcanized rubber in 1844, sports such as rugby and soccer needed inflatable balls for play. Animal bladders were easy to obtain and were well-suited for the purpose. In the early days of football, animal bladders were still in wide use, with pig's bladders being the choice of discerning sportsmen. The balls were known as "pigskins," presumably because players didn't want to be reminded of what part of the pig the balls came from.

By the late nineteenth century, animal bladders were replaced with rubber bladders, and the modern football contains no pig parts. The nickname, however, remains.

Why is a touchdown worth six points?

In an early form of the game, teams could only score by kicking. When a touchdown was made, it only allowed a team to kick for a point. (Points could also be scored by kicking without the benefit of a touchdown.)

In the early 1880s, it was decided that touchdowns should be more valuable than kicks from the field, and a points system was introduced. At first, a touchdown counted as four points, and the subsequent kick was worth another four points. Then, in 1897, the value of a touchdown increased to five points, while the kick after was reduced to a single point.

The touchdown became worth six points in American football in 1912. Canadian football stuck with the traditional five points until 1956, when the touchdown increased from five to six points.

According to NFL rules …

- If a team is late coming onto the field at the beginning of a game, they can be penalized 15 yards and automatically lose the coin toss.
- When a punt is blocked and the ball travels past the line of scrimmage, touches a member of the blocking team, then falls to the ground, whichever team recovers the ball — even the kicking team — gets a first down.
- When the opposing team fakes a punt and passes the ball instead, the two outside defenders cannot be called for pass interference.

Why is a field goal worth three points?

Football started out as a kicking-oriented game, and the scoring reflected this. At first, the only way a team could score was by kicking. Later, when the touchdown became a point-getter of its own, a scoring system was introduced and a field goal was worth a whopping five points, and carried more value than a touchdown.

As the touchdown became a source of excitement — and proved to be a tougher feat than a field goal — the scoring changed and in 1904 the value of a field goal was reduced to four points. Five years later, in 1909, it was devalued again to three points.

Where does the word *tackle* come from?

The Middle Dutch word *tacken* meant "to grab" or "to hold." The word evolved in English and by the eighteenth century *tackle* referred to harnessing equipment used on horses. The word was borrowed by early rugby to refer to the grabbing or "harnessing" of another player, and ultimately was adopted as a football term.

When was instant replay introduced as a means of reviewing calls in the NFL?

Although criticized by many as a dehumanizing of the game, instant replay was approved for use in the NFL in 1986. At the time, only the officials could call for an instant replay. The system suffered from a limited number of cameras — resulting in poor angles for many disputed plays — and was ultimately abandoned in 1992.

In 1999, technology, and the number of available cameras, had increased considerably and the league decided to give it another go. This time, the "coach's challenge" was introduced, allowing teams to call for reviews of up to two plays per game. (Later, a third challenge was allowed for teams that had been successful on their two previous challenges.) For several years, instant replay was only used during the regular season, but was approved for use in the playoffs beginning in 2005.

The system was considered temporary until 2007, when the NFL owners voted by an overwhelming 30–2 margin to make instant replay a permanent part of the game.

When was instant replay introduced as a means of reviewing calls in the CFL?

While instant replay had been in use off and on in the NFL since 1986, and regularly since 1999, the CFL's board of governors did not approve the officiating aid until 2006.

Notable Rule Changes in American Football

1906:	Forward pass legalized
1912:	Value of a touchdown increased to six points
1942:	NFL requires players to wear protective headgear
1946:	Free substitution forbidden, replaced by limited substitution
1948:	Plastic helmets forbidden
1949:	Free substitution restored
1956:	Grabbing the facemask made illegal
1962:	AFL makes the scoreboard clock the official clock
1967:	Slingshot goal posts became the NFL standard
1974:	Sudden-death overtime adopted for regular-season games and NFL goal posts moved to the back of the end zone
1980:	45-second clock replaces the 30-second clock
1994:	Two-point conversion an option after touchdowns
1995:	Quarterbacks permitted to receive communication from the bench via radio transmitters in their helmets
1999:	Instant replay for the review of calls returns to the NFL on a temporary basis
2007:	Instant replay for the review of calls is accepted as a permanent facet of the game

Where does the term *snap* come from?

In the early days of the game, when rugby was evolving into football, the hands were not used to put a ball in play. Instead, a player put his foot on the ball and, with a snapping motion, caused it to go to his teammate. While later rule changes allowed the use of the hands to deliver the ball from the line of scrimmage to a teammate, the term "snap" remained.

Quickies

Did you know ...

that according to NCAA rules, a snap is considered a backward pass the moment it leaves the snapper's hands? The rules also say that a snap does not need to be between the legs. A centre can snap from the side, if they're ever possessed to do so.

You CAN Tell the Players Without a Program — NFL Positional Numbering

1–19:	Quarterbacks and kickers
10–19:	Tight ends and receivers, but only when higher numbers are unavailable
20–49:	Running backs and defensive backs
50–59:	Centres and linebackers
60–79:	Defensive and offensive linemen
80–89:	Tight ends and receivers
90–99:	Defensive linemen and linebackers

Why are players' numbers determined by their position?

At one time, players were allowed to wear whatever number they wanted. But in the interest of making things easier for officials to identify eligible receivers, regulations were brought in. College and professional regulations differ somewhat, but are relatively close to the model brought in by the NFL in 1973.

What is the "Emmitt Smith Rule"?

Critics occasionally refer to the NFL as the "No Fun League" because of its frequent rules to eliminate on-field celebrations. One such rule became known as the "Emmitt Smith Rule." The Dallas Cowboys running back was known for celebrating his touchdowns by removing his helmet. The NFL felt that this encouraged taunting and excessive celebration, and in 1997 adopted a rule forbidding players from removing their helmets on the field, except during timeouts or breaks between quarters.

Football Slang

- **Alligator arms**: When a receiver does not extend his arms far enough to catch a ball.
- **Blutarsky**: A quarterback with a 0.0 rating in a game.
- **Coffin corner**: The corner of the playing field in front of the end zone, but next to the sidelines.
- **Garbage time or junk time**: The period at the end of a blowout, where the outcome is known but the teams are still playing out the clock.
- **Pooch punt**: A kick purposely made short of the opposing goal line.
- **Sidewalk alumni**: Fans of a college or university team who have never actually attended that school.
- **Taxi squad**: Reserve players who are technically on a team, but never get into a game.

What is a "rouge"?

While fans of the Canadian game rarely use the term *rouge* nowadays, the word is still used in the official rules.

A rouge is a single point that is scored when a ball is either kicked through the end zone, or kicked into the end zone and not returned past the goal line by the receiving team. This can occur on punts, missed field goal attempts, or kickoffs. A point after a touchdown is not considered a "rouge," nor is the three-point field goal.

The rouge, or single, is unique to the Canadian game. It is not clear how the word *rouge* came to be applied to the score.

What is the origin of the word *scrimmage*?

The word *scrimmage*, as used in North American football, evolved from the rugby term *scrummage*, which is generally shortened to *scrum* and refers to the mass of players fighting for the ball to start play.

Interestingly, though the North American term sprung from the rugby term, they both have a common origin that is, in fact, closer to the North American word. *Scrummage* comes from *scrimish*, which is an older variation of the modern word, *skirmish*.

Who supplies the balls for professional football games?

Generally, the home team is responsible for supplying footballs in most leagues. The NFL, for example, requires that home teams provide 36 balls for outdoor games, and 24 for indoor games. The balls must be given to the referee at least two hours before game time so that he can test them with a pressure gauge.

In addition, for every game, 12 new balls are shipped to the stadium, sealed in a box that can only be opened by the referee. These balls are to be used exclusively for kicking.

Who first decided to pick up the ball and carry or throw it?

According to one legend, a student at the British Public School of Rugby named William Webb Ellis was playing a kicking game, and decided to pick up the ball and run with it. In doing so, he invented a new sport, called *rugby*. Much doubt has been cast on this legend, but many still treat the story with reverence.

As rugby evolved into the modern game of football, many variations of the North American sport existed, and in 1874, versions of "football" varied greatly. That year, Montreal's McGill University football team was invited to visit Harvard in the United States for a match against their squad. On arrival, it was discovered that the two teams were playing very different brands of "football." The version played by McGill University was a form of rugby, and involved carrying the ball and throwing it. The Harvard version was a kicking game closer to soccer.

The teams solved the problem by playing two games — one under each school's rules. The Harvard team was so excited by the McGill version of the game that they adopted the new rules, and this variety of football spread rapidly in the United States, ultimately becoming a base on which the modern game was built.

Who created the Statue of Liberty play?

One of the more famous, but rarely used, trick plays in football is the Statue of Liberty play. In the simplest and most common version of the play, the quarterback rolls back, and moves his throwing hand in position to pass, but retains the ball in his non-throwing hand, and holds it behind his back. A receiver or back then takes the ball and runs in a direction opposite to where the quarterback is apparently throwing.

At the point of the fake, the positioning of the quarterback's arms are similar to the pose of the Statue of Liberty, giving the play its name.

The play was invented by the Grand Old Man of College Football, Amos Alonzo Stagg. The legendary coach and pioneer of the game was not responsible for its popularity, though — credit for the play's spread goes to University of Michigan coach Fielding Yost.

Why is Canadian football considered a "passing" game while American football is considered a "running" game?

The rules and the size of the playing field have made the Canadian game a haven for the quarterback who loves big passing plays.

With only three downs to work with, short yardage gains put Canadian teams in down trouble, meaning that the grind-it-out tactic often employed by American teams to gain a few yards at a time on the ground is risky.

Also, the Canadian field is much larger than the American field. It's longer, 110 yards from goal line to goal line, with 20-yard end zones, making it a total of 30 yards longer than the American field. It's also wider, measuring 65 yards from sideline to sideline, compared to the 53 1/3-yard width of American fields. With so much more room, passing plays are more difficult to defend against.

> **The 1989 San Francisco 49ers**
>
> They could beat you in the air or on the ground. Quarterback Joe Montana and receivers Jerry Rice and John Taylor made the Niners' passing attack one of the best in the history of the game — Montana averaged nearly 10 yards for every pass attempt. But they could also run the ball — Roger Craig running for more than 1,000 yards. It surprised no one that they not only won the Super Bowl, but won handily, 55–10, over the Denver Broncos.

When was the two-point conversion introduced?

In 1958 the NCAA adopted its first new scoring rule in 46 years with the introduction of the two-point conversion. Teams made good use of it on the first weekend, with five games turning on the success or failure of two-point converts.

The AFL followed suit in 1960, but the NFL was slow to warm up to the rule, and when the two leagues completed their merger in 1970, the rule was snuffed out. Eventually, the NFL came to see merit in the rule, and adopted it in 1994.

> **The 1981 Edmonton Eskimos**
>
> The Eskimos of the late 1970s and early 1980s were one of the great dynasties in football, winning five straight Grey Cups, thanks in large part to Warren Moon, one of the greatest quarterbacks ever to play the game. The 1981 Esks might have been the best team of that dynasty, finishing with a 14–1–1 record and winning one of the most memorable Grey Cup games ever played.

How often are two-point conversions successful?

The success rate of two-point conversions has varied wildly over the years. In the early days of the rule's existence it was estimated that two-point attempts were successful only 35 percent of the time.

By the time the NFL adopted the rule in 1994, success rates had improved; estimates generally place the success rate for both the NFL and NCAA around 43 percent. For comparison, one-point attempts are successful around 98 percent of the time.

When was the term *Hail Mary* pass first used?

In the 1975 Wild Card game against the Minnesota Vikings, the Dallas Cowboys found themselves at midfield with 24 seconds remaining, trailing 14–10. Needing a touchdown, quarterback Roger Staubach took the snap and rolled back to his own 40-yard line. "I closed my eyes," Staubach said after the game, "and said a 'Hail Mary' prayer." He then hurled the ball 55 yards to Drew Pearson, who caught it at the five-yard line and took it to the end zone for a touchdown.

The media took Staubach's "Hail Mary" description and began applying it to any last-ditch, desperation pass.

Where does the shotgun formation get its name?

The term *shotgun formation* became popular when the San Francisco 49ers made heavy use of the formation in the 1960s. The formation spreads receivers widely, and the scattering of these receivers is likened to the scattering of a shotgun blast.

Who created the Run and Shoot Offence?

While credit is often given to long-time coach and offensive coordinator Darell "Mouse" Davis, the Run and Shoot was actually invented by Glenn "Tiger" Ellison, a high-school football coach who developed the offence for his teams, and published a book about the strategy called *Run and Shoot Football: Offense of the Future* in 1965.

The basic Run and Shoot Offence uses four receivers, one running back, a quarterback, and five linemen. The receivers run short and medium routes in a passing-centric offence, while spreading out the defence to create running lanes.

Mouse Davis took to the strategy, and employed it as a coach with Portland State University. He later brought the offence to professional football, first with the Toronto Argonauts (who won a Grey Cup using the Run and Shoot after Davis's departure) and then the USFL's Houston Gamblers.

The Run and Shoot gained some popularity in the NFL in the late 1980s and early 1990s, most notably with Warren Moon and the Houston Oilers, but is seldom used at the professional level today.

What is the "flying wedge"?

The flying wedge was easily the most controversial formation in the history of football. Introduced by Harvard in 1892, the flying wedge was a dangerous manoeuvre that called for offensive players to link arms and form a V-shaped wedge with the ball carrier tucked behind them, and drive the point of the V toward the defence to move the ball carrier forward. The wedge was difficult to penetrate, and defenders found that the "best" way to defend against the formation was to throw themselves at the legs of the rushing players.

It was extraordinarily dangerous, and resulted in many injuries. After President Theodore Roosevelt threatened to ban the sport if violence was not eliminated, the Intercollegiate Athletic Association of the United States (which later became the NCAA) made a number of rule changes, including banning mass-momentum plays such as the flying wedge.

Police riot squads now use a manoeuvre called the flying wedge — similar to the football play — to break up unruly mobs.

What is an "Alley Oop"?

The "Alley Oop" in football was a more formalized version of (and a predecessor to) the Hail Mary pass.

While a Hail Mary pass is generally a chaotic, last second desperation pass, the Alley Oop was a coordinated, practiced play employed by the San Francisco 49ers in the 1950s.

Wide receiver R.C. Owens, who was often considerably taller than the defensive backs guarding him, would run to the back of the end zone and quarterback Y.A. Tittle would throw a high, arching pass. Owens would leap to a ball beyond the reach of the defenders and haul it in for a touchdown.

While the use of the term "Alley Oop" is uncommon in football today, the term was adopted in basketball in the 1960s, and is a common play in that sport.

> **The 1972 Miami Dolphins**
>
> Though some have felt their schedule was light, it's hard to improve on a perfect season — the only perfect season in NFL history. The Miami Dolphins featured such greats as Bob Griese, Mercury Morris, and Larry Czonka. Almost inexplicably, they were underdogs going into the Super Bowl, but silenced their critics with a 14–7 win over the Washington Redskins. Call them overrated if you will, but they beat all comers.

How often are onside kicks successfully recovered by the kicking team?

The onside kick is a high-risk strategy used by kicking teams to attempt to retain control of the ball. The best rate of success comes with catching the opposing team by surprise, but even then, the risk is high. Only 20 percent of onside kicks are successfully recovered by the kicking team.

Take away the element of surprise and the odds are even longer. Late in the game, when a team is attempting to catch up and can't afford to let the other team have the ball, an onside kick is often a necessity, and the opposition knows it. When the onside kick is anticipated, the success rate drops to between 12 and 14 percent.

What is a "West Coast Offence"?

"West Coast Offence" is a name given to the style of offence developed and perfected by Bill Walsh, first as offensive coordinator with the Cincinatti Bengals, and then, to great success, as head coach of the San Francisco 49ers.

The West Coast Offence is a pass-oriented offence. The bulk of plays in the West Coast Offence are short, horizontal passes, and the frequency of these plays forces the defence to defend accordingly. With the defence stretched out, running and passing lanes are opened up, creating holes for the running backs and opportunities for longer passes.

Unlike other pass-oriented offences, the West Coast Offence generally employs two or more running backs.

Ironically, the term "West Coast Offence" was first used with disdain. After his New York Giants defeated the 49ers in the 1985 playoffs, coach Bill Parcels scoffed at the strategy in a post-game scrum, saying, "What do you think of that West Coast Offence now?"

Where did the "Wildcat Formation" get its name?

The Wildcat Formation is one that has gained popularity in recent years. It's most notable feature is that the quarterback does not line up behind the centre. Instead, a running back sets up behind the centre and takes the snap.

There are competing claims to the origins of the formation, both stemming from teams named the "Wildcats." One credits Hugh Wyatt, coach of the La Center High School Wildcats, who published an article that detailed the formation in *Scholastic Coach* magazine. The other major claim points to Steve Bush, who is currently an assistant coach with the Miami Dolphins, but supposedly developed the formation while coaching the West Genesee High School Wildcats.

Whatever the origins, most NFL teams have now begun using variations of the Wildcat Formation. Meanwhile, the CFL, specifically seeking to allow the formation, revised their longstanding rule that required the quarterback to be in position to take the snap.

Who was the only NFL player to rush for more than 2,000 yards in a fourteen-game season?

As a member of the 1973 Buffalo Bills, O.J. Simpson barely eclipsed the mark, rushing for 2,003 yards on the season. Five years later, the NFL season expanded to sixteen games, leaving O.J. Simpson as the only player to surpass the plateau in the fourteen-game format.

Though he has dropped well down the list over the years, Simpson ended his career after the 1979 season in second place on the all-time rushing list with 11,236 career yards.

Quickies

Did you know ...

that it was NFL commissioner and former Philadelphia Eagles owner Bert Bell who spoke the words, "On any given Sunday, any team can beat any other team"?

Why is the Pro Football Hall of Fame in Canton, Ohio?

According to the Pro Football Hall of Fame, Canton was selected as the home for the NFL's shrine for three reasons. First, it was in Canton that the American Professional Football Association — now known as the NFL — was founded. Second, Canton was the home of one of the first great football teams, the Canton Bulldogs, who featured the likes of Jim Thorpe. Third, the citizens of Canton organized a feverish campaign to become home to the Hall in the early 1960s.

Who was the first drafted player to go on to a Hall of Fame career in the NFL?

In the early years of the NFL Draft, busts were common, as were players simply electing not to go into professional football. So, with the number six pick in the first-ever NFL Draft in 1936, the Chicago Bears lucked out in drafting Joe Stydahar. The offensive tackle out of West Virginia University played with the Bears from 1936 to 1942, then, after serving in World War II, from 1945 to 1946. He was a four-time all-star and helped the Bears to win NFL Championships in 1940, 1941, and 1946.

Number six seems to have been a lucky number in the early years of the draft. The following season, the Washington Redskins used the number six slot to draft Sammy Baugh, the first drafted quarterback elected to the Hall of Fame.

> **The Magnificent Seven: Football's Humanitarians**
>
> - **Rosey Grier**: inspirational speaker, helps provide homes and training for the disadvantaged.
> - **Steve Largent**: inducted into Sports Humanitarian Hall of Fame for various contributions.
> - **Travis LaBoy**: started a foundation to support autistic children.
> - **Gene Upshaw**: numerous humanitarian awards for his work with charities and the community.
> - **Michael McCrary**: founded Mac's Miracle Fund, offering programs for children.
> - **Byron "Whizzer" White**: became a Supreme Court Justice and had a humanitarian award named after him.
> - **Jerome Bettis**: started "The Bus Stops Here" foundation to aid underprivileged children.

Who is the only player elected to both the Pro Football Hall of Fame and the Canadian Football Hall of Fame?

Many players have had success in both the NFL and CFL, but none have been as accomplished in both leagues as Warren Moon.

After a solid college career, Moon went undrafted by the NFL, and had to look north of the border for work. He joined the Edmonton Eskimos, and quickly became one of the most dominant players in league history, leading his team to five consecutive Grey Cup wins between 1978 and 1982.

Moon then converted his CFL success into NFL interest and signed with the Houston Oilers. While Moon never made it to the Super Bowl, he became one of only two quarterbacks to pass for more than 4,000 yards in consecutive seasons, and was named to the Pro Bowl nine times.

When he retired, his combined totals in the CFL and NFL established several professional football records, including most career passing yards, and most career passing touchdowns. He was elected to the Canadian Football Hall of Fame in 2001, and the Pro Football Hall of Fame in 2006.

Who extended his middle finger for a cover photo on an issue of *Sports Illustrated*?

An August 1972 issue of *Sports Illustrated* ran a feature on Larry Csonka and Jim Kiick. The two were members of the stellar Miami Dolphins team that was favoured by many to win the Super Bowl, and, in fact, did, completing a perfect season. But the issue that ran prior to the '72 season created a furor that the Dolphins weren't expecting. Csonka is seated, his hand on his ankle, with his middle finger slyly extended. Somehow the obscene gestured was missed by the photographer and staff at the magazine, but not by the public, who were divided between the amused and the outraged.

What action by NFL commissioner Pete Rozelle caused Joe Namath to announce his retirement?

In the summer of 1969, only months after Joe Namath and the New York Jets upset the Baltimore Colts in Super Bowl III, commissioner Pete Rozelle took exception to Namath's part-ownership of a nightclub, Bachelors III. The club was frequented by what Rozelle called "undesirables," including co-owners with ties to gamblers. Rozelle ordered Namath to sell his interest in the club or face suspension.

Namath then stunned everyone by announcing his retirement. However, after negotiations with Rozelle, Namath eventually agreed to sell the club and returned to football less than a month into his "retirement."

What team has the most inductees in the Pro Football Hall of Fame?

With representation from such legends as George Halas, Red Grange, Dick Butkus, and Walter Payton, the Chicago Bears have had the most players and executives elected to the Pro Football Hall of Fame, with 26. Their nearest competitors are the Green Bay Packers, who boast 21 hall of famers.

Who declared "It will take an act of God to beat us on Saturday" prior to a 1969 CFL playoff game?

The Toronto Argonauts faced the Ottawa Rough Riders in the two-game total-points Eastern Division final in 1969. The Argos won the first game handily, 22–14. Coach Leo Cahill, confident that his team had Ottawa's number, despite the fact that they had only beaten the Riders twice in their last 12 encounters, told the media that "It will take an act of God to beat us on Saturday."

That weekend, the act of God actually occurred. The field at Ottawa's Lansdowne Park was frozen, and the Argos were only equipped with standard cleats and running shoes. The Rough Riders, meanwhile, had broomball style shoes that provided excellent traction on the slippery surface. The Riders pounded the Argos 32–3 to advance to the Grey Cup.

Who said "Winning isn't everything; it's the only thing"?

While credit is often given to Vince Lombardi, who repeated it many times over the course of his life, it actually originates with Henry Russell "Red" Sanders, the long-time coach of the UCLA Bruins. He first made the comment at a physical-education workshop in 1950, saying, "I'll be honest. Winning isn't everything. Men, it's the only thing." Then, in 1955, in an interview with *Sports Illustrated*, he repeated the philosophy, saying, "Sure, winning isn't everything. It's the only thing."

Lombardi's first-known use of the expression didn't come until 1959.

Who was "The Gipper"?

The phrase "Win one for the Gipper" has become a sports cliché. The line was originally uttered by the Gipper himself — George Gipp.

Gipp was a legendary member of the Notre Dame Fighting Irish, playing at multiple positions — most notably, quarterback and halfback. His team-record of 2,341 rushing yards stood for more than 50 years.

In late November 1920, Gipp contracted strep throat, which developed into pneumonia. He died on December 14. In his final days, Notre Dame coach Knute Rockne visited Gipp in the hospital. Gipp reportedly said the following: "Some time, Rock, when the team is up against it, when things are wrong and the breaks are beating the boys, ask them to go in there with all they've got and win just one for the Gipper."

Rockne found the opportunity to fulfill this request prior to a 1928 game against Army, using Gipp's line to inspire the Irish to an upset victory.

Who was the youngest coach ever to win one hundred games in the NFL?

John Madden achieved his most lasting fame in the broadcast booth, popularizing the word "Doink!" and using his telestrator at every conceivable opportunity. He became so prominent as a colour commentator that *John Madden Football* became the most dominant football product in the gaming market for many years.

Because of his 30 years as a broadcaster, it's almost easy to forget that he was also an outstanding football coach. In 10 years as coach of the Oakland Raiders between 1969 and 1978, he compiled a 103–32–7 record, winning one Super Bowl. He left coaching at the age of 42 as the youngest coach ever to reach 100 wins.

What was the "Fog Bowl"?

Toronto's lakeside Exhibition Stadium was always a favourite prey of the elements, and the 1962 Grey Cup was no exception.

The December 1, 1962, game pitted the Hamilton Tiger-Cats against the Winnipeg Blue Bombers. In the second quarter, clear skies gave way to a thick fog. Visibility was so poor that not only could fans not see the action, but the players were having trouble. Receivers could not see passes thrown their way, and punt returners had to wait until the ball hit the ground before they could see it.

With the score 28–27 for the Bombers in the fourth quarter, officials gave in and suspended play with just over nine minutes remaining. The game was resumed the following day, December 2, and Winnipeg held on for the win. It was the only game in Grey Cup history to be played over two days.

The name "Fog Bowl" was later borrowed and applied to a 1988 NFL playoff game between the Philadelphia Eagles and the Chicago Bears. While the game was not suspended, visibility was limited to less than 20 yards. The Eagles ultimately prevailed, 20–12.

"It's Good!" — Four Famous Field Goals

- **Adam Vinatieri**: Vinatieri kicked a 48-yard field goal on the final play of Super Bowl XXXVI to give the New England Patriots a 20–17 win over the St. Louis Rams.
- **Tom Dempsey**: With two seconds remaining in a critical regular season matchup, Dempsey kicked a record-setting 63-yard crossbar-scraper to give the New Orleans Saints a 19–17 win over the Detroit Lions.
- **Jim O'Brien**: In Super Bowl V, O'Brien kicked a 32-yard field goal with nine seconds remaining as the Baltimore Colts defeated the Dallas Cowboys, 16–13.
- **Lui Passaglia**: Passaglia's field goal on the last play of the 1994 Grey Cup won the title for the B.C. Lions as they defeated to Baltimore Stallions, 26–23.

Whose cereal did Jimmy Johnson stomp on?

When Doug Flutie left the CFL to join the Buffalo Bills in the NFL, a minor mania was touched off, thanks to Flutie's spark-plug play on the field. The surge in Flutie's popularity led to the introduction of a new breakfast cereal, Flutie Flakes. Proceeds from sales of the cereal went to the Doug Flutie Jr. Foundation for Autism, which the star quarterback named in honour of his autistic son.

Apparently unaware of the charitable purpose of the cereal, Miami Dolphins coach Jimmy Johnson celebrated his team's victory over Flutie's Bills by pouring a box of Flutie Flakes on the floor of his team's dressing room and stomping on them. Johnson later apologized.

> **"Wide Right!" — Four Famous Missed Field Goals**
>
> • **Scott Norwood**: In the dying moments of Super Bowl XXV, the Buffalo Bills quarterback missed a 47-yard attempt, and the Bills lost 20–19.
> • **Gary Anderson**: In the NFC Championship Game on January 17, 1999, Anderson missed a 38-yard attempt late in the game that would have clinched a win for the Minnesota Vikings. Instead, the Atlanta Falcons followed the miss with a 71-yard drive that culminated in a game-tying touchdown. The Falcons won in overtime.
> • **Mike Vanderjagt**: The Indianapolis Colts kicker missed a 46-yard attempt with 18 seconds left in an AFC Divisional Playoff game against the Pittsburgh Steelers on January 14, 2006. The Colts lost the game, 21–18.
> • **Paul McCallum**: The Saskatchewan Roughriders kicker missed an 18-yard attempt in overtime of a playoff game against the B.C. Lions. The Lions went on to win the game.

Who first called the winning play of the 1972 AFC Championship Game "the Immaculate Reception"?

Trailing 7–6 to the Oakland Raiders with 22 seconds to play in the fourth quarter, the Pittsburgh Steelers faced a fourth and ten situation on their own 40-yard line. Quarterback Terry Bradshaw, unable to find his primary receiver, opted to throw the ball to fullback John Fuqua. Fuqua was hit as the ball arrived, and the pass was deflected into the arms of running back Franco Harris, who carried the ball all the way into the Raiders end zone for a game-winning touchdown.

The play was controversial. Many felt the ball actually hit the intended receiver, Fuqua. Under an NFL rule in place at the time, the play would have been illegal as the same pass had been touched by two receivers in succession. However, the officials ruled that the ball had bounced off the Raiders defender, and the touchdown stood.

Afterwards, a pair of Steelers season-ticket holders, Sharon Levosky and Michael Ord, called the team's radio announcer on his postgame show and suggested the miraculous play be known as "the Immaculate Reception."

Who caught Doug Flutie's Hail Mary pass when Boston College defeated Miami in 1984?

After the University Miami scored a touchdown with 28 seconds remaining to take a 45–41 lead, it looked like they had secured a victory over Boston College. When Boston

College's final drive seemed stalled at the Miami 48-yard line with six seconds to play, the BC fate seemed sealed.

Then, on the final play of the game, quarterback Doug Flutie took the snap, dropped back, eluded a tackler, and from his own 36-yard line found Gerry Phelan in the end zone to win the game.

What was the Great Rose Bowl Hoax?

Students at the California Institute of Technology (Caltech) often joked that their football team played in front of more empty seats than any team in the nation. After all, they played at the massive Rose Bowl but garnered little attention or fan interest.

A group of Caltech students — later named the "Fiendish Fourteen" — grew tired of being ignored while the stadium and its annual game achieved nationwide fame. Prior to the 1961 Rose Bowl Game, they learned that cheerleaders for one of the competing teams, the Washington Huskies, had planned a special gimmick for halftime. Spectators were given cards that they were to hold over their heads — each card being coloured as part of an overall pattern that would display images for the delight of television viewers.

The night before the game the Fiendish Fourteen broke into the cheerleaders' hotel rooms and replaced the cards with ones of their own.

At halftime, when the cards were raised, some of the cheerleaders' planned images remained intact, but the Huskies logo was replaced by a Caltech Beavers logo, and the word "Caltech" was raised at one end of the stadium. The cheerleaders were not amused.

> **The 1979 Pittsburgh Steelers**
>
> The names of the players on the 1979 Steelers speak volumes: Terry Bradshaw, Lynn Swann, John Stallworth, Franco Harris, "Mean" Joe Greene, Jack Lambert, and Jack Ham. The team had 10 Pro Bowlers, and after a 12–4 regular season breezed through the playoffs, ultimately winning the Super Bowl with a 31–19 win over the Los Angeles Rams. It was the second straight Super Bowl win for one of the most celebrated teams of their era.

Who scarred the left eye of a future American president?

U.S. President Gerald Ford was often mocked by comedians for his apparent clumsiness, but at least one of his injuries was sustained in an intentional act of athleticism.

Ford was a centre for the University of Michigan. In 1934, Michigan played the University of Chicago, who featured the first-ever Heisman Trophy winner, Jay Berwanger. Ford tackled Berwanger, but Berwanger's heel caught Ford's cheekbone, opening a three-inch gash. The incident left a scar that Ford carried with him for the rest of his life.

Who was the recipient of the first "Gatorade shower"?

During their 1986 season and run toward a Super Bowl title, the New York Giants became known for celebrating big wins by dumping an icy bucket of Gatorade on head coach Bill Parcells. The ritual received massive attention in the media and became a phenomenon that spread throughout the sport at every level — thanks to the ingenuity of Parcells and the Giants.

Or not. The story of the tradition beginning with the 1986 Giants is a myth. The first Gatorade shower actually took place two years earlier when the 1984 Chicago Bears were on the verge of clinching the Central Division title. Steve McMichael grabbed coach Mike Ditka, while Mike Singeltary and Dan Hampton moved in and dumped the Gatorade bucket on Ditka. For years, the Bears were content to let the Giants take the credit, until 1999, when Hampton, fed up with the misattributed recognition, told the story to the *Daily Herald* in Chicago. The *Daily Herald* went to the game tapes and confirmed Hampton's claim.

Who were the passer and receiver on the 1982 play known as "The Catch"?

The San Francisco 49ers trailed the Dallas Cowboys 27–21 with less than a minute to play in the 1982 NFC Championship Game. On third down from the Cowboys' six-yard line, Joe Montana took the snap and looked for his intended receiver, Freddie Solomon. But Solomon was covered, and Montana had to scramble to escape rushing Cowboys defenders. He spotted the secondary receiver, Dwight Clark, and lofted a pass to the right side of the end zone that appeared to be out of reach. But Clark leaped, grasped the ball with his fingertips, and pulled it down for the game-winning touchdown.

The play soon became known as "The Catch" and is one of the most-storied plays in NFL history.

Who was the ball carrier on the final play of Super Bowl XXXIV in 2000?

After falling behind the St. Louis Rams 23–16 late in the game, quarterback Steve McNair led his Tennessee Titans down to the Rams' 10-yard line with only six seconds remaining. With no timeouts, the Titans had one play to find the end zone and force overtime.

McNair passed to an open Kevin Dyson at the five-yard line, but Mike Jones, covering another player, spotted the pass and turned to grab Dyson's legs. Dyson reached in vain for the goal line, but was brought down at the one-yard line as time expired.

What was the "Ice Bowl"?

The Green Bay Packers' home stadium, Lambeau Field, is often referred to as "The Frozen Tundra." Never was this nickname more apt than in the 1967 NFL Championship Game between the host Packers and the Dallas Cowboys.

Quickies

Did you know ...
that the Super Bowl XXXVI was the first Super Bowl played in February? Prior to that, all Super Bowls had been played in January. Since that time, all but one (Super Bowl XXXVII) has been played in February.

With a game-time temperature of -13°F (-25°C), it was the coldest game ever played in the NFL, without wind chill being taken into account. It was so cold that the turf heating system failed, and the field was rock-hard. The officials were unable to use their whistles as they froze to their lips, and so, they had to replace whistle-blowing with shouting.

The game itself was a classic. The Cowboys overcame a 14–0 deficit to take a 17–14 lead in the fourth quarter. Then, with six seconds remaining on the clock, Packers quarterback Bart Starr executed a quarterback sneak and ran into the end zone for a 21–17 win, and the Packers' third straight NFL Championship.

What was memorable about the 1948 Grey Cup?

The fact that the Calgary Stampeders won the 1948 Grey Cup in Toronto and completed a perfect season is almost a side note. The game itself featured memorable moments, such as the "sitting touchdown," a trick play in which receiver Norm Hill lay on his back in the end zone, virtually hidden, then sat up to receive the touchdown pass. But the real excitement occurred at the Royal York Hotel, where celebrating Stampeders fans carried the goal posts into the lobby and rode horses through the front doors and onto the elevators.

The 1971 Nebraska Cornhuskers

Wingback Johnny Rodgers thrilled fans with his kickoff and punt returns to help Nebraska to a 13–0 record and a National Championship in 1971. The team was phenomenal: they averaged 39 points a game on offence, and only eight points a game on defence. They were only seriously challenged once, when the number one ranked Huskers defeated the number two ranked Oklahoma Sooners 35–31 in what was dubbed the "Game of the Century."

Who fumbled in the dying minutes of the 1971 Grey Cup?

The hard-luck Toronto Argonauts had not won a Grey Cup since 1952, but were on the verge of ending their drought in 1971. Led by future NFL great Joe Theismann, the Argos advanced to the Grey Cup against the Calgary Stampeders. Late in the game, trailing 14–11, the Argos' Dick Thornton intercepted a Stamps pass and returned it to their 11-yard line. After advancing a further four yards, the Argos elected to run on second down to ensure a chance to tie the game with a field goal if they were unable to find the end zone.

Theismann handed off to Leon McQuay, who saw an opening and headed for the end zone. Just then, his foot slipped on the wet turf and his elbow hit the ground, jarring the ball loose. The Stampeders recovered and won the game, while the Argos would have to wait another 12 years to break their Grey Cup drought.

Who were the first inductees into the Pro Football Hall of Fame?

When the Pro Football Hall of Fame first opened its doors on September 7, 1963, a whopping 17 members were enshrined as the first inductees. They were: Sammy Baugh, Bert Bell, Joe Carr, Earl "Dutch" Clark, Harold "Red" Grange, George Halas, Mel Hein, Wilbur "Pete" Henry, Robert "Cal" Hubbard, Don Hutson, Earl "Curly" Lambeau, Tim Mara, George Preston Marshall, John "Blood" McNally, Bronko Nagurski, Ernie Nevers, and Jim Thorpe.

Who was professional football's first superstar?

Jim Thorpe was already a household name long before playing professional football. The versatile, multi-sport athlete had received a tickertape parade down Broadway in New York after winning gold medals in the pentathlon and decathlon at the 1912 Olympic Games. The following year, he was stripped of his medals after it was learned that he had played two seasons of professional baseball in the East Carolina League.

In 1913, Thorpe signed with the New York Giants baseball team, playing with them for three seasons. In 1915, he became a member of professional football's Canton Bulldogs. With Thorpe's arrival, the team's attendance skyrocketed from an average of 1,200 fans a game to 8,000. Thorpe helped lead the team to three titles before Canton became one of the founding members of the American Professional Football Association — soon renamed the National Football League — in 1920. Thorpe continued playing on several NFL teams until retiring in 1928. In 1950, the Associated Press named him the top American athlete of the first half of the twentieth century.

Career Rushing Yards Leaders	
NFL	
Emmitt Smith	18,355
Walter Payton	16,726
Barry Sanders	15,269
CFL	
Mike Pringle	16,425
George Reed	16,116
Damon Allen	11,920

What was the first non-Canadian team to win the Grey Cup?

A shining light amid an otherwise dismal attempt by the CFL to expand south of the border, the Baltimore football club (playing without a name) made a splash in their first season, reaching the 1994 Grey Cup against the B.C. Lions. They lost, however, on a field goal by Vancouver-born Lui Passaglia on the last play of the game.

The following year, now playing as the Baltimore Stallions, they reached the Grey Cup again, prevailing over the Calgary Stampeders, 37–20.

Career Passing Yards Leaders	
NFL	
Brett Favre	61,655
Dan Marino	61,361
John Elway	51,475
CFL	
Damon Allen	72,381
Danny McManus	53,165
Anthony Calvillo	53,050

Who holds the record for the longest field goal?

At the professional level, two men are tied for the longest-ever field goal at 63 yards. Tom Dempsey first accomplished this feat on November 8, 1970. Kicking with a club foot that had no toes, he nailed the 63-yard attempt with two seconds left on the clock as the New Orleans Saints defeated the Detroit Lions 19–17. It was one of only two wins for the Saints that year. Dempsey's record was matched on October 25, 1998, by Jason Elam of the Denver Broncos.

But the longest field goal in history at any level was kicked by Ove Johansson of Abilene Christian University in the NAIA on October 16, 1976. It turned out to be the peak of Johansson's football career. While he did manage to catch on with the NFL's Philadelphia Eagles, his stint was short-lived and disastrous. He appeared in only two games, and was one for four in field goal attempts, and one for three in extra-point attempts.

Quickies

Did you know …
that more pizza is sold on Super Bowl Sunday than on any other day of the year? It sounds like a tough gig for the poor pizza-delivery person who has to miss the game, but there is a bright side: tips also skyrocket on Super Sunday.

Who has won the most Super Bowls?

Thanks to two championships in the 2000s, the Pittsburgh Steelers hold the record for the most Super Bowl wins with six. Their nearest challengers are the Dallas Cowboys and San Francisco 49ers, both of whom have won five Super Bowls.

As far as individual players go, Charles Haley has won the most Super Bowl rings, winning twice as a San Francisco 49er and three times as a Dallas Cowboy.

Who has won the most Grey Cups?

If we count the entire history of the Grey Cup, including the years prior to the CFL when amateur teams competed for the trophy, the Toronto Argonauts lead the pack with fifteen Grey Cup wins.

It is generally felt, though, that the modern era of Canadian football didn't begin until the mid-fifties, by which time, the championship was played exclusively between professional teams in the organizations that, a few years later, became known as the Canadian Football League.

Beginning in 1954, the Edmonton Eskimos have been the winningest team in Grey Cup history, taking the trophy home 12 times.

Most Career Yards Gained	
NFL	
Jerry Rice	22,895
Tim Brown	14,934
Isaac Bruce	14,109
CFL	
Allen Pitts	14,891
Milt Stegall	14,695
Darren Flutie	14,359

When was the first Grey Cup played?

On December 4, 1909, the University of Toronto met the Parkdale Canoe Club at Rosedale field to determine the Rugby Football Championship of Canada. Although Lord Earl Grey's trophy was not ready yet, it had already been determined that the winner of this game would be the inaugural recipient of the Grey Cup. Led by kicker Hugh Gall, who kicked a record eight singles, the University of Toronto team prevailed by a score of 26–6 before a crowd of 3,807.

What was the first NFL team to have cheerleaders and a mascot?

The Baltimore Colts of the late 1950s produced a number of NFL firsts, including the first fan clubs (the Colt Corrals) and the first helmet logos. They were also the first NFL team to have cheerleaders and a mascot. The mascot was, originally, a live horse named Dixie who would do a victory lap around the stadium after every Baltimore touchdown. Dixie was later replaced by two humans in a horse suit.

What was the first football team to play on artificial turf?

When the Houston Astrodome first opened in 1965 the field was made from natural grass. However, baseball outfielders found that the glass panels in the dome's ceiling — which were necessary in order to keep the grass alive — created a glare that made fielding impossible, and the panels were painted over.

This meant it was necessary to install artificial grass in the stadium.

The first football game played on artificial turf saw the University of Houston take on Washington State on September 23, 1966.

Who was the first African-American to play in the NFL?

In the early days of the NFL, there was no official colour barrier, though African-American players were not commonplace. When the NFL (known then as the American Professional Football Association) began play in 1920, two African-Americans took the field: the Akron Pros' Frederick "Fritz" Pollard and the Rock Island Independents' Bobby Marshall.

But in the 1930s, things changed. George Preston Marshall, owner of the Boston Braves (who later became the Washington Redskins), refused to allow African-Americans on his team, and put pressure on other owners to adopt the same policy. By 1934, no African-American players were on the rosters of any team in the NFL.

Most Career Touchdowns	
NFL	
Jerry Rice	208
Emmitt Smith	175
Marcus Allen	145
CFL	
Milt Stegall	144
George Reed	137
Mike Pringle	137

In 1946 the colour barrier was broken when the Cleveland Rams moved to Los Angeles. The team was to play in the Los Angeles Coliseum, but the commissioners of the stadium had a major stipulation: the team had to be racially integrated. Woody Strode and Kenny Washington — UCLA alumni who played college football with baseball's Jackie Robinson — debuted that season as the first African-American players in the NFL's modern era.

What college has produced the most NFL players?

Footballers looking for the best path to the pros will want to take note. As of the beginning of the 2009 season, the University of Notre Dame has had the most alumni appear in the NFL, with 459. Next in line is the University of Southern California with 441.

When was the first NFL regular-season game played outside the United States?

In recent years, the Buffalo Bills gained the ire of some fans by choosing to play one game each year in Toronto. But the Bills' international experiment was not the first time that the NFL has staged regular-season games outside the United States.

The first such international venture took place in 2005 when the Arizona Cardinals took on the San Francisco 49ers before a crowd of 103,467 in Mexico City. The Cardinals won, 31–14.

When was the first CFL game played outside Canada?

The collapse of the original World League of American Football was followed shortly by the CFL's first attempt at expansion into the United States. Fred Anderson, owner of the WLAF's Sacramento Surge, jumped at the chance to be among the first American teams in the Canadian league. He started a new team, the Sacramento Gold Miners, using similar uniforms and some of the same players as his old WLAF team.

Originally the CFL planned to have multiple American teams in the 1993 season, but only the Gold Miners were ready to take the field.

The Gold Miners played a short preseason schedule and two road games before playing host to the first CFL game outside of Canada on July 17, 1993. They lost to the Calgary Stampeders, 38–36.

Two years later, the Gold Miners moved to San Antonio, where they lasted one year before folding.

Most Career Field Goals	
NFL	
Morten Anderson	565
Gary Anderson	538
Matt Stover	435
CFL	
Lui Passaglia	1,203
Paul Osbaldiston	927
Mark McLoughlin	909

What was the biggest comeback in NFL history?

On January 3, 1993, the Buffalo Bills hosted the Houston Oilers in the wild card game. The Bills were hoping to use the game as a stepping stone to their third consecutive Super Bowl appearance, but with star quarterback Jim Kelly out with a ligament injury, Frank Reich was called into action.

And it looked like a disaster. The Oilers, with Warren Moon as quarterback, surged to an early lead, and by the third quarter held a devastating 35–3 lead.

But this was familiar territory for Frank Reich. In 1984, while a college player, he had lead the Maryland Terrapins to a stunning comeback against the Miami Hurricanes, turning a 31–0 deficit into a 42–40 win.

Drawing on the spirits of comebacks past, the Bills scored 28 points in the third quarter. In the fourth quarter, an Andre Reed touchdown gave the Bills the lead, though it was countered by an Oiler field goal, sending the game into overtime. Steve Christie then kicked a 32-yard field goal to complete the biggest comeback in NFL history, turning a 32-point deficit into a 41–38 win.

What was the first college bowl game?

The first college bowl game was not actually referred to as a "bowl" game, and did not even go by its present name until more than two decades after the annual game was first played.

On January 1, 1902, the tradition of New Year's Day college football clashes began when Michigan overwhelmed Stanford 49–0 in what was called the Tournament East-West Football Game. The beating was so severe that Stanford actually quit after three quarters, and the "annual" game was scrubbed for the next 14 years.

In 1916, the game was revived and the State College of Washington defeated Brown College. From then on, the game was held every year, but it did undergo a major change. After the original host facility for the game — Tournament Park — was deemed unsuitable, the game moved to a new stadium, and that stadium gave the annual game its new name: the Rose Bowl.

What team has won the most Rose Bowls?

Given that they have also appeared in far more games than any other school, it comes as no surprise that the University of Southern California also has the most Rose Bowl wins, taking home the title 24 times in 33 appearances, as of 2009. The nearest competitor is the University of Michigan with eight wins in 20 games.

Most Career Combined Yards Gained

NFL	
Jerry Rice	23,546
Brian Mitchell	23,330
Walter Payton	21,803

CFL	
Mike "Pinball" Clemons	25,438
Henry "Gizmo" Williams	23,927
Mike Pringle	23,20

Who is the coach with the most wins in CFL history?

Don Matthews, who coached six different teams in the CFL, amassed the most wins of any coach with 231.

In addition to his overall win totals, Matthews also holds the record for most Grey Cup appearances (nine) and most Grey Cup wins (five).

> **The 1972 USC Trojans**
>
> The 1972 edition of the Trojans may have been the greatest in the history of the school's storied football program. A perfect 12–0 season included a decisive win against Notre Dame, and a dismantling of Ohio State at the Rose Bowl. The strength of this team was a trio of running backs: Sam "Bam" Cunningham, Anthony Davis, and Rod McNeill.

Who is the coach with the most wins in NFL history?

Don Shula, the long-time coach of the Miami Dolphins, racked up an astonishing total of 328 victories over the course of his career, including the only perfect season in NFL history in 1972.

But for all his victories, he does not hold the record for most Super Bowl wins. That honour goes to Chuck Knoll, the man at the helm of the Pittsburgh Steelers dynasty that won four Super Bowls in six years between 1975 and 1980.

Who is the coach with the most wins in NCAA history?

Longevity has its merits, and Joe Paterno, who, as of the end of the 2008 season, had coached the Penn State Nittany Lions for 59 years, has the records to prove it. Between 1966 and 2008, Penn State teams won 383 games under Paterno's stewardship. He also holds the record for most Bowl victories with 23. Along the way, he has won two National Championships and three Big Ten Championships.

Paterno had opportunities to take his coaching skills to professional football — he was offered head coaching positions with the Pittsburgh Steelers and the New England Patriots (the latter included an offer of part-ownership), but he elected to remain with Penn State, and is currently signed to coach the team through the 2011 season. He will be 85 years old upon the completion of his contract.

Why did the USFL sue the NFL?

The USFL was on shaky ground after just three seasons, and they made a decision to become a fall league in 1986, in direct competition with the NFL.

But it was not to be. The USFL could not get networks to cover their games, and many teams were in deep financial trouble.

The USFL blamed the NFL for its woes, and launched an antitrust suit, claiming that the NFL engaged in predatory practices. Among other things, the NFL was accused of using its influence to limit the USFL's access to venues and network broadcast deals, and targeting the league as a whole and franchises in particular in an attempt to squash the competing league.

A jury found in favour of the USFL, but awarded the fledgling league only one dollar in compensation. The league put its 1986 season on hold, and ultimately folded.

What celebrity billionaire was part owner of the USFL's New Jersey Generals?

The New Jersey Generals, while lacklustre on the field, grabbed headlines in their brief existence by signing high-profile players like Heisman-winners Herschel Walker and Doug Flutie.

It's no surprise then that the Generals' ownership group included a man known for spending and grabbing attention: Donald Trump.

What was the XFL?

The XFL was the much-mocked attempt by World Wrestling Federation owner Vince McMahon to establish an American football league to rival the NFL.

Like the earlier USFL, the XFL set itself up as a spring league to avoid direct competition with the NFL. But it was clear from the start that the gloves were off, as the XFL encouraged its players to be an over-the-top alternative to the "No Fun League." Touchdown celebrations were encouraged, roughing penalties were limited, and stadium announcers were encouraged to taunt the opposition. Pre-game coin tosses were replaced by players fighting for a ball, and that sissy fair-catch rule was eliminated.

Curiosity drew 14 million viewers to the league's debut game between the New York/New Jersey Hitmen and the Las Vegas Outlaws on February 3, 2001. But few fans were impressed by the new product, and ratings and attendance dwindled as the season went on.

After only one season, the league folded.

Who won the Most Valuable Player Award in the XFL's first and only championship game?

Jose Cortez, the placekicker for the Los Angeles Xtreme, kicked three field goals to help his team to a 38–6 drubbing of the San Francisco Demons in the first and only XFL Championship Game in 2001. He was also the league's leading scorer that season, having kicked 20 field goals.

Ironically, despite his value to his team, kickers under the XFL's pay structure were the lowest-paid players in the league.

The much-travelled kicker also spent time in the NFL, the Arena Football League, and NFL Europe.

XFL Players Who Also Played in the NFL

- John Avery
- Ron Carpenter
- Jose Cortez
- Eric England
- Mike Furrey
- Steve Gleason
- Kelly Herndon
- Corey Ivy
- Kevin Kaesviharn
- Tommy Maddox
- Yo Murphy
- Rashaan Salaam
- Kevin Swayne
- Rod Smart
- Brad Trout

What is the Lingerie Football League?

The most improbable league ever to emerge may be the Lingerie Football League. The idea began as a single pay-per-view event, the Lingerie Bowl, which aired opposite the Super Bowl halftime show in 2003. Two female teams played on a 50-yard field, but the outcome wasn't the draw: the women were wearing helmets, shoulder pads, and underwear. And that's it.

The idea was so successful that it was repeated the following two years, and by 2005 organizers had decided to go beyond a single game and form an actual league. Originally the league consisted of only four teams, but has since expanded to 10, with plans for future expansion.

Who was the first former USFL player elected to the Pro Football Hall of Fame?

He was one of the greats of the short-lived USFL, winning league-MVP honours in 1984, but Jim Kelly achieved his greatest fame as a member of the NFL's Buffalo Bills.

Kelly had spent two years with the USFL's Houston Gamblers and was slated to be the starting quarterback for the New Jersey Generals when the league folded. Kelly soon hooked up with the Bills, and went on to lead them to five division championships, and four straight Super Bowl appearances. Although Kelly's Bills are best known for their failure to win the grand prize, Kelly established himself as a legend of the game, and was inducted into the Pro Football Hall of Fame in 2002 — the first former USFL player to receive that honour.

What quarterback was a first-round draft pick in the NFL, but elected to play in the USFL instead?

In a surprising career move, the Buffalo Bills' top pick in the 1983 draft, Jim Kelly, decided that the USFL was the place to be. Kelly cited cold weather and poor attendance as reasons

The 1948 Calgary Stampeders

While the team is overshadowed in the history books by the wild celebration of Stamps fans at the Grey Cup, the team itself was phenomenal, featuring such legends as Normie Kwong, Paul Rowe, and Woody Strode. Their Grey Cup win capped off a perfect season.

for snubbing the Bills. However, the Bills retained rights to Kelly, and when the USFL folded in 1986, Kelly joined the team and became one of the city's most accomplished and popular athletes.

How many non-U.S. teams were part of the World Football League?

The World Football League was a failed attempt to provide competition for the National Football League.

League founder Gary Davidson, who also had the dubious distinction of helping to launch the World Hockey Association and the American Basketball Association, had ambitious plans to make the new football league a global one.

Unfortunately, attempts to deliver non-American entries were fruitless. The Toronto Northmen were to be the league's lone Canadian representative until Prime Minister Pierre Trudeau attempted to block the move with the Canada Football Act, which was designed to prevent foreign leagues from competing with the Canadian Football League on Canadian soil.

Though the proposed act was never passed into law, the threat was sufficient to cause the Northmen to change homes, becoming the Memphis Southmen.

No international teams played in the WFL, which folded in 1975, partway through its second season.

Who came up with the idea of arena football?

While attending a Major Indoor Soccer League game at Madison Square Garden in 1981, Jim Foster — a former NFL and future USFL executive — found inspiration. If one brand of "football" could be moved indoors and onto a smaller field, why not American football?

He jotted down some ideas, including such off-beat concepts as the rebound nets at the back of the end zones. Then, while he worked with the USFL, he put the idea on hold. When the USFL folded, he returned to his dream and set about starting a league. By 1987, he'd found investors and host cities and launched the Arena Football League. Foster was the league's first commissioner, and later became owner of the Iowa Barnstormers.

The 1994 Toronto Argonauts

The line up was impressive: Paul Masotti, Pinball Clemons, Derrell Mitchell, Mike Vanderjagt, and a host of tremendous players helped the team to a 15–3 record and a Grey Cup win. But the heart of the team may have been quarterback Doug Flutie, who dazzled fans with the brand of football that had come to be known as "Flutie Magic."

The league had only novelty appeal at first, but eventually built up a large enough fan base to maintain itself until 2008 before electing to take the 2009 season off due to financial circumstances. The AFL plans to return in 2010.

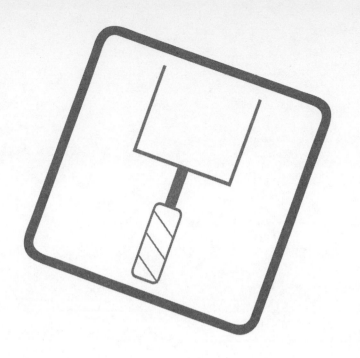

rugby

How did rugby get its name?

Rugby takes its name from the Rugby School, an English private school founded in 1567, in the town of Rugby, Warwickshire. It has been contended by some that the sport was invented at this school in the early nineteenth century. The sport was originally called Rugby football, because it was a variant on traditional football associated with the school, which used an oval ball and permitted handling of the ball.

Who was William Webb Ellis?

At the Rugby School in England there stands a statue of student William Webb Ellis with a plaque commemorating the moment in 1823 when the boy supposedly picked up what we would today call a soccer ball and ran with it during a football game, thus inventing the game of rugby. There were no formally codified rules of football at the time, nevertheless it was completely outside the norm to take such action. The original claim that Ellis did this was made in 1876, four years after Ellis's death, by Matthew Bloxam, an assistant master at Rugby School, who himself heard the story second hand. The claim has been widely disputed and debated, yet the legend lives on.

Quickies
Did you know ...
that the trophy for the Rugby Union World Cup is named the William Webb Ellis Cup?

Who invented the rugby ball?

A shoemaker on St. Matthews Street, in the town of Rugby, named William Gilbert is credited with the invention of the oval rugby ball around 1840. Gilbert, whose shop was across the street from Rugby School's playing field, provided the students with soccer balls made from inflated pigs' bladders covered in leather. The irregular shape of the bladders gave the balls their distinctive plum shape. As the oddly shaped footballs were specially designed and made for the Rugby School, they came to be known as "Rugby footballs."

Who set down the first rules of rugby?

The first rules of rugby were set down by three students at the Rugby School in August, 1845, at the instructions of the

Quickies
Did you know ...
that in 1851 William Gilbert displayed the Rugby School Football at The Great Exhibition in London?

school. The three were William Delafield Arnold, W.W. Shirley, and Frederick Hutchins. They submitted 37 Rules which were immediately passed and a Rule Book was printed.

Who was Richard Lindon?

A shoemaker on Lawrence Sheriff Street, in the town of Rugby, Richard Lindon became the first official supplier of Rugby footballs to the Rugby School. In 1862 Lindon had innovated the use of inflatable vulcanized rubber inner-tubes instead of pigs' bladders, providing his balls a uniform oval shape. He also invented a brass hand pump used to inflate the balls.

What is the difference between rugby union and rugby league?

In 1895, English rugby, which was governed by the Rugby Football Union, split into two groups: those who favoured strict amateurism and those who supported paying players as professionals. On August 29 that year, 22 rugby clubs from across the north of England held a meeting in the George Hotel in Huddersfield. These clubs, which supported professionalism, voted to secede from the Rugby Football Union and set up the Northern Rugby Football Union, which later became known as the Rugby Football League. Today, both rugby union and rugby league are professional. Rugby union has 15 players in a match, whereas rugby league has 13 players. Most of the rules of play are similar or identical, but there are some differences. Union puts emphasis on the use of scrums and line-outs (when the ball goes out of play). League has both also, but these elements are somewhat incidental to the League game. On the other hand, a league team has only six tackles to score a try before the ball goes to the opposition, whereas in union there is no set number of tackles before possession is lost.

What clubs founded the Northern Rugby Football Union?

The 22 clubs that founded the Northern Rugby Football Union on August 29, 1895, were as follows: Batley, Bradford, Brighouse Rangers, Broughton Rangers, Dewsbury, Halifax, Huddersfield, Hull, Hunslet, Leeds, Leigh, Liversedge, Manningham, Oldham, Rochdale Hornets, St. Helens, Tyldesley, Wakefield Trinity, Warrington, Widnes, Wigan, and Stockport. Dewsbury withdrew a few days later and were replaced by Runcorn.

Quickies
Did you know ...
that rugby union did not turn professional until 1995?

Why were no finals contested at the 1957 and 1960 Rugby League World Cup competitions?

From 1954 until 1972 the Rugby League World Cup used a format in which each team competing (there were only four) played every other team in an initial group stage. The two teams that sat atop the points table at the end of the group stage advanced to the final. In the 1957 and 1960 competitions, Australia and Great Britain, respectively, won all of their matches in the group stage and sat atop the points table alone and could not be caught. Thus they were declared champions in those years without the need of a final match.

Quickies
Did you know ...
that in Australia rugby is called football?

What is the modern rugby ball made of?

The modern rugby ball is made of polyurethane, synthetic leather, laminated polyester, latex, and glue. It designed to keep its shape and withstand the elements.

What is a "Test"?

International rugby union matches with full status are called Test matches. Like in cricket, the term "Test" is thought to arise from the idea that the matches are a "test of strength and competency" between the sides involved. The term is always capitalized.

When was the first Rugby Football Union Test?

The Rugby Football Union was formed in January 1871, two months before the first-ever Test was played at Raeburn Place in Edinburgh between Scotland and England, in which Scotland defeated England 4–1.

What was the first rugby union club in Australia?

The first rugby union club in Australia — the Sydney University Rugby Union Club — was formed in 1864.

When did an Australian team first compete in a Test match?

An Australian team played their first-ever Test in June 1899 against a touring Great Britain team. Australia won 13–3 at the Sydney Cricket Ground.

What is a "maul"?

When a rugby ball carrier is held up (without being tackled) by both an opposing player and a player from his own team, the formation is called a maul. The offside line becomes the last foot of the last man on each side of the maul. Players can only join in from behind that teammate. Anyone who comes in from the sides will be penalized by the referee. Hands are allowed to be used in the maul as the struggle ensues for possession of the ball. If either team deliberately collapses the maul then that side will be penalized by the referee. The objective is to move the ball out of the maul backwards to your team. If the ball does not come out in a timely fashion, the referee will award a scrum to the team that did not take the ball into the maul.

Quickies

Did you know ...

that from 1896 until 1956 the South Africa's Springboks played 54 Tests, winning 38, drawing five, and losing only 11?

When do players form a "truck and trailer"?

A "truck and trailer" occurs when a rugby player carrying the ball leaves a maul, followed by one or more of his teammates. The ball carrier is the truck and the followers are the trailer.

What is a "scrum"?

In a rugby union scrum, the eight forwards (rugby league uses six forwards) from each team bind together and push against each other. The formation for each team consists of a row of three players, behind which is a row of two, behind which is another row of three. The players in each row lock arms over each others' backs. The ball is fed by the team with possession down the space between the two opposing front rows. A pushing contest ensues to move the opposing team backwards off the ball as the player at the center of each front row — called the hooker — attempts to kick the ball to the back of the scrum where it can be received by the player in at the center of the back row, who always wears the number 8. In rugby league, a scrum uses only six players and the rear line consists of only one player, called the "loose forward."

What is the "tunnel"?

When a scrum is formed, the gap between the three players from each team who form the scrums' opposing front rows is called the tunnel.

What is a "grubber kick"?

A grubber kick is a low-trajectory kick that causes the ball to roll and tumble across the ground, producing irregular bounces that make it very hard for the defending team to catch without causing a knock-on.

What is a "knock-on"?

Also called a knock-forward, a knock-on is when a player loses possession of the ball as it bounces forward off his hands or arms and hits either the ground or another player. It results in a scrum.

What is a "ruck"?

In rugby a ruck is formed when the ball is on the ground and two opposing players meet over it. As with a scrum, they may not touch the ball with their hands and the offside line becomes the last foot of the last man on each side of the ruck. Players can join the ruck only from behind. They compete for the ball by attempting to drive the opposition backwards off the ball while also attempting to 'ruck' the ball backwards with their feet. Rucks commonly form at tackles, but can form anywhere in the field of play where the ball is on the ground. When the ball emerges from the ruck, it may be picked up and the player with possession can attempt to move it forward.

What is a "mulligrubber"?

A mulligrubber is a style of kick in rugby where the ball is directed toward the ground and forced to bounce. The tactic is often used in situations where either the ball needs to be placed in a specific position or to intentionally stop the opponent from being able to catch the ball.

Where is Garryowen?

Garryowen Football Club is a rugby union club in Limerick, Ireland. In the 1920s the club pioneered the use of the punt now called a Garryowen, or an "up and under." It is a very high, short punt that drops the ball onto or behind the defending team.

The height of the punt allows the offence to close distance before the ball drops.

What is a *haka*?

The *haka* is a traditional Maori dance performed by the All Blacks, the international rugby union team of New Zealand, immediately prior to international matches. It serves as a challenge to the opposing team.

What is a *Sipi Tau*?

The *Sipi Tau* is a war dance performed by the Tongan national rugby union team before each of their international matches.

What is a "try"?

In rugby a try is the primary method of scoring. A try is worth five points. It is scored when a player places the ball on the ground with downward pressure in the in-goal area between (and including) the goal line and up to but not including the dead ball line of the opposition's half.

How do you score a goal in rugby?

A goal in rugby, as opposed to a try, is scored by kicking the ball between the uprights and above the crossbar of the goal posts. There are three ways to score a goal:

- **a dropped goal** — scored in open play where the ball must hit the ground immediately before it is kicked;

- **a penalty goal** — awarded after the opposing side infringes the laws of rugby and may be kicked from a stationary ground position or by drop kick; and
- **a conversion** — awarded after a try is scored; it must be done by either a drop kick or a place kick.

baseball

How was the distance between home plate and the pitching mound established in baseball?

Baseball has gone through dozens of changes since 1845, when 25-year-old Alexander Cartwright set the ideal distance between bases at 90 feet. Back then the pitchers threw underhanded from a distance of only 45 feet, but because this seemed to give an advantage to the pitcher it was increased to 50 feet in 1881, which initiated the argument that the batter had the advantage. To address this, overhand pitching was introduced in 1884, which completely overwhelmed the batters. So in 1893 a distinguished committee settled on placing the pitching rubber on a mound 60 feet from home plate. But, like most committee decisions, there was a slight misreading between conception and inception and the rubber was mistakenly placed 60 feet and six inches from the batter, where it remains to this day. "The pitcher's plate shall be 10 inches above the level of home plate. The degree of slope from a point six inches in front of the pitcher's plate to a point six feet toward home plate shall be one inch to one foot, and such degrees of slope shall be uniform."

> **Major League Baseball's Longest-Standing Unbroken Single-Season Records**
>
> - **Batting Average**: .426 — Nap Lajoie (1901)
> - **Pitcher Wins**: 41 — Jack Chesbro (1904)
> - **Triples Hit**: 36 — Chief Wilson (1912)
> - **Extra-Base Hits**: 119 — Babe Ruth (1921)
> - **Runs Scored**: 177 — Babe Ruth (1921)
> - **Total Bases**: 457 — Babe Ruth (1921)
> - **Runs Batted In**: 191 — Hack Wilson (1930)
> - **Doubles Hit**: 67 — Earl Webb (1931)
> - **Hitting Streak**: 56 games — Joe DiMaggio (1941)

Who invented baseball?

The New World Settlers from Britain brought with them a game called "rounders." It was a common man's variation of cricket and was recorded as being widely played in the mid-eighteenth century. In rounders a batter tried to hit a pitched ball and then run around from one to five bases in an attempt to reach home without being "plugged" or hit by a ball thrown by the fielders. A plugged runner was out. The bases were posts in the ground. There is a reference to the game as "base-ball" in a children's book dated 1744.

In 1907 an American Commission decided that baseball was invented in 1839 by Abner Doubleday in Cooperstown, New York, but it was Alexander Cartwright who established the modern field and drafted the first rules of the new game, which included plugging for an out as was a ball caught on first bounce. The winner of the game was the first team to score 21 runs.

It's interesting to note that the first form of baseball played in Canada was in Beachville, Ontario, on June 4, 1838, the

> **Quickies**
> *Did you know ...*
> that in 1849 the New York Knickerbockers were the first baseball team to wear a uniform?

Major League Baseball's Longest-Standing Unbroken Career Records

- **Pitcher Wins**: 511 — Cy Young (retired 1911)
- **Pitcher's Lowest Earned Run Average**: 1.82 — Ed Walsh (retired 1917)
- **Triples Hit**: 309 — Sam Crawford (retired 1917)
- **Doubles Hit**: 792 — Tris Speaker (retired 1928)
- **Highest Batting Average**: .366 — Ty Cobb (retired 1928)

year before Doubleday played at Cooperstown and seven years before Cartwright and his New York Knickerbockers established his new rules.

A game similar to rounders that was played by British soldiers was called "bat'" and is recorded as being played in places as diverse as Red River, Manitoba, and Huntington, Quebec, during the 1830s.

What's in a baseball?

The baseball got its present size and weight as a result of a rule change in 1872, but the ball's rubber core made home runs difficult to hit. A lively bounce came from the introduction of a cork centre in 1910, and homerun hitters began to be commonplace. In 1931, the stitching that held the cover on the ball was raised, allowing pitchers to throw a greater variety of pitches. The last major change occurred in 1974, when the horsehide cover was replaced by cowhide.

The weight of a baseball must be between five and five and a quarter ounces and its circumference from nine to nine and a quarter inches.

The formation of the ball begins with a 1/2 ounce, 2.9 inch diameter cork core. A layer of black rubber is then applied followed by a layer of red rubber each weighing 7/8 of an ounce. Afterwards, 121 yards of blue-gray wool followed by 45 yards of white wool yarn are added to the outside. The ball is then wrapped in cowhide covering held together by 216 stitches and some rubber cement. Red stitches are placed on the ball to allow pitchers to throw curve balls. Curve balls curve since the air resistance on the stitches is non-uniform.

Why were spitballs outlawed?

Spitball pitches used to be very common in the early days of baseball, when the lack of raised stitching on the ball made putting a spin on it very difficult. When the ball is moistened by saliva or some other lubricant like petroleum jelly, the pitcher can release it more smoothly. From the batter's point of view, the pitch leaves the pitcher's hand looking like a fastball, when it is, in fact, travelling much slower. In 1920, a series of rule changes designed to help hitters resulted in spitballs being outlawed in major-league baseball.

Some pitchers continued to use the spitball after the rule change. Perhaps the most famous was a Hall of Fame pitcher, Gaylord Perry, who won 314 games. At 43, he was thrown out of the game for wetting the ball.

Today, a pitch called the split fingered fastball is in the arsenal of several leading major-league pitchers. It is legal, but its behaviour is said to closely resemble a spitball.

Where did the term "ballpark" come from?

"Ballpark" was first used to refer to a baseball stadium back in 1899. With the dawn of the space age in the 1960s, "ballpark" was used in an article in the San Francisco Examiner to refer to the safe zone for the splashdown of a space capsule. "Ballpark figure" was first recorded in print in the late 1960s, in the *Wall Street Journal*, to indicate a sum of money that is roughly correct.

Why do baseball socks just have a strap on the foot?

Stirrup stockings are holdover from baseball's early days when fabric dyes were not colourfast and spike wounds were commonplace. Spike wounds happened because runners often used their cleats to intimidate infielders when sliding into bases. In order to reduce the chance that dyes would get into a wound and infect it, stirrup stockings were developed, and a plain white sock, called a "sanitary" because it prevented infection, was worn underneath.

What did the Florida Marlins do that no other baseball team in history has done?

In April 1993, the Florida Marlins began to play baseball in the National League's Central Division. In October 1997, they became the first team to win a World Series from the wild-card position, beating the Cleveland Indians in seven games. They also achieved the feat faster than any other expansion team. During the postseason, the team was dismantled to cut costs. The next year, they set a record for ineptitude, posting a record of 54–108, making them the first team to lose over 100 games the year after winning a World Series.

How many pitchers for Canadian baseball teams have thrown a perfect game?

Dennis Martínez is the only pitcher for a Canadian team to throw perfect game. He threw to 27 batters in a game against the Los Angeles Dodgers on July 28, 1991, which the Expos won, 2–0. Dave Stieb was pitching for the Toronto Blue Jays in 1988, when he became one of only two pitchers to give up a hit to the 27th batter after retiring the first 26. He went on to lose the game.

What does a batting coach mean by a "roundhouse swing"?

Roundhouses used to be common in railway yards as places to store, switch, and maintain locomotives. They featured a round turntable used to put locomotives on new tracks. The turntable's motion gave rise to the expression "roundhouse swing" used in boxing to describe a punch that starts at the side of the body and is delivered in a wide arc. Roundhouse swing is also often used to describe an inefficient power swing in baseball.

Baseball also has a "roundhouse curve," which was the bread and butter pitch of early Hall of Famer Christy Matheson.

When was softball invented?

Softball was invented by George Hancock. In November of 1887, George was among a group of young Harvard and Yale alumni who were fooling around inside the Farragut Boat Club Gymnasium in Chicago awaiting the outcome of a Harvard-Yale football game. When word came that Yale had won, an enthusiastic supporter picked up a discarded boxing glove and tossed it at the Harvard group who then tried to send it back by hitting the glove in the air with a stick. Hancock took the boxing glove and tied it into a ball with the laces, then chalked off an indoor baseball diamond consisting of a home plate, three bases, and a pitcher's box. The group divided into two teams and softball had begun!

It was moved outside in the spring and was played on fields that were too small for baseball. The game, at that time, was alternately referred to as "indoor-outdoor," "kitten ball," or "mush ball." Eventually the rules and equipment evolved into the softball we know today, which is played by millions of people in over 100 countries.

Why does "balk" mean to stop short?

Those who know baseball understand that when a pitcher makes a deceptive move by interrupting what appears to be an intention to throw to a batter, it's called a balk, an infraction of the rules, and base runners all advance. A balk is much more than a baseball term. A horse can balk, or stop short when spooked by an obstacle or a person might balk at continuing with a commitment when a problem becomes clear. Balk is from the ancient Anglo Saxon word *balca*, meaning ridge, and was commonly used as a reference to the mounds of dirt between plowed furrows. This concept of being a ridge or obstacle, allowed the word to evolve into a description of a wooden beam, especially one used to bar a door before the common use of locks and keys. It became an obstruction to thieves. In baseball, when the pitcher toes the rubber, it limits his options to move and it was originally a small wooden plank or beam on the mound or ridge, which is how the word balk entered the game in 1845.

> **Quickies**
> *Did you know …*
> that Jack Norworth wrote two versions of "Take Me Out to the Ball Game"? The first, from 1908, was about a "baseball mad" woman named Katie Casey imploring her beau to take her to a game. In the second, from 1927, Norwich updated the lyrics and changed the girl's name to Nelly Kelly. It is the latter version that today's fans hear — and sing! — during the seventh inning stretch at the ballpark. Both versions have the same chorus.

Who wrote the song "Take Me Out to the Ball Game"?

In 1908 vaudeville entertainer Jack Norworth scribbled the words to "Take Me Out to the Ball Game" on an envelope after spotting a sign on the New York subway that read: "Baseball Today — Polo Grounds." That scrap of paper now resides in the permanent collection of memorabilia at the National Baseball Hall of Fame in Cooperstown, New York. Norworth's words were set to music by composer Albert von Tilzer. Interestingly, neither Norworth nor von Tilzer had ever attended a professional baseball game before penning the tune.

> **The 16 Founding Teams of the National Association of Base Ball Players**
>
> - **Brooklyn Clubs**: Atlantics, Bedford, Continental, Eckfords, Excelsior, Harmony, Nassau, Olympic, Putnam.
> - **Morrisania Club (Bronx)**: Union.
> - **New York Clubs**: Baltic, Eagle, Empire, Gotham, Harlem, Knickerbockers.

What was the National Association of Base Ball Players?

The National Association of Base Ball Players (NABBP) was American baseball's first organizing body. Sixteen clubs met in New York City in January of 1857 at the invitation of Daniel "Doc" Adams, owner of the Knickerbocker Base Ball Club. Adams was elected president of the convention and was also named chairman of the Committee on Rules and Regulations. Just over a year later, on March 10, 1858, 22 clubs attended a second meeting and agreed to form the National Association of Base Ball Players — this despite the fact that all the teams were from the New York City area. The new association, which established standards for teams and players, grew to include teams from New Jersey in 1859, and from Pennsylvania in 1860. After the Civil War, the association's membership

Teams in the National Association of Professional Base Ball Players

- Boston Red Stockings (1871–1875)*
- Chicago White Stockings (1871; 1874–1875)*
- Cleveland Forest Citys (1871–1872) [sic]
- Fort Wayne Kekiongas (1871)
- New York Mutuals (1871–1875)*
- Philadelphia Athletics (1871–1875)*
- Rockford Forest Citys (1871)
- Troy Haymakers (1871–1872)
- Washington Olympics (1871–1872)
- Brooklyn Atlantics (1872–1875)
- Brooklyn Eckfords (1872)
- Baltimore Canaries (1872–1874)
- Middletown Mansfields (1872)
- Washington Nationals (1872–1873; 1875)
- Washington Blue Legs (1873)
- Baltimore Marylands (1873)
- Philadelphia White Stockings (1873–1875)
- Elizabeth Resolutes (1873)
- Hartford Dark Blues (1874–1875)*
- Philadelphia Centennials (1875)
- New Haven Elm Citys (1875)
- St. Louis Brown Stockings (1875)*
- St. Louis Red Stockings (1875)
- Keokuk Westerns (1875)

*These 6 teams went on to found the National League, along with the Cincinnati Red Stockings and the Louisville Grays.

expanded rapidly, to 91 clubs in 1865, 202 in 1866, and more than 300 in 1867. It dissolved after 1870, following disputes between amateur and professional players.

What was the National Association of Professional Base Ball Players?

The National Association of Professional Base Ball Players, also known as the National Association, was an offshoot of the NABBP formed in 1871 after disputes between amateur players and pros. It was disbanded in 1875 and many of its teams went on to form the National League.

What was the first professional baseball team?

Up until 1869, the National Association of Base Ball Players did not permit players to receive payment for their games. That year, with a rule change admitting professionals into the Association, the Cincinnati Red Stockings became the first all-pro baseball team, with ten players on salary. The team which had been formed in 1866 was managed by Harry Wright, a jeweler by trade who played centerfield and also shared pitching duties with Asa Brainard. Wright's younger brother George played shortstop and is widely considered one of the greatest players of the era. In the 1869 season the team posted a record of 57 wins–0 losses. The 1870 team posted a record of 66 wins–7 losses–1 tie. The team was disbanded after 1870 due to poor financial success. Today's Cincinnati Reds, formed in 1882, adopted their name from the original Red Stockings team.

Quickies
Did you know ...
that a new team under the name Cincinnati Red Stockings was formed in 1876 as a charter member of the new National League? They were thrown out of the League in 1881 for selling beer at the ballpark and allowing games to be played at their ballpark on Sundays.

What is the "Senior Circuit"?

Founded on February 2, 1876, to replace the National Association of Professional Base

Annual Salaries in 1869 of Baseball's First Pro Team, the Cincinnati Red Stockings

Player	Position	Salary
Harry Wright	Center Field	$1,200
George Wright	Shortstop	$1,400
Asa Brainard	Pitcher	$1,100
Fred Waterman	Third Base	$1,000
Doug Allison	Catcher	$ 800
Charlie Gould	First base	$ 800
Charlie Sweasy	Second Base	$ 800
Andy Leonard	Left Field	$ 800
Cal McVey	RightField	$ 800
Dick Hurley	Substitute	$ 600

Ball Players, the National League of Professional Baseball Clubs, or simply the National League (NL), is the older of two leagues constituting today's Major League Baseball. The other is the American League, established in 1901. The NL is sometimes referred to as the "Senior Circuit" in contrast to the "Junior Circuit" of the American League.

Who invented baseball's shin guard?

That would be Bud Fowler, whose real name was John Jackson, born March 16, 1858, in Cooperstown, New York. Fowler, who had a prolific career, was the first African American to cross the colour line and play on a professional team with white players. He had been pitching for an amateur team in Chelsea, Massachusetts, when a nearby all-white professional team, the Lynn Live Oaks, lost their ace hurler to an illness. On May 17, 1878, Fowler was brought in as a replacement, pitching the Live Oaks to a 3–0 victory over the Tecumsehs of London, Ontario. Fowler is also credited with inventing the first baseball shin guards because white players spiked him so often that he taped pieces of wood to his legs to protect himself.

Founding Teams of the National League

- Chicago White Stockings
- Philadelphia Athletics
- Boston Red Stockings
- Hartford Dark Blues
- Mutual of New York
- St. Louis Brown Stockings
- Cincinnati Red Stockings
- Louisville Grays

Who won the first World Series?

There were a number of post-season competitions played in American baseball in the late nineteeth century, but it wasn't until 1903, when the National League and American

Founding Teams of the American League (1901)

- Baltimore Orioles
- Boston Americans
- Chicago White Stockings
- Cleveland Blues
- Detroit Tigers
- Milwaukee Brewers
- Philadelphia Athletics
- Washington Senators

League established a working relationship, that the first championship playoff was played between the top two teams from each league. In what is now officially recognized by Major League Baseball as the first World Series, in October 1903 the Boston Pilgrims took a best-of-eight series against the Pittsburgh Pirates, 5–3.

Who pitched the first-ever World Series shut out?

That was Bill Dinneen of the Boston Pilgrims, who took his team to a 3–0 win over the Pittsburgh Pirates in game two of the 1903 World Series.

Who was the first person named MVP of a World Series?

The first time an MVP was named in a World Series was in 1955 as the Brooklyn Dodgers defeated the New York Yankees four games to three. Dodgers pitcher Johnny Podres, called the "Yankee Killer," was named MVP of the series after pitching two complete-game victories, including a shut-out in game seven.

Quickies

Did you know ...
that foul hits first became strikes in baseball's rules in 1901?

Results from the 1903 World Series

Game	Date	Winning Team (and pitcher)	Losing Team (and pitcher)
1	Oct. 1	Pittsburgh (Phillippe) 7	Boston (Young) 3
2	Oct. 2	Boston (Dinneen) 3	Pittsburgh (Leever) 0
3	Oct. 3	Pittsburgh (Phillippe) 4	Boston (Hughes) 2
4	Oct. 6	Pittsburgh (Phillippe) 5	Boston (Dinneen) 4
5	Oct. 7	Boston (Young) 11	Pittsburgh (Kennedy) 2
6	Oct. 8	Boston (Dinneen) 6	Pittsburgh (Leever) 3
7	Oct. 10	Boston (Young) 7	Pittsburgh (Phillippe) 3
8	Oct. 13	Boston (Dinneen) 3	Pittsburgh (Phillippe) 0

What was the "Chicago Black Sox" scandal?

On September 28, 1920, Chicago White Sox (later named Black Sox) players Eddie Cicotte and "Shoeless" Joe Jackson appeared before a Chicago Grand Jury and implicated themselves and six teammates — Chick Gandal, Charles "Swede" Risberg, Fred McMullin, Oscar "Happy" Felsch, Claude "Lefty" Williams, and Buck Weaver — in a conspiracy with bookmaker Joe "Sport" Sullivan and gangsters Arnold Rothstein and Abe Attell to intentionally loose the 1919 World Series against the Cincinnati Reds.

Although Cicotte and Jackson later recanted their confessions, and although none of the players were convicted in a court of law, all were permanently banned from the game by baseball's new commissioner, Kenesaw Mountain Landis.

> **Quickies**
> *Did you know ...*
> that on Oct 1, 1903, facing legendary pitcher Cy Young, Pittsburgh right fielder Jimmy Sebring hit the first-ever World Series home run — and it was a grand slam to boot, as the bases were loaded?

> **Quickies**
> *Did you know ...*
> that in nine World Series attempts between 1916 and 1956 (seven of which were against the Yankees), 1955 was the only time the Dodgers would take the championship before moving to Los Angeles in 1957?

How did "Shoeless" Joe Jackson get his nickname?

In 1908 Joseph Jefferson Wofford Jackson — as he was named at birth — was 19 years-old and playing for the Greenville Spinners in the Carolina Association baseball league. Because a new pair of cleats were causing blisters on his feet during one game, he took them off and played in his stockings. Sports writer Scoop Latimer later called him "Shoeless" Joe Jackson in the Greenville News.

Pay-Off Money Received by Each of the Chicago White Sox

Player	Position	Take
Chick Gandal	First base	$35,000
Charles "Swede" Risberg	Shortstop	$15,000
Eddie Cicotte	Pitcher	$10,000
Fred McMullin	Utility infielder	$ 5,000
Oscar "Happy" Felsch	Center field	$ 5,000
Claude "Lefty" Williams	Pitcher	$ 5,000
"Shoeless" Joe Jackson	Left field	$ 5,000
Buck Weaver*	Third base	$ 0

*Weaver knew about the fix but did not participate.

Who was the "ninth man out"?

St. Louis Browns' second baseman, Joe Gedeon, may not have been a part of the 1919 Black Sox conspiracy to throw the World Series, but he certainly knew about it. Gedeon learned about the fix from his friend Swede Risberg, the White Sox's corrupted shortstop, and placed bets against the White Sox. In 1920 he admitted this fact before a Grand Jury. As a result, the Commissioner of baseball banned him from the game for life, making him the ninth and final such outcast resulting from the Black Sox scandal — and the only one who did not play for Chicago.

Quickies
Did you know ...
that Shoeless Joe Jackson was illiterate?

Who were the first people elected into the National Baseball Hall of Fame?

The Baseball Hall of Fame in Cooperstown, New York, was opened on June 12, 1939. The first inductees, elected that year, were Ty Cobb, Babe Ruth, Honus Wagner, Christy Mathewson, and Walter Johnson. Since then, 289 people have been elected to the Hall of Fame, including eight umpires.

Quickies
Did you know ...
that in the first game of the 1919 World Series, when Chicago's starting pitcher Eddie Cicotte hit Cincinnati's leadoff batter, Morrie Rath, on the second pitch, it was the prearranged signal that the fix was going forward?

How are people elected into the Baseball Hall of Fame?

Election to the National Baseball Hall of Fame is possible through one of two ways. The Baseball Writers' Association of America (BBWAA) considers the candidacies of players who have played at least ten major league seasons and have been retired five seasons. The Veterans Committee considers players, managers, umpires, and executives whose careers have been over for twenty-one seasons or more.

Quickies
Did you know ...
that on October 8, 1956, in game 5 of the World Series against the Brooklyn Dodgers, Yankees pitcher Don Larsen recorded what is still the only perfect game in the history of the World Series?

Why is former Cincinnati Reds player Pete Rose ineligible for election into the Baseball Hall of Fame?

In August 1989, three years after he retired as manager of the Cincinnati Reds, Pete

Rose — who also played for the Reds from 1963 to 1978 and from 1984 to 1986 — voluntarily agreed to become permanently ineligible from participating in baseball amidst accusations that he gambled on baseball games while playing for and managing the Reds. After Rose's ban was instated, the Baseball Hall of Fame formally voted to ban those on baseball's "permanently ineligible" list from induction. Rose denied the accusations until 2004 when he admitted in his autobiography, and in later media interviews, that he had regularly made baseball wagers, betting on the Reds while managing the team.

The Eight Umpires in the Hall of Fame	
Umpire	**Year Inducted**
Tom Connolly	1953
Bill Klem	1953
Billy Evans	1973
Jocko Conlan	1974
Cal Hubbard	1976
Al Barlick	1989
Bill McGowan	1992
Nestor Chylak	1999

Who brought baseball to Cuba?

In 1864, a student named Nemisio Guillo returned from the U.S. where he had been studying at Spring Hill College, in Mobile, Alabama. With him he brought Cuba's first baseballs and bats. Along with his brother, Ernest, he was later instrumental in forming Cuba's first professional baseball team, Club Habana, in 1868, as well as the Cuban Professional League. Club Habana won six league championships from 1878 to 1887.

Who was "The Cuban Sylph"?

Esteban "Steven" Bellán was a Cuban national who attended St. John's College (now Fordham University) in New York in the 1860s. During his time there, he played for the college's Fordham Rose Hill Base Ball Club, and afterwards, in 1968, played one season for the Union club of Morrisania (Bronx) under the National Association of Base Ball Players, which was still an amateur league at that time. He went on to play with the Troy Haymakers, of Lansingburgh, New York, in 1871 and 1872. Troy was a professional club under baseball's newly formed National Association, making Bellán the first Latin American to play professional baseball in the U.S. He was nicknamed "The Cuban Sylph" for his elegant and stylistic play at third base. He finished his American career in 1873 with the New York Mutuals before returning to Cuba where he became a player-manager for Club Habana.

Quickies

Did you know ...
that during the Ten Years' War — Cuba's first war for liberation from Spain, which spanned from 1868 to 1878 — Spanish authorities banned baseball in Cuba because it was distracting the citizenry from bullfights?

What was the Mitchell Report?

The Mitchell Report, or as it is formally titled "The Report to the Commissioner of Baseball of an Independent Investigation into the Illegal Use of Steroids and Other Performance Enhancing Substances by Players in Major League Baseball," was a damning report released on December 13, 2007, which presented findings and recommendations compiled by former United States Senator George J. Mitchell and his law firm, DLA Piper, following a 20-month investigation into the use of anabolic steroids and human growth hormone in Major League Baseball. The 409-page report, which implicated dozens of players for substance abuse, stated that "For more than a decade there has been widespread illegal use of anabolic steroids and other performance enhancing substances by players in Major League Baseball, in violation of federal law and baseball policy. Club officials routinely have discussed the possibility of such substance use when evaluating players. Those who have illegally used these substances range from players whose major league careers were brief to potential members of the Baseball Hall of Fame. They include both pitchers and position players, and their backgrounds are as diverse as those of all major league players."

Who was "Murdoch"?

"Murdoch" was the nickname of Kirk J. Radomski, a batboy and clubhouse employee for the New York Mets from 1985–1995, who also happened to have a little side business. On April 27, 2007, he pleaded guilty in United States District Court to money laundering and the illegal distribution of steroids and other performance-enhancing drugs to dozens of players throughout Major League Baseball. He faced a maximum prison sentence of 25 years and a $500,000 fine, but was sentenced to only five years probation and ordered to pay a fine of $18,575 due to his cooperation with the federal government and the Mitchell Report. Radomski provided Mitchell with the names of dozens of his clients, also providing such material evidence as cashed cheques made out to his account from players, personal notes, and shipping documents.

What was the first non-American team in the major leagues?

The first major league team outside the U.S. was the Montreal Expos, or as they were known to hometown fans, *Les Expos de Montréal*. The Expos were formed in 1969 and their name refers to the International and Universal Exposition, or Expo '67 as it was commonly known, the World's Fair held in Montreal, Canada, from April 27 to October 29, 1967. After the 2004 season, the franchise was relocated by Major League Baseball (its owners since 2002) to Washington, D.C., and became the Washington Nationals.

Who is Youppi!?

Youppi! is the giant, shaggy, orange-haired creature that was mascot of the Montreal Expos for 25 years. It was designed by Bonnie Erickson, formerly a designer for Jim Henson, and the creator of Miss Piggy, Statler & Waldorf, and other Muppets. After the Expos moved to Washington D.C., Montreal's NHL team, the Canadiens, bought Youppi! in a reported six-figure deal, making Youppi! the first mascot in pro sports to switch leagues.

> **Quickies**
>
> *Did you know ...*
> that prior to the Montreal Expos, Montreal had a minor league team called the Royals which served as the main farm team for the Dodgers up until 1960? Famous Royals players included Jackie Robinson, Roberto Clemente, Roy Campanella, and Tommy Lasorda.

Who did the Montreal Expos face in their first and last games?

Coincidentally, the Expos played both their first and last games against the same team, the New York Mets. On April 8, 1969, the newly formed Montreal squad made their professional debut at Shea Stadium to defeat the Mets 11–10. Thirty-five years later, they ended their run in the same stadium, losing to the Mets 8–1 on October 3, 2004.

> **Quickies**
>
> *Did you know ...*
> that during the Expos' longest game ever — a 22-inning marathon that they lost against the Los Angeles Dodgers on August 23, 1989 — Montreal's mascot Youppi! jumped noisily on the roof of the Dodgers' dugout in the 11th inning and L.A. manager, Tommy Lasorda, complained to the umpire causing Youppie! to become the first team mascot ever to be ejected from a game?

Why did the Expos unfurl a banner commemorating their 1994 team at their final home game?

In August of 1994, the Montreal Expos were in first place with a record of 74–40 and showed every sign that they would advance to the post-season for only the second time in their career. The Major League Baseball Players Association had other plans, however, as the players went on strike on August 12, bringing the season to a premature close, and resulting in the cancellation of the entire post-season including the World Series. At their final home game on September 29, 2004, Montreal unfurled a banner reading "1994 Meilleure Équipe du Baseball / Best Team in Baseball" commemorating their 1994 team. Ironically, the only time the Expos actually did make it to

> **Quickies**
>
> *Did you know ...*
> that Pittsburgh Pirate Willie Stargell hit the longest home run ever recorded at Montreal's Olympic Stadium on May 20, 1978, smacking the ball an estimated 535 feet into the "Big O's" second deck over right field? A yellow seat now marks the location where the ball landed.

the post-season was in 1981, another year shortened by — though not completely lost to — a players' strike.

Have any teams based outside the U.S. ever won the World Series?

The only non-American team to have won the World Series is the Toronto Blue Jays, who actually took the pennant twice, first in 1992 and again in 1993. Founded in 1976, the Blue Jays are a member of the Eastern Division of Major League Baseball's American League. Their first official game was played March 11, 1977.

How did the Toronto Blue Jays get their name?

While Toronto is indeed in blue jay territory, the pesky, screeching birds that can be seen throughout the metropolis in the summer were only a convenient marketing device for Labatt Breweries, the initial majority owner of the city's major league baseball team. While a contest was held to name the new team, "Blue Jays" was eventually chosen by Labatt Breweries because Labatt's Blue was (and remains) its premier brand of beer, which was sold at ball games. The brewery had hoped Torontonians would call their team "The Blues" for short, but locals opted instead for "The Jays."

What other major league team still playing was once called the Blue Jays?

After the Philadelphia Phillies' owner William Cox became embroiled in a betting scandal and was banned from baseball in 1943, the club's new owner, Bob Carpenter, Jr., unofficially changed the team's name to the Blue Jays. However, Phillies fans never embraced the new moniker and it was discreetly retired after the 1948 season. The Phillies are one of major league baseball's oldest teams, debuting in the National League as the Quakers in 1883. The club adopted "Philadelphians," Phillies for short, as its name in 1890. Philadelphia holds a lesser distinction as the team that has lost the most games in major league baseball history. In fact, during its long and storied history it has only won two World Series — in 1980 (defeating the Kansas City Royals) and in 2008 (triumphing over the Tampa Bay Rays).

Why do the Toronto Blue Jays have the name "Ted" on their uniforms?

In 2009 the Toronto Blue Jays' uniforms saw the addition of a small black armband with the name "Ted" printed on it in memory of their owner, media magnate Ted Rogers, who died on December 2, 2008. Rogers bought the Blue Jays for $160 million CDN in 2000. The Blue Jays' stadium, once called the SkyDome because of its retractable roof, was rechristened the Rogers Centre in February 2005, after Rogers Communications purchased that facility, as well.

> **Quickies**
> *Did you know …*
> that in addition to an NHL team named the Maple Leafs, Toronto was home to an imortant minor-league baseball team of the same name from 1896 to 1967, a club that enjoyed affiliations with such major league clubs as the Pittsburgh Pirates, the St. Louis Browns, and the Boston Red Sox?

What is the highest scoring game in World Series history?

In game 4 of the 1993 World Series between the Toronto Blue Jays and Philadelphia Phillies, home team Philadelphia was up 14–9 in the top of the eighth when the Blue Jays rallied to score six runs on hits from Paul Molitor, Tony Fernández, Rickey Henderson, and Devon White. The Jays took the game 15–14 and the game remains the highest scoring in the history of the World Series.

> **Quickies**
> *Did you know …*
> that the first Toronto Blue Jays game, on April 7, 1977, was played in a snowstorm?

Why did Roberto Alomar donate $50,000 U.S. to Adrenoleukodystrophy (ALD) research?

On September 27, 1996, during a game against his former team, the Blue Jays, Roberto Alomar got into a heated argument over a called third strike with umpire John Hirschbeck and spat in the official's face. Alomar was castigated in the press and shunned by fans but nonetheless attempted to defend himself by claiming Hirschbeck had uttered a racial slur and that the umpire had become "bitter" since his young son had died of ALD. Upon hearing this the next day, Hirschbeck had to be physically restrained from confronting Alomar in the players' locker room. Alomar was suspended for only five games and donated $50,000 to ALD research, which was matched by the Orioles. The two men eventually made apologies to each other by standing at home plate and shaking hands in front of the crowd before an Orioles game on April 22, 1997.

Former Toronto Maple Leafs in the National Baseball Hall of Fame

- Sparky Anderson
- Ed Barrow
- Dan Brouthers
- Hugh Duffy
- Charlie Gehringer
- Burleigh Grimes
- Carl Hubbell
- Willie Keeler
- Joe Kelley
- Ralph Kiner
- Nap Lajoie
- Heinie Manush

What did pitcher Randy Johnson do to a dove in 2001?

Call it a fowl play, if you will. In a freak accident on March 24, 2001, in Tuscon Arizona, Diamondbacks hurler Randy Johnson threw a routine fastball pitch during the seventh inning of a spring training game against the San Francisco Giants. As the pitch sped towards batter, a dove flew across the infield between the mound and home plate and was struck by the ball. The event was captured on video, and the bird is seen exploding in a cloud of feathers. Johnson's fastballs have been clocked at over 100 mph, so not surprisingly the bird was instantly killed. The official call was "no pitch."

Quickies

Did you know ...
that Blue Jays short stop Marco Scutaro is known by the nickname Li' Papi because since the 2004 season only one player has more game-ending hits than him — Boston's David Ortiz, whose nickname is Big Papi?

Has the MLB All-Star game ever been played outside the U.S.?

The All-Star Game has been played outside the U.S. only twice, both times on Canadian soil. On July 13, 1982, the Montreal Expos hosted the All-Star Game at Olympic Stadium. The National League won 4–1 before a crowd of 59,057. The second time was in Toronto, on July 9, 1991, as the Blue Jays hosted the Midsummer Classic at the SkyDome. The American League won 4–2 before 52,383 fans.

What was the Pearson Cup?

The Montreal Expos and Toronto Blue Jays were for many years rivals in major league baseball simply because they were the only two Canadian teams. The Pearson Cup was an annual mid-season exhibition game between them, named after former Canadian Prime Minister Lester B. Pearson. The series began in 1978 and ran until 1986, although due to a strike, no game was played in 1981. In 2003 and 2004 the series was revived, but after the 2004 season the Expos moved to Washington, D.C., and became the Washington Nationals. The cup itself is now on display in the Canadian Baseball Hall of Fame.

Quickies

Did you know ...
that Major League Baseball does not recognize radar speed as an official statistic?

The 100+ mph Club: Pitchers Whose Fastballs have been Clocked at Over 100 mph.

Pitcher	Speed	Date	Place
Joel Zumaya	104.8 mph	10-10-2006	McAfee Coliseum
Armando Benitez	102.0 mph	05-24-2002	Shea Stadium
Bobby Jenks	102.0 mph	08-27-2005	Safeco Field
Randy Johnson	102.0 mph	07-09-2004	Pacific Bell Park
Matt Lindstrom	102.0 mph	05-16-2007	PNC Park
Robb Nen	102.0 mph	10-23-1997	Jacobs Field
Justin Verlander	102.0 mph	06-12-2007	Comerica Park
Jonathan Broxton	101.0 mph	06-26-2007	Chase Field
A.J. Burnett	101.0 mph	05-31-2005	PNC Park
Joba Chamberlain	101.0 mph	08-24-2007	Comerica Park
Rob Dibble	101.0 mph	06-08-1992	Candlestick Park
Kyle Farnsworth	101.0 mph	05-26-2004	Minute Maid Park
Eric Gagne	101.0 mph	04-16-2004	Pacific Bell Park
Jose Mesa	101.0 mph	05-01-1993	Cleveland Stadium
Seth McClung	101.0 mph	08-21-2007	Chase Field
Guillermo Mota	101.0 mph	07-24-2002	Qualcomm Stadium
Tony Pena	101.0 mph	06-07-2007	AT&T Park
Billy Wagner	101.0 mph	07-30-2003	Turner Field
Nolan Ryan	100.9 mph	08-20-1974	Anaheim Stadium

What was the Seitz decision?

Prior to 1975 baseball player contracts contained a reserve clause, which stated that, upon a contract's expiration, the rights to the player were to be retained by the team to which he had been signed. Under the reserve clause, although both the player's obligation to play for the team as well as the team's obligation to pay the player were terminated, the player was not free to enter into another contract with another team. The reserve clause was long a point of contention been players and owners and removing it eventually became a major goal of the Major League Baseball Players Association in their negotiations with owners. The reserve clause was eventually struck down when arbitrator Peter Seitz ruled on December 23, 1975, that since Los Angeles Dodger Andy Messersmith had played the entire 1975 season without a contract, and since Expo Dave McNally had done likewise, the two players could become free agents. By not signing contracts they had opened a loophole in the reserve clause. Seitz's decision was upheld on appeal in

Quickies
Did you know ...
that in 1993 Blue Jays' John Olerud, Robbie Alomar, and Paul Molitor finished 1–2–3 in the major league batting race — the first time teammates had done so in 100 years?

Federal court and, despite the owners' attempts to fight the decision by locking players out of training camp in spring 2006 (a move vetoed by baseball Commissioner Bowie Kuhn), the free agency era was born. In their 1976 collective-bargaining agreement, the players and owners finally agreed to a system of free agency.

Pearson Cup Results

When played as a single game:

Season	Winning team	Losing team	Series
1978	Montréal 5	Toronto 4	MTL 1–0
1979	Montréal 4	Toronto 4	MTL 1–0–1
1980	Montréal 3	Toronto 1	MTL 2–0–1
1981	No game due to player's strike.		
1982	Montréal 7	Toronto 3	MTL 3–0–1
1983	Toronto 7	Montréal 5	MTL 3–1–1
1984	Toronto 2	Montréal 1	MTL 3–2–1
1985	Montréal 2	Toronto 2	MTL 3–2–2
1986	Toronto 5	Montréal 2	Tied 3–3–2

When played as a three-game series:

Season	Winning team	Losing team	Series
2003	Montréal 3	Toronto 3	Tied 3–3–3
2004	Montréal 3	Toronto 3	Tied 3–3–4

Who was the first player to make $1 million annual salary?

Not only was he the first pitcher to reach 5,000 strikeouts, and the first pitcher to throw five no-hitters (and then six, and then seven), Hall of Famer Nolan Ryan was also the first baseball player to pass the $1 million annual salary threshold. Ryan, at 32, signed a free agent contract worth $4.5 million over four years with the Houston Astros, on November 19, 1979.

Quickies
Did you know ...
that when the Blue Jays won the World Series in 1993, they were the first team to achieve back-to-back championships since the New York Yankees did it in 1977 and 1978?

Annual Salaries of Baseball's Top Players, Pre- and Post-Free Agency

Pre-free agency, in 1975:
Dick Allen $200,000
Johnny Bench $175,000
Ferguson Jenkins $175,000

Post-free agency, in 1977:
Mike Schmidt $560,000;
Reggie Jackson $525,000;
Joe Morgan $400,000

Who is baseball's highest paid player?

The New York Yankees' third baseman, Alex Rodriguez, currently holds the title of baseball's top salary dog with a $275 million U.S. contract through 2018, that garners him $27.5 million per year.

The Evolution of Highest Paid Player Salaries

Year	Salary/Yr	Player	Team/Organization
1927	$ 70,000	Babe Ruth	New York Yankees
1930	$ 80,000	Babe Ruth	New York Yankees
1949	$ 100,000	Ted Williams	Boston Red Sox
1966	$ 130,000	Willie Mays	San Francisco Giants
1972	$ 200,000	Hank Aaron	Atlanta Braves
1975	$ 740,000	Catfish Hunter	New York Yankees
1979	$ 1,000,000	Nolan Ryan	Houston Astros
1981	$ 2,000,000	Dave Winfield	New York Yankees
1985	$ 2,130,300	Mike Schmidt	Philadelphia Phillies
1986	$ 2,800,000	George Foster	New York Mets
1990	$ 3,000,000	Rickey Henderson	Oakland Athletics
1991	$ 4,700,000	José Canseco	Oakland Athletics
1992	$ 5,800,000	Bobby Bonilla	New York Mets
1993	$ 5,975,000*	Ryne Sandberg	Chicago Cubs
1995	$ 9,237,500	Cecil Fielder	Detroit Tigers
1997	$10,000,000	Albert Belle	Chicago White Sox
1998	$14,936,667	Gary Sheffield	Florida Marlins
2000	$15,714,286	Kevin Brown	Los Angeles Dodgers
2001	$22,000,000	Alex Rodriguez	Texas Rangers
2005	$26,000,000	Alex Rodriguez	New York Yankees

*Ryne Sandberg's 1993 contract was originally for $7,100,000 per year, but he retired before the contract expired and forfeited the end of the contract.

Why were the New York Yankees originally called the Highlanders?

In 1903 Frank Farrell, who was involved with gaming and gambling in New York City, along with the city's former police chief, Bill Devery, purchased the Baltimore Orioles, a defunct franchise of the American League, for $18,000 and moved the team to Manhattan. Approved as a franchise member of the American League, the new New York team played in a hastily constructed, all-wood park at 168th Street and Broadway. Because the site was one of the highest spots in Manhattan, the team was named the "Highlanders" and their home field "Hilltop Park."

Quickies

Did you know ...
that baseball was the first sport to see players become free agents?

What was the Curse of the Bambino?

In the off-season of 1919–1920, the owner of the Boston Red Sox, Harry Frazee, made the less-than-brilliant decision to sell none other than Babe Ruth to the New York Yankees. Ruth, then 25, was one of the most valuable players in professional baseball, yet Frazee balked at the prospect of doubling his salary to $20,000 as the Bambino — as Ruth was nicknamed — was demanding for the next season. The Curse of the Bambino was a superstition in Boston that held that because of this foolish deal, the Red Sox — who had won five World Series since the first Fall Classic in 1903 — were cursed never to win the supreme baseball championship again. And there might have been something to the "curse," because the Red Sox didn't win the World Series again for 86 years. The hex was finally lifted when Boston swept the St. Louis Cardinals in the 2004 World Series. Any lingering doubts about the jinx were completely vanquished when the Red Sox won the Series again in 2007, sweeping the Colorado Rockies.

Where did Babe Ruth hit his first professional home run?

In 1914 Babe Ruth was still in the minor leagues, playing with the AAA Providence Grays. On September 5, the Grays played an away game against the Toronto Maple Leafs at Hanlan's Point on Toronto Island. It was here that Babe Ruth hit his first professional home run, and the only home run of his minor league career as he was recruited into the major leagues for the next season. Hanlan's Point is now considered a historic site and there are three commemorative plaques marking the first home run of the Bambino's career.

What did the Boston Red Sox get for Babe Ruth?

In exchange for Babe Ruth, the Red Sox received from the New York Yankees $125,000 in cash and a $350,000 loan against the mortgage on Fenway Park.

What is a grand salami?

This, quite simply, is slang for a grand slam, when a batter hits a home run with the bases loaded.

Who hit the first and last home runs in Old Yankee Stadium?

The original Yankee Stadium opened in the Bronx on April 18, 1923, with the home team defeating the Boston Red Sox 4–1 before a reported crowd of 74,200 fans. Babe Ruth hit the stadium's first home run that day, with a three-run dinger in the third inning. Because of Ruth's tremendous fan draw, the new stadium quickly became known as the House That Ruth Built. Old Yankee Stadium saw its last baseball game on September 21, 2008, with the Yankees beating the Baltimore Orioles 7–3. In the fourth inning of that game, Yankees catcher José Molina hit the ball over the left-field fence to record the final home run ever in the park.

Slang Terms for Home Runs

Big fly, blast, bomb, circuit clout, dinger, ding-dong, dong, four-bagger, four-base knock, funk blast, goner, gopher ball, homer, jack, long ball, moonshot, quadruple, round-tripper, shot, slam, swat, tape-measure shot, tater, wallop, going deep, going yard, going home, clearing the table, and dialled eight (from the practice of having to dial eight from a hotel room telephone to dial long distance).

Who was New York's first batter at the New Yankee Stadium?

In the spring of 2009, demolition began on Yankee Stadium with plans to convert the area where it stands into a public green space called Heritage Field. Concurrently, the New Yankee Stadium opened on April 16 literally across East 161st Street from the old ballpark. In the first game, on opening day, captain and shortstop Derek Jeter was the first

Players with Longest Hitting Streak Against Yankees

Player	Dates	Team	Streak
Charlie Gehringer	1935–1936	Tigers	31 games
Alexis "Alex" Rios	Sep 9, 2006–Jun 5, 2008	Blue Jays	26 games
Nomar Garciaparra	Sep 19, 1996–May 25, 1999	Red Sox	21 games
Paul Molitor	Sep 13, 1983–Apr 18, 1986	Brewers	21 games
Harold Baines	Apr 30, 1984–Aug 14, 1985	White Sox	21 games
Albert Belle	Sep 5, 1993–Aug 13, 1995	Indians	19 games

Players with Hitting Streaks of 40 Games or More

Player	Dates	Team	Streak
Joe DiMaggio	May 15–Jul 16, 1941	Yankees	56 games
Denny Lyons	Jun 24–Aug 26, 1887	Athletics	52 games
Pete Rose	Jun 14–Jul 31, 1978	Reds	44 games
Willie Keeler	Apr 22–Jun 18, 1897	Orioles	44 games
Bill Dahlen	June 20–August 6 1894	Colts	42 games
George Sisler	July 27–September 17, 1922	Browns	41 games
Ty Cobb	May 15–July 2, 1911	Tigers	40 games

Yankee batter at plate. After pretending he was going to hit with the actual bat that Babe Ruth used to hit the first homer in the old Yankee Stadium — which had been placed at home plate for the opening ceremonies — Jeter handed the artifact to a bat boy, took a new bat, and flied out to center field off Cleveland Indians pitcher Cliff Lee.

Other New Yankee Stadium Firsts on the Ballpark's Opening Day, April 16, 2009

- **First final score**: Cleveland Indians 10–New York Yankees 2
- **First ceremonial pitch thrown by**: Yogi Berra
- **First home plate umpire**: Tom Hallion
- **First batter**: Cleveland Indians center fielder Grady Sizemore
- **First out**: Grady Sizemore grounded out to first
- **First batter struck out swinging**: Cleveland first baseman Victor Martinez, 1st inning
- **First hit**: Yankee left fielder Johnny Damon, single to center field, 1st inning.
- **First batter hit by a pitch**: Yankee first baseman Mark Teixeira, third up, 1st inning
- **First baserunner to advance to second**: Yankee Johnny Damon, off walk to Mark Teixeira hit by pitch, 1st inning
- **First double**: Cleveland's right fielder Ben Francisco, 2nd inning
- **First walk**: Cleveland's catcher Kelly Shoppach, 2nd inning
- **First double play**: Cleveland's Martinez popped to shortstop, batter-runner Mark DeRosa thrown out at first, 3rd inning
- **First baserunner to advance to third**: Yankee Damon, off double to left field by Nick Swisher, 3rd inning
- **First run scored**: Cleveland's Francisco off a double to left field by Shoppach, 4th inning
- **First steals**: Yankee DH Hideki Matsui to third, and center fielder Brett Gardner to second on wild pitch by Cleveland's Cliff Lee, 4th
- **First baserunner caught stealing**: Cleveland's Sizemore on throw by Yankee catcher Jorge Posada to second base, 5th inning
- **First Home Run**: Yankee Posada hits solo homer over center-field fence, 5th inning
- **First error**: throwing error by Cleveland second baseman Tony Graffanino off Matsui's single to second advances Robinson Canó to third
- **First pitching change**: Yankee CC Sabathia relieved by Edwar Ramirez, 6th inning
- **First Grand Slam**: Cleveland's Sizemore puts it over right field fence to bring Kelly Shoppach, Ben Francisco, and Trevor Crowe home, 7th inning
- **First winning pitcher**: Cleveland southpaw Cliff Lee
- **First losing pitcher**: NY's José Veras
- **First crowd**: 48,271 fans

What is a "Yogiism"?

Yogi Berra got his nickname from a childhood friend who said that when his pal sat cross-legged with his arms folded he looked like a Hindu holy man. Ironically, the Hall of Famer and former Yankee catcher is renowned today for his less-than-sagacious bon mots, called Yogiisms. Here are a few Yogi gems:

- "It ain't over till it's over."
- "Never answer an anonymous letter."
- "I usually take a two hour nap from one to four."
- "When you come to a fork in the road, take it."
- "I didn't really say everything I said."
- "You can observe a lot by watching."
- "The future ain't what it used to be."
- "If the world were perfect, it wouldn't be."
- "If the people don't want to come out to the ballpark, nobody's going to stop them."

Where did the tradition of the rally cap start?

The rally cap refers to the superstitious act of wearing one's baseball cap inside-out as a talisman to induce a rally from your team for a win. The superstition first arose during game 5 of the 1945 World Series. The Detroit Tigers and Chicago Cubs were tied in the sixth inning, with the series itself standing at 2–2, when a radio announcer noted that some of the Tigers players in the dugout were wearing their caps inside out. Subsequently, the Tigers scored four runs that inning after a ball rolled between the legs of Chicago first baseman Phil Cavarretta. The Tigers won the game 8–4 and eventually went on to become that year's World Series Champions. The rally cap has been a tradition in baseball ever since.

Quickies
Did you know …
that on April 16, 1929, the New York Yankees became the first team to make numbers permanent on their uniforms? They would become standard for all teams by 1932.

What are those wire necklaces some players wear?

In 1991 Yankees pitcher Randy Johnson was in Japan on an all-star tour when he learned about Phiten necklaces, which are made of nylon coated with titanium. The company's website says "Phiten products regulate and balance [the] flow of energy throughout your body. Proper energy balance helps to alleviate discomfort, speed recovery, and counter-act fatigue by restoring the body's natural healing powers." The necklaces have become extremely popular through MLB with players who believe in their ability to promote good health. On April 7, 2009, the *St. Petersburg Times* newspaper in Florida asked a sports scientist about the efficacy of the necklaces. "There are no studies that have looked at whether or not wearing one of these necklaces or bands has any impact or any change in one's body," said Jeff Konin, executive director for the Sports Medicine and Athletic Related Trauma Institute at the University of South Florida.

What is the Curse of Colonel Sanders?

The victims of the Curse of Colonel Sanders are Japan's Hanshin Tigers, who have won only one title in 68 years, taking Japan's Central League championship in 1985. In celebration that year, fans who looked like players on the team jumped into Osaka's polluted Dotonbori River. Because no one looked like the Tigers' burly and bearded American star Randy Bass, fans threw in a large statue of Colonel Sanders stolen from a nearby Kentucky Fried Chicken outlet. The statue disappeared, and in subsequent years the Tigers dropped back into the basement. According to legend, the curse won't be lifted until the entire colonel statue is found. Part of the statue was raised from the deep in March 2009 — a portion consisting of its torso, head (without glasses), and arms (without hands).

What was the longest game in major league baseball history?

The longest game in major league baseball history was a matchup between the Chicago White Sox and the Milwaukee Brewers on May 8, 1984, at Comiskey Park in the Windy City. Scoring stalled at six runs a side in the eighth inning and play went on for an astonishing 25 innings and a total playing time of eight hours and six minutes before Chicago scored to win 7–6.

What was the longest game without extra innings in major league baseball history?

The longest game in major league baseball history without extra innings was a contest between the New York Yankees and the Boston Red Sox on August 18, 2006, at Fenway Park. The game lasted four and three-quarter hours, with New York emerging victorious 14–11.

What was the shortest game in major league baseball history?

The shortest game in major league baseball history was held on September 28, 1926, and saw the New York Yankees defeating Philadelphia Athletics 6–1 in just 51 minutes.

Who was the first player to steal a base while the ball was being pitched, but before it was hit?

In 1865 Eddie Cuthbert of the Philadelphia Keystones decided on his own to make a go for second base rather than wait for the hit. He made it, and base stealing has been a tradition in baseball ever since. Stealing bases was codified in baseball's rules in 1898.

What is defensive indifference?

If a baserunner makes an attempt to steal and the defence makes no attempt to put that baserunner out, the play is scored as "defensive indifference" and no stolen base is credited to the runner.

Who holds the record for most steals of home plate?

The great Ty Cobb, who played for the Detroit Tigers (1905–1926) and the Philadelphia Athletics (1927–1928), holds the record for most steals of home, with 54 thefts. During the 1912 season alone, Cobb stole the plate eight times, setting the record for most single-season steals of home. Cobb also holds the record for most steals of second base, third base, and home plate during the same inning, completing that feat four times in his career.

Where is the strike zone?

Imagine that home plate is column of light shinning straight up into the sky. The strike zone is a section of that column defined by MLB as follows: "that area over homeplate the upper limit of which is a horizontal line at the midpoint between the top of the shoulders and the top of the uniform pants, and the lower level is a line at the hollow beneath the kneecap." Of course, for each batter the strike zone is different, so the rules further stipulate that: "the Strike Zone shall be determined from the batter's stance as the batter is prepared to swing at a pitched ball." If any part of the ball passes through any part of the strike zone and is not hit, it should be called as a strike by the Umpire.

Baseball's Top 20 Thieves		
Rank	Player	Stolen Bases
1	Rickey Henderson	1406
2	Lou Brock	938
3	Billy Hamilton	912
4	Ty Cobb	892
5	Tim Raines	808
6	Vince Coleman	752
7	Eddie Collins	744
8	Arlie Latham	739
9	Max Carey	738
10	Honus Wagner	722
11	Joe Morgan	689
12	Willie Wilson	668
13	Tom Brown	657
14	Bert Campaneris	649
15	Kenny Lofton	622
16	Otis Nixon	620
17	George Davis	616
18	Dummy Hoy	594
19	Maury Wills	586
20	George Van Haltren	583

Quickies

Did you know …
that if a batter reaches base due to a fielding mistake, he is not credited with a hit — instead, the responsible fielder is charged with an error?

Who was the first player to hit a grand slam in the World Series?

On October 10, 1920, the Cleveland Indians outfielder Elmer Smith hit the first-ever World Series grand slam. In game 5 of the series against the Brooklyn Robbins, Smith knocked it out of League Park with the bases loaded in the first inning. Burleigh Grimes was pitching. Cleveland took the series 5–2.

Why was Cleveland's baseball team called the Naps from 1903 to 1914?

Today's Cleveland Indians were once named the Cleveland Naps after their star second baseman Nap Lajoie who, on September 27, 1914, became the first player to reach the 3,000-hit mark in a Cleveland uniform.

Why were manager Jack O'Connor and pitching coach Harry Howell fired by the 1909 St. Louis Browns?

When Nap Lajoie, playing for Cleveland, staged a duel with Ty Cobb for the 1909 season's batting title, something of a scandal erupted after the season's final game. Lajoie got eight hits in eight at bats in that game against the St. Louis Browns. But six of them were bunts and obviously gifts from the Browns. Johnny "Red" Corriden, the Browns' third baseman, had been ordered by his manager, Jack O'Connor, to move back into the grass of left field so that Lajoie could get on base by bunting down the third-base line. Ban Johnson, the American League president, later investigated the incident, and although Corriden was absolved, O'Connor and his pitching coach, Harry Howell, were fired by the Browns. The two had launched their scheme out of dislike for Cobb, wanting to see him lose the

Quickies

Did you know …
that in the fifth inning of game 5 of the 1920 World Series, Bill Wambsganss made an unassisted triple-play? The feat has never been repeated in a World series.

duel against Lajoie. It didn't work, as Cobb recorded a final batting average that season of .3848 to Lajoie's .3841.

Who was the first African-American manager in major league baseball?

April 8, 1975, marked a great stride for baseball and the Cleveland Indians as Frank Robinson became the first African-American manager in major league history. He was also a player for the Indians and debuted that day in grand style, hitting a homer in his first at bat.

Who are the "twins" of Minnesota?

The question is not who, but where. On October 26, 1960, Calvin Griffith, president of the Washington Senators, made the historic decision to move his club — which the Griffiths had controlled in D.C. since 1912 — to the Minneapolis/St. Paul area, thereby giving birth to the "Minnesota Twins" baseball team, named after the two Upper Midwest, American cities.

How did the Chicago Cubs get their name?

Prior to 1907, the Chicago Cubs were officially known as the Chicago Orphans, and prior to 1902, the nickname "Cubs" did not exist. The alias was created that year by a local newspaper when it was noted that the team had a disproportionate number of

Five Ways a Baseball Player Can Be Called "Out"

- **Strikeout**: the batter is out when three strikes are recorded at bat, only two of which can be called on fouls.
- **Flyout**: the batter-runner is out when a hit ball is caught by a fielder before it touches the ground.
- **Ground out**: the batter-runner is out when, after a hit ball lands in fair territory, a fielder in possession of the ball either touches first base or relays the ball to another fielder who touches first base before the batter-runner can touch that base.
- **Force out**: a baserunner is out when, having been forced to advance because another baserunner is headed for the base he is on, he is unable to touch the next base before a fielder in possession of the ball does so.
- **Tag out**: a baserunner is out when he is in fair territory* not touching any base and a fielder touches him with the ball or a glove holding the ball. If a runner is not forced to advance, they must be tagged out.

*Exception to the tag out rule: a batter-runner who has safely touched first base may safely overrun that base without worry of being tagged provided he returns to first base through foul territory and does not turn into fair territory towards second base.

Quickies
Did you know ...
that in a game on May 23, 1901, Nap Lajoie was intentionally walked while the bases were loaded? With a batting average of .426, Lajoie, then playing for the Philadelphia Athletics, was considered such a threat at home plate that Chicago White Sox pitcher Clark Griffith, who was also the Sox's pitcher-manager, walked Lajoie with no outs in the ninth inning with three runners on. The Sox were ahead 11–7, and Griffith feared Lajoie would hit a grand slam. The strategy paid off, as the next three Athletics batters went out on ground balls and the Sox won 11–10.

Only 14 Major League Players Have Turned Unassisted Triple Plays

American League

Player, Team	Position	Date	Inning
Asdrubal Cabrera, Cleveland	2B	05-12-2008	5th
Randy Velarde, Oakland	2B	05-29-2000	6th
John Valentin, Boston	SS	07-08-1994	6th
Ron Hansen, Washington	SS	07-30-1968	1st
Johnny Neun, Detroit	1B	05-31-1927	9th
George Burns, Boston	1B	09-14-1923	2nd
Bill Wambsganss, Cleveland	2B	10-10-1920	5th
Neal Ball, Cleveland	SS	07-19-1909	2nd

National League

Player, Team	Position	Date	Inning
Troy Tulowitzki, Colorado	SS	04-29-2007	7th
Rafael Furcal, Los Angeles	SS	08-10-2003	5th
Mickey Morandini, Philadelphia	2B	09-20-1992	6th
Jimmy Cooney, Chicago (NL)	SS	05-30-1927	4th
Glenn Wright, Pittsburgh	SS	05-07-1925	9th
Ernie Padgett, Boston (NL)	SS	10-06-1923	4th

young players. Indeed, out of thirty-nine players on the roster, thirty-four were under 30, and twelve of them were under 25. The nickname stuck and the team officially adopted it as their name in 1907.

Only Three Batters Have Ever Been Intentionally Walked with Bases Loaded

- Nap Lajoie of the Philadelphia Athletics, May 23, 1901.
- Bill Nicholson of the Chicago Cubs, July 23, 1944.
- Barry Bonds of the San Francisco Giants, May 28, 1998.

Quickies

Did you know ...

that the melody of the tomahawk chop "war chant" song sung by fans of the Atlanta Braves is from the opening notes of composer Antonin Dvorak's *New World Symphony*?

Who was Albert Spalding?

Yes, the Spalding sporting goods brand does have a player heritage. Albert Spalding, who was born in 1850, was a pitcher who started out as an amateur; but following the formation of the National Association, baseball's first professional league, in 1871, he joined the Boston Red Stockings, winning 205 games as a pitcher and batting .323. He started the Spalding Sporting Goods company in Chicago in 1876, manufacturing all manner of baseball equipment, including the official game balls used for the National League. While playing for the Chicago White Stockings in 1877, Spalding became the first pro player to use a glove to protect his hand.

Who holds the record for winning the most Cy Young Awards?

The Cy Young Award is an honor given annually in baseball to the best pitcher in Major League Baseball (MLB), one each for the American and National leagues. The award was first introduced in 1956 by Baseball Commissioner Ford Frick in honor of Hall of Fame pitcher Cy Young, who died in 1955. The award was originally given to the single best pitcher in the major leagues, but in 1967, after the retirement of Frick, the award was given to one pitcher in each league. The record holder for most Cy Young Award wins is Roger Clemens, who took the trophy seven times.

Quickies
Did you know ...
that the only Minnesota Twins player to have ever recorded six hits in a game was Kirby Puckett — and he did it twice? The first time was against Milwaukee on August 30, 1989, and the second was against Texas on May 23, 1991.

Quickies
Did you know ...
that in 1957, Warren Spahn, playing for the Boston Braves, became the first left-handed pitcher to win the Cy Young Award?

Pitchers with Multiple Cy Young Awards

Pitcher	Wins	Awards Years
Roger Clemens	7	1986, 1987, 1991, 1997, 1998, 2001, 2004
Randy Johnson	5	1995, 1999, 2000, 2001, 2002
Steve Carlton	4	1972, 1977, 1980, 1982
Greg Maddux	4	1992, 1993, 1994, 1995
Sandy Koufax	3	1963, 1965, 1966
Pedro Martínez	3	1997, 1999, 2000
Jim Palmer	3	1973, 1975, 1976
Tom Seaver	3	1969, 1973, 1975
Bob Gibson	2	1968, 1970
Tom Glavine	2	1991, 1998
Denny McLain	2	1968, 1969
Gaylord Perry	2	1972, 1978
Bret Saberhagen	2	1985, 1989
Johan Santana	2	2004, 2006

What was the Continental League?

What the Continental League was, was *not*. In 1958 after New York's two National League teams, the Giants and Dodgers, moved to California — to San Francisco and Los Angeles, respectively — lawyer William Shea made attempts bring other National League teams to the Big Apple, but the Cincinnati Reds, Philadelphia Phillies, and Pittsburgh Pirates all refused his proposals. When the National League further declined Shea's request to create a new New York Team (the Yankees are in the American League), Shea announced plans, in 1959, to form a third pro-baseball league, called the Continental League. Although the cites of Denver, Houston, Minneapolis–St. Paul, New York City, and Toronto were

Players with Multiple MVP Titles

- **7 wins**: Barry Bonds
- **3 wins**: Yogi Berra, Roy Campanella, Joe DiMaggio, Jimmie Foxx, Mickey Mantle, Stan Musial, Alex Rodriguez, Mike Schmidt
- **2 wins**: Ernie Banks, Johnny Bench, Mickey Cochrane, Lou Gehrig, Juan Gonzalez, Hank Greenberg, Rogers Hornsby, Carl Hubbell, Walter Johnson, Roger Maris, Willie Mays, Joe Morgan, Dale Murphy, Hal Newhouser, Albert Pujols, Cal Ripken, Frank Robinson, Frank Thomas, Ted Williams, Robin Yount

lined up for teams in the new league, many have surmised that Shea's move was something of a bluff. To head off the new league, baseball's National and American Leagues almost immediately announced plans for expansion. They added four teams: the American League's Washington Senators (moved to Texas to become the Rangers in 1972) and Los Angeles Angels, and the National League's Houston Colt .45s (now the Astros) and New York Mets. When the expansion was announced, Shea dropped plans to launch the Continental League. Shea Stadium, home of the New York Mets from 1964–2008, was named in his honor. The Mets played their first official game in franchise history on April 11, 1962, in an 11–4 loss to the Cardinals in St. Louis.

Major League Players Who Have Hit Home Runs in at Least Six Consecutive Games

American League

Player	Team	Homers	Year	Dates
Ken Griffey Jr.	Mariners	8	1993	July 20–28
Don Mattingly	Yankees	8	1987	July 8–18
Kevin Mench	Rangers	7	2006	April 2–28
Jim Thome	Indians	7	2002	June 25–30, July 2–3
Travis Hafner	Indians	6	2005	Sept. 18–23
Reggie Jackson	Orioles	6	1976	July 18–23
Frank Howard	Senators	6	1968	May 12–18
Roger Maris	Yankees	6	1961	Aug. 11–16
Roy Sievers	Senators	6	1957	July 29–31, Aug. 1–3
Lou Gehrig	Yankees	6	1931	Aug. 28–31, Sept. 1
Ken Williams	Browns	6	1922	July 28–July 31, Aug. 1–2

National League

Player	Team	Homers	Year	Dates
Dale Long	Pirates	8	1956	May 19–28
Barry Bonds	Giants	7	2004	April 12–20
Barry Bonds	Giants	6	2001	April 12–18
Walker Cooper	Giants	6	1947	June 22–28
Morgan Ensberg	Astros	6	2006	April 15–21
George Kelly	Giants	6	1924	July 11–16
Willie Mays	Giants	6	1955	Sept. 14–20
Graig Nettles	Padres	6	1984	Aug. 11–22

What is the symbolism behind the New York Mets' logo?

The circular Mets logo, created by sports cartoonist Ray Gatto, was designed to represent many facets of New York City as well as its relationship with baseball. Of course, the round insignia with its orange stitching represents a baseball. The bridge in the foreground symbolizes that the Mets represent all five of the city's boroughs. The skyline in the background shows a church spire at the left, symbolic of Brooklyn, the borough of churches. The second building from the left is the Williamsburg Savings Bank, the tallest building in Brooklyn. Next is the Woolworth Building. At center is the Empire State Building. At the far right is the United Nations Building. The Mets' colours are Dodger blue and Giant orange, symbolic of the return of National League baseball to New York after the Dodgers and Giants moved to California. Blue and Orange are also the official colors of New York State.

The 40–40 Club: The Only Four Major League Players that have Recorded 40 Home Runs and 40 Stolen Bases In a Single Season

American League

Year	Player	Homers	Steals
1998	Alex Rodriguez, Seattle	42	46
1988	Jose Canseco, Oakland	42	40

National League

Year	Player	Homers	Steals
2006	Alfonso Soriano, Washington	46	41
1996	Barry Bonds, San Francisco	42	40

Have any World Series ever been played by two teams that shared a ballpark as their home field?

Actually, this has happened three times in the history of the Fall Classic.

The first two were at New York's Polo Grounds. In 1921 the Giants beat the Yankees five games to three (in a best of nine series) and in 1922 the Giants took it again, beating the Yankees in five games (in a best of seven series). The third time was in 1944 in St. Louis when the Cardinals defeated Browns four games to two (in a best of seven) at Sportsman's Park.

What was "Merkle's boner"?

In 1908, the New York Giants and the Chicago Cubs finished the regular season with identical 98–55–1 records and needed to play a decisive makeup game on September 23 to determine the National League championship. In the bottom of the ninth, with runners on first and third and two out, New York's Al Bridwell made an apparent game-winning hit. The runner on third, Moose McCormick, ran to home scoring what all thought was the winning run. But the runner advancing from first to second base, Fred Merkle, upon seeing McCormick cross home plate and thinking the game was over, mistakenly veered towards the clubhouse without touching second base as required by the rules. Chaos ensued as the celebrating Giants fans stormed the field and Cubs players, realizing Merkle's error, attempted to get to get the ball to second base for a force out. They eventually did and because order could not be restored, the next day the umpire ruled the game a 1–1 tie. The match was replayed October 8 with Chicago posting a 4–2 victory and ultimately advanced to the World Series where they defeated Detroit. Mrekle's error has ever since been known as Merkle's boner.

Who was Milt Mason?

The mustachioed mascot for the Milwaukee Brewers — named Bernie Brewer — is based on a fan named Milt Mason who, at the age of 69 in 1970, climbed atop the scoreboard

at County Stadium in late June and sat in a trailer refusing to come down until the team drew a crowd of 40,000 fans. He was there until August 16, when the crowd reached 44,387.

What pitcher has thrown the most career strikeouts?

That would be none other than Nolan Ryan. On August 22, 1989, Ryan, pitching for the Texas Rangers, struck out Oakland's Rickey Henderson to become the first pitcher in Major League history to record 5,000 career strikeouts. Of the pitch, Henderson said, "I don't think nobody could have hit that pitch. He got me on the best pitch he threw." No other pitcher has broken the 5K barrier. Nolan was 42-years-old at the time and would continue to play until 1993 to record a total of 5,714 career strikeouts.

Why did the Detroit Tigers players stage a one-day strike on May 18, 1912?

While playing a game on May 15, 1912, against the hometown New York Highlanders, Tigers superstar pitcher Ty Cobb took exception to comments repeatedly heckled at him by a fan named Claude Lueker. Cobb ascended into the bleachers and proceeded to savagely beat the man. Lueker, it turned out, had only one hand, which itself was missing fingers and could not defend himself against the notoriously violent Cobb. The next day, league president Ban Johnson suspended Cobb from play. Cobb's teammates staged a strike to oppose the suspension, but after Tigers ownership put together a sandlot team for one game, leading to a 24–2 loss at Philadelphia on May 18, Cobb told his team to end their strike. He would remain suspended for ten days.

Top Players With at Least One Hit in at Least 30 Consecutive Games in One Season

Rank	Year	Name	Team	Consecutive Games with Hits
1	1941	Joe DiMaggio	New York (AL)	56
2	1897	Willie Keeler	Baltimore (NL)	44
	1978	Pete Rose	Cincinnati	44
4	1894	Bill Dahlen	Chicago (NL)	42
5	1922	George Sisler	St. Louis (AL)	41
6	1911	Ty Cobb	Detroit	40
7	1987	Paul Molitor	Milwaukee	39
8	1945	Tommy Holmes	Boston (NL)	37
9	2005	Jimmy Rollins	Philadelphia (NL)	36
10	1895	Fred Clarke	Louisville (NL)	35
	1917	Ty Cobb	Detroit	35
	2002	Luis Castillo	Florida	35
	2006	Chase Utley	Philadelphia (NL)	35

What is Lou Gehrig's disease?

Lou Gehrig's disease, as it is colloquially known, is Amyotrophic Lateral Sclerosis (ALS), a progressive, fatal disease caused by the degeneration of motor neurons, the cells in the central nervous system that control voluntary muscle movement. Yankees star Lou Gehrig was diagnosed with the disease in 1939 and died from it two years later at age 37. In his career, he had set a record for most consecutive games played, at 2,130, which was not broken until 1995 by Cal Ripken.

Seventeen Pitchers that Have Tossed Perfect Games in Major League History

American League

Pitcher	Date	Result
David Cone	07-18-1999	New York 6, Montreal 0
David Wells	05-17-1998	New York 4, Minnesota 0
Mike Witt	09-30-1984	California 1, Texas 0
Kenny Rogers	07-28-1994	Texas 4, California 0
Len Barker	05-15-1981	Cleveland 3, Toronto 0
Catfish Hunter	05-08-1968	Oakland 4, Minnesota 0
Don Larsen	10-08-1956	New York 2, Brooklyn 0
Charlie Robertson	04-30-1922	Chicago 2, Detroit 0
Addie Joss	10-02-1908	Cleveland 1, Chicago 0
Cy Young	05-05-1904	Boston 3, Philadelphia 0

National League

Pitcher	Date	Result
Randy Johnson	05-18-2004	Arizona 2, Atlanta 0
Dennis Martinez	07-28-1991	Montreal 2, Los Angeles 0
Tom Browning	09-16-1988	Cincinnati 1, Los Angeles 0
Sandy Koufax	09-09-1965	Los Angeles 1, Chicago 0
Jim Bunning	06-21-1964	Philadelphia 6, New York 0
Monte Ward	06-17-1880	Providence 5, Buffalo 0
Lee Richmond	06-12-1880	Worcester 1, Cleveland 0

How do you calculate a pitcher's ERA?

ERA stands for "earned run average." In baseball statistics, ERA is the mean of earned runs given up by a pitcher per nine innings pitched. That is, the ERA is a calculation of the average number of runs a pitcher would have surrendered over the course of a full game had he been kept in for the full nine innings. It is determined by dividing the number of earned runs allowed by the number of innings pitched and multiplying by nine. An earned run is any run for which the pitcher is held accountable. Unearned runs, resulting from batters who reached base on errors (even errors by pitchers) do not count toward ERA. To a pitcher, obviously, a low ERA is preferable.

Quickies
Did you know ...
that Lou Gehrig's disease, or Amyotrophic Lateral Sclerosis (ALS), is the same disease that afflicts renowned physicist Stephen Hawking?

Quickies
Did you know ...
that the 1963 San Francisco Giants boasted an all-brother outfield, with siblings Jesus, Matty, and Felipe Alou?

**Players Who Have Recorded the Most in Home Runs, Runs Batted In,
and Batting Average in a Single Season**

American League

Year	Player, Team	HR	RBI	AVG
1967	Carl Yastrzemski, Boston	44	121	.326
1966	Frank Robinson, Baltimore	49	122	.316
1956	Mickey Mantle, New York	52	130	.353
1947	Ted Williams, Boston	32	114	.343
1942	Ted Williams, Boston	36	137	.356
1934	Lou Gehrig, New York	49	165	.363
1933	Jimmie Foxx, Philadelphia	48	163	.356
1909	Ty Cobb, Detroit	9	115	.377
1901	Nap Lajoie, Philadelphia	14	125	.422

National League

Year	Player, Team	HR	RBI	AVG
1937	Joe Medwick, St. Louis	31	154	.374
1933	Chuck Klein, Philadelphia	28	120	.368
1925	Rogers Hornsby, St. Louis	39	143	.403
1922	Rogers Hornsby, St. Louis	42	152	.401
1912	Heinie Zimmerman, Chicago	14	103	.372
1894	Hugh Duffy, Boston	18	145	.438
1878	Paul Hines, Providence	4	50	.358

Who coined the phrase "walk-off home run"?

A walk-off home run is a home run that ends the game. It must give the home team the lead — and consequently, the win — in the bottom of the final inning of the game. It is called a "walk-off" because the teams walk off the field immediately after the winning run crosses home plate. The phrase first appeared in the San Francisco Chronicle on April 21, 1988, when Lowell Cohn used it in an article about Oakland pitcher Dennis Eckersley, whose slang term for the last at-bat of a game was "walkoff pieces."

What is a Lawrence Welk?

The famous TV personality and band leader Lawrence Welk was noted for setting the tempo for song with the phrase "and a 1, and a 2, and a 3." In baseball, a Lawrence Welk play is a 1–2–3 double play. This occurs when the bases are loaded and the batter hits a ground ball to the pitcher (No. 1 position), who throws it to the catcher (No. 2 position) to force out the baserunner coming home from third, and who then throws it to the first baseman (No. 3 position), who steps on first to force the batter-runner out.

Pitchers Who Have Recorded the Best Totals in Wins, Earned Run Average, and Strikeouts in a Single Season

American League

Year	Player, Team	Wins	ERA	K's
2006	Johan Santana, Minnesota	19	2.77	245
1999	Pedro Martinez, Boston	23	2.07	313
1998	Roger Clemens, Toronto	20	2.65	271
1997	Roger Clemens, Toronto	21	2.05	292
1945	Hal Newhouser, Detroit	25	1.81	212
1937	Lefty Gomez, New York	21	2.33	194
1934	Lefty Gomez, New York	26	2.33	158
1931	Lefty Grove, Philadelphia	31	2.06	175
1930	Lefty Grove, Philadelphia	28	2.54	209
1924	Walter Johnson, Washington	23	2.72	158
1918	Walter Johnson, Washington	23	1.27	162
1913	Walter Johnson, Washington	36	1.14	243
1905	Rube Waddell, Philadelphia	27	1.48	287
1901	Cy Young, Boston	33	1.62	158

National League

Year	Player, Team	Wins	ERA	K's
2007	Jake Peavy, San Diego	19	2.54	240
2002	Randy Johnson, Arizona	24	2.32	334
1985	Dwight Gooden, New York	24	1.53	268
1972	Steve Carlton, Philadelphia	27	1.97	310
1966	Sandy Koufax, Los Angeles	27	1.73	317
1965	Sandy Koufax, Los Angeles	26	2.04	382
1963	Sandy Koufax, Los Angeles	25	1.88	306
1939	Bucky Walters, Cincinnati	27	2.29	137
1924	Dazzy Vance, Brooklyn	28	2.16	262
1918	Hippo Vaughn, Chicago	22	1.74	148
1916	Grover Alexander, Philadelphia	33	1.55	167
1915	Grover Alexander, Philadelphia	31	1.22	241
1908	Christy Mathewson, New York	37	1.43	259
1905	Christy Mathewson, New York	31	1.28	206
1894	Amos Rusie, New York	36	2.78	195
1889	John Clarkson, Boston	49	2.73	284
1888	Tim Keefe, New York	35	1.74	335
1884	Old Hoss Radbourn, Providence	59	1.38	441
1877	Tommy Bond, Boston	40	2.11	170

What is a Baltimore Chop?

No, this is not dinner after the game at a Baltimore steakhouse. This was a method of hitting popularized by the Baltimore Orioles in the late nineteenth and early twentieth centuries. The batter would intentionally hit the ball downward to the hard ground in front of home plate in the hopes that a high bounce would allow him to reach first base safely before the opposing team could field the ball. The Baltimore groundskeeper packed the dirt tightly around home plate and mixed it with clay. Speedy Orioles players like John McGraw, Joe Kelley, Steve Brodie, and Wee Willie Keeler — who once legged out a double off a Baltimore chop — were the best practitioners of the hit.

What is a T-card?

In what would be an advertising scandal by today's standards, from the 1870s till the First World War, collectable baseball-player cards came in cigarette packages. Companies, such as the American Tobacco Company and the Imperial Tobacco Company of Canada, used the cards as promotional devices to lure customers. Decades later, the cards became highly valuable memorabilia because they were disposable and hence became very rare by the time most serious collectors took notice. The American Tobacco Company (ATC) released the largest number of baseball cards, beginning in 1909 with the issue of their T206 White Border Set. The T206 cards are some of today's rarest and most valuable cards. Subsequent ATC issues were similarly numbered — ie: T205, T3, T204 — and such cards are today called T-cards because of their "T" prefix, which of course stands for tobacco.

Baseball Idioms and Their Meanings

- **In the ballpark**: within a particular sphere of influence, comparison, knowledge or activity.
- **Batting a thousand**: to get everything right.
- **Big league**: activity performed at a high level of seriousness.
- **Bush league**: derogatory term for amateurism.
- **Clean up hitter**: a problem solver.
- **Cover all the bases**: making sure all aspects of a problem or challenge are receiving attention.
- **Threw a curveball**: an unexpected and often unpredictably drastic action or comment from another person.
- **Play hardball**: seriously competitive and tough level of activity, often in business.
- **Hit it out of the park**: a spectacularly successful accomplishment.
- **Hit or miss**: success or failure as only options.
- **Out of left field**: unusual, unexpected or irrational offering, comment or other action from another person.
- **Off base**: not paying attention; also being misguided, mistaken, or working on faulty assumptions.
- **Pinch hit**: to act as a substitute, often in an emergency situation.
- **Play ball**: to start an activity or resume after a delay.
- **Rain check**: a promise of future activity after a cancellation.
- **Right off the bat**: initially; for starters; immediately.
- **Step up to the plate**: to rise to an occasion or challenge.
- **Strike out**: fail in an endeavor.
- **Touch base**: to make contact, especially in business.
- **Whole 'nother ball game**: when circumstances surrounding an event change drastically; also when something is unrelated to the topic at hand.

What has been the top price fetched by a vintage baseball card?

There are a number of vintage baseball cards that can fetch six figures at auction. For example, a 1914 Baltimore News Babe Ruth card is worth $500,000 in good condition,

Naughty Baseball Metaphors and Their Meanings

- **First base**: kissing; French kissing
- **Second base**: sexual petting, especially over clothes
- **Third base**: oral sex or naked genital fondling
- **Home run**: sexual intercourse
- **Pitcher and catcher**: participants in homosexual anal intercourse
- **Switch-hitter**: bisexual
- **Bat and balls**: penis and testicles

Top Ten Baseball Movies

- *Bull Durham* (1988), directed by Ron Shelton and starring Kevin Costner
- *Field of Dreams* (1989), directed by Phil Alden Robinson and starring Kevin Costner
- *Bang the Drum Slowly* (1973), directed by John D. Hancock and starring Robert de Niro
- *Eight Men Out* (1988), directed by John Sayles and starring John Cusack
- *The Pride of the Yankees* (1942), directed by Sam Wood and starring Gary Cooper
- *The Bad News Bears* (1976), directed by Michael Ritchie and starring Walter Mathau
- *The Natural* (1984), directed by Barry Levinson and starring Robert Redford
- *A League of Their Own* (1992,) directed by Penny Marshal and starring Geena Davis
- *The Sandlot* (1993), directed by David M. Evans and starring Tom Guiry
- *Major League* (1989), directed by David S Ward and starring Charlie Sheen

Top Ten Baseball Books

- *The Boys of Summer* by Roger Kahn (1971)
- *Ball Four* by Jim Boulton (1970)
- *Bang the Drum Slowly* by Mike Harris (1956)
- *The Summer Game* by Riger Agnell (1972)
- *The Long Season* by Jim Brosnan (1960)
- *The Natural* by Bernard Malamud (1952)
- *Babe: The Legend Comes to Life* by Robert Creamer (1974)
- *Joe DiMaggio: The Hero's Life* by Richard Ben Cramer (2000)
- *Veeck as in Wreck* by Bill Veeck and Ed Linn (1962)
- *A False Spring* by Pat Jordan (1975)

and a 1909 Honus Wagner rookie card in comparable condition can bring in $300,000. But one card in particular has achieved spectacular "highest pricetag" status not just because it is rare, but also because of who used to own it. In 1991, a Honus Wagner card that was designed and issued by the American Tobacco Company from 1909 to 1911 as part of their T206 series, was purchased from a memorabilia collector by none other than NHL legend Wayne Gretzky for $451,000. "The Great One" resold the card four years later to Wal-Mart and Treat Entertainment for $500,000, for use as the top prize in a promotional contest. The next year, a Florida postal worker won the card and auctioned it at Christie's for $640,000 to collector Michael Gidwitz. In 2000, the card was sold in an auction on eBay to Brian Seigel for $1.27 million. In February 2007, Seigel sold the card to an anonymous collector for $2.35 million. Less than six months later, the card was sold to another anonymous California collector for $2.8 million. These transactions have made the Wagner card the most valuable baseball card in history.

basketball

What internationally played indoor team sport was invented by a Canadian?

James Naismith, from Bennie's Corners in Ontario's Ottawa Valley, became interested in sports when he was a theological student at McGill University. His favourite game was football, and his fellow ministers-in-training would pray for his soul because they considered football to be a tool of the devil. In 1891, as a physical education instructor at the YMCA school in Springfield, Massachusetts, Naismith realized that his students found the regimen of indoor calisthenics and exercises boring. He decided to invent a new indoor game that would be easy to learn and fun to play. After some failed experiments with football, soccer, and lacrosse, Naismith came up with basketball. When he could not find square boxes to use as targets, he used a pair of half-bushel peach baskets. In the first basketball game ever played, a man on a ladder had to retrieve the ball every time a basket was scored.

Quickies
Did you know ...
that James Naismith also invented the original football helmet?

Why are basketball players called "cagers"?

When James Naismith introduced basketball, the game was played with a soccer ball and the baskets were peach buckets nailed to the balcony at each end of the gym. The early games were rough and crude before Naismith introduced his thirteen rules in 1892 — so rough that the Trenton basketball team, playing in the first YMCA League, built a fence around the court to keep the ball in play. This fence was like a cage, and so the players were called cagers.

Who originated the "High 5" hand salute?

The celebratory gesture of raising hands to slap palms was first referred to in print as a "High 5" in 1980 because it was introduced by the University of Louisville basketball team during their 1979/80 NCAA championship season. Derek Smith claims to have invented the gesture and named it a "High 5" after he and two other Louisville players, Wiley Brown and Daryl Cleveland, created and practiced the hand gesture during the preseason (1979) and then introduced it during regular league play.

Quickies
Did you know ...
that the Fort Wayne Pistons were moved to Detroit in 1957 to become the Detroit Pistons?

How were the NBA's New York Nets named?

A charter member of the American Basketball Association in 1967, this team was first known as the Americans. When they moved to Commack, New York, a year later they chose the name Nets because nets were an important part of the game and the name rhymed with other pro teams from New York: the Mets and the Jets.

How did the NBA team, the Boston Celtics, get their name?

The Irish people are descendants of the Celts with a hard C (Kelts). The word began as the Greek word *Keltoi* which is what they (and the Romans) called the peoples of Europe who once lived in parts of Gaul, Spain, and Britain. The Celts were to Europe what the Native American Indians are to North America. They were tribal and nomadic without a central capital. As the Romans conquered these nations, the people moved north concentrating mainly in Brittany, The Isle of Man, Wales, Scotland, Cornwall, and Ireland. The soft C (Selts) pronunciation is from the French who called these people Celtique (selteek) and through their political liaisons with France against England, the Scots began using this French pronunciation to describe themselves. So the Scots are "Selts" while the Irish and the rest are "Kelts". This explains the Scottish Glasgow Celtics (seltics) soccer club but not the Boston Celtics (seltics) basketball team. When that team was formed in 1949, the owner, Walter Brown decided to pander to the huge Irish population of his city by naming his team the Celtics but apparently no one picked up that using the soft C (S) wasn't Irish and so the name remains with a Scottish pronunciation.

What's the origin of the expression "My bad"?

The slang expression "My bad" popped up in the 1970s as an acknowledgement of personal responsibility for making a mistake. The first written reference is in C. Wielgus and A. Wolff's 1986 book, *"Back-in-your-face": A Guide to Pick-up Basketball*. The phrase became popularized through the 1995 film *Clueless*, starring Alicia Silverstone.

Quickies
Did you know ...
that in the 1950s NBA pay was so low that Don Meineke worked in heating and air-conditioning sales in the off season?

What player won the first-ever NBA Rookie of the Year Award?

The NBA has been handing out the Rookie of the Year Award since the 1952–53 season. The first winner was forward Don "Monk" Meineke of the Fort Wayne Pistons, who posted a season total of 726 points in 68 games, logging 2,250 minutes of playing time. Meineke stayed with the Pistons through the 1955–56 season and then played two more NBA seasons, one each with the Rochester Royals and Cincinnati Royals, but was never able to post such numbers again. He retired from basketball in 1958.

Quickies

Did you know ...
that only once in NBA history have two African-American coaches faced each other in the Finals? In 1975 Al Attles led Golden State Warriors to victory over K.C. Jones' Washington Bullets.

Who was the first black NBA player?

He played just seven games that season logging 43 points, but on October 31, 1950, forward Earl Lloyd cemented his place in basketball history by becoming the first African-American to play in the NBA. Going by the nicknames "Big Cat" and "moon Fixer," the 6'5" Lloyd — a future hall of famer — played that season for the Washington Capitals then played for the Syracuse Nationals from 1952 till the end of the 1957–58 season. He finished his NBA career playing the next two seasons for the Detroit Pistons.

Who was the first recipient of the J. Walter Kennedy Citizenship Award?

Each year the Professional Basketball Writers Association recognizes one NBA player or coach for outstanding service and dedication to the community with the J. Walter Kennedy Citizenship Award. Named after the NBA's second commissioner of the NBA, the award was first given during the 1974–75 season to center Wes Unseld of the Washington Bullets.

Quickies

Did you know ...
that in the 1950–51 NBA season, the Boston Celtics became the first team to draft a black player, whose name was Chuck Cooper?

Quickies

Did you know ...
that in 1969 Wes Unseld became only the second NBA player besides Wilt Chamberlain to be named Rookie of the Year and MVP in the same season?

What is the Sixth Man Award?

In basketball there are those players — five in number — who head straight for the court at the beginning of a game and there are those who head for the bench. The former are referred to as "starters" because they start the game. They are typically the best players on the team, though players who later come off the bench as substitutes can be invaluable to a team's success. The NBA recognizes such bench players with its annual Sixth Man Award, given to the league's most valuable player coming off the bench. The player must have come off of the bench more than they started games to be eligible.

Who is Joe Dumars?

Joe Dumars, the President of Basketball Operations with the Detroit Pistons, gave his name to the trophy of the NBA's annual Sportsmanship Award when he became its first recipient after the 1995–96 season. The Joe Dumars Trophy is given to the player who most exemplifies the ideals of sportsmanship, on the court ethical behavior, fair play, and integrity. Dumars played 14 seasons with Detroit, from 1985–86 till 1998–99.

Which NBA player has missed the most 3-point shots in a single game?

A 3-point shot in basketball is any basket sunk from outside an arc extending from the end-line of the court exactly 19'9" from the center of the basket. The line of this arc painted on the floor is called, appropriately, the "three point line." An extra point is awarded because it is a more difficult shot — as proven by the Boston Celtics' Antoine Walker, who on December 17, 2001, set an NBA record by missing 11 3-point shots in a match against the 76ers.

Top Ten Basketball Movies

- *Hoosiers* (1986), starring Gene Hackman
- *Basketball Diaries* (1995), starring Leonardo DiCaprio
- *Hoop Dreams* (1994), starring William Gates
- *Glory Road* (2006), starring Josh Lucas
- *Rebound: The Legend of Earl 'The Goat' Manigault* (1996), starring Don Cheadle
- *He Got Game* (1998), starring Denzel Washington
- *Love & Basketball* (2000), starring Omar Epps
- *Finding Forrester* (2000), starring Sean Connery
- *Above the Rim* (1994), starring Duane Martin
- *Teen Wolf* (1985), starring Michael J. Fox

Who holds the NBA single-season record for the highest points-per-game average?

While playing for the Philadelphia Warriors in the 1961–62 season, center Wilt Chamberlain averaged an astonishing 50.4

points per game to set the record for the highest points-per-game average in a single NBA season. What was his best effort that season? Well, on March 2, 1962, Chamberlain set the NBA single-game scoring record by tallying 100 points for Philly in a 169–147 victory over the New York Knicks.

Quickies

Did you know ...

that in his 1961–62 season with Philadelphia, Wilt Chamberlain became the only NBA player ever to score over 4,000 points (4,029 to be precise)?

What became of the American Basketball Association?

The American Basketball Association (ABA) was a professional basketball league founded in 1967. The league existed for ten years and consisted, on average, of ten teams per season with two divisions of five teams each. Unable to secure a television deal its revenues remained low, and in 1976 a merger occurred between the ABA and the older NBA, with 4 ABA teams being absorbed into the NBA. Those teams were the New York Nets (now the New Jersey Nets), Denver Nuggets, Indiana Pacers, and San Antonio Spurs. Following the merger, the ABA was disolved.

American Basketball Association Champions and MVPs

Season	Finals Winner	Loser	Games	Playoffs MVP
1967–68	Pittsburgh Pipers	New Orleans Buccaneers	4–3	Connie Hawkins
1968–69	Oakland Oaks	Indiana Pacers	4–1	Warren Jabali
1969–70	Indiana Pacers	Los Angeles Stars	4–2	Roger Brown
1970–71	Utah Stars	Kentucky Colonels	4–2	Zelmo Beaty
1971–72	Indiana Pacers	New York Nets	4–2	Freddie Lewis
1972–73	Indiana Pacers	Kentucky Colonels	4–3	George McGinnis
1973–74	New York Nets	Utah Stars	4–1	Julius Erving
1974–75	Kentucky Colonels	Indiana Pacers	4–1	Artis Gilmore
1975–76	New York Nets	Denver Nuggets	4–2	Julius Erving

Why is the shot clock set at 24 seconds?

The shot clock is a 24-second timer designed to eliminate stalling tactics and to increase the pace and score of basketball games. Upon taking possession of the ball, the offensive team must attempt to score before the shot clock expires. The ball must either touch the basket's rim or enter the basket for the shot clock to stop. If the shot clock expires before that occurs, the offensive team is assessed a violation resulting in loss of possession. The idea for the shot clock came from Howard Hobson, who coached at the University of Oregon and later Yale University, and it was first tested by the NBA's Syracuse Nationals,

The NBA's Highest and Lowest Game Scores

- **Lowest**: Fort Wayne Pistons defeat Minneapolis Lakers 19–18, Nov 22, 1950
- **Highest**: Detroit Pistons defeat Denver Nuggets 186–184, Dec 13, 1983

in 1954. Syracuse owner Danny Biasone devised the 24-second duration of the shot clock by dividing the number of seconds in a 48-minute game (2,880) by the average number of shots in a game (120).

Who posted the first triple double in WNBA playoff history?

A triple double in basketball is when a player accumulates double-digit totals (i.e., 10 or more) for a single game in three of these categories: points, rebounds, assists, steals, or blocked shots. It is considered to be one of the most difficult basketball accomplishments to achieve. The first player in the Women's National Basketball Association to record a triple double during the playoffs was forward Sheryl Swoopes, who posted 14 points, 10 rebounds, and 10 assists on August 30, 2005, to help the Houston Comets defeat the Seattle Storm 75–67 in game three of round one of that year's conference semi-finals. Houston advanced to the next round on the win but were stopped in the conference finals by the Sacramento Monarchs.

Quickies

Did you know ...
that Sheryl Swoopes was the first WNBA player to have a Nike shoe named after her: the "Air Swoopes"?

WNBA Champions and MVPs

Year	Winner	Opponent	Format	Result	Finals MVP
1997	Houston Comets	New York Liberty	Single game	65–51	Cynthia Cooper
1998	Houston Comets	Phoenix Mercury	Best-of-three	2–1	Cynthia Cooper
1999	Houston Comets	New York Liberty	Best-of-three	2–1	Cynthia Cooper
2000	Houston Comets	New York Liberty	Best-of-three	2–0	Cynthia Cooper
2001	Los Angeles Sparks	Charlotte Sting	Best-of-three	2–0	Lisa Leslie
2002	Los Angeles Sparks	New York Liberty	Best-of-three	2–0	Lisa Leslie
2003	Detroit Shock	Los Angeles Sparks	Best-of-three	2–1	Ruth Riley
2004	Seattle Storm	Connecticut Sun	Best-of-three	2–1	Betty Lennox
2005	Sacramento Monarchs	Connecticut Sun	Best-of-five	3–1	Yolanda Griffith
2006	Detroit Shock	Sacramento Monarchs	Best-of-five	3–2	Deanna Nolan
2007	Phoenix Mercury	Detroit Shock	Best-of-five	3–2	Cappie Pondexter
2008	Detroit Shock	San Antonio Silver Stars	Best-of-five	3–0	Katie Smith

Who scored the first basket in the WNBA?

The first player to score a basket in the WNBA was point guard Penny Toler playing for the Los Angeles Sparks against the New York Liberty at the Great Western Forum in Inglewood, California, in the first-ever league game on June 21, 1997.

What is the name of the NBA Championship trophy?

The annual NBA champions are awarded the Larry O'Brien NBA Championship Trophy. The trophy was given that name in 1984 in honour of former NBA commissioner Larry O'Brien. Prior to 1984 it was called the Walter A. Brown Trophy, named after the original owner of the Boston Celtics.

Quickies

Did you know ...

that the first player to record 1,000 points in the WNBA was 4-times finals MVP Cynthia Cooper, who would go on to become the first to score 2,000 and then 2,500 before retiring?

Who was the first NBA player to win back-to-back Finals MVP titles?

In 1992, none other than Michael Jordan became the first-ever NBA player to be named Finals MVP in two consecutive seasons, after having also won the title in 1991. But of course, Jordan was just getting started. In 1993 he added a third Finals MVP title and then, in 1996, 1997, and 1998, he added a second Finals MVP hat trick for an NBA record-setting career total of six Finals MVP wins.

Quickies

Did you know ...

that Willis Reed of the New York Knicks was the first player to be named NBA Finals MVP multiple times, getting the nod in 1970 and again in 1973?

Quickies

Did you know ...

that during the 2009 NBA All-Star Weekend, NBA Commissioner David Stern announced that the Finals MVP award would be renamed the "Bill Russell NBA Finals Most Valuable Player Award" in honor of 11-time NBA champion, Bill Russell?

Who was the NBA's first Coach of the Year?

1962–63 was the inaugural season for the NBA's Coach of the Year award, and that year Harry Gallatin, coach of the St. Louis Hawks, became the first NBA coach to receive the honour. Although the Hawks were ultimately eliminated by the Los Angeles Lakers in the Western Division Finals that season, it was still something of a fitting first, since it was also Gallatin's first year coaching in the NBA.

Only Three NBA Players Have Won the MVP Triple Crown in One Year			
Player	**All-Star Game MVP**	**NBA MVP**	**NBA Finals MVP**
Willis Reed	1970	1970	1970
Michael Jordan	1996	1996	1996
Shaquille O'Neal	2000	2000	2000

What team won the first NBA game?

The first NBA game was played on November 1, 1946, in Toronto. The New York Knicks defeated the Toronto Huskies 68–66. The Huskies folded the next year.

Why did Toronto Raptors fans wear baby bibs printed with the number 15 on April 15, 2005?

On April 15, 2005, Toronto fans at a home game showed their scorn for former-Raptor Vince Carter, who wears number 15, by donning baby bibs with his number printed on them. It was the first time Carter had returned to Toronto after being traded to the New Jersey Nets. Carter, once a superstar in Toronto, fell out of favour with fans after suffering chronic injuries and then making it clear through the poor quality of his play that he wanted a trade. By wearing the bibs, Toronto fans were calling him a big baby.

> **Quickies**
> *Did you know ...*
> that the Minneapolis Lakers were the first team to win three consecutive NBA championships, taking top spot in 1951–52, 1952–53, and 1953–54?

What NBA team was first to lose the finals three years running?

In the NBA season of 1950–51, the New York Knicks faced the Rochester Royals, (now the Sacramento Kings) in the finals and lost 4–3. The next season the Knicks returned to the finals only to lose again, defeated this time by the Minneapolis Lakers, 4–3. In the 1952–53 season they tried it again against Minneapolis, only to lose the finals 4–1. The three losses made the Knicks the first team to lose the finals three years running. They would not return to the finals until 1970, when they would actually manage to win. They won again in 1973, but have not made it to the finals since.

> **Quickies**
> *Did you know ...*
> that the Boston Celtics won eight NBA Championships in a row from the 1958–59 season to the 1965–66 season?

What team has posted the NBA's best regular season record?

The 1995–96 Chicago Bulls set the record for the all-time best regular season with 72 wins and 10 losses. They went on to win the NBA championship that year. They are followed by: the 1971–72 LA Lakers (69–13), the 1996–97 Chicago Bulls (69–13), and the 1966–67 Philadelphia 76ers (68–13), all of whom went on to win the NBA championship in their respective seasons.

Multiple NBA League MVP Award Winners

Winner	Year
Bob Pettit	1955–56, 58–59
Bill Russell	1957–58, 61–62, 62–63, 64–65
Wilt Chamberlain	1959–60, 65–66, 66–67, 67–68
Kareem Abdul-Jabbar	1971–72, 73–74, 75–76, 76–77, 79–80
Moses Malone	1978–79, 81–82, 82–83,
Larry Bird	1983–84, 84–85, 85–86
Magic Johnson	1986–87, 88–89, 89–90
Michael Jordan	1990–91, 91–92, 95–96, 97–98
Karl Malone	1996–97, 98–99
Tim Duncan	2001–02, 02–03
Steve Nash	2005–06, 06–07

When was the first NBA All-Star Game played, who was the MVP, and who was the winning coach?

The first NBA All-Star Game was played in 1951 in Boston at the Boston Garden. The East won the game 111–94. The MVP of the game was Ed Macauley of the Boston Celtics. The winning coach was Joe Lapchick, who was the coach of the New York Knicks at the time.

The Founding Teams of the NBA from 1949 and Where They Are Now

Then	Now
Syracuse Nationals	Philadelphia 76ers
New York Knicks	same
Washington Capitols	defunct
Philadelphia Warriors	Golden State Warriors
Baltimore Bullets	defunct
Boston Celtics	same
Minneapolis Lakers	Los Angeles Lakers
Rochester Royals	Sacramento Kings
Chicago Stags	defunct
Fort Wayne Zollner Pistons	Detroit Pistons
St. Louis Bombers	defunct
Indianapolis Olympians	defunct
Anderson Packers	defunct
Tri-Cities Blackhawks	Atlanta Hawks
Sheboygan Redskins	defunct
Waterloo Hawks	defunct
Denver Nuggets*	defunct

*The Denver Nuggets team in today's NBA evolved out of the Denver Rockets of the defunct American Basketball Association, which merged with the NBA in 1976. The Rockets were renamed the Nuggets in 1974 in honour of the original NBA team.

What was the original name of the NBA?

The Basketball Association of America (BAA), founded in June, 1946, was the forerunner to the NBA. In 1949, its name was changed to the National Basketball Association when it merged with a rival organization, the National Basketball League.

What player has the most NBA championship rings?

Bill Russell holds the record with a total of 11 championship rings acquired with the Boston Celtics over a 13-year career spanning 1957 through 1959. The runner-up is his former teammate Sam Jones, who was part of 10 championship teams.

What NBA team has lost the NBA Finals the most times?

One team has lost over two times more NBA Finals than their nearest competition. The Los Angeles/Minneapolis Lakers, winners of 14 NBA championships, have also *lost* 14 NBA championships. They lost in the finals once as the Minneapolis Lakers (5 wins–1 loss), and 13 times as the Los Angeles Lakers (9 wins–13 losses).

Have any NBA teams won every finals tournament in which they have competed?

Five teams have won all the NBA Finals in which they have competed, but only two of them have multiple wins. The Chicago Bulls have appeared in six NBA Finals so far and have won them all (1991, 1992, 1993, 1996, 1997, 1998). The San Antonio Spurs have appeared in, and won, four NBA Finals (1999, 2003, 2005, 2007). Meanwhile, three teams each have just one appearance and one win: the Baltimore Bullets (now defunct) in 1948, the Rochester Royals (now the Sacramento Kings) in 1951, and the Miami Heat in 2006.

What is March Madness?

March Madness is the unofficial name given to the U.S.'s National Collegiate Athletic Association (NCAA) Men's Division I basketball tournament which is held each March.

The tournament takes place over three weeks at sites across the United States and culminates with national semifinals, called the Final Four because by then there are only four teams left.

Quickies

Did you know ...

that two teams are tied in second place for the most NBA Finals losses, with six each: the New York Knicks, and the Philadelphia 76ers?

What American college won the first NCAA Division I Basketball Championship?

In 1939, the Oregon Ducks of the university of Oregon won the first NCAA Men's Division I basketball championship. Nicknamed "The Tall Firs," the Ducks beat the Ohio State Buckeyes 46–33 in the championship game. The Ducks have not taken the NCAA title again since that first win.

What American college was the first to win back-to-back NCAA Men's Division I basketball championships?

Oklahoma State was the first school to win back-to-back NCAA Men's Division I basketball championships. They accomplished this in 1945 and 1946. The second school to accomplish this feat was Kentucky in 1948 and 1949.

What American college was the first to win back-to-back NCAA Women's Division I basketball championships?

The University of Southern California (USC) women's basketball team was the first to win back-to-back NCAA Women's Division I basketball championships. They accomplished this in 1983 and 1984, the second and third year of the women's basketball tournament.

Who was the youngest coach in the history of the NBA?

Dave DeBusschere played for 12 years in the NBA with the Detroit Pistons and New York Knicks. During the 1964–64 season with Detroit, at the age of just 24, he

Quickies

Did you know ...

that UCLA holds the record for the most Consecutive NCAA Division I Men's basketball championships, with seven straight wins from 1967 to 1973?

was appointed player-coach of the team, becoming the youngest ever NBA coach.

After labouring for almost three seasons at the helm, DeBusschere withdrew from coaching duties during the 1966–67 season, with a 79–143 record and no playoff appearances, to return to become a full-time player.

What is the NBA record for the longest losing streak in a single season?

The record for longest single-season losing streak in NBA history is shared by the Vancouver Grizzlies (now the Memphis Grizzlies) who suffered 23 consecutive losses in the 1995–96 season, and the Denver Nuggets, who served up 23 back-to-back duds in the 1997–98 season.

Who was the first NBA player to score a three-point basket?

Chris Ford, who played for the Boston Celtics at the time, scored the first three-point basket in NBA history on October 12, 1979, in a game against the Houston Rockets at the Boston Garden. Two years later, Ford was part of the 1981 Celtics NBA Championship team. In 1990 he became head coach of the Celtics, a position he held for five years during which he led his team to the NBA playoffs four times.

lacrosse

Why is Canada's national sport called "lacrosse"?

Lacrosse, "the little brother of war" was considered good training for Native American warriors. Teams consisting of hundreds of players often involved entire villages in brutal contests that could last as long as three days. To the French explorers who were the first Europeans to see the game, the stick resembled a bishop's ceremonial staff, called a "crozier", surmounted by a cross, or *la crosse* — and the sport had a new name.

Who invented lacrosse?

The game that eventually came to be called lacrosse was created by Native Americans before European settlers arrived in North America. Its name was dehuntshigwa'es in Onondaga ("men hit a rounded object"), da-nah-wah'uwsdi in Eastern Cherokee ("little war"), Tewaarathon in Mohawk language ("little brother of war"), and baaga'adowe in Ojibwa ("bump hips"). These games, played on large open plains, could last several days with as many as 100 to 1,000 men from opposing villages or tribes taking part.

Quickies
Did you know ...
that lacrosse is Canada's official national sport of summer, but Canada's official national sport of winter is ice hockey?

What were early lacrosse sticks and balls made of?

Native Americans used three types of lacrosse sticks. Communities such as Cherokee, Choctaw, and Seminole in the South-eastern United States played a version called "toli", which used two sticks per-player, each measuring around 60 centimetres long. One stick was held in each hand and the player cupped a ball of stuffed deer hide between small, netted hoops on the ends of the two sticks. In the Great Lakes region, bands such as the Ojibwa, Winnebago, and Menominee used only one stick per player, which measured about 90 centimetres long. A round, netted pocket measuring 7–10 centimetres in diameter on the end of the stick was used to carry a wooden ball. Meanwhile, in the Northeast, the Iroquois and others used a stick that became the model for contemporary equipment, which were typically longer

Quickies
Did you know ...
that in 1900, lacrosse was banned among the Oklahoma Choctaw when it was found that players were attaching lead weights to their sticks to crack each other's skulls?

Quickies
Did you know ...
that Great Lakes Natives used the extremely dense wood from tree knots to make lacrosse balls?

than 90 centimetres. Curved into a hook at one end, they were strung with netting inside the hook and down the shaft of the stick. Balls were made of deer hide stuffed with hair.

What is a modern lacrosse ball made of?

The modern lacrosse ball is made of solid rubber. It is typically white or yellow. It is usually between 19–20 centimetres in circumference, about 6.5 centimetres in diameter, and weighs between 140–150g.

Who was Dr. W. George Beers?

Dr. William George Beers was a Montreal dentist who founded the Montreal Lacrosse Club in 1856, completed the first set of codified rules for lacrosse in 1867 (by which time there were some 80 lacrosse clubs in Canada), and also introduced the use of a rubber ball to the game.

What is an "air Gait"?

The air Gait is a lacrosse move invented by player Gary Gait at Syracuse University in the 1980s. Gait would leap upwards behind the goal, reaching over crossbar to shoot the ball downwards into the goal behind the goalie. The move has since been made illegal in the rules of the game.

What is an "armadillo"?

In an "armadillo" five lacrosse players lock arms around one player in the middle of the group who carries the ball in a shortened goalie stick with a very deep pocket. The tactic makes it almost impossible for the opposing team to dislodge the ball as the huddled players advance up-field. It was invented in 1983 by the men's team at Virginia's Washington & Lee University and was very quickly banned.

What is *baggataway*?

Baggataway is the Ojibwa word for the game more widely known as lacrosse. The early French settlers saw the Natives playing the game, and named it for the sticks they used to toss the ball. The Native way of playing lacrosse was a wild, no-holds-barred melee that could involve as many as 500 men on each team, and often resulted in broken bones and even death. In 1867, William George Beers of Montreal formed the National Lacrosse Association of Canada, which promoted a set of rules by which the game was to be played. There is no record that lacrosse was ever made Canada's official national game. Beers also made such Native-related activities as snowshoeing and tobogganing popular recreational activities.

What is a "Baltimore crab"?

Also called an "Indian pick-up," a Baltimore crab is a method of picking up a ball by sliding the top of the stick's scoop over the ball to start it rolling, while also turning the stick's head under the ball quickly to collect it up in one motion.

Quickies

Did you know ...

that on June 4, 1763, the Ottawa Chief Pontiac invited the British garrison of Fort Michilimackinac to watch a game of baggataway outside the walls of the fort? While the soldiers watched, with the gates of the stockade wide open, the teams gradually worked their way closer to the fort. Suddenly the ball was tossed over the wall. This was the signal to attack. The men grabbed weapons from the women, who'd been hiding them under their blankets. They rushed into the fort and massacred everybody except a few Frenchmen. This was the beginning of Pontiac's War.

What is a "Canadian egg roll"?

This is not the post-game snack. Canadian egg roll is slang for a shot where a player with his back to the net catches a pass and then swoops the stick downward in one motion and shoots the ball backwards at the net from knee-height.

What is a "Yard Sale"?

This is not a way to get rid of your old lacrosse equipment. Rather, "yard sale" is slang for when a ball carrier has the ball and stick completely knocked out of his hands by a stick check.

Quickies

Did you know ...

that Bob Scott's book *Lacrosse: Technique and Tradition* is referred to as "The Bible" within the sport due to its comprehensiveness and expertise?

What were the founding four teams of the National Lacrosse League?

The National Lacrosse League (NLL), a men's professional indoor league in North America, was originally called the Eagle Pro Box Lacrosse League. It was established in 1986 by businessmen Chris Fritz and Russ Cline and saw it's first season of play early the next year. The founding teams were the Philadelphia Wings, New Jersey Saints, Washington Wave, and Baltimore Thunder. The league changed its name to the Major Indoor Lacrosse League (MILL) in the first post season and added two more teams, the Detroit Turbos and New England Blazers. In 1997, the MILL merged with a new lacrosse league called the National Lacrosse League, adopting the newer league's name.

What teams played the first game in National Lacrosse League history?

The first National Lacrosse League season began on January 31, 1987, when the New Jersey Saints defeated the Philadelphia Wings on home turf by a score of 11–8 before a crowd of 5,976 fans at the Wachovia Spectrum.

What National Lacrosse League team won the first league championship?

The first National Lacrosse League season came to an end on March 22, 1987, when the Baltimore Thunder, coached by Bob Griebe, defeat the Washington Wave by a score of 11–10 to capture the first-ever League Championship. A crowd of 7,019 was on hand at Baltimore's Capital Centre.

Who are Paul and Gary Gait?

Coming out of Syracuse University and joining the NLL in 1990, identical twins Paul and Gary Gait were drafted and signed to play with the Detroit Turbos. The Gaits, who hailed originally form Victoria, B.C., were the leaders on the Syracuse NCAA Championship teams of 1988, 1989, and 1990. In their first NLL season, Paul scored a record 47 goals, while Gary was second in the league with 32. Gary also established new records with 36 assists and 68 points. Gary is currently signed to the Rochester Knighthawks of the National Lacrosse League and the Toronto Nationals of Major League Lacrosse. Paul is currently the head coach of the Rochester Knighthawks.

Quickies

Did you know ...
that in 2006 both Gait brothers were among the five charter members to be voted into the National Lacrosse League Hall of Fame?

What is Major League Lacrosse?

Major League Lacrosse (MLL) is a professional men's outdoor lacrosse league that was founded in May 1999 by businessmen Jake Steinfeld, Dave Morrow, and Tim Robertson. The six founding teams were Baltimore Bayhawks, Boston Cannons, Bridgeport Barrage, Long Island Lizards, New Jersey Pride, and Rochester Rattlers. On June 7, 2001, Major League Lacrosse played its first regular-season game as Baltimore defeated Long Island by a 16–13 score.

What was the first Major League Lacrosse team to win back-to-back championships?

With their championship victory in 2007, the Philadelphia Barrage became the first team to win back-to-back Major League Lacrosse (MLL) championships, in 2006 and 2007.

Quickies

Did you know ...
that Baltimore's Chris Turner scored the first goal in MLL regular season history on June 7, 2001?

Quickies

Did you know ...
that the Major League Lacrosse team with the most championships since the league's founding in 2001 is the Philadelphia Barrage, with wins in 2004, 2006, and 2007?

What country has won the most International Lacrosse Federation World Lacrosse Championships?

The International Lacrosse Federation (ILF) World Lacrosse Championship started as a four-team invitational tournament in 1967. It is contested every four years. The 2006 World Lacrosse Championships saw teams from 21 nations compete. Since its inception in 1967, the United States has won the ILF World Lacrosse Championship 8 times, taking top honours in 1967, 1974, 1982, 1986, 1990, 1994, 1998, and 2002. Canada won in 1978 and 2006. No other nation has won the World Lacrosse Championship.

When was the first women's lacrosse game?

Native Americans — both men and women — played lacrosse, but the first game amongst European women was played in 1890 at the St. Leonards School in Fife, Scotland. The school's headmistress, Louisa Lumsden, brought the game to Scotland after watching a men's lacrosse game between the Canghuwaya Indians and the Montreal Lacrosse Club.

Quickies

Did you know ...

that in 1926 Rosabelle Sinclair, a student of Louisa Lumsden's, established the United States' first women's lacrosse team at Baltimore's Bryn Mawr School?

Results of the Women's Lacrosse World Cups

Year	Winners	Opponents
1982	United States	Australia
1986	Australia	United States
1989	United States	England
1993	United States	England
1997	United States	Australia
2001	United States	Australia
2005	Australia	United States

curling

Why is the game with rocks on ice called "curling"?

The first reference to the game we call curling was recorded in Scotland in 1541 and has nothing to do with the curling path of some stones. The game was, and in many places still is called, "the roaring game" because of the rumbling sound the rocks make while sliding over pebbled ice. This rumbling sound was called a curr in the Scots language and is how the game became known as curling. (In the Scots language, a curr is, among other things, the sound a dove makes when cooing — related to purring). The word "curling" surfaced in 1620 as the name of the roaring game which would be brought to Canada by Scottish immigrants in the early nineteenth century.

Where did the word *bonspiel* come from?

The first recorded occurrence of the word *bonspiel* is found in a Scottish reference to an archery match held in 1565, when the word was spelled *bonspiell*. The word, however, was never used as a general term for sport or games in Scotland and since the eighteenth century has referred specifically to curling matches. Its root, scholars speculate, is the old Dutch, *bondspel*, meaning alliance or league (*bond*) and game (*spel*).

Why do we call the foothold in the ice a "hack"?

The foothold in the ice from which a curler pushes off when delivering a stone is called the *hack*. Hack, of course, means to chop, as with an axe or hoe. It is also a word for the spot that has been chopped, as when saying someone made a hack into a tree — or into ice — and there's the answer. While the hack in modern curling is a fixture attached to the surface of the ice, in the early days of curling, the hack was a shallow hole or indentation hacked into the ice surface with an axe.

Quickies

Did you know ...
that two paintings from the year 1565 by the Flemish Artist Pieter Bruegel (1530–1569) depict an activity similar to curling being played on frozen ponds?

What is "The Brier"?

Called simply "The Brier," the Tim Horton's Brier, which has been sponsored by the donut shop chain since 2005, is the annual Canadian men's curling championship, sanctioned by the Canadian Curling Association (CCA). Since its founding in 1927, it has also been sponsored by Macdonald Tobacco (1927–79), Labatt Brewery (1980–2000), and Nokia (2001–04). It is a competition hosting provincial and regional teams, the winner of which goes on to represent Canada at the World Curling Championships.

In 1927, the tournament trophy was called the MacDonald Brier Tankard after the name of MacDonald's most popular pipe tobacco. Brier is the name of a plant from which the roots are used to make tobacco smoking pipes. That first Dominion Curling Championship led to the establishment of the Canadian Curling Association in 1935.

Top Three Finishers in the "The Brier" by Province or Region				
Province/Region	1st	2nd	3rd	Total
Manitoba	26	13	13	52
Alberta	24	17	8	49
Ontario	9	16	11	36
Saskatchewan	7	15	15	37
British Columbia	4	12	14	30
Northern Ontario	4	5	10	19
Nova Scotia	3	3	6	12
Quebec	2	4	4	10
Newfoundland & Labrador	1	1	1	3
New Brunswick	0	3	7	10
Yukon/Northwest Territories	0	1	0	1
Toronto	0	0	5	5
Prince Edward Island	0	0	2	2

What is the origin of the "hog-line"?

Today, the hog-line on the ice marks the spot before which a curler delivering a stone must release the stone. But it was originally created to mark the minimum distance the curler had to propel the stone. This might sound preposterous, given that curling stones weigh about 35–40 lbs and there are not many curlers so weak that they could not get a stone past at least that spot, 10 meters from the hack. But in the seventeenth and eighteenth century things were different. Back then curling stones could weigh up to 115 lbs and presented a major test of physical strength between competitors. If your stone couldn't pass the hog line, it was called a "hog" or "hogger" because, like the beast, it was so lazy.

What is the oldest curling stone in existence?

The earliest known curling stone is called the "Stirling Stone," and was discovered in the bed of an old pond that was drained at Dunblane, Scotland. Into the stone is carved the number 1511 and the words "St. Js B Stirling." It is believed that these markings indicate when and where the stone was made. The town of Stirling is just south of Dunblane.

World Curling Federation Top Ten Rankings — Men		
Country	Points	2008–09 Ranking
Canada	916	1
Scotland	748	2
Norway	617	3
United States	561	4
Germany	492	5
Switzerland	476	6
Finland	396	7
Sweden	352	8
France	285	9
Denmark	272	10

What was the first curling club in Canada?

The first curling club in Canada was formed in Montreal in 1807 by 20 merchants who called themselves the Montreal Curling Club. It has been operating continuously since then and celebrated its 200th anniversary in 2007. In 1835, members of the Montreal Curling Club took part in the very first inter-city game in Canada, competing against the Quebec Curling Club in Trois-Rivières. Quebec won and Montreal had to pay for the dinner. Legend has it there was no whisky available and there were many complaints about having only wine and champagne to drink.

Quickies
Did you know …
that in curling the ice is called the "sheet" and the target is called the "house"?

National Championship Briers and Founding Years

- **Men — Canada**: Tim Hortons Brier, 1927
- **Men — U.S.**: United States Curling Men's Championships, 1957
- **Men — Scotland**: Bruadar Scottish Men's Championship, 1963
- **Men — France**: Championnat de France Messieurs, 1951
- **Men — Russia**: Russian Men's Curling Championship, 1992
- **Women — Canada**: Scotties Tournament of Hearts, 1961
- **Women — U.S.**: United States Curling Women's Championships, 1977
- **Women — Scotland**: Columba Cream Scottish Women's Championship, 1977
- **Women — France**: Championnat de France Dames, 1971

What is a *loofie*?

Old curling stones from the sixteenth century, such as the Stirling Stone, did not have handles. Instead, a groove and holes would be carved into the stone similar to those now used in bowling balls. The old Scots word for hand was "loof," and since these stones were specially made to fit the hand, these old stones were called *loofies*.

What is on Ailsa Craig?

In the Firth of Clyde off the western coast of Scotland, and south of the Isle of Arran, is Ailsa Craig, a dome of volcanic rock that rises steeply out of the water some 340 metres. It is sometimes called "Paddy's Milestone" because it is halfway between Glasgow and Belfast. These days there is not much on Ailsa Craig except for an automated lighthouse and gannets (bird sanctuaries), but from the mid-nineteenth to mid-twentieth centuries, the island was quarried for a rare type of granite known as "Ailsite" which was used to make curling stones. The unique quality of Ailsite is that it is extremely dense and its water absorption is negligible. Were it not so, expansion and contraction due to freezing and thawing of water absorbed into the stone would cause the rock to pit and crack.

What is the Tournament of Hearts?

The Scotties Tournament of Hearts is the annual Canadian Women's Curling Championship, sanctioned by the Canadian Curling Association. The winner goes on to represent Canada at the Women's World Curling Championships. The Tournament of Hearts is a competition hosting provincial teams, although since ince 1985, the winner gets to return the following years as "Team Canada." The tournament is sponsored by Kruger Products, a paper manufacturer which make Scotties tissues.

Top Three Finishers in the "The Tournament of Hearts" by Province or Region

Province/Region	1st	2nd	3rd	Total
Saskatchewan	9	6	7	22
Manitoba	8	10	6	24
British Columbia	8	7	9	24
Canada	7	5	4	16
Alberta	6	8	4	18
Nova Scotia	5	3	4	12
Ontario	4	6	12	22
Quebec	1	2	3	6
New Brunswick	1	2	1	4
Newfoundland and Labrador	0	3	3	6
Prince Edward Island	0	1	2	3
Yukon/ Northwest Territories	0	0	1	1

Where is the world's oldest curling pond?

Kilsyth Curling Club, in Kilsyth, Scotland, lays claim to being the first curling club in the world, having been formally constituted in 1716. It is still in existence today. Kilsyth also claims the oldest purpose-built curling pond in the world at Colzium Estate.

What was the first curling club in the United States?

The first curling club in the United States was organized in 1831, only thirty miles from Detroit at Orchard Lake, Michigan. Called the Orchard Lake Curling Club, the club used hickory block "stones." Organized at the home of Dr. Robert Burns, the Orchard Lake group curled on Lake St. Clair. The club no longer exists.

Quickies
Did you know …
that in 2002, permission was given to the Ayrshire firm Kays of Scotland, who have been manufacturing curling stones since 1851, to remove 1,500 tons of loose granite boulders from Aislas Craig provided no quarrying was done?

Quickies
Did you know …
that in early Canada, garrison officers created curling stones called "irons" by filling the metal-rimmed hubs of gun carriages with molten metal and inserting iron handles?

When was the first-ever world curling championship?

The first world curling championship was limited to men and was known as the "Scotch Cup" held in Falkirk and Edinburgh, Scotland, in 1959. The first title was won by the Canadian team from Regina, Saskatchewan, skipped by Ernie Richardson.

Quickies
Did you know …
that the Milwaukee Curling Club, founded in 1846, is the oldest continuously operating curling club in the United States?

World Curling Federation Top Ten Rankings — Women

Country	Points	2008–09 Ranking
Canada	795	1
Sweden	736	2
Switzerland	587	3
Denmark	547	4
China	542	5
United States	488	6
Scotland	439	7
Russia	372	8
Norway	362	9
Japan	353	10

olympics

What do the five Olympic rings and their colours represent?

The five Olympic rings were formally introduced in 1920 and represent the union of the five continents or regions of the world that are linked by the Olympic spirit and credo during the Games. The six colours of the Olympic flag, including the rings and white background, are taken from all of the nations' flags. At least one Olympic colour appears on every flag in the world.

Why is a small sporting facility called a "gymnasium" while a larger one is a "stadium"?

The word *gymnasium* is from the Greek word *gymnos*, which means "nude." Thus, *gymnasium* literally means "a school for naked exercise." The first Olympic event for the nude male athletes, or gymnasts, was a foot race known as a *stade*, which was a Greek unit of measurement for the distance of the race (which was six hundred feet), and that is why the facility was called a stadium.

> **Quickies**
> *Did you know ...*
> that in early years of the modern Olympic Games it was permissible for teammates in team sports to be from different nations? For example, in the Games of the I Olympiad, held in Athens in 1896, the tennis doubles gold medal was taken by the team of Great Britain's John Pius Bolad and Germany's Friedrich Traun.

What does it mean to "rest on your laurels"?

The practice of using laurels to symbolize victory came from the ancient Greeks. After winning on the battlefield, great warriors were crowned with a wreath of laurels, or bay leaves, to signify their supreme status during a victory parade. Because the first Olympics consisted largely of war games, the champions were honoured in the same manner, with a laurel: a crown of leaves. To "rest on your laurels" means to quit while you're ahead.

> **Quickies**
> *Did you know ...*
> that the 1912 Olympics in Stockholm were the first Games to welcome competitors from all five continents?

> **Quickies**
> *Did you know ...*
> that for the five Olympic Games from 1900 to 1920, Tug of War was an official sport?

Why do we say that someone well conditioned has been "whipped into shape"?

During the ancient Olympics, athletes were expected to go into training ten months before the start of the games. The last month was spent at the site, where — regardless of the weather or bodily injuries, while on a strictly limited diet, and without shoes, shorts, or the right to complain — whenever they faltered, they were whipped by their trainers. These Olympians were literally whipped into shape.

What were the most medals ever won by a Canadian at the Olympics?

At the Torino Winter Olympics in 2006, Cindy Klassen became the first Canadian Olympian to win five medals in a single Olympic Games. In doing so she broke a record shared by swimmers Elaine Tanner and Anne Ottenbrite. A short and long distance speed skater, Klassen won gold in the 1,500m, silver in the women's team pursuit, silver in the 1,000m, bronze in the 3,000m, and bronze in the 5,000m. When a bronze won at Salt Lake City in 2002 is added to the total, she is the biggest overall medal winner in Canadian Olympic history.

Top Ten Most Successful Olympic Movies		
Title	**Lifetime Gross (USD)**	**Opening Date**
Blades of Glory	$118,594,548	3/30/07
Cool Runnings	$68,856,263	10/1/93
Miracle	$64,378,093	2/6/04
Chariots of Fire	$58,972,904	9/25/81
The Cutting Edge	$25,105,517	3/27/92
Running	$6,012,556	11/2/79
Personal Best	$5,672,311	2/5/82
American Anthem	$4,845,724	6/27/86
Running Brave	$3,000,000	11/4/83
Goldengirl	$1,247,376	6/15/79
Without Limits	$777,423	9/11/98
Prefontaine	$589,304	1/24/97

Which Paralympian was named Canadian Athlete of the Year in 2008?

In 2008, wheelchair racer Chantal Petitclerc was awarded both the Lou Marsh Trophy and Canadian Press's Bobbie Rosenfeld Award as Canada's Female Athlete of the Year. Petitclerc, who lost the use of both legs in an accident at the age of 13, had been competing in the Paralympic Games since 1992. Over five Games she had amassed an astounding 21 Paralympic medals, including five gold medals at the 2004 Summer Games in Athens. She holds world records in the 100-, 200-, 400-, 800-, and 1,500-metre distances. A truly inspirational athlete, a municipal ice hockey arena in her home town of Saint-Marc-des-Carrières now bears her name.

> **Quickies**
> *Did you know ...*
> that the 1928 Winter Games, hosted by St. Moritz, Switzerland, were the first to be held in a different nation than the Summer Games of the same year? The Summer Games of 1928 were held in Amsterdam.

Which Olympian had a doll created in her image?

Barbara Ann Scott was the first Canadian woman to win an Olympic gold medal in figure skating. After her win at the 1948 Winter Olympics in St. Moritz, Switzerland, she returned home to Canada to a hero's welcome. The girl who became known as "Canada's Sweetheart" was thrown a huge civic reception, presented with a new car by the mayor of her hometown of Ottawa (which she had to return in order to retain her amateur athlete status), and honoured by the Reliable Toy Company with the creation of a Barbara Ann Scott doll. She was a great inspiration for many girls born in the late 1940s and 1950s, quite a few of whom had been named after the popular skater.

> **Quickies**
> *Did you know ...*
> that in the early twentieth century, in addition to sports contests, the Olympics included amateur art competitions, featuring the disciplines Architecture, Literature, Music, Painting, and Sculpture?

Who was Pierre de Coubertin?

At an international congress on June 23, 1894, at the Sorbonne in Paris, a French educator and historian named Pierre de Frédy, Baron de Coubertin, proposed a revival of the ancient Olympic Games. The Paris congress led to the establishment of the International Olympic Committee, of which de Coubertin became the general secretary. It was also decided that the first of these IOC-organized Olympics would take place in Athens, Greece and that they would be held every four years. Today, de

> **Sports on the Program for the First Modern Olympic Games, 1896**
>
> - Aquatics
> - Athletics
> - Cycling
> - Fencing
> - Gymnastics
> - Shooting
> - Tennis
> - Weightlifting
> - Wrestling

Coubertin is considered the founder of the modern Olympic Games and, since 1964, the Pierre de Coubertin medal has been given by the International Olympic Committee to those athletes who demonstrate the spirit of sportsmanship in Olympic events.

What stadium was used for the first modern Olympic Games?

Amazingly, the Games of the I Olympiad, which were held in Athens in 1896, used the Panathinaiko Stadium — a white-marble stadium that had been used in ancient Greece to host the Panathenaic Games in honour of the Goddess Athena. The stadium was refurbished a second time in 1895 for the 1896 Summer Olympics, with completion funding provided by the Greek benefactor George Averoff (whose marble statue now stands at the entrance), based on designs by architects Anastasios Metaxas and Ernst Ziller. The stadium is still in use today and in the 2004 Olympic Games it hosted the archery competition and the finish of the Marathon.

Who wrote the Olympic theme song?

The Olympic Anthem heard at the opening and closing ceremonies of today's Olympic Games was written by Greek composer Spiros Samaras, with lyrics by Greek poet Kostis Palamas. It was composed for and first played at the Games of the I Olympiad in Athens, 1896, but it did not become the official Olympic Anthem until the 1960 Olympic Games. A variety of other musical pieces were used for opening and closing ceremonies up until that time.

What did winners receive at the first modern Olympics in 1896?

Winners in the first modern Olympics — officially called the Games of the I Olympiad — did not receive gold medals. That's because there was no three-tier medal system as there is now. Rather, first place finishers were awarded a silver medal, an olive branch, and a diploma. Athletes who finished in second place were given a copper medal, a branch of laurel, and a diploma.

Quickies
Did you know ...
that the Lake Placid Winter Olympic Games of 1932 were the first to use a podium for the official presentation of medals to event winners?

When were the first Winter Olympics?

In 1921, the International Olympic Committee gave its patronage to what was termed a "Winter Sports Week" to take place in 1924 in Chamonix, France. There were only six sports on the program, but the week saw over 10,000 paying spectators attend. Because the week was such a success, in 1926, during the 25th Session of the International Olympic Committee in Lisbon, the Chamonix Games were recognized as the first Olympic Winter Games.

Quickies
Did you know ...
that the Lake Placid Winter Games of 1932 marked the first time ice hockey was played at the Olympics in a covered arena?

Why were the 1976 Winter Olympics moved from Denver to Innsbruck?

The 1976 Winter Olympics were originally awarded to the city of Denver, Colorado, but in a referendum, the people of Colorado voted to prohibit public funds from being used to support the Games out of concerns for increasing costs and opposition to the ecological impact of the proposed Olympic facilities, so the Games were shifted to Innsbruck, Austria.

Who was the first modern Olympic champion?

On April 6, 1896, American athlete James Connolly became the first modern Olympic champion in more than 1,500 years when he won the triple jump at the Games of the I Olympiad in Athens.

Cities that Have Hosted the Modern Olympics Multiple Times

Summer Games
- Athens: 1896, 2004
- Paris: 1900, 1924
- London: 1908, 1948
- Los Angeles: 1932, 1984

Winter Games
- St. Moritz: 1928, 1948
- Innsbruck: 1964, 1976
- Lake Placid: 1932, 1980

What was on the medals at the Games of the I Olympiad?

One side of the medal showed the face of Zeus, king of the ancient Greek gods, along with his hand holding a globe with the winged victory on it. The caption in Greek read simply "Olympia." The other side had the Acropolis site with the caption in Greek "International Olympic Games in Athens in 1896."

Who invented the Olympic torch relay?

Sadly, the first Olympic torch relay was an invention of Hitler's Nazis. Although an Olympic flame had been lit at the Games since Amsterdam, 1928, it was not until Berlin, 1936 — the "Nazi Olympics" — that the first torch relay happened. The innovation was conceived by Dr. Carl Diem, head of the German organizing committee and a fervent supporter of the Third Reich, as a propaganda tool to draw a parallel between Nazi Germany and the splendor of Classical Greece. Diem proposed that a lit torch be relayed from Ancient Olympia, in Greece, to the Berlin Stadium to light the Olympic Flame. On July 20, 1936, fifteen Greek maidens clad in short, belted smocks representing the robes of priestesses, gathered on the plain at Ancient Olympia and the flame was lit there by the rays of the Greek sun off a reflector manufactured by the German optical firm, Zeiss. The torch itself, which was fueled with magnesium, was manufactured by the German firm, Krupp. A high priestess presented the flame to Kyril Kondylis, the first Greek runner, to begin a torch relay. After several thousand miles, the flame arrived in Berlin where it was used, in front of Adolph Hitler and an audience of thousands, to light the stadium flame by German runner Fritz Schilgen who had been chosen for the duty because of his blonde "Aryan" looks.

Sports on the Program at the Chamonix "Winter Sports Week," 1921

- Biathlon
- Bobsleigh
- Curling
- Ice Hockey
- Skating
- Skiing

Why did protesters line the route of the Olympic torch in major cities prior to the 2008 Summer Games?

During the spring of 2008, as China staged the Olympic torch relay from Greece to Beijing, the flame's route in many major cities outside China was lined with protesters. The reason? A month prior, Chinese troops had begun pouring into Tibet to suppress protests by Buddhist monks over China's occupation of their country. The Tibetans knew that the Olympics were the perfect forum to raise awareness of China's terrible human rights record in Tibet. The tactic worked as activists drew worldwide media attention to the state of Tibet by staging protests in such cities as London, San Francisco, Paris (where the torch had to be extinguished and the relay cancelled), Canberra, and Delhi. Sadly, little of this news made it back to China, where media is controlled by the State.

Medal Results by Country in the First Modern Olympics, Athens 1896

Country	Gold	Silver	Bronze	Total
Australia	2	0	0	2
Austria	2	1	2	5
Bulgaria	0	0	0	0
Chile	0	0	0	0
Denmark	1	2	3	6
France	5	4	2	11
Germany	6	5	2	13
Great Britain	2	3	2	7
Greece	10	17	19	46
Hungary	2	1	3	6
Italy	0	0	0	0
Sweden	0	0	0	0
Switzerland	1	2	0	3
United States	11	7	2	20

Note: Although the practice of handing out gold, silver, and bronze medals at Olympic Games did not begin until 1904, the International Olympic Committee has recorded the first, second, and third place finishers for all events and has retroactively assigned medal standings for the 1896 and 1900 Olympic Games.

How many demonstrations were held in Beijing's designated "demonstration zones" during the 2008 Summer Olympic Games?

Bowing to pressure from the International Olympic Committee, Chinese Olympic officials announced prior to the Beijing Games that three of the city's parks had been designated "demonstration zones" where people could gather to stage demonstrations. Government guidelines required that those seeking a demonstration permit had to report to the Public Security Bureau five days before their planned demonstration and present identification along with a written application. Although over seventy applications were submitted, no demonstrations were approved and a number of applicants were detained by police. When outside journalists visited the parks, they were unable to find the supposed demonstration zones.

Who were those men in blue track suits surrounding the Beijing Olympic torch on it's relay?

Beijing Olympic organizers called them "flame attendants" but others called them thugs. Officially, they were the "29th Olympic Games Torch Relay Flame Protection Unit" and they consisted of a group of 30 Chinese paramilitary police sent by Beijing to serve as the torch's last line of defence against protestors. Upon encountering them during the London relay, even Sebastian Coe, a two-time Olympic gold medallist and the chairman of the London 2012 Games, was shocked at their aggressive behaviour. "They tried to push me out of the way three times," Coe told the BBC. "They are horrible. They did not speak English. They were thugs." After the Chinese flame attendants were seen manhandling protestors in London and Paris, Australian officials issued warnings that they — the attendants — would be arrested if they laid hands on Australian citizens.

Which Olympics were the first to be broadcasted on television?

In 1936, at the behest of Hitler's propaganda minister Joseph Goebbels, the Berlin Olympics became the first Games to be broadcast on television. Twenty-five television viewing rooms were set up in the Greater Berlin area, allowing the locals to follow the Games free of charge. In addition, 20 radio transmitting vans were made available to foreign media, along with 300 microphones. Radio broadcasts at the 1936 Olympics were given in 28 languages.

Quickies

Did you know ...

that when the 2008 Olympic torch relay reached Islamabad, Pakistan, authorities scrapped the original two-mile route through city streets out of security concerns? Instead, the torch bearers simply ran around the grounds of Jinnah cricket stadium, which was surrounded by police and soldiers.

What happened to the Summer Games of the VI, XII, and XIII Olympiads?

Astute observers with a knowledge of Roman numerals will note that while the Beijing Summer Olympics of 2008 were officially titled the "Games of the XXIX Olympiad" — or for those who don't count in Roman, the Games of the 29th Olympiad — only 26 cities have ever hosted the Summer Games since the birth of the modern Olympics in 1896. (Prior to 1924, there were *only* Summer games.) Three Summer Olympics are missing: the Games of the VI, XII, and XIII Olympiads. These were the three Olympics that, had they not been cancelled, would have fallen on years during the First and Second World Wars. All three Games had actually been approved and assigned to host cities before the outbreak of any conflicts. The Games of the VI Olympiad were to take place in Berlin in 1916, the Games of the XII Olympiad were scheduled for Tokyo in 1940, and the Games of the XII Olympiad had been slotted for London in 1944. Obviously none of these cities could host the Olympics during those years, so while the Roman numerals assignments remained attached to those years, the events themselves were not held.

Quickies

Did you know ...

that on the first day of the 1936 Olympics, Hitler shook hands only with the German victors and then left the stadium? Olympic committee officials later insisted Hitler greet each and every medallist or none at all. Hitler opted for the latter and skipped all further medal presentations.

Quickies

Did you know ...

that unlike the Summer Olympics, if any Winter Olympics are cancelled, such as the 1940 and 1944 Winter Games which were cancelled due to WWII, the next Winter Games to actually be held take the next numerical assignment? So, the Winter Olympic Games of 1936 were officially called the "IV Olympic Winter Games," and after a 12-year hiatus during WWII, the Winter Olympic Games of 1948 were officially called the "V Olympic Winter Games."

Who lit the torch at the 1964 Summer Olympics in Tokyo?

Though he was a runner who would go on to win gold and silver in the 1966 Asian Games in Bangkok, 19-year-old Yoshinori Sakai was not an Olympian, nor would he ever be. Nonetheless, the young athlete was chosen to light the Olympic torch for the 1964 Summer Olympics in Tokyo because of where and when he had been born: Hiroshima, Monday, August 6, 1945 — the day the U.S. had dropped an atomic bomb on the city. The choice, it is said, was made in homage to the victims and as a call for peace in the world.

Why were the 1956 Summer Games held from November 22 to December 8?

In 1956, for the first time, the Summer Olympics were held in the southern hemisphere, in Melbourne, Australia. Summer, of course, hit down under during the northern hemisphere's winter months, so the games had to be postponed until the weather was warmer.

Who were the first women to compete in the modern Olympics?

The first women to compete in the modern Olympics appeared in the 1900 games in Paris. They were named Mme. Brohy and Mlle. Ohnier, of France, and both competed in croquet. Women also competed in golf and tennis at the 1900 games.

What was femininity testing?

Starting in 1968 and continuing till 1999, International Olympic Committee rules indicated that any woman competing in the Olympics had to undergo what was called a "femininity test" to verify she was in fact a woman and not a male imposter. Early tests were physical examinations, while later tests were done using mouth swabs to test chromosomal make up. The rationale for this test was that should a man successfully pose as a woman and compete, he might experience an unfair advantage in strength. The practice never uncovered such an imposter, although certain athletes from the Soviet Union suspiciously dropped out of international competition once such testing was introduced. As it became increasingly apparent that the newer chromosome tests were unreliable, the practice of gender testing was dropped all together.

> **Quickies**
> *Did you know ...*
> that the only woman athlete in the 1976 Montreal Olympics to not have a sex test was Princess Anne of the United Kingdom, who competed in equestrian events? As the daughter of the host country's head of state, Queen Elizabeth II, such a test was seen as improper.

> **Quickies**
> *Did you know ...*
> that Janet Evans' 1988 Olympic swimming record of 4:03.85 in the women's 400m freestyle was faster than all men's times in the same event before the 1972 Olympics?

Who was the first Olympic athlete caught using a banned substance?

Doping controls were first instituted by the International Olympic Committee in 1968 at the Grenoble Winter Olympics. It was not until that year's Summer Games in Mexico, however, that the first Olympic athlete was disqualified for failing the banned-substances testing. Hans-Gunnar Liljenwall, a Swedish competitor in the modern pentathlon, tested positive for alcohol at those games. Liljenwall, it has been reported, claimed to have had "two beers" prior to the event to calm his nerves. The entire Swedish pentathlon team eventually had to return their bronze medals.

Who has had to return the most Olympic medals due to doping?

At the 2000 Summer Olympics in Sydney, American Marion Jones scored big on the track, taking gold in the 100m, 200m, and 4x400m relay, as well as bronze in the long jump and 4x100m relay. Although she was not caught doping during those games, rumours of Jones' use of steroids had dogged her since high school and in 2007, she finally confessed to having used steroids at the Sydney Games. The International Olympic Committee stripped Jones of her medals and she was found guilty of perjury before a 2003 grand jury had been investigating the use of banned substances in sports. Jones was sentenced to six months in jail.

> **Quickies**
> *Did you know ...*
> that at the 2002 Salt Lake City Winter Games, $3 million was spent on drug testing?

What was BALCO?

On September 3, 2003, U.S. federal law enforcement officials conducted a raid on a company named the Bay Area Laboratory Cooperative, or Balco, a California lab that specialized in nutritional supplements. Records from the Balco raid along with statements from its its founder and president, Victor Conte Jr., implicated dozens professional and Olympic athletes in the possible use of the banned substance tetrahydrogestrinone (TGH), an anabolic steroid developed for the company by chemist Patrick Arnold.

SUMMER OLYMPICS

Who was Duke Kahanamoku?

Duke Paoa Kahinu Mokoe Hulikohola Kahanamoku (Duke was his given name, not a title) was the first Hawaiian to win Olympic gold, making his debut at Stockholm on July 6, 1912, competing in the 100m freestyle event. Though he was not royalty, he was known as "The Duke" and appropriately became the king of Hawaiian aquatics in the early twentieth century. While swimming the race, Kahanamoku pulled so far ahead of the other swimmers that at the halfway point he was able to stop and look back to survey the field. Despite this pause, he won by two meters, not only taking the gold but also setting a new Olympic record of 63.4 seconds. Kahanamoku also helped the U.S. 800m freestyle team take the silver medal in that event. In 1920 at the Antwerp Games, 30-year-old Kahanamoku did it again, first matching his 100m freestyle record in the semifinals and then breaking it in the final with a time of 61.4 seconds. However, the result was nullified after some countries protested the outcome. The race was re-swam and, as if to proved his mastery of the event, Kahanamoku shaved another full second off his time to come in at 60.4 seconds. No one protested. Kahanamoku added a third career gold medal to his collection that year in the 4x200m freestyle relay. He became one of Hawaii's most famous athletes and there is a statue of him today on Waikiki Beach.

> **Quickies**
> *Did you know ...*
> that Duke Kahanamoku acted in minor parts in 28 Hollywood films, was elected to the post of sheriff of Honolulu in 1936, and played a major role in introducing the sport of surfing around the world?

> **Quickies**
> *Did you know ...*
> that in January 1913, Olympic champion Hawaiian swimmer Duke Kahanmoku was attacked by a 10 foot eel while training for the Australian swimming championships in the waters off the coast of California? The swimmer managed to choke the eel to death but not before losing an index finger to its jaws.

How many Olympic swimming records were broken at the Beijing Games in 2008?

The Beijing games of 2008 were themselves a record breaker — for most swimming records broken. At those Games, out of 64 swimming events (which were split evenly between men and women) 62 saw records broken. The only swimming records that were not broken at the Beijing games were American Ian Thorpe's time of 3:40.59 for the 400m freestyle, set at the 2000 Sydney Games, and Dutchwoman Inge de Bruijn's time of 66.61 for the 100m butterfly, also set at Sydney. Never before at an Olympic Games have so many swimming records been broken, and coincidentally, Beijing took the record away from Sydney, where 14 records were broken.

Men's Swimming Olympic Records, as of 2008

Event	Record	Name	Nation	Games
50m freestyle	21.30	César Cielo Filho	Brazil	2008 Beijing
100m freestyle	47.05	Eamon Sullivan	Australia	2008 Beijing
200m freestyle	1:42.96	Michael Phelps	United States	2008 Beijing
400m freestyle	3:40.59	Ian Thorpe	Australia	2000 Sydney
1500m freestyle	14:38.92	Grant Hackett	Australia	2008 Beijing
100m backstroke	52.54	Aaron Peirsol	United States	2008 Beijing
200m backstroke	1:53.94	Ryan Lochte	United States	2008 Beijing
100m breaststroke	58.91	Kōsuke Kitajima	Japan	2008 Beijing
200m breaststroke	2:07.64	Kōsuke Kitajima	Japan	2008 Beijing
100m butterfly	50.58	Michael Phelps	United States	2008 Beijing
200m butterfly	1:52.03	Michael Phelps	United States	2008 Beijing
200m individual medley	1:54.23	Michael Phelps	United States	2008 Beijing
400m individual medley	4:03.84	Michael Phelps	United States	2008 Beijing
4×100m freestyle relay	3:08.24	Michael Phelps	United States	2008 Beijing
		Garre Weber-Gale	United States	2008 Beijing
		Cullen Jones	United States	2008 Beijing
		Jason Lezak	United States	2008 Beijing
4×200m freestyle relay	6:58.56	Michael Phelps	United States	2008 Beijing
		Ryan Lochte	United States	2008 Beijing
		Ricky Berens	United States	2008 Beijing
		Peter Vanderkaay	United States	2008 Beijing
4×100m medley relay	3:29.34	Aaron Peirsol	United States	2008 Beijing
		Brendan Hansen	United States	2008 Beijing
		Michael Phelps	United States	2008 Beijing
		Jason Lezak	United States	2008 Beijing

Women's Swimming Olympic Records, as of 2008

Event	Record	Name	Nation	Games
50m freestyle	24.06	Britta Steffen	Germany	2008 Beijing
100m freestyle	53.12	Britta Steffen	Germany	2008 Beijing
200m freestyle	1:54.82	Federica Pellegrini	Italy	2008 Beijing
400m freestyle	4:02.19	Federica Pellegrini	Italy	2008 Beijing
800m freestyle	8:14.10	Rebecca Adlington	Great Britain	2008 Beijing
100m backstroke	58.77	Kirsty Coventry	Zimbabwe	2008 Beijing
200m backstroke	2:05.24	Kirsty Coventry	Zimbabwe	2008 Beijing
100m breaststroke	1:05.64	Leisel Jones	Australia	2008 Beijing
200m breaststroke	2:20.22	Rebecca Soni	United States	2008 Beijing
100m butterfly	56.61	Inge de Bruijn	Netherlands	2000 Sydney
200m butterfly	2:04.18	Liu Zige	China	2008 Beijing
200m individual medley	2:08.45	Stephanie Rice	Australia	2008 Beijing
400m individual medley	4:29.45	Stephanie Rice	Australia	2008 Beijing
4×100m freestyle relay	3:33.76	Inge Dekker	Netherlands	2008 Beijing
		Ranomi Kromowidjojo	Netherlands	2008 Beijing
		Femke Heemskerk	Netherlands	2008 Beijing
		Marleen Veldhuis	Netherlands	2008 Beijing
4×200m freestyle relay	7:44.31	Stephanie Rice	Australia	2008 Beijing
		Bronte Barratt	Australia	2008 Beijing
		Kylie Palmer	Australia	2008 Beijing
		Linda Mackenzie	Australia	2008 Beijing
4×100m medley relay	3:52.69	Emily Seebohm	Australia	2008 Beijing
		Leisel Jones	Australia	2008 Beijing
		Jessicah Schipper	Australia	2008 Beijing
		Libby Trickett	Australia	2008 Beijing

Why were so many swimming records broken at the Beijing 2008 Olympics?

There were some great swimmers at the Beijing Games. Take American Michael Phelps, who won eight gold medals in China, single handedly breaking four Olympic records (three of which were also world records), and in relays breaking three more Olympic records (all also worlds) with his teammates. Australian Grant Hacckett chopped over four seconds off the 1500m freestyle record. Japan's Kōsuke Kitajima shaved over a second off the records for both the 100m and 200m breaststroke. Meanwhile in the women's events, the UK's Rebecca Adlington knocked over 5.5 seconds off the 800m freestyle record. Australian Stephanie Rice cut the records for the 200m and 400m individual medleys down by over two and three seconds, respectively. In the women's relays, the Aussies shattered the 4x200m medley record by over 9.5 seconds! Even if all of these athletes were the very best to have ever swum in an Olympic pool, in a sport that measures times in 1/100ths of a second, such differentials are like aeons and thus highly unusual. So what was happening?

It turns out it was that Water Cube the Chinese hosts built. Olympic rules require that a regulation swimming pool be at least 2 meters deep, but they do not specify a maximum depth. The pool at the Water Cube is 3 meters deep, making it 50% deeper than any official

Olympic pools used in the past. In swimming, when athletes propel themselves through the water, their movements send shockwaves down through the water which bounce up off the bottom of the pool. When those waves reach the surface, they create turbulence. The deeper the water, the farther those waves have to travel, and the farther they travel, the more energy they lose. So quite simply, the swimmers in the Water Cube had to fight less turbulence than they would have if racing in a pool with a depth of 2 meters, which meant they could swim faster. This was a major factor in all that record breaking.

How did Olympic champion Johnny Weissmuller come to play Tarzan in the movies?

Johnny Weissmuller was one of the all-time great American Swimmers. In his career, he set 67 world records, won 56 American national championships, and took five Olympic gold medals and one bronze swimming at the 1924 and 1928 Games. He also appeared as Tarzan in 12 Hollywood movies between 1932 and 1948. Legend has it that, while working on the adaptation of Tarzan the Ape Man, screen writer Cyril Hume noticed Weissmuller swimming in the pool at his hotel and suggested him to MGM studios for the role of Tarzan. MGM hit a stumbling block, however, as Weissmuller at the time was under contract to BVD to model underwear and swimsuits. MGM got him released from the contract by agreeing to pose many of its female stars in BVD swimsuits.

> **Quickies**
> *Did you know ...*
> that Johnny Weissmuller was born in Romania, but lied and claimed to have been born in Pennsylvania so that he could swim for the American team?

How did Zhang Juanjuan of China shock South Korea's women archers at the 2008 Summer Games?

Quite simply, Zhang Juanjuan won gold in the women's individual archery competition — a shock because since 1984 the South Korean women had dominated archery at the Olympics, having taken gold in the individuals at every Games, as well four silvers and four bronzes. Additionally, since the advent of team archery competitions at the Seoul Games of 1988, the South Korean women had won gold at every Olympic Games. Zhang Juanjuan defeated defending gold medallist and Olympic record holder Park Sung-Hyun by a margin of just 1 point.

Women's Individual Archery since 1984			
Year	Gold	Silver	Bronze
1984	South Korea	China	South Korea
1988	South Korea	South Korea	South Korea
1992	South Korea	South Korea	Unified team
1996	South Korea	China	Ukraine
2000	South Korea	South Korea	South Korea
2004	South Korea	China	Chinese Taipei
2008	China	South Korea	South Korea

Who was the first woman to win gold in Olympic archery?

Archery was first competed in the Olympics of 1900 in Paris, but a women's competition was not added until the St. Louis Olympics of 1904. There, Matilda Howell of the U.S. took gold in both the Women's Double National Round (24 arrows at 60 yards and 12 arrows at 50 yards) and the Women's Double Columbia Round (12 arrows at each of 50, 40, and 30 yard distances), becoming the first female Olympic archery champion. Howell, who won 17 national championships of the 20 she contested between 1883 and 1907, was one of the greatest all-time women archers.

Quickies

Did you know ...

that at the 1904 Olympics, because the archery competition doubled as the United States National Championship, only archers from the U.S. competed?

Who was Sir Anthony Dod of Edge?

Sir Anthony Dod of Edge was commander of the English archers at the Battle of Agincourt, where the British famously defeated the much larger French army in the year 1415 under the leadership of King Henry V. Dod was also the ancestor of the Olympic archers Willy Dod and Charlotte "Lottie" Dod, who became the first brother-sister medallists in Olympic history, when Willy took gold and Lottie took silver at the London Games of 1908.

Quickies

Did you know ...

that in Olympic archery the target is 1.22 meters (48 inches) in diameter, but to the archer, who shoots from 70 meters (86.4 yards) away, it appears about the size of a thumbtack held at arm's length?

What was pole archery?

In the 1920 Olympics at Antwerp two types of archery contests were held. One was the round-target type we are familiar with today, but the other, called pole archery, appeared for the first and last time at those games. The targets for pole archery were dead birds set on four beams running between two 31 metre-high poles. The sport was designed to simulate hunting, so the birds varied according to the types of birds that might be shot down from tree branches in a forest. There were two sizes, large birds and small birds, with medals awarded in each class for individuals competition and team competition. All of the competitors in the pole archery competition were from Belgium.

Who won the first marathon of the modern Olympic Games?

At the Games of the I Olympiad, held in Athens in 1896, there was no event that the Greek hosts wanted more to win than the 40,000m marathon race, which was created to honor the legend of Pheidippides, who, it is said, carried the news of the Greek victory at the Battle of Marathon in 490 B.C. by running from Marathon to Athens. On April 10, 1896, Spyridon Louis, a 24-year-old Greek shepherd, wearing shoes that had been donated by his fellow villagers, set off from Marathon with sixteen other runners. He took the lead four kilometers from the Panathenaic Stadium and, to the great joy of the 100,000 spectators in and around the stadium, won the race by more than seven minutes.

Men's Olympic Archery Records

Event	Result	Name	Country	Games
Individual12 arrows	117pts	Lee Chang-Hwan	South Korea	2008 Beijing
Individual 72 arrows/70m	684pts	Michele Frangilli	Italy	1996 Atlanta
Team 24 arrows	227pts	Park Kyung-Mo	South Korea	2008 Beijing
		Im Dong-Hyun	South Korea	2008 Beijing
		Lee Chang-Hwan	South Korea	2008 Beijing
Team 3x72 arrows	2031pts	Jang Yong-Ho	South Korea	1996 Atlanta
		Kim Bo-Ram	South Korea	1996 Atlanta
		Oh Kyo-Moon	South Korea	1996 Atlanta

Women's Olympic Archery Records

Event	Result	Name	Country	Games
Individual 12 arrows	115pts	Park Sung-Hyun	South Korea	2008 Beijing
Individual 72 arrows	673pts	Lina Herasymenko	Ukraine	1996 Atlanta
Team 3x72 arrows	1994pts	Kim Soo-Nyung	South Korea	2000 Sydney
		Kim Nam-Soon	South Korea	2000 Sydney
		Yun Mi-Jin	South Korea	2000 Sydney

Who were the Flying Finns?

In the early twentieth century a group of three Finnish middle and long-distance runners so dominated Olympic competition that they were dubbed the "Flying Finns." The nickname was first used of Hannes Kolehmainen, who took home three gold medals and broke two world records during the 1912 Summer Olympics in Stockholm. The other two were Paavo Nurmi, who took a total of nine golds and three silvers over the 1920, 1924, and 1928 Games, and Ville Ritola who spread his take of five golds and three silvers between 1924 and 1928. Ever since, champion Finnish runners, such as Volmari Iso-Hollo, the winner of the 3000m steeplechase at the 1932 and 1936 Summer Olympics, have also been nicknamed Flying Finns.

Who was the first runner to finish the 5000m race in under 15 minutes?

Not surprisingly, the first runner to finish the 5000m race in under 15 minutes was Finnish. In the early twentieth century, Finnish runners dominated middle and long-distance events. At the 1912 Olympics in Stockholm, Hannes Kölehmainen won the 5,000m race, setting a new world record, with a time of 14:36.35. It was the first time anyone had broken the 15 minute barrier. That year, the great Finn also took gold in the 10,000m race and the individual cross country, as well as silver in the team cross country. In the 1920 Games at Antwerp Kölehmainen took gold in the marathon.

What did Finnish runner Paavo Nurmi accomplish despite opposition from Finnish officials?

At the Paris Games of 1924, Finn Paavo Nurmi cemented his place in Olympics athletics history as one of the greatest runners of all time. Nurmi came into those Games already in possession of three golds and one silver from the Antwerp games of 1920, where amongst other things he had won the 10,000m track race. On July 10, 1924, at the Paris Games, Nurmi performed one of the greatest feats in Olympic history. First he won the 1,500m race. Then, two hours later, he won the 5,000m. Two days later, in the midst of a blistering heat wave that saw temperatures climbing to 45 degrees Celsius, Nurmi won the 10,000m cross-country race by 1 minute 24.6 seconds and gained another gold medal in the team cross-country event. It was to be the last time cross country races would be held in the Olympics, because so many of the runners collapsed from heat exhaustion

and had to be rushed to a hospital. Indeed, of 38 entrants only 15 made it to the finish, and of these, eight were carried off on stretchers. Despite the heat wave, the following day Nurmi finished first in the 3,000m team race. He had hoped to break a record in the 10,000m title, but Finnish officials, fearing for his health, refused to enter him in the event. Upon returning to Finland, an angry Nurmi later accomplished what those officials had prevented him from doing. On August 31 he ran a time of 30:06.2 in a 10,000m race in the city of Kupio, setting a world record that would stand until 1937.

Men's Athletics Olympic Records

Event	Athlete	Result	Country	Location
100m	Usain Bolt	9.69	Jamaica	2008 Beijing
200m	Usain Bolt	19.30	Jamaica	2008 Beijing
400m	Michael Johnson	43.49	U.S.	1996 Atlanta
800m	Vebjørn Rodol	1:42.58	Norway	1996 Atlanta
1500m	Noah Ngeny	3:32.07	Kenya	2000 Sydney
5000m	Kenenisa Bekel	12:57.82	Ethiopia	2008 Beijing
10000m	Kenenisa Bekele	27:01.17	Ethiopia	2008 Beijing
Marathon	Samuel Wanjiru	2:06:32	Kenya	2008 Beijing
110m Hurdles	Xiang Liu	12.91	China	2004 Athens
400m Hurdles	Kevin Young	46.78	U.S.	1992 Barcelona
3000m Steeplechase	Julius Kariuki	8:05.51	Kenya	1988 Seoul
4x100m Relay	Nesta Carter	37.10	Jamaica	2008 Beijing
	Michael Frater	37.10	Jamaica	2008 Beijing
	Usain Bolt	37.10	Jamaica	2008 Beijing
	Asafa Powell	37.10	Jamaica	2008 Beijing
4x400m Relay	LaShawn Merritt	2:55.39	U.S.	2008 Beijing
	Angelo Taylor	2:55.39	U.S.	2008 Beijing
	David Neville	2:55.39	U.S.	2008 Beijing
	Jeremy Wariner	2:55.39	U.S.	2008 Beijing
20km Walk	Robert Korzeniowski	1:18:59	Poland	2000 Sydney
50km Walk	Alex Schwazer	3:37:09	Italy	2008 Beijing
High Jump	Charles Austin	2.39 m	U.S.	1996 Atlanta
Long Jump	Bob Bemon	8.90 m	U.S.	1968 Mexico City
Pole Vault	Steve Hooker	5.96 m	Australia	2008 Beijing
Triple Jump	Kenny Harrison	18.09 m	U.S.	1996 Atlanta
Shot Put	Ulf Timmermann	22.47 m	Germany	1988 Seoul
Discus Throw	Virgilijus Alekna	69.89 m	Lithuania	2004 Athens
Hammer Throw	Sergey Litvinov	84.80 m	Soviet Union	1988 Seoul
Javelin Throw	Andreas Thorkildsen	90.57 m	Norway	2008 Beijing
Decathlon	Roman Sebrle	8893 pts	CZE	2004 Athens

What was gold medallist Micheline Ostermeyer's profession?

Micheline Ostermeyer undoubtedly holds the distinction of being the only concert pianist in history to have won gold at the Olympics. At the 1948 London Games, Ostermeyer, who was a great-niece of author Victor Hugo, competed in athletics for France and won gold in both the shot put and discus throw. All that piano playing must have made her arms stronger than her legs, however, as she was only able to achieve bronze in the high jump.

Women's Athletics Olympic Records

Event	Athlete	Result	Country	Location
100m	Florence Griffith Joyner	10.62	U.S.	1988 Seoul
200m	Florence Griffith Joyner	21.34	U.S.	1988 Seoul
400m	Marie-Jose Perec	48.25	France	1996 Atlanta
800m	Nadezhda Olizarenko	1:53.43	Russia	1980 Moscow
1500m	Paula Ivan	3:53.96	Romania	1988 Seoul
5000m	Gabriela Szabo	14:40.79	Romania	2000 Sydney
10000m	Tirunesh Dibaba	29:54.66	Ethiopia	2008 Beijing
Marathon	Naoko Takahashi	2:23:14	Japan	2000 Sydney
100m Hurdles	Joanna Hayes	12.37	U.S.	2004 Athens
400m Hurdles	Melanie Walker	52.64	Jamaica	2008 Beijing
3000m Steeplechase	Gulnara Galkina-Samitova	8:58.81	Russia	2008 Beijing
4x100m Relay	Romy Müller	41.60	Germany	1980 Moscow
	Bärbel Wöckel	41.60	Germany	1980 Moscow
	Ingrid Auerswald	41.60	Germany	1980 Moscow
	Marlies Göhr	41.60	Germany	1980 Moscow
4x400m Relay	Tatyana Ledovskaya	3:15.17	USSR	1988 Seoul
	Olga Nazarova	3:15.17	USSR	1988 Seoul
	Mariya Pinigina	3:15.17	USSR	1988 Seoul
	Olga Bryzgina	3:15.17	USSR	1988 Seoul
20km Walk	Olga Kaniskina	1:26:31	Russia	2008 Beijing
High Jump	Yelena Slesarenko	2.06 m	Russia	2004 Athens
Long Jump	Jackie Joyner-Kersee	7.40 m	U.S.	1988 Seoul
Pole Vault	Yelena Isinbayeva	5.05 m	Russia	2008 Beijing
Triple Jump	Françoise Mbango Etone	15.39 m	Cameroon	2008 Beijing
Shot Put	Ilona Slupianek	22.41 m	Germany	1980 Moscow
Discus Throw	Martina Hellmann	72.30 m	Germany	1988 Seoul
Hammer Throw	Aksana Miankova	76.34 m	Belarus	2008 Beijing
Javelin Throw	Osleidys Menendez	71.53 m	Cuba	2004 Athens
Heptathlon	Jackie Joyner-Kersee	7291	U.S.	1988 Seoul

Who won the first-ever women's athletics event held in the Olympics?

When American Betty Robinson ran in the 100m race at 1928 Olympics it marked the very first time a women's athletics competition was held in the Games. For the 16-year-old Robinson, who had been discovered only four months earlier by a high-school track coach who noted how fast she was when he saw her running for a train, the Olympic appearance was only the fourth time she'd run the 100m race. Robinson won the race by half a metre, equalling the world record. She also earned a silver that year in the 4x100m relay.

What remarkable comeback did Betty Robinson achieve in the 1936 Summer Games?

In 1931, three years after Betty Robinson had won gold in the 100m race at the Amsterdam Olympics, she was badly injured in an airplane crash. The man who found her thought she was dead, so he put her in the trunk of his car and drove to a mortuary, where his mistake was discovered. Robinson spent eleven weeks in a hospital with severe head injuries and a broken leg and arm. A metal rod and pin were inserted to stabilize the leg, which was placed in a hip-to-heel cast. For four months, she was in a wheelchair or on crutches, and the leg became a half-inch shorter. Robinson wanted to return to competitive sprinting, but she was no longer able to bend her leg fully at the knee, so she could not assume the crouched starting position. She could, however, run in relays because only the starting runner had to crouch. In 1936, at the Los Angeles Olympic Games, Robinson appeared with fellow Americans Harriet Bland, Annette Rogers, and Helen Stephens in the 4x100m relay, running the third leg. The quartet captured the gold when a member of the record-setting and heavily favoured German team fumbled the baton pass before the last hand-off. Robinson's comeback remains one of the most remarkable in Olympic history.

Why did it take 48 years for a particular Canadian woman to win an Olympic race?

The winner of the women's 100m race at the 1932 Los Angeles Olympics was a Polish athlete named Stanislawa Walasiewicz. The silver medallist was Canadian Hilde Strike. In 1980, when the Polish gold medallist was tragically killed as an innocent bystander during a bank robbery, the ensuing autopsy discovered that *she* was a *he*, and Strike was ultimately declared the winner.

Who was the first black African to win gold?

It was Abebe Bikila, and he ran barefoot. Yes, literally. The Ethiopian long-distance runner became the first black African to win gold in the Olympics when he won the 1960 marathon at the Summer Games in Rome. Bikila returned to the Olympics in 1964 — this time with shoes and socks — to do it again, taking a clear lead by the halfway mark and steadily pulling away to win by more than four minutes. His time, 2 hours 12 minutes 11.2 seconds, marked not only a world record for the marathon, but also the first time anyone had ever won the race twice.

Why were Tommie Smith and John Carlos expelled from the Olympic Village at the Summer Games in 1968?

1968 was a tumultuous year for the U.S. The military was engaged in a deeply unpopular conflict in Vietnam. Anti-war and civil rights protests raged across the U.S., resulting in violent and lethal clashes between police and civilians. Both Martin Kuther King Jr. and Senator Bobby Kennedy were both assassinated. To add to the trouble, at the Summer Olympics in Mexico, American runners Tommie Smith and John Carlos — the gold and bronze medal winners in the 200m race — raised black-gloved fists and hung their heads when their country's national anthem was played during the medal presentation ceremony. Their "Black Power" salute was made to protest racial segregation in the U.S. The two were subsequently expelled from the Olympic Village, having been accused by the International Olympic Committee of politicizing the event.

What is the "Fosbury flop"?

At the 1968 Summer Games in Mexico, American high jumper David Fosbury revolutionized the event, debuting a new technique that would come to be known as the "Fosbury flop". Prior to 1968, Olympic high jumpers used a scissor kick motion to clear the bar. Fosbury innovated the method — now extremely popular — of using a twisting, backwards, head-first dive to clear the bar. Fosbury not only took the gold in high jump that year, but also beat the Olympic record by a full 6 centimetres with his winning jump of 2.24 metres. By the 1980 Games in Moscow, 13 of the 16 Olympic high jump finalists were using the Fosbury flop.

Why was the Olympic flag raised exactly 15.21 metres at the Tokyo Olympics in 1964?

The first time the Olympics were held in Asia was 1964, when Tokyo hosted the Games. At the opening ceremony, the Olympic Flag was raised exactly 15.21 metres to commemorate another first. In 1928 Mikio Oda, of Hiroshima Prefecture in Japan, became Asia's first Olympic champion in an individual event when he edged Levi Casey of the United States by four centimetres to win the gold medal in the triple jump at the Amsterdam Olympics. Thirty-six years later, when the Olympics were held in Tokyo, the Olympic flag was raised to a height of 15.21 metres to honour the exact distance of Oda's gold-medal Olympic jump.

> **Quickies**
> *Did you know ...*
> that Chuhei Nambu, who won gold in the triple jump and bronze in the long jump at the 1932 Los Angeles Olympic Games, was once banned from a department store in his home city of Sapporo, in northern Japan? Nambu tried to practice indoors during the winter and he would do his workouts by weaving among the store's customers while running up and down the stairs. The store's management was not impressed.

How much faster can a man run the 100m event since the first Olympics?

An American named Thomas Burke won the first gold medal in the 100m race at the first modern Olympics in Athens, Greece, in 1896 with a time of exactly 12 seconds. Another American, Justin Gatlin, won with a time of 9.85 seconds in 2004 in Barcelona, Spain. The best time ever recorded in the Olympic 100m event was in Seoul Korea in 1988 by Canadian Ben Johnson, who posted a time of 9.79 seconds. He was later disqualified after testing positive for steroid use. Ben Johnson has recently been seen on Canadian television, in advertisements for an energy drink called "Cheetah."

Though not an Olympic record, in May of 2008, Jamaican sprinter Usain Bolt set a new 100m world record — with a time of 9.72 seconds — while competing in the Reebok Grand Prix in New York.

> **Quickies**
> *Did you know ...*
> that in the 1904 games, American Alvin Kraenzlein won the 60m, 110m, and 200m hurdles, as well as the long jump? His record of four individual victories at one Olympic Games still stands for a track and field athlete.

Who were the first Africans to compete in the modern Olympics?

In the 1904 games in Chicago, marathon runners Len Tau and Jan Mashiani, Tswana tribesmen who were in St. Louis as part of the Boer War exhibit at the World's Fair, became the first Africans to compete in the Olympics.

Why was Fred Lorz disqualified from the 1904 marathon?

At the St. Louis Olympic Games of 1904 the marathon race was staged on a sweltering afternoon over such a hilly course that only 14 of the 32 runners managed to finish. One of them was American Fred Lorz. First in, after 3 hours 13 minutes, Lorz was proclaimed winner and had already been photographed with Alice Roosevelt, the daughter of the President Roosevelt, and was about to be given the gold medal, when it was exposed that he had travelled much of the race route as the passenger in a car. Lorz was disqualified and Fellow American Thomas Hicks was awarded the gold.

Who did the King of Sweden call "The greatest athlete in the world."?

At the 1912 Olympics in Stockholm, American Jim Thorpe won both the pentathlon and decathlon by huge margins, setting world records in both events. At the awards ceremony, Gustav V, King of Sweden, told Thorpe, "Sir, you are the greatest athlete in the world." But the following year Thorpe's name was struck from the roll of Olympic champions after it was revealed that he had earlier been paid for playing minor league baseball. The amount involved was only $15 U.S. per week, but at that time the Olympics followed strict rules of amateurism. It was not until 1982 that the IOC reversed its decision and returned Thorpe's medals, posthumously, to his family. Born with the Sac-and-Fox Indian name Wa-tho-huck, meaning "Bright Path", Thorpe attended Carlisle Indian School, where he established an awesome reputation as a football running back, being voted

All-American in 1911 and 1912. He later played professional football for the Canton Bulldogs and was actually the first President of the National Football League, although the title was largely ceremonial. Thorpe also played major league baseball for the New York Giants, Boston Braves, and Cincinnati Reds.

Who was the "Buckeye Bullet"?

American Jesse Owens was the son of sharecroppers and the grandson of slaves. He was also one of the greatest Olympic champions in history. Given his prowess on the running track and in the long-jump, Owens would likely have shone brightly at any Olympic games, but the fact that he appeared in the 1936 Games cemented his name in history. The 1936 Games were, of course, the "Nazi Olympics" held in Berlin during Hitler's Third Reich. It was Hitler's twisted belief that the Berlin Olympics would demonstrate the superiority of the Aryan race. Never before or since has such an offence to the Olympic spirit been committed.

But Owens' performance at those games would shame Hitler in front of the world. It all started before the Games, on May 25, 1935, when Owens, 22, broke five world records and equaled a sixth in the space of 45 minutes in Ann Arbor, Michigan, at the Big Ten Championships, America's Division I college athletic conference. At Owens' school, Ohio State, athletes are called "Buckeyes" after the state tree, and Owens was known as the "Buckeye Bullet" because of his speed. It was obvious to all that the young student was headed for the Olympics. Indeed, Owens later qualified for the U.S. Olympic team in both sprints and the long jump. In Berlin, before Hitler and a stadium crowd of over 100,000, he began by equaling the Olympic record in the first round of the 100m race. In the final, he led from the first stride and held off the closing rush of fellow American Ralph Metcalfe to win by one metre. Owens barely qualified for the final of the long jump, but once there he won the gold medal easily, as no one could beat any of his three best jumps. The next day, Owens effortlessly pulled away from the field to win the 200m by four metres. This earned him his third gold medal in three days. Four days later, Owens ran the leadoff leg for the U.S. team in the 4x100m relay. The quartet set a world record that would last for 20 years. Adolf Hitler and the Nazis had hoped that the 1936 Olympics would prove their vile theories of racial superiority, but Jesse Owens had other plans.

Why did Olympic athletes Susi Santi and Allan Budi Kusuma receive a two hour parade in Jakarta in 1992?

Indonesians have been competing in the Olympics since 1952, but up until 1992, they managed to take home just one medal: silver, won by their women's archery team in 1988. However, when badminton was added to the Olympic roster at the Barcelona Games of 1992, all that changed. That year alone, Indonesians took home six badminton medals, including one bronze, three silvers, and two golds. Those golds were won by Susi Santi, in women's singles, and Allan Budi Kusuma, in men's singles, and because they were the first-ever gold medals won by Indonesia, the couple — who were engaged to be married — received a two-hour parade through the streets of Jakarta upon their return home.

Indonesia's Complete Olympic Medal Record

Sport	Gold	Silver	Bronze
Badminton	7	6	7
Weightlifting	0	2	4
Archery	0	1	0

Who holds the record for fastest shuttlecock smash?

The badminton smash is a shot hit with power and speed downward into the opponent's court. It can be done either forehand or backhand and oftentimes incorporates a jump by the player into the air to add force. It can send the shuttlecock hurtling at astonishing velocities. Indeed, the fastest shuttlecock smash on record was hit by men's doubles player Fu Haifeng of China, who set the official world record of 332 km/h (206 mph) on June 3, 2005, in the Sudirman Cup. Along with partner Cai Yun, the powerful Fu Haifeng took silver in Men's Doubles at the 2008 Beijing Olympics.

Has any athlete from outside Asia ever won a gold medal in badminton?

Ever since badminton was introduced to the Olympic Games in 1992, only one gold medal in the sport has ended up outside Asia, with Denmark's Paul-Erik Hoyer-Larsen winning the men's singles in Atlanta in 1996.

Top Olympic Badminton Medal Winners by Country Since 1992

Rank	Nation	Gold	Silver	Bronze	Total
1	China	11	6	13	30
2	South Korea	6	7	4	17
3	Indonesia	6	6	6	18
4	Denmark	1	1	2	4
5	Malaysia	0	2	2	4
6	Great Britain	0	1	1	2
7	Netherlands	0	1	0	1
Total		24	24	28	76

When did baseball become an Olympic sport?

Prior to the Barcelona Summer Games of 1992, baseball had been played at 12 Olympics as a demonstration sport. As of 1992, it was decided by the International Olympic Committee to eliminate all demonstration sports from the Games and baseball was elevated to an official Olympic sport. It was not until 2000 in Sydney that professional players were allowed to participate. Softball was introduced in Atlanta in 1996.

Why did the U.S., the birthplace of baseball, not dominate the sport at the Olympics?

Of the five gold medals available in the history of Olympic baseball after it became an official sport, Cuba has taken three, while the U.S. has taken only one (South Korea took the other). You would have thought the U.S. should have dominated Olympic baseball, but the problem was that prior to 2000, professional players were not allowed to compete, and after 2000, Major League Baseball refused to build an Olympic break into their season so that the pros could play in the Games. The U.S. did manage to take gold in 2000, but their team was made up of minor leaguers, many of who would eventually play for Major League Baseball.

Olympic Baseball Medal Rank by Country

Rank	Country	Gold	Silver	Bronze	Total
1	Cuba	3	2	0	5
2	United States	1	0	2	3
3	Japan	0	1	2	3
4	South Korea	1	0	1	2
5	Australia	0	1	0	1
6	Chinese Taipei	0	1	0	1

How many games have American softball teams lost at the Olympics?

Softball became an official Olympic sport at the Barcelona games in 1996 and the Americans dominated the gold platform until 2008. Out of 37 games played over four Olympics, the American women lost just five games. The only loss that really mattered, however, was the last one, in which Japan, by winning 3–1, unseated the champions in the final at the 2008 Beijing Games. Japan's win not only forced the Americans to have to settle for softball silver for the first time in the Olympics, but also broke a 22-game American winning streak.

Why was the score of the first Olympic basketball final so low?

Basketball was introduced to the Olympics in Berlin in 1936 with teams representing 23 countries. By today's standards, scores in the tournament were remarkably low. There was good reason. The International Basketball Federation, which is the governing body of international basketball, used the 1936 tournament to experiment with outdoor basketball. Rather than cement courts, lawn tennis courts were used for the competition. This caused problems when the weather was adverse, especially during the final game, which was played in a rainstorm. Unable to dribble the ball, players had to be content to play a passing game, and the end result saw the U.S. taking gold over Canada with a score of just 19–8.

Olympic Softball Results by Year

Year	Gold	Silver	Bronze
2008	Japan	United States	Australia
2004	United States	Australia	Japan
2000	United States	Japan	Australia
1996	United States	China	Australia

In the 1936 Olympics, why did the Polish basketball team win their fourth-round game against Peru with a score of just 2–0?

That would be because the Peruvian athletes were on their way home. It all began on the soccer pitch. In the quarter-finals of the soccer tournament, Peru rallied from a two-goal deficit in the final 15 minutes of normal time to tie the game. During extra-time, Peru scored twice and won, 4–2. However, Austria protested that Peruvian players had manhandled them, and that spectators, one brandishing a revolver, had swarmed down on the field before the game was over. Officials ordered a replay without any spectators, but Peru refused and their entire Olympic squad, from every sport, left Berlin in protest.

When the basketball game against Poland came around, since Peru didn't show up, all Poland had to do was sink a single basket for a walkover.

Why has the American basketball team from the 1972 Olympics never accepted their silver medals?

The final of the men's basketball tournament at the 1972 Olympics was a time keeper's nightmare. With three seconds left on the clock, American guard Doug Collins had just sunk his second of two free throws to give his team a lead of 50–49 over Cold War rivals USSR. But as play resumed, the Soviet coach protested that he had legally called for a time out between Collins' two free throws, and indeed, video tape reveals that a time out horn had sounded between the two foul shots but it had been ignored by officials. Play was stopped with just one second remaining and officials decided to restore three seconds to the clock. However, play was restarted by the referee before the clock could be properly reset and as the Soviets inbounded the ball and attempted to make a pass down court, the scorer's table sounded the horn again to try to stop play. The Americans misinterpreted this horn as the signal for the end of the game and began celebrating, but officials insisted that the three seconds still had to be restored to the clock. The game was not over. Once the clock was properly reset, Soviet player Ivan Edshko inbound the ball with a court-length pass to teammate Aleksander Belov, who made a lay up to score the winning basket for the Soviets. The American team, convinced that they had won the game, refused to accept their silver medals and have never relented.

Why did Canadian basketball player Toots Meretsky not receive his silver medal at the 1936 Olympics?

In the first-ever Olympic basketball tournament at the 1936 Games in Berlin, the Canadian basketball team won silver. It remains the only time a Canadian basketball team have taken a medal at the Olympics. But player Irving "Toots," who passed away in 2006, didn't receive a medal at those games because there were nine players on the Canadian squad and the Berlin officials had only prepared eight medals. It was not until 1996, on the sixtieth anniversary of the Berlin Games, that his family contacted the IOC, who had a silver medal cast for Toots from the original mold.

What was the "Dream Team"?

For the 1992 Summer Olympics in Barcelona, the International Olympic Committee relaxed the rules and, for the first time, allowed NBA players to participate in basketball. The U.S. assembled a line up dubbed the "Dream Team" because of their superstar status. The team swept their way to gold in six games defeating all opponents by a margin of at least 32 points and averaging 117 points per game.

Canada's 1936 Olympic Silver Basketball Team

Player	Games Played	Points Scored
Doug Peden	5	42
Art Chapman	6	39
James Stewart	6	27
Al Allison	6	26
Gordon Aitchison	6	20
Malcolm Wiseman	6	12
Chuck Chapman	4	4
Irving "Toots" Meretsky	2	4
Edward Dawson	1	0

Why did controversy swirl around Spain's Olympic basketball teams in 2008?

Spain's men's and women's basketball teams came under fire during the 2008 Summer Olympics in Beijing after photos surfaced that were interpreted by many people as offensive to the Chinese people. The pictures, some of which were made for a Spanish courier company that sponsors the teams, showed Spanish basketball team members pushing the sides of their eyes back with their index fingers to mimic the stereotype of Asian eye shape. Spanish NBA players Pao Gascol and Jose Calderon, both of whom were on Spain's Olympic squad, as well as Jose Luis Saez, the head of the Spanish Basketball Federation, said that the photos were not racist, but meant as a gesture of affection towards the Chinese people.

The 1992 Dream Team's Olympic Stats

Athlete	Age	Games played	Points	Rebounds	Assists
Charles Barkley	29	8	144	33	19
Michael Jordan	29	8	119	9	38
Karl Malone	29	8	104	42	9
Chris Mullin	28	8	103	13	29
Clyde Drexler	30	8	84	24	29
Patrick Ewing	29	8	76	42	3
Scottie Pippen	26	8	72	17	47
David Robinson	26	8	72	33	7
Larry Bird	35	8	67	30	14
Earvin "Magic" Johnson	32	6	48	14	33
Christian Laettner	22	8	38	20	3
John Stockton	30	4	11	1	8

Who was László Papp?

László Papp was undoubtedly one of the greatest fighters to have ever stepped into the Olympic boxing ring. After winning the Olympic middleweight title in 1948, Hungary's Papp won the light-middleweight contests in both 1952 and 1956 to become the first boxer to win three Olympic gold medals — something only two others have done since. His finest moment in the Olympic ring came in the 1956 final when he beat American José Torres, a future world professional champion. A skillful, hard-punching southpaw, Papp was the first fighter from the Soviet bloc allowed to turn professional and he won the European middleweight title in 1962. However, in 1965, the Hungarian authorities withdrew their permission for him to fight professionally and the chance of a world title bout was denied him. Papp later served as the coach of the Hungarian national boxing team from 1971–92.

Quickies
Did you know ...
that boxing was not part of the 1912 Stockholm games because Swedish laws banned the sport?

Quickies
Did you know ...
that Olympic boxers are assigned opponents in their weight class through random selection?

Who is Teófilo Stevenson?

Cuban Teófilo Stevenson cemented his place in boxing history by becoming the first fighter to win the gold medal in the same division three times, and only the second fighter ever to take home three golds. Competing in what is now known as the super-heavyweight division, Stevenson began his Olympic career at the 1972 Munich Games. That year he met American Duane Bobick in the quarterfinals delivering a TKO to the

American in the third round. Advancing to the semifinals, Stephenson faced Peter Hussing of Germany, who later called Stephenson's punch the hardest he'd felt in over 200 bouts. Stevenson earned a TKO in the second round of that fight and went on to take gold by a walkover when his final round opponent forfeited due to a broken thumb. At the 1976 Montreal Games, Stevenson was in peak form, disposing of his first three opponents in just 7 minutes and 22 seconds. In the final, Mircea Simion of Romania managed to make it to the third round before his handlers threw in the towel, giving Stephenson a second gold. Stevenson won his third gold four years later in Moscow by defeating Pyotr Zayev of the USSR with a 4–1 decision in the final. Zayev was only the second Olympic boxer to have ever gone a full three rounds against Stephenson.

Who is Félix Savón?

Cuban heavyweight boxer Félix Savón made his Olympic debut at the 1988 Games in Barcelona — but he arrived in Spain with a thoroughbred's record, having won the amateur world title in 1986, 1989, and 1991. After taking gold at Barcelona, he went on to do the same at the 1996 Games in Atlanta and at the 2000 Games in Sydney to join his countryman Teófilo Stevenson and Hungarian László Papp in the elite group of the only boxers to have ever won three Olympic championships.

What is the Val Barker Cup?

Named after the first Honorary Secretary of the *Federation Internationale de Boxe Amateur* (FIBA), the Val Barker Trophy is awarded by FIBA — the world governing body for amateur boxing — to the boxer who shows the best style and is the most proficient at the Olympic Games. The award, first given out in 1936, is voted on by the members of FIBA's executives that are in attendance at Olympic matches.

Have any Canadians won gold in Olympic boxing?

Canada has seen three boxers emerge from the Olympic ring as gold-medal champions. The first was Bert Schneider, from Montreal, who fought in the welterweight division at the 1920 games in Antwerp. Schneider defeated four opponents over the space of three days, defeating Britain's Alexander Ireland in the final. The second Canadian gold-winning boxer was Horace "Lefty" Gwynne, from Toronto, who defeated three opponents to take the Olympic bantamweight tile at the 1932 Games in Los Angeles. The third, and most famous, Canadian gold medallist in boxing is super-heavyweight Lennox Lewis, from Kitchener, Ontario, who took the championship in his division at the Seoul Games in 1988. Lewis went on to win the professional world heavyweight title in 1993.

Val Barker Trophy Winners

- **Louis Laurie** (U.S.): flyweight, bronze, 1936
- **George Hunter** (South Africa): light heavyweight, gold, 1948
- **Norvel Lee** (U.S.): light heavyweight, gold, 1952
- **Richard McTaggart** (United Kingdom): lightweight, gold, 1956
- **Nino Benvenuti** (Italy): welterweight, gold, 1960
- **Valery Popenchenko** (Soviet Union): middleweight, gold, 1964
- **Philip Waruinge** (Kenya): featherweight, bronze, 1968
- **Téofilo Stevenson** (Cuba): heavyweight, gold, 1972
- **Howard Davis** (U.S.): lightweight, gold, 1976
- **Patrizio Oliva** (Italy): light welterweight, gold, 1980
- **Paul Gonzales** (U.S.): light flyweight, gold, 1984
- **Roy Jones** (U.S.): light middleweight, silver, 1988
- **Roberto Balado** (Cuba): super heavyweight, gold, 1992
- **Vassily Zhirov** (Kazakhstan): light heavyweight, gold, 1996
- **Oleg Saitov** (Russia): welterweight, gold, 2000
- **Bakhtiyar Artayev** (Kazakhstan): welterweight, gold, 2004
- **Bakhtiyar Artayev** (Kazakhstan): welterweight, gold, 2004
- **Vasyi Lomachenko** (Ukraine): featherweight, gold

Who did Cassius Clay defeat to win gold?

On September 5th at the Rome Olympics of 1960, a young boxer named Cassius Marcellus Clay, who would later change his name to Muhammad Ali and become one of the greatest competitors the sport has ever seen, stepped into the ring against a formidable opponent for the final bout. Veteran Polish light-heavyweight Zbigniew Pietrzykowski was ten years Clay's senior and had by then already won three European Amateur Championships — 1955, 1957, and 1959. By the end of the fight, however, the 18-year-old Clay had shown the world what he was made of, defeating Pietrzykowski 5–0 with a third round that left the Pole bloodied and reeling against the ropes.

Quickies
Did you know ...
that Muhammad Ali has said that he threw his Olympic gold medal into the Ohio River after being refused service in a "whites only" restaurant?

Medal Record for Canoeist Birgit Fischer-Schmidt				
Games	Age	Event	Team	Medal
1980, Moscow	18	Women's Kayak Singles, 500m	East Germany	Gold
1988, Seoul	26	Women's Kayak Singles, 500m	East Germany	Silver
1988, Seoul	26	Women's Kayak Doubles, 500m	East Germany	Gold
1988, Seoul	26	Women's Kayak Fours, 500m	East Germany	Gold
1992, Barcelona	30	Women's Kayak Singles, 500m	Germany	Gold
1992, Barcelona	30	Women's Kayak Fours, 500m	Germany	Silver
1996, Atlanta	34	Women's Kayak Singles, 500m	Germany	4th
1996, Atlanta	34	Women's Kayak Doubles, 500m	Germany	Silver
1996, Atlanta	34	Women's Kayak Fours, 500m	Germany	Gold
2000, Sydney	38	Women's Kayak Doubles, 500m	Germany	Gold
2000, Sydney	38	Women's Kayak Fours, 500m	Germany	Gold
2004, Athens	42	Women's Kayak Doubles, 500m	Germany	Silver
2004, Athens	42	Women's Kayak Fours, 500m	Germany	Gold

Who is the Olympic canoeist with the most medals?

The all time top medal winner on Olympic canoeing and kayaking — and one of the greatest athletes to have ever competed in the Games — is Germany's Birgit Fischer-Schmidt. Her 12 medals — eight gold and four silver — in the sport place her second in the all-time Olympic medal race, behind Soviet gymnast Larisa Latynina, who won 18 medals total.

Who was Kolo?

With a record of 19 gold medals, 27 silvers, and 25 bronzes Hungary holds the title for most Olympic medals outright in canoeing and kayaking (though it should be noted that Germany and the Soviet Union each have 29 golds). The greatest Hungarian canoeist was György Kolonics, whose nickname was Kolo. In addition to his two Olympic gold medals and two bronzes, Kolo won 14 world canoeing championships between 1993 and 2007. On July 15, while training in Budapest for the Beijing Games, Kolo died of heart failure. His doubles partner György Kozmann wore a black arm band in his honour at the Beijing Games, paddling to a bronze medal win in the 1,000m race with Tamás Kiss taking Kolo's place.

Quickies

Did you know ...

that after losing the men's doubles 500m race by just 0.032 seconds at the 1996 Olympics in Atlanta, Italian canoeist Beniamino Bonomi took no chances at the 2000 Sydney Games and shaved off his left sideburn for good luck? The strategy paid off as Bonomi and partner Antoni Rossi paddled to gold in the 1,000m doubles race that year.

How did Canadian cyclist Clara Hughes win gold in the Winter Olympics?

Canadian cyclist Clara Hughes made her Olympic debut competing in the road race and time trail competition at the 1996 Games in Atlanta. She took bronze in both events, finishing the 104.4km road race just 31 one-hundredths of a second behind French gold medallist Jeannie Longo-Ciprelli. When Hughes rode in the same events in the Sydney Games of 2000 and did not take any medals, it would be the last time she'd appear in the Summer Olympics — though not the last time she'd appear in the Olympics. In 2001, Hughes took up speed skating and, after just seven weeks of training, made the Canadian team and accompanied them to the 2002 Winter Olympics in Salt Lake City, where she garnered bronze in the 5,000m race. She wasn't done yet. Hughes donned the skates once more for the Turin Winter Olympics in 2006 where she upgraded her medal standing first to silver, coming in second with fellow Canucks in the team pursuit, and then to gold, finishing a full second ahead of the pack in the 5,000m race.

Quickies

Did you know ...

that only two athletes have ever won multiple medals at both the Winter and Summer Olympics: Germany's Christa Luding Rothenburger and Canada's Clara Hughes? Both did it in cycling and speed skating.

The Top 10 Olympic Canoeing and Kayaking Countries

Rank	Country	Gold	Silver	Bronze	Total
1	Hungary	19	27	25	71
2	Germany	29	19	18	66
3	Soviet Union	29	13	9	51
4	Romania	10	10	14	34
5	France	5	8	18	31
6	Sweden	15	11	4	30
7	East Germany	14	7	9	30
8	Canada	4	9	8	21
9	Australia	2	7	11	20
10	Bulgaria	4	5	8	17

Medals won by Clara Hughes, Canada's Cycling Skater

Games	Discipline	Events	Medal
Atlanta 1996	Cycling Road	Individual road race	Bronze
Atlanta 1996	Cycling Road	Individual time trial	Bronze
Salt Lake City 2002	Speed skating	5,000m Women	Bronze
Turin 2006	Speed skating	Team pursuit Women	Silver
Turin 2006	Speed skating	5,000m Women	Gold

What woman cyclist has raced in the most consecutive Olympic Games?

France has given the world some legendary cyclists, but on the Olympic stage, none match the special achievement of Jeannie Longo-Ciprelli. She made her first appearance in the Games in 1984 at Los Angeles at age 25, where she finished sixth in the women's individual road race. Since then, she has competed in every Summer Olympics, picking up one gold, two silvers, and one bronze along the way. She made her most recent appearance in the women's individual time trial on August 13, 2008, in Beijing at the tender age of 49. She came in fourth, missing the medal podium by just 1.63 seconds. The next oldest person in the race was 38-year-old fifth-place finisher Christie Thorburn. Jeannie Longo-Ciprelli may not have the highest medal standing ever, but with eight consecutive Olympic appearances to her credit, there is little doubt that she is one of history's greatest — and most durable — Olympic cyclists.

Women's Olympic Cycling Records

Event	Result	Name	Country	Games
Sprint individual	10.963	Victoria Pendleton	UK	2008 Beijing
Individual pursuit	3:24.537	Sarah Ulmer	New Zealand	2004 Athens

Who was Paul Nassom?

For reasons unknown, after winning three gold medals at the 1896 Olympics, French cyclist Paul Masson turned his surname backwards and competed on the professional cycling circuit as Paul Nassom. He placed third in the world professional sprint championship in 1897.

Quickies

Did you know ...
that France holds the most gold medals in Olympic cycling, with 41? Italy is second, with 36, and Great Britain third, with 20.

Quickies

Did you know ...
that French cyclist Léon Flameng, who won gold, silver, and bronze medals at the 1896 Olympics, became a sergeant-pilot with France's 2nd Aviation Group during WWI? He was killed in action when his parachute failed to open.

What inspired British cyclist Chris Hoy to take up the sport?

When cyclist Chris Hoy won gold in the team sprint, the 1,000m sprint, and the keirin race at the 2008 Beijing Olympics, the three wins added to his 2004 Athens gold for the 1,000m time trial to make him the most successful gold medallist in Olympic men's cycling history. Only one other person holds four Olympic cycling golds, and that is Dutchwoman Leontien Zijlaard-van

Moorsel. Hoy, who also won a silver medal at the 2000 Sydney Olympics in the team sprint event, told London's Telegraph newspaper that he was inspired to first take up bicycling at the age of six after seeing the BMX scenes in Steven Spielberg's movie *E.T. The Extraterrestrial*. As a teen, Hoy was a top-rated BMX racer in England.

> **Quickies**
> *Did you know ...*
> that Dutchwoman Leontien Zijlaard-van Moorsel, who holds the record for most Olympic Cycling medals, with four golds, one silver, and one bronze, once suffered from anorexia?

What was the last event competed in the first modern Olympics, held in Athens in 1896?

It was the last event, and the last time the event would be held in the Olympics. The Games of the I Olympiad culminated in the grueling men's 12-hour cycling track race. Of the seven cyclists who began the race, only two had the endurance to finish: Austrian Adolf Schmal, who took gold, and Great Britian's Frederick Keeping. Schmal's winning tactic was to lap all the other cyclists by the tenth lap, after which he refused to budge from the pack.

> **Quickies**
> *Did you know ...*
> that Victor Johnson, the Olympic gold medallist in the 660 yard sprints held at the London games of 1908 (the only Olympics at which this race would be held), was the son of a bicycle maker who built England's first unicycles?

What is the longest race ever held in the Olympics?

The 1912 Stockholm games presented cyclists with a major endurance test. The course for the cycling road race was 320 km, and it remains the longest race of any kind in Olympic history.

> **Quickies**
> *Did you know ...*
> that Austria's gold-medal cyclist Adolf Schmal did double duty at the 1896 Olympics, also competing in fencing?

Men's Olympic Cycling Records

Event	Result	Name	Country	Games
Sprint individual	9.815	Chris Hoy	UK	2008 Beijing
Individual pursuit	4:15.031	Bradley Wiggins	UK	2008 Beijing
Team pursuit (4,000m)	3:53.314	Ed Clancy	UK	2008 Beijing
		Paul Manning	UK	2008 Beijing
		Geraint Thomas	UK	2008 Beijing
		Bradley Wiggins	UK	2008 Beijing

When did BMX become an Olympic sport?

BMX, which stands for bicycle moto-cross, made its Olympic debut at the 2008 Games in Beijing. The Men's competition saw 32 riders competing, with world champion Māris Štrombergs, of Latvia, taking gold. The women's contest saw 16 entrants, with France's Anne-Caroline Chausson emerging as champion.

The First-Ever Olympic BMX Medallists, from Beijing 2008

Men

Athlete	Age	Team	Medal
Māris Štrombergs	21	Latvia	Gold
Mike Day	23	United States	Silver
Donny Robinson	25	United States	Bronze

Women

Athlete	Age	Team	Medal
Anne-Caroline Chausson	30	France	Gold
Laetitia le Corguille	22	France	Silver
Jill Kintner	26	United States	Bronze

Why are the official host cities of the 1956 Summer Olympics listed as Melbourne and Stockholm?

The official host of the 1956 Summer Olympics was the Australian city of Melbourne. It was the first time the Olympics had gone to Oz. Unfortunately for equestrian athletes, there was to be no trip "down under" as Australian quarantine laws were so strict that the Olympic horses were not permitted in the country without a 6-month quarantine. This was impractical for the athletes and horses, so it was decided to contest separate Olympic Equestrian Games in Europe, where most of the athletes lived. That June, a mini-Olympics of sorts took place in Stockholm, Sweden, complete with an opening ceremony led by King Gustav VI Adolf and the Olympic torch and flame. This was the only time in the history of the modern Olympics that unity of time and place, as stipulated in the Olympic Charter, has not been observed.

What does "dressage" mean?

You've seen those horses at the Olympics that can perform elaborate, elegant movements — trotting sideways, prancing with various gaits, skipping, walking in place —

all with minimal instruction from their top-hatted riders. Some people call it "horse ballet." Its real name is *dressage*, a French term that means "training" or "breaking in." Through standardized progressive training methods, dressage develops a horse's natural athletic ability and willingness to perform. At the peak of a dressage horse's development, it can respond to a rider's minimal aids by performing requested movements while remaining relaxed and appearing effortless.

Who was the most successful Olympic dressage rider?

With a record six Olympic gold medals and two bronzes, German rider Reiner Klimke was the most successful dressage Olympian ever. In addition, at the time of his death in 1999, Klimke held six World Championship gold medals, as well as eight European Championship golds and one bronze.

Reiner Klimke's Olympic Dressage Dominance

Games	Age	Event	Team	Medal
1964 Tokyo	28	Mixed Dressage, Team	Germany	Gold
1968 Mexico	32	Mixed Dressage, Individual	West Germany	Bronze
1968 Mexico	32	Mixed Dressage, Team	West Germany	Gold
1976 Montreal	40	Mixed Dressage, Individual	West Germany	Bronze
1976 Montreal	40	Mixed Dressage, Team	West Germany	Gold
1984 Los Angeles	48	Mixed Dressage, Individual	West Germany	Gold
1984 Los Angeles	48	Mixed Dressage, Team	West Germany	Gold
1988 Seoul	52	Mixed Dressage, Team	West Germany	Gold

Who were the D'Inzeo brothers?

Italian Olympic equestrian Raimondo D'Inzeo and his brother, Piero, were the first Olympians to compete in eight Olympic Games, a mark since equaled by only five Olympians. The sibling show jumpers appeared in every Summer Games between 1948 and 1976. During that time the younger Raimondo tallied two silver medals, three bronzes, and one gold. His gold was for the individual show jumping event at the 1960 Games in Rome, where brother Piero took silver in the same event. Piero never won gold, but did manage to take home one more silver and four bronzes in his Olympic career.

Why was Canadian equestrian Eric Lamaze twice banned from Olympic competition for life?

Show jumper Eric Lamaze had a wild ride getting to Olympic gold. Prior to the 1996 Games in Atlanta, Lamaze tested positive for cocaine use and was disqualified from competition. In July 2000, prior to the Sydney Games, he tested positive for use of the banned substances pseudoephedrine and ephedrine. Under Olympic rules, the second strike brought an automatic lifetime suspension. But the ban would not stick. The pseudoephedrine, which came from an Advil cold remedy, was not enough alone to warrant a ban. And the ephedrine, it turned out, had been an unlisted ingredient in a dietary supplement Lamaze had used. Because he didn't know he'd taken it, the ban was lifted that August. But when Lamaze tested again a few days later, cocaine was once again found in his system and the Canadian Centre for Ethics in Sport slapped him with his second lifetime ban. Through arbitration, Lamaze was eventually reinstated and at the Beijing Games in 2008 he finally got his Olympic chance. He brought home silver in the team jumping competition and gold in the individual.

What is capsaicin?

Did you ever eat a chilli pepper? That painful burning sensation in your mouth is caused by capsaicin, a compound in the peppers that acts as an irritant on the skin. It may seem counterintuitive, but capsaicin is used as an ointment in equestrian show jumping to

Horses Ejected from the Beijing Games for Doping			
Horse	**Rider**	**Country**	**Dope**
Lantinus	Denis Lynch	Ireland	capsaicin
Camiro	Tony Andre Hansen	Norway	capsaicin
Chupa Chup	Bernardo Alves	Brazil	capsaicin
Coster	Christian Ahlmann	Germany	capsaicin

numb pain in the legs of horses. How does it do that? When capsaicin comes in contact with a nerve, it stimulates the release of a chemical called "substance P," which transmits the nervous signal for pain to the brain. Repeated applications of capsaicin depletes the nerve's stores of substance P, and halts the transmission of the pain signal. Therefore capsaicin is a banned substance in Olympic competition.

Who was "Disonischenko"?

Boris Onischenko, a half-colonel of the KGB from Ukraine, entered the 1976 Olympics in Montreal a respected modern pentathlete who competed for the USSR and had won a silver medal in the individual competition at Munich 1972 games. He exited Montreal in disgrace, however, with headlines around the world denouncing him as "Disonischenko" and "Boris the Cheat". The pentathlon is a five-discipline event that includes fencing, but Onischenko's épée was something of a secret weapon. It had been wired so that he could trigger the electronic scoring system with his hand and register a hit at will. When Jim Fox, the British pentathlon team's captain and a sergeant in the British army, protested during a bout that Onischenko was scoring on him without actually make hits, officials relieved the Soviet athlete of his sword. Onischenko continued with a replacement weapon and still beat Fox, but afterwards he was disqualified because officials discovered the secret trigger in his sword's grip. The Brits went on to win gold in the event.

Has any country's sitting Olympic committee president ever won a medal in competition?

At the 1912 Stockholm games one member of the Austrian team finished second in the team sabre fencing event, taking a silver medal. He was Otto Herschmann, president of the Austrian Olympic Committee. Herschmann is the only sitting national Olympic committee president to have won an Olympic medal.

In fencing, what is the difference between an épée and a foil?

The épée is the duelling sword from days gone by. It is the same length as a foil but the blade is much thicker and is fluted (to allow blood to drain away!). The target in épée is the entire body but points may only be scored with the tip of the weapon in a thrusting motion. The foil was the sword used by duellers to practice their art and is much lighter than the épée. The foil is considered by many to be a weapon of greater finesse and the target area is restricted to just the torso.

What year was soccer introduced in the Olympics?

Both the 1900 and 1904 Olympic games featured men's soccer tournaments as demonstration matches, with three teams competing at each tournament. The IOC has subsequently upgraded the tournaments to official status with medals attributed to the teams based upon the match results, though FIFA does not recognize them as official. In 1908, in London, soccer was an official Olympic game with eight teams competing.

Olympic Soccer Gold-Medal Holders, Ranked By Country

Rank	Country	Gold	Silver	Bronze	Total
1	Hungary	3	1	1	5
2	Great Britain	3	0	0	3
3	Argentina	2	2	0	4
4	Soviet Union	2	0	3	5
5	Uruguay	2	0	0	2
6	Yugoslavia	1	3	1	5
7	Poland and Spain	1	2	0	3
8	East Germany	1	1	2	4
9	Czechoslovakia	1	1	0	2
	France	1	1	0	2
	Nigeria	1	1	0	2
10	Italy and Sweden	1	0	2	3
11	Belgium	1	0	1	2
12	Cameroon and Canada	1	0	0	1

What is the individual scoring record for a single player in an Olympic soccer game?

In 1908 Denmark's Sophus "Krølben" Nielsen set an Olympic record by scoring 10 goals in a 17–1 win against France. His team went on to take the silver in the final against Great Britain. Gottfried Fuchs achieved the same feat scoring 10 goals for Germany against Russia at the 1912 Olympics.

In the 1920 final, why did the Czech team walk from the field of play without finishing the match?

The 1920 Olympic games were held in Antwerp, Belgium, and saw the host nation's soccer team advanced to the final against Czechoslovakia. It was an unruly and violent game. Shortly after Czech left-back Karel Steiner was ejected in the 39th minute for a bad foul, the Czech team walked off the field in protest. They were unhappy with the performance of the 65-year-old English referee, John Lewis, as well as the English linesmen, Charles Wreford-Brown and A. Knight. They were also unnerved by the appearance of Belgian soldiers who surrounded the pitch during the match. Belgium, who led 2–0, took the gold medal by default.

Soccer Teams With the Most Olympic Outings and No Medals

Country	Olympiads Attended
Egypt	10
Mexico	8
South Korea	8
Australia	7
Morroco	6
Turkey	5
Luxembourg	5

What year were professional players first allowed to compete in Olympic soccer?

For the 1984 Los Angeles Games, the IOC decided to admit professional players to Olympic soccer. But a conflict arose with FIFA, who did not want the Olympics to rival the World Cup. A compromise was struck that allowed teams from Africa, Asia, Oceania, and CONCACAF (the Confederation of North, Central American, and Caribbean Association Football) to field their strongest professional players, while only allowing the historically stronger nations in UEFA (Union of European Football Associations) and CONMEBOL (South American Football Confederation) to pick players who had not previously played in a World Cup.

Quickies
Did you know ...
that soccer was the first team sport admitted to the Olympics?

Has the Olympic gold medal in soccer ever been decided in a shootout?

Only once — at the 2000 Sydney Games. On September 30, Pierre Wome of Cameroon scored the winning penalty kick as his team outscored Spain 5–3 in the shootout, after the two teams were tied 2–2 after two overtimes. The following Monday was declared a national holiday by Cameroon's president.

Stadiums to be used for Soccer in the 2012 London Olympic Games

City	Stadium
London	Wembley Stadium
Glasgow	Hampden Park
Cardiff	Millennium Stadium
Manchester	Old Trafford
Newcastle upon Tyne	St. James' Park
Birmingham	Villa Park

When was women's soccer introduced into the Olympics?

Sadly, it was only in 1996 that women's soccer became an official Olympic sport.

Why haven't England, Scotland, Wales, or Northern Ireland fielded women's Olympic Soccer teams?

England and the other three British Home Nations are not eligible to compete as separate entities in women's Olympic soccer because the International Olympic Committee does not recognize their FIFA status as separate nations. As a result, Great Britain has not yet fielded a team.

What is the largest instance of death related to a soccer match?

On May 24, 1964, more than 300 soccer fans died and another 500 were injured in Lima, Peru, in a riot during an Olympic qualifying match between Argentina and Peru.

Men's Olympic Soccer Medallists

Year	Gold	Silver	Bronze
1900	Great Britain	France	Belgium
1904	Canada	United States	
1908	Great Britain	Denmark	Netherlands
1912	Great Britain	Denmark	Netherlands
1920	Belgium	Spain	Netherlands
1924	Uruguay	Switzerland	Sweden
1928	Uruguay	Argentina	Italy
1936	Italy	Austria	Norway
1948	Sweden	Yugoslavia	Denmark
1952	Hungary	Yugoslavia	Sweden
1956	USSR	Yugoslavia	Bulgaria
1960	Yugoslavia	Denmark	Hungary
1964	Hungary	Czechoslovakia	East Germany
1968	Hungary	Bulgaria	Japan
1972	Poland	Hungary	USSR
1976	East Germany	Poland	USSR
1980	Czechoslovakia	East Germany	USSR
1984	France	Brazil	Yugoslavia
1988	USSR	Brazil	West Germany
1992	Spain	Poland	Ghana
1996	Nigeria	Argentina	Brazil
2000	Cameroon	Spain	Chile
2004	Argentina	Paraguay	Italy
2008	Argentina	Nigeria	Brazil

Women's Olympic Soccer Medallists

Year	Gold	Silver	Bronze
1996	United States	China	Norway
2000	Norway	United States	Germany
2004	United States	Brazil	Germany
2008	United States	Brazil	Germany

What Olympian has won the most medals?

Ukraine-born Soviet gymnast Larisa Latynina holds the distinction of having won the most medals of any athlete in Olympic history. Between 1956 and 1964 she competed in 19 Olympic gymnastic events and took a medal in all but one, the balance beam at the 1956 Melbourne games. Her record stands at nine gold medals, five silvers, and four bronzes.

Record Medallist Larisa Latynina's Remarkable Olympic Gymnastics Career			
Games	Age	Event	Finish
1956 Melbourne	21	Floor Exercise	Gold
1956 Melbourne	21	Horse Vault	Gold
1956 Melbourne	21	Uneven Bars	Silver
1956 Melbourne	21	Balance Beam	4th place
1956 Melbourne	21	Individual All-Around	Gold
1956 Melbourne	21	Team All-Around	Gold
1956 Melbourne	21	Team Portable Apparatus	Bronze
1960 Rome	25	Floor Exercise	Gold
1960 Rome	25	Horse Vault	Bronze
1960 Rome	25	Uneven Bars	Silver
1960 Rome	25	Balance Beam	Silver
1960 Rome	25	ndividual All-Around	Gold
1960 Rome	25	Team All-Around	Gold
1964 Tokyo	29	Floor Exercise	Gold
1964 Tokyo	29	Horse Vault	Silver
1964 Tokyo	29	Uneven Bars	Bronze
1964 Tokyo	29	Balance Beam	Bronze
1964 Tokyo	29	Individual All-Around	Silver
1964 Tokyo	29	Team All-Around	Gold

What male athlete has won the most Olympic Medals?

Gymnast Nikolay Andrianov won more Olympic medals than any male athlete in any sport while representing his native Soviet Union and Russia. Between 1972 and 1980 he won seven gold medals (six individual, one team), five silver, and three bronze, for a record total of 15 medals. He won three Olympic medals in 1972, seven in 1976, and five in 1980.

Quickies
Did you know ...
that in the 1904 summer Olympics in Chicago, American gymnast George Eyser took six medals including golds in parallel bars, long horse vault, and rope climbing? It was an accomplishment made that much more remarkable given that Eyser had a prosthetic left leg made of wood.

What man has won the most gold medals in gymnastics?

The Olympic male gymnastics competitor most weighed down by gold is Japan's Sawao Kato, who is the proud owner of eight champion medals. He took his first at the 1968 Games in Mexico, then grabbed another two at Munich in 1972, and got his final two in Montreal in 1976. In addition, Kato also took three silver medals and one bronze over the space of those Games for an Olympic career total of 12.

Who was the first Olympic gymnast to be awarded a perfect score?

At the age of just 14, Romanian gymnast Nadia Comăneci made her Olympic debut in Montreal in 1976. She competed in a number of events, eventually taking home three gold medals, one silver, and one bronze. But it was her routine on the uneven bars that cemented her reputation as one of the greatest gymnasts ever, as the judges awarded her a perfect score of 10.0. No gymnast had ever achieved that score before, but before the Montreal Games were over, Comăneci would do it six more times. The feat would land her on the cover of *Time* magazine.

Why did controversy swirl around the Chinese women's gymnastics team at the 2008 Olympics in Beijing?

Before, during, and after the Beijing Summer Games of 2008, questions were being raised about the ages of some members on China's women's gymnastics team. Olympic regulations state that gymnasts must be at least 16 years old. Looking at the diminutive Chinese competitors, He Kexin, Jiang Yuyuan, and Yang Yilin, it seemed obvious to many that they were younger than 16. Documentary evidence appeared to point in that direction also. Newspaper articles, records at a local Chinese sports bureau and from previous competitions, and the website of the State General Administration of Sports all variously had the girls listed as being born in years that would put them under the age of 16 during the Beijing Games. When confronted with these facts, Chinese authorities insisted that the birthdates on the girls' passports — which put them over 16 — were accurate. The girls won gold in the team competition.

What was club swinging?

No, this was not a racy after-hours event for sexually adventurous married Olympians. Nor was it juggling, as many people think it was. Club swinging, which was only contested at the 1904 and 1932 Games, was a men's gymnastics event in which a competitor whirled and swung two bowling pin-like clubs — called "Indian clubs" — around his head and body in a variety of patterns in a complicated routine. Americans dominated the event, taking all medals in both 1904 and 1932.

Have any Canadians ever won gold medals in Olympic gymnastics?

Canada's overall medal count in Olympic gymnastics stands at seven, two of which are gold. At the 1984 Los Angeles Olympics, Vancouver-born Lori Fung became not only Canada's first gold medallist in gymnastics, but she became the first-ever medal recipient in rhythmic gymnastics, which were being contested for the first time at those Games. Canada had to wait twenty years for the next gymnastics gold, which was won by Kyle Keith Shewfelt in the floor exercise at the 2004 games in Athens.

> **Quickies**
>
> *Did you know ...*
> that 1932 club swinging gold medallist George Roth was so poor during the Great Depression that after accepting his gold medal in front of a packed stadium at the Los Angeles Games, he had to hitch-hike his way home to East Hollywood?

What is rhythmic gymnastics?

Rhythmic gymnastics, which used to be called "modern gymnastics," is strictly a women's competition. The gymnasts, accompanied by music, perform on a 13-metre-square floor area with ribbon, rope, ball, clubs, and hoop. In the individual event athletes perform different routines with four of the five apparatus. In the team competition, teams of five perform together once using clubs and once with two using hoops and three using ribbons. It was first contested at the 1984 Games.

Who is "The Hose"?

Handball player Magnus Wislander of Sweden was given the nickname "The Hose" because of his ability to slither through the defence on the handball court. He played in over 380 international matches for the Swedish national team from 1985 through 2004, averaging three goals per game. He helped his team win silver at three consecutive Olympics: 1992, 1996, and 2000.

Who are the top medal-winning players in Olympic field hockey?

It's a draw, though they both played for the same country. India's Leslie Claudius and Udham Singh are the only two players in Olympic field hockey to have won four medals each. Both players have three gold medals and one silver.

> **Quickies**
> *Did you know ...*
> that at the 1956 Olympics in Melbourne, India's Udham Singh was the leading goal scorer in the field hockey tournament, with 14 goals?

What was Pakistan's first Olympic gold win?

Pakistan's first-ever trip to the medal podium came with their silver win in men's field hockey at the 1956 Olympics in Melbourne, where they were defeated 1–0 by their arch rivals, India, in the final. Four years later, at the 1960 Olympics in Rome, Pakistan turned the tables and defeated India 1–0 in the final to secure the nation's first-ever gold medal. Their only other medal in those games was a bronze won by welterweight freestyle wrestler Muhammad Bashir.

Why did the Court of Arbitration for Sport exonerate the Spanish women's team just before the 2008 Olympics despite two of their players having failed a doping test?

A week before the Beijing Olympic Games, the Azerbaijan Hockey Federation appealed to the Court of Arbitration for Sport against the participation of the Spanish women's field hockey team in the Olympics. Spain had won the Olympic Qualification Tournament held in Baku, Azerbaijan, in April, but two Spanish players had tested positive for doping after defeating the host nation 2–1 in the final, thus knocking them out of Olympic contention. At the time, the International Hockey Federation had exonerated the two Spanish players, who claimed the positive test was part of an Azeri plan to thwart the Spanish women. During the Qualification Tournament the Spanish team had suffered phone bombardments, ill air in their hotel, and tampered drinking water. The Court of Arbitration also dismissed the Azeri charges, allowing the Spanish women to compete in Beijing, where they finished in seventh place.

> **Quickies**
> *Did you know ...*
> that between 1928 and 1960, Indian field hockey teams won six straight gold medals?

What did Anton Geesnik do to shock Japanese spectators at the 1964 Tokyo Olympics?

Judo first appeared at the Olympic Games in 1964 at Tokyo. Although Judo traditionally does not use weight classes, three were established for those games, as well as an open class in which anyone could compete. Japanese judoka (as the fighters are called) took gold in the three weight classes — lightweight, middleweight, and heavyweight — but when it came to the open category, a 130 kg Dutch giant named Anton Geesnik defeated Japanese national champion Akio Kaminaga, deeply shocking the Japanese people who were convinced of their superiority in the sport. Of course, time would prove them right, as Japan has gone on to dominate Olympic Judo, winning 35 of the 109 gold medals handed out to judoka since 1964.

> **Quickies**
>
> *Did you know ...*
> that even though "judo" means "the gentle way" in Japanese, the martial art is the only Olympic event where choke holds are not outside the rules?

Who is the judoka with the most Olympic medals?

Seven-times World Champion in the women's extra-lightweight class, Japan's Ryoko Tamura-Tani also holds the record for most Olympic judo medals, with two gold, two silver, and one bronze. Known as 'Yawara-chan' in her home country, after a popular manga comic character, she is married to professional baseball player Yoshitomo Tani, who played for Japan's Olympic baseball team at the 1996 and 2004 games, bringing home silver and bronze medals, respectively.

What are the five events in the modern pentathlon?

The modern pentathlon was invented in the late nineteenth century by the founder of the modern Olympics, Baron Pierre de Coubertin. The name combines the Greek words penta- "five" and -athlon "contest", as the sport consists five contests: pistol shooting, épée fencing, 200m freestyle swimming, show jumping, and a 3km cross-country run. The addition of "modern" to the name distinguished it from the original pentathlon of the ancient Olympic Games, which consisted of a foot race, wrestling, long jump, javelin, and discus — all skills of the ancient Greek soldier. Coubertin modeled his pentathlon to simulate the skills that might be required of a then-modern cavalry soldier.

> **Quickies**
>
> *Did you know ...*
> that at the 1904 Olympics an Americanized version of croquet called "rogue" was contested?

What did rower Bobby Pearce do that delighted crowds at the 1928 Olympics in Amsterdam?

At the 1928 Amsterdam Olympics, Bobby Pearce, a third-generation sculling champion from the Sydney suburb of Double Bay, faced an unexpected challenge in the middle of his quarterfinal single-sculls race against Victor Saurin of France. As he propelled his craft across the water a family of ducks swam into the path of his scull. Remarkably, and much to the delight of the Dutch onlookers, Pearce stopped to let the birds pass! He then sculled to victory, winning by 20 lengths and breaking the course record. Pearce returned to the Olympics for the Los Angeles Games of 1932 and again rowed to victory in single sculls — without ducks this time! — becoming the first rower ever to win gold in the event twice.

Why did Silken Laumann almost not compete at the 1992 Olympics?

Prior to the 1992 Olympics in Barcelona, Canadian rower Silken Laumann was seen as a strong contender to win gold in the single skulls race. But in May of that year, while training for the Games, her skull was involved in a collision with the boat of German coxless pair team Colin von Ettinghausen and Peter Hoeltzenbein. The collision resulted in horrible wounds to Laumann's leg that required five operations and weeks in hospital. Doctors doubted she would be able to row at world class levels again, but Laumann was determined to prove them wrong and by late June she was back in her skull. Her leg severely weakened, Laumann nonetheless managed to win a bronze medal in the single sculls event in Barcelona on July 28th. She achieved silver in the event four years later in Atlanta.

What is a cox box?

That small person who sits at the stern or bow of a rowing scull, calling out "Stroke! Stroke! Stroke!" through a megaphone to the rowers, is known as the coxswain, or the cox. In addition to setting the rhythm of the rowers' strokes, it is the cox's job to steer the boat. These days megaphones are rare because the cox typically communicates with the rowers by use of a cox box, an electronic device that combines a digital stroke-rate monitor and elapsed-time readout with a voice amplifier.

Who holds the record for competing in the most Olympic games?

With nine appearances, Austrian sailor Hubert Raudaschl holds the absolute record for competing in the most Olympics. Raudaschl sailed in every Summer Games from 1964 to 1996. He won silver medals in the 1968 Mixed One Person Dinghy and the 1980 Mixed Two Person Keelboat competitions. His number of appearances could have been even higher, as he was present at the 1960 Olympics as an 18-year-old. However, he was only a substitute for the Austrian sailing team there.

Who was Israel's first Olympic champion?

The first and only Israeli athlete so far to bring home the gold is Gal Fridman, who took first place in the 2004 windsurfing competition at Athens. Fridman also took bronze in the windsurfing competition at the 1996 Atlanta Games. Of the seven Olympic medals won by Israeli athletes, three are for windsurfing.

Who was the first competitor to win the same individual event at four consecutive Olympics?

Danish yachtsman Paul Elvstrøm competed in eight Olympic Games from 1948 to 1988. It was his first four appearances that cemented his reputation as one of history's greatest

Israel's Complete Olympic Medal Record

Games	Athlete	Event	Medal
Beijing 2008	Shahar Zubari	Windsurfing	Bronze
Athens 2004	Arik Ze'evi	Judo	Bronze
Athens 2004	Gal Fridman	Windsurfing	Gold
Sydney 2000	Michael Kolganov	500m Kayak	Bronze
Atlanta 1996	Gal Fridman	Windsurfing	Bronze
Barcelona 1992	Shay-Oren Smadga	Judo	Bronze
Barcelona 1992	Yael Arad	Judo	Silver

Olympic competitors. At London (1948), Helsinki (1952), Melbourne (1956), and Rome (1960), Elvstrøm triumphed in the one-person dinghy event becoming the first athlete to win gold at four consecutive Olympics.

> **Quickies**
> *Did you know …*
> that yachtsman Paul Elvstrøm competed in the 1984 and 1988 Games in the mixed multihull event with his daughter Trine as crew? Though they did not take any medals, the duo remain the only father/daughter team to have competed in the Olympics.

Who was Hong Kong's first Olympic champion?

Hong Kong has competed as an independent team at the Olympics since 1952. Their first and only Olympic champion is Lee Lai Shan who won gold in the women's windsurfing competition at the 1996 Atlanta Olympics.

Who is Brazil's most accomplished Olympian?

> **Quickies**
> *Did you know …*
> that at London's 1948 Olympics, when U.S. sailors Paul and Hilary Smart won the mixed two-person keelboat event, they became the first father and son in the same sport to win Olympic gold?

Yachtsman Torben Grael competed in all six Summer Games from 1984 to 2004. Along the way, he scooped up two gold medals, one silver, and one bronze. All of his medals, except the silver, were won in the mixed two-person keelboat. The silver was won in the three-person keelboat. Grael's medal record makes him not only the Brazilian athlete with the most Olympic medals but also the most accomplished sailor in Olympic history.

What was the highest number of sailors to compete at an Olympic Games?

The Atlanta Games of 1996 saw astounding 436 sailors compete in the Olympic Regatta representing 77 countries, more than any other Olympics before or since. Ten events were contested off the coast of Savannah, Georgia, with 22 nations dividing the spoils of the 30 medals available.

Hong Kong's Complete Olympic Medal Record

Games	Athlete	Event	Medal
Athens 2004	Li Ching	Table Tennis	Silver
Athens 2004	Ko Lai Chak	Table Tennis	Silver
Atlanta 1996	Gal Fridman	Windsurfing	Bronze

Who is the oldest competitor in the Olympics to have won a medal?

Not just *one* medal, six medals! In 1908, Swedish shooter Oscar Swahn was 60 years old when he won his first Olympic gold medal. He won the running deer single-shot event and took a second gold the next day in the team event. Swahn also earned a bronze in the running deer double-shot contest. In the 1912 Stockholm games, Swahn returned to win bronze in the double-shot and gold in the team single-shot. And he wasn't finished! After World War I, Swahn returned to the Olympics at the age of 72 to take silver in the running deer double-shot team event at the Antwerp games of 1920. Swahn remains the oldest person to have won an Olympic medal.

Quickies

Did you know ...

that the oldest Olympic class sailboat still in competition is the Starboat, a 6.9 m two-person keelboat first raced at the 1932 Los Angeles games?

Teams with Only One Gold Win in Olympic History

Team	Games	Event	Athlete
Armenia	Atlanta 1996	Wrestling	Armen Nazaryan*
Bahrain	Beijing 2008	Men's 1,500m run	Rashid Ramzi
Burundi	Atlanta 1996	Men's 5,000m run	Vénuste Niyongabo
Colombia	Sydney 2000	Weightlifting	María Isabel Urrutia
Costa Rica	Atlanta 1996	200m freestyle swim	Claudia Poll
Ecuador	Atlanta 1996	20k walk	Jeffersón Pérez
Hong Kong	Atlanta 1996	Women's windsurfing	Lee Lai Shan
Israel	Athens 2004	Men's windsurfing	Gal Fridman
Mozambique	Sydney 2000	Women's 800m run	Maria Mutola
Panama	Beijing 2008	Long jump	Irving Saladino
Peru	London 1948	Pistol shooting	Edwin Vásquez
Suriname	Seoul 1988	100m butterfly	Anthony Nesty
Syria	Atlanta 1996	Women's heptathlon	Ghada Shouaa
Trinidad & Tobago	Montreal 1976	Men's 100m run	Hasley Crawford
Uganda	Munich 1972	400m hurdles	John Akii-Bua
United Arab Emirates	Athens 2004	Shooting	Ahmed Al-Maktoum
Venezuala	Mexico 1968	Boxing	Francisco Rodriguez

*Armen Nazaryan also won gold wrestling for Bulgaria at the 2000 Sydney Games. Bulgaria has 52 gold medals.

Who was Vice-Admiral Willis Augustus Lee, Jr.?

Olympic shooter Willis Lee was a distant relative of Gen. Robert E. Lee and the great-great-grandson of the third Attorney General of the United States, Charles Lee. A 1908 graduate of the U.S. Naval Academy, he was a member of the Navy rifle teams of 1908, 1909, 1913, 1919, and 1930. Lee served during both World War I and World War II, making a stop between the two at the Antwerp Olympic Games of 1920 to win five gold medals, one silver and one bronze in the shooting competition. In 1942 he commanded the task force which defeated the Japanese on Guadalcanal. At the time of his death in 1945 he was a Vice-Admiral.

What athlete competed in the most events in one Olympics?

In 1920, First Lieutenant Lloyd Spooner of the U.S. Army's 47th Infantry competed in 12 shooting events at the Antwerp Olympic Games — it remains the standing record for most events competed in by one person during one Olympics. Spooner took home four gold medals, one silver, and two bronzes, a record medal haul that would stand until the 1980 Moscow Olympics when the USSR's Aleksandr Dityatin won eight gymnastics medals.

Men's Olympic Shooting World Records

Event	Result	Name	Country	Games
10m air rifle (60 shots)	599pts	Zhu Qinan	China	2004 Athens
50m rifle prone (60 shots)	600pts	Christian Klees	Germany	1996 Atlanta
50m rifle 3 positions (3x40 shots)	1177pts	Rajmond Debevec	Slovakia	2000 Sydney
50m pistol (60 shots)	581pts	Aleksandr Melentiev	USSR	1980 Moscow
25m rapid fire pistol (60 shots)	583pts	Keith Sanderson	U.S.	2008 Beijing
10m air pistol (60 shots)	591pts	Mikhail Nestruev	Russia	2004 Athens
Trap (125 targets)	124pts	Alexei Alipov	Russia	2004 Athens
Trap (125 targets)	124pts	Michael Diamond	Australia	1996 Atlanta

Why did Karoly Takacs switch from shooting with his right hand to his left?

A member of the Hungarian pistol shooting team in 1938, Karoly Takacs was also a sergeant in the army. One day, a defective grenade exploded in his right hand — his pistol hand — and shattered it completely. He spent a month in hospital, and then afterwards secretly taught himself to shoot with his left hand. The following year he won the Hungarian pistol shooting championship and was a member of the Hungarian team that won the automatic pistol event at the world championships. He went on to win gold in the 25m rapid fire pistol (60 shots) competition at both the 1948 and 1952 Olympics, beating the world record by ten points at the later.

Women's Olympic Shooting World Records				
Event	Result	Name	Country	Games
10m air rifle (40 shots)	399pts	Lioubov Galkina	Russia	2004 Athens
50m rifle 3 positions (3x20 shots)	589pts	Du Li	China	2008 Beijing
50m rifle 3 positions (3x20 shots)	589pts	Renata Mauer-Rozanska	Poland	1996 Atlanta
25m pistol (30+30 shots)	590pts	Tao Luna	China	2000 Sydney
10m air pistol (40 shots)	390pts	Tao Luna	China	2000 Sydney
10m air pistol (40 shots)	390pts	Marina Logvinenko	Russia	1996 Atlanta
Trap (75 targets)	71pts	Daina Gudzineviciute	Lithuania	2000 Sydney
Skeet (75 targets)	72pts	Chiara Cainero	Italy	2008 Beijing

What controversy swirled around Chinese shooter Hu Binyuan at the 2008 Beijing Olympics?

Much to the astonishment of spectators and other competitors, Chinese shooter Hu Binyuan won bronze in the men's double trap event at the Beijing Games after having clearly missed the target a number of times. On at least three occasions, it was reported by the media and other shooters, Hu was awarded a hit by the Chinese judges although his shots had not found home.

Has any non-Asian competitor won a gold in table tennis?

Of the 24 gold medals awarded in table tennis since the sport first appeared at the 1988 Seoul Olympics, China has taken 20 and South Korea 3. The 1992 gold in the men's singles competition, which was won by Swedish competitor Jan-Ove Waldner, remains the only Olympic gold medal in table tennis not won by an Asian athlete.

Why was Cuban taekwondo fighter Angel Matos banned for life from Olympic competition?

After being disqualified from the taekwondo heavyweight bronze-medal bout at the Beijing 2008 Summer Games, Cuban competitor Angel Matos stepped way over the line. Matos was winning the August 23rd match 3–2 against Kazakhstan's Arman Chilmanov with 1:02 left in the second round when he sustained a broken toe on his left foot. The referee temporarily stopped the match so that Matos could receive medical treatment. By the rules, fighters are permitted one minute for such treatment, but Matos exceeded that time limit and Swedish referee Chakir Chelbat disqualified him. Rising to his feet, Matos immediately disputed the call, arguing with Chelbat, but when Chelbat signaled that Chilmanov was victor in the fight, Matos lashed out and kicked the ref in the face. He then pushed another official and spat on the mat before leaving. Chelbat's mouth required stitches. Matos and his coach, Leudis González, were ejected from the tournament and banned for life from sanctioned competition by the The World Taekwondo Federation, which governs the sport.

Who was the first male Olympic tennis champion?

In 1896 John Boland was an Oxford student who enjoyed the study of Greek mythology. When he learned about the Olympics revival, Boland traveled to Athens to watch the Games of the I Olympiad. However, upon his arrival, his friend, Thrasyvoalos Manaos, Secretary of the Athens 1896 Organising Committee, convinced Boland to enter the tennis competition. Despite competing in leather-soled shoes with heels, Boland won the competition and became the first-ever Olympic tennis champion.

Who was the first female Olympic tennis champion?

The first female Olympic tennis champion was Charlotte Cooper of Great Britain who played to victory in women's singles at the 1900 games in Paris. Her defeat of Helène Prevost in the women's singles final that year made her the very first woman to win Olympic gold in any sport.

How long has tennis been an Olympic sport?

Tennis has been played at the modern Olympics since the start — if you don't include a 64 year hiatus, that is. Tennis was part of the first modern Olympic Games in 1896 and continued through 1924, but it was not competed again until 1988. A large part of what kept tennis out of the Olympics between 1924 and 1988 was the difficulty of excluding professional players under the Olympic amateurism requirement. That rule was overturned in 1986, making it the responsibility of individual sports groups to determine whether or not professionals should be allowed to compete in the Olympics. This new rule allowed tennis to return to the Games.

Why did Pete Sampras skip the 2000 Olympics in Sydney?

Pete Sampras and other professional tennis players skipped the 2000 Olympics in Sydney because of the distance required to travel to Australia and because of the amount of effort

it was going to take to win once they got there. Sampras complained that there was a 128-player draw at the Games, and that rivaled what pros played in a whole year. He was wrong. The singles competition had "only" a 64-player draw, and doubles at 32-teams — still a lot of tennis in ten days!

How did Novak Đoković celebrate his bronze tennis win in 2008?

Serbian tennis player Novak Đoković was the world's No. 3 ranked male tennis player, behind Roger Federer and Rafael Nadal, going into the Beijing Games. He was defeated in the semis by Spain's Nadal, who went on to take gold, but he won the bronze match against American James Blake. To celebrate he ripped his shirt off, draped himself in the flag of Serbia, and threw the contents of his racquet bag into the crowd.

Who was FedRinka?

In three Olympic attempts, tennis star Roger Federer won his only medal playing men's doubles. It was the gold at Beijing, which he won with fellow Swiss player Stanislas Wawrinka. Together the golden duo became known as FedRinka.

> **Quickies**
> *Did you know ...*
> that Canada's only Olympic medal in tennis was won in 2000 by Daniel Nestor and Sébastien Lareau at the men's doubles tournament in Sydney? They took gold, defeating Aussies Todd Woodbridge and Mark Woodforde in the final.

What is the "Golden Slam"?

In 1988 Steffi Graf did something no other tennis player, man or woman, has ever done. That year the German athlete not only completed a single-season grand slam on the professional tour, winning at the Australian Open, French Open, Wimbledon, and the U.S. Open, but she also took gold at the Seoul Olympics to complete what the media dubbed the first-ever "Golden Slam."

When did Triathlon become an Olympic sport?

The 2000 Summer Olympics in Sydney saw the first appearance of the triathlon. Forty-eight women and 52 men competed in separate triathlons. The 2004 triathlon was identical to the first in distance, but the 100-athlete quota was evened between 50 women and 50 men. The quota was further increased to 55 women and 55 men for the 2008 Beijing Olympics.

Which triathletes hold the unofficial Olympic records for triathlon?

The IOC does not maintain official Olympic record times for the triathlon because of the variability of the courses. Nonetheless, the unofficial record for fastest male triathlon belongs to Canada's Simon Whitfield, who finished in 1:48:24.02 at the 2000 Sydney Games. The women's record is held by Australian Emma Snowsill, who clocked in at 1:58:27.66 in Beijing 2008.

> **Olympic Triathlon Total Distance: 51.5 km**
>
> - Swim: 1.5km (0.93 miles)
> - Cycle: 40km (24.85 miles)
> - Run: 10km (6.21 miles)

How many countries have sent both men and women to compete in the triathlon at every Olympics since 2000?

Of the 43 countries that have competed in Olympic triathlon, only 13 have sent both men and women to compete at every Games since triathlon was introduced in 2000. They are: Australia, Brazil, Canada, Czech Republic, France, Germany, Great Britain, Hungary, Japan, New Zealand, Spain, Switzerland, and the United States.

Are there any multiple medal winners in Olympic triathlon?

Only two people have managed so far to snag more than one medal in Olympic triathlon. Simon Whitefield of Canada won gold at the Sydney Olympics in 2000 and silver at the Beijing Games in 2008. Bevan Docherty of Australia took silver at the Athens race in 2004, and he won bronze in Beijing. No triathlon gold medallist has managed a return trip to the gold podium yet.

Olympic Triathlon Medallists Since 2000

Men

Games	Gold	Silver	Bronze
Sydney 2000	Simon Whitfield (CAN)	Stephan Vuckovic (GER)	Jan Řehula (CZE)
Athens 2004	Hamish Carter (NZL)	Bevan Docherty (NZL)	Sven Riederer (SUI)
Beijing 2008	Jan Frodeno (GER)	Simon Whitfield (CAN)	Bevan Docherty (NZL)

Women

Games	Gold	Silver	Bronze
Sydney 2000	Brigitte McMahon (SUI)	Michellie Jones (AUS)	Magali Di Marco Messmer (SUI)
Athens 2004	Kate Allen (AUT)	Loretta Harrop (AUS)	Susan Williams (U.S.)
Beijing 2008	Emma Snowsill (AUS)	Vanessa Fernandes (POR)	Emma Moffatt (AUS)

Who holds the record for the most Olympic gold medals in volleyball?

This is a three-way split — because they all played for the same team. In 1992, 1996, and 2000, the women's Cuban volleyball team dominated competition at the Olympic Games taking gold each year. Of the players on the various Cuban squads, just three were at all three Olympics: Regla Bell, Mireya Luis, and and Regla Torres, who at just 17.5- years-old remains the youngest Olympic volleyball gold medallist.

What controversy surrounded Brazillian Olympic volleyball player Kiki?

In October 2000, Time Asia magazine revealed that Brazillian volleyball player Erika Coimbra, who was known by the nickname Kiki and who had helped the Brazillian women's team win bronze in Sydney the month prior, was a hermaphrodite. The report said that she, as well as Brazillian female judo competitor Edinanci da Silva (who did not win any medals), had both been born with "non-functioning male genitalia that were surgically removed." After the news broke, some people questioned the gender of the two athletes but both women had passed mandatory genetic gender testing prior to the games.

> **Quickies**
> *Did you know …*
> that when Canadian Simon Whitfield arrived at the 2000 Sydney Games to compete in the first-ever Olympic Triathlon — which he would win — he was ranked just 13th in the world for the sport?

> **Quickies**
> *Did you know …*
> that volleyball, invented in 1895, was originally called "mintonette"?

Why do women wear those skimpy bikinis for Olympic beach volleyball?

Believe it or not, those bikinis — or rather, swimsuits — are mandated in the rules of Olympic women's beach volleyball as set out by the Federation Internationale de Volleyball (FIVB). While the rules state that male volleyball players may wear tank tops and shorts, the FIVB has ruled that women must wear either one-piece or two-piece bathing suits. It is left up to the teams themselves to choose which.

> **Quickies**
> *Did you know …*
> that American Volleyball two-time gold medallist Misty May is married to Major League Baseball catcher Matt Treanor?

Who were the "iron hammer" and the "Tiananmen wall"?

The 1984 Games at Los Angeles saw the debut of volleyball as an Olympic sport. Even though Eastern Bloc countries were boycotting the L.A. Games, the four top volleyball teams from the 1982 Women's World Championships — China, Peru, Japan, and the United States — were all present in California. China, the reigning world champions, lost only two sets on their way to gold in the Olympic tournament, thanks in large part to star players Ping Lang, nicknamed "iron hammer" for her powerful

> **Quickies**
> *Did you know …*
> that volleyball was the first team sport for women in the Olympics? It made its debut at the Tokyo Summer Games in 1964.

offensive capabilities, and Zhou Xiaolan, nicknamed the "Tiananmen wall" for her shot-blocking defensive skills.

Why did weightlifter Paul Anderson defeat Humberto Selvetti in the 1956 Melbourne Games despite the fact that the two men hoisted the same weight?

They may have lifted the same weight, but they themselves did not weigh the same. And in weightlifting that is key. American weightlifter Paul Anderson weighed 137.9kg. In weightlifting, ties are broken by awarding the higher place to the athlete with the lower body weight. Incredibly, this worked to Anderson's advantage when he tied for first with Humberto Selvetti of Argentina. Selvetti weighed 143.5kg, so Anderson took the gold.

Who is Tommy Kono?

American Tommy Kono was a World and Olympic champion weightlifter who was the only man to set World records in four different weight classes: lightweight (148 lb or 67 kg), middleweight (165 lb or 75 kg), light-heavyweight (181 lb or 82 kg), and middle-heavy-weight (198 lb or 90 kg). Between 1953 and 1959 he was undefeated in World and Olympic competition, adding six straight world titles to his two Olympic gold medals. He was also a body builder and won the Mr. Universe title in 1954, 1955, and 1957.

Who is the "Pocket Hercules"?

Bulgarian-born Turkish featherweight weightlifter Naim Süleymanoğlu is one of the most powerful men to have ever competed at the Olympics. Nicknamed "The Pocket Hercules" because he is only 4'10" tall, he set his first world record at age 15 in 1982, and at the 1984 European Championships he became only the second man to lift three times his body-weight overhead. Prior to the 1988 Olympics, he had set 32 world records. He took gold medals at the Seoul, Barcelona, and Atlanta Games. At the 1988 Olympics, Süleymanoğlu lifted a weight which would have won the weight class above his.

Who was Naum Shalamanov?

Don't be confused if you see this name in the weightlifting record books. Naum Shalamanov is none other than Naim Süleymanoğlu. A Turk born into Soviet Bloc Bulgaria, Süleymanoğlu was forced by the state, along with other Turkish Bulgarians, to adopt Bulgarian names. He defected to Turkey in 1986 and changed his name to the Turkish Naim Süleymanoğlu.

Who was the first female Olympic weightlifting champion?

On September 16 at the 2000 Sydney Olympics, Bulgaria's Izabela Dragneva lifted a combined total of 190kgs in the 48kg category to become the first Olympic gold medallist in woman's weightlifting, which was making its debut at those Games. But it turned out to be a false start. Three days later it was announced Dragneva had tested positive for steroid use — the third Bulgarian weightlifter to fail drug testing at the Sydney Games. She was stripped of her medal and the entire Bulgarian weightlifting team — men and women — were booted out of the Games. Two Bulgarian men also had to return medals. Silver medallist Tara Nott of the United States, who lifted 185kgs in the category, was subsequently awarded Dragneva's gold to become the first-ever Olympic women's weightlifting champion.

> **Quickies**
> *Did you know ...*
> that Greek Olympic weightlifter Halil Mutlu, who holds three gold medals, has been able to lift four times his body weight?

Who was Junpim Kuntatean?

Junpim Kuntatean was the former name of a Thai female weightlifter. For good luck, and on the advice of a fortune teller, prior to the Beijing Olympics in 2008, she changed her name to Prapawadee Jaroenrattanatarakoon. The strategy worked: she won the gold medal in the women's featherweight class in Beijing.

What is the difference between a "snatch" and a "clean-and-jerk"?

In weightlifting, Olympic competitors perform two types of lifts — the snatch and the clean-and-jerk. For the snatch, they must lift the barbell to arm's length above their head all in one continuous, swift movement, finishing with straight arms and an upright body.

In the clean-and-jerk, the lifter first pulls the barbell up from a squatting position to the shoulders while moving into a standing position — that's the "clean" — then the lifter pushes the barbell straight up overhead finishing with arms fully extended and an upright body — that's the "jerk."

The snatch is performed in the first half of the competition. Lifters are permitted three attempts at each lift. Their best snatch and best clean-and-jerk figures are added to determine the winners.

What is the difference between Greco-Roman wrestling and freestyle wrestling?

Greco-Roman wrestling made its Olympic debut in the year 776 B.C. with the very first Games in ancient Greece. It would be resurrected after 1500 years with the first modern Olympics in 1896. In Greco-Roman wrestling, the wrestlers use only their arms and upper bodies to attack, and can hold only those same parts of their opponents. Meanwhile, in the late nineteenth century, another form of wrestling had become popular, called "catch as catch can," in which wrestlers could use their legs for pushing, lifting, and tripping, and they could hold opponents above or below the waist.

In 1904, the Olympic Games added the second wrestling event and called it "freestyle." Both forms of wrestling are still contested at the Olympics.

What did Swedish wrestler Ara Abrahamian do with his Olympic medal?

Swedish wrestler Ara Abrahamian won bronze in the Greco-Roman 84 kilo category at the 2008 Beijing Olympics, but he'd become enraged at a penalty call in the semifinal match against Italian Andrea Minguzzi, who went on to win the gold medal. At the medal ceremony, Abrahamian took the medal off his neck and dropped it on the wrestling mat before walking out of the gymnasium. He later made accusations of corruption against an Italian judge, requesting a formal revue along with the National Olympic Committee of Sweden. The International Olympic Committee stripped Abrahamian of his medal, calling his actions at the podium disrespectful. An investigation led by the International Federation of Associated Wrestling Styles, the governing body of the sport, resulted in fines and two-year suspensions for Abrahamian and his coach Leo Myllari. In the case of Abrahamian, the suspension came too late, as he had announced his retirement immediately following Beijing.

Who is the Siberian Bear?

Between the time of his debut in international competition in 1987 to the time of his retirement after the 2000 Sydney Olympics, Russian Greco-Roman super-heavyweight wrestler Aleksaner Karelin lost only one match — his last. During his career, Karelin won gold medals at the 1988, 1992, and 1996 Olympic Games. He was world champion nine times and European champion 12. Prior to the 2000 Sydney Games he had not given up a single point on the wrestling mat in six years. His only loss came at those Games in an astonishing upset when, in the gold medal match, he faced an American Mormon farmhand named Rulon Gardner. Gardner had never competed in an Olympics before, though he had secured the U.S. Championship in 1995 and 1997 as well as the Pan Am

championship in 1998. He'd faced Karelin once before at the 1997 World Championships, losing 5–0. But at Sydney, Gardner scored first and then held the Russian to zero points to take gold. Karelin retired from wrestling after the Sydney Games.

> **Quickies**
> *Did you know ...*
> that Swedish Greco-Roman wrestler Carl Westergren, who won three gold medals in Olympic competition between 1920 and 1932, was a bus driver by trade?

Why was Canadian press attaché Barb Wilson asked to leave a wrestling match at the Atlanta Olympics?

When reporter Barb Wilson showed up at a men's wrestling bout during the Atlanta Olympics in 1996 wearing a Canadian jersey and a pair of shorts, officials from one of the Islamic nations present protested because her legs were showing and distracting their athletes. Wilson was initially asked to leave, but refused and authorities eventually acknowledged her right to remain. The distracted wrestlers just had to make due.

Have any Canadian women won Olympic medals in wrestling?

Yes, one of each — gold, silver, and bronze. Women's wrestling made its debut at the 2004 Games in Athens, where Canada's Tonya Verbeek won a silver in the 55kg freestyle event (there is no women's Greco-Roman wrestling at the Olympics). At the 2008 Beijing Games Verbeek again "medaled," taking bronze in the same weight class. Meanwhile, also at Beijing, Canadian Carol Huynh, competing in the 48kg class, won Canada's first Olympic gold in women's wrestling. Appropriately, Huynh's last name is pronounced "win."

> **Quickies**
> *Did you know ...*
> that Russian wrestler Aleksaner Karelin weighed 15lbs at birth?

WINTER OLYMPICS

What is a biathlon?

Based on the practice of using skis for hunting or for military activities during the winter in northern European countries, the biathlon is a sport that combines two disciplines: cross-country skiing and rifle shooting. It was first contested at the 1960 Winter Olympics in Squaw Valley with the men's 20 km individual event. Other distances, including sprints and relays, have since been added. Women's events made their debut at the 1992 Albertville Olympics. The biathlon is considered to be the winter cousin of the Summer Olympics' modern pentathlon.

Quickies

Did you know ...
that biathletes shoot 0.22-calibre rifles?

How did the Canadian women's biathlon team raise money for training?

The five-member Canadian women's biathlon team, in need of funding to attend the 2010 Vancouver Olympics, issued a 2009 wall calendar which features "tasteful" nude photos of themselves posing with their rifles.

Has anyone ever won gold medals in both the Summer and Winter Olympics?

Only one person has ever won gold medals in both the Summer and Winter Olympics. American Eddie Eagan holds that special place in Olympic history. In 1920, the Yale, Harvard, and Oxford educated Eagan defeated Sverre Sörsdal of Norway to win the light heavyweight boxing championship at the Antwerp Olympics. Twelve years after his victory at the Summer Games, Eagan reappeared at the 1932 Lake Placid Winter Olympics as a member of Billy Fiske's four-man bobsleigh team. The Fiske foursome won the event by two seconds and Eagan achieved his unique double.

Quickies

Did you know ...
that in the early twentieth century, the Winter Olympics included a skiing and shooting competition similar to biathlon called "military patrol"?

Why was there no bobsleigh competition at the 1960 Winter Games?

There was no bobsleigh competition at the 1960 Winter Games in Squaw Valley, California, because there was no bobsled run. When it was discovered that only nine of the 30 nations participating in the Games intended to send bobsled teams, organizers refused to build a bobsled run. It remains the only time in the history of the Winter Games that bobsleigh events have not been held.

Was the movie *Cool Runnings*, about a Jamaican bobsled team, based on reality?

As strange as this may sound, the Jamaican four-man bobsled team was and is a reality. Although the characters in the film Cool Runnings are fictional, the story is based on the exploits of Jamaica's first four-man team which competed at the 1988 Winter Olympics in Calgary. They placed 21st during that competition after having crashed their sled. Jamaica has since sent bobsledders, including two-man sleds, to four other Winter Games and they plan to have a team at Vancouver 2010.

Why does the world Olympic medal leader in skeleton not have a gold medal?

The skeleton medal standings have a peculiar feature: while there are two competitors who have medaled twice in the history of the Winter Games, no one has ever won gold twice. That said, skeleton has only been competed four times in the Olympics — 1928, 1948, 2002, and 2006 — so it seems there hasn't been enough opportunity yet for anyone to repeat gold. Thus, at present, the Olympic medal leaders in skeleton are American Jack Heaton, who won silver in both 1928 and 1948, and Gregor Stähli, of Switzerland, who won bronze in 2002 and 2006. Six men are tied behind them for third place with single-gold wins.

Complete Results for Jamaica's Olympic Boblsleigh Teams

Games	2 Man	4 Man
Calgary 1988	30th	crashed
Albertville 1992	35th	25th
Lillehammer 1994	disqualified*	14th
Nagano 1998	29th	21st
Salt Lake City 2002	28th	n/a†

*The sled and crew were over regulation weight limit.
†no 4-man team entered

What is Team Gushue?

Curling teams traditionally name themselves after their skippers, or captains. Team Gushue is the name by which the Canadian men's curling team that won gold at the 2006 Turin Winter Olympics calls itself. The team is skippered by Newfoundlander Brad Gushue.

Who was Sandra Schmirler?

When Sandra Schmirler was a kid in Biggar, Saskatchewan, she wanted to play hockey, but since there was no girls' hockey team in town she opted for a broomstick over a hockey stick and took to the curling rink. She curled all through school and eventually, as an adult, Schmirler would use that broomstick to lead the Canadian women's curling team to gold at the Nagano Olympics of 1998 — the first year women's curling appeared in the Games. Schmirler died of cancer two years later at the young age of 36.

Quickies

Did you know ...
that no individual has ever won gold twice in Olympic curling?

Who manufactures the curling stones for the Olympics?

When it was announced that curling was to be included in the Nagano 1998 Winter Olympics as a medal sport, the International Olympic Committee requested that the firm Kays of Scotland, in Ayrshyre, manufacture the curling stones using rare Ailsite granite from Ailsa Craig in the Firth of Clyde.

Men's Olympic Curling Medallists by Country

Games	Gold	Silver	Bronze
Turin 2006	Canada	Finland	United States
Salt Lake 2002	Norway	Canada	Switzerland
Nagano 1998	Switzerland	Canada	Norway
Chamonix 1924	Great Britain	Sweden	France

When was the first Olympic competition for ice hockey staged?

Oddly enough, the first time hockey was played at the Olympics was in April 1920, at the Summer Games in Antwerp, as a demonstration sport. Seven nations took part: Canada, the United States, Sweden, France, Belgium, Switzerland, and Czechoslovakia. Canada's amateur Winnipeg Falcons won gold, with the United States and Czechoslovakia taking silver and bronze respectively. Canada beat Sweden 12–1 in the gold-medal match. The Canadian team was so superior, and so much more sophisticated, that Europeans embraced both the nation and the game. In late January and early February of 1924, a separate Winter Olympics were staged for the first time at Chamonix, France. This time Canada was represented by the Toronto Granites, who easily took the gold medal, with the United States and Great Britain taking silver and bronze respectively. Canada's dominance was awesome. The Granites walloped Czechoslovakia 30–0, Sweden 22–0, Switzerland 33–0, and Great Britain 19–2. Their only competition was the United States, who they handily defeated 6–1 in the gold-medal final.

Women's Olympic Curling Medallists by Country

Games	Gold	Silver	Bronze
Turin 2006	Sweden	Switzerland	Canada
Salt Lake 2002	Great Britain	Switzerland	Canada
Nagano 1998	Canada	Denmark	Sweden

Who beat Canada's hockey team in the gold-medal match at the 1936 Winter Olympics?

After winning gold in hockey without breaking a sweat at the 1920, 1924, 1928, and 1932 Olympics, Canada finally encountered some competition at the 1936 Winter Olympics in Garmisch-Partenkirchen, Germany, as storm clouds of future war were already beginning to gather and the Nazis used both the Winter and Summer Games as a showcase for their delusions of Aryan superiority. Represented by the Port Arthur Bearcats, Canada easily vanquished its opponents in the first round, but in the semi-finals the Bearcats came up against a Great Britain team stocked with a number of men who held British passports but who lived and played hockey in Canada. The Bearcats lost 2–1 to the British, who didn't lose any hockey matches during the Games (though they did tie 0–0 with the United States). Britain

Quickies

Did you know ...

that the first Canadian Olympic ice hockey team, which played at the first Winter Olympics in Chamonix, France in 1924, won gold with only three goals scored against them? In fact, in their first three matches, the Canucks scored 85 times without conceding any goals!

284 • NOW YOU KNOW BIG BOOK OF SPORTS

won the gold medal, while Canada had to settle for the silver and the United States got bronze. There would not be another Olympics until 1948.

Who was Father David Bauer and what did he do for Canadian hockey?

Born in Goderich, Ontario, Father David Bauer was the brother of Bobby Bauer, one of the famed members of the Boston Bruins' Kraut Line. As a youth, Bauer was an outstanding left winger at St. Michael's High School in Toronto, an educational facility noted for its junior hockey program. He also played with the Oshawa Generals Junior A team when it won the Memorial Cup in 1944. (The Memorial Cup is the championship trophy for amateur junior hockey in Canada, while the Allan Cup does the same service for amateur senior hockey.) Later, Bauer returned to St. Michael's and coached its Junior A club to a Memorial Cup in 1961. The next season the Basilian priest was transferred to St. Mark's College at the University of British Columbia. Esteemed as a hockey coach, Bauer had his plan for a national team approved by the Canadian Amateur Hockey Association in 1962. In 1968 the national team, helmed by Father Bauer, won a bronze medal at the Grenoble Winter Olympics in France. Two years later Canada withdrew from international hockey, citing the impossibility of competing against much-improved European teams without the participation of Canadian professionals. Father Bauer's national team was then terminated, but the priest continued his dedicated pursuit of coupling education with athletic skill. He was elected to the Hockey Hall of Fame posthumously in 1989, having died the year before. Fortunately, he did live to see Canadian professionals finally play at the World Championships when the International Ice Hockey Federation and North American hockey officials brokered a "deal" in 1977, but he died long before his country won its first gold in an Olympics since the 1950s. No doubt Father Bauer was smiling somewhere on that auspicious occasion in Salt Lake City in 2002.

Who were the first three Canadians to win the Stanley Cup, the gold medal in hockey at the Winter Olympics, and the World Hockey Championship?

Prior to the Winter Olympics in Salt Lake City in 2002, only 10 people had won a Stanley Cup as well as Olympic gold and a World Championship in hockey, and all of them were Europeans: Viacheslav Fetisov (Soviet Union), Igor Larionov (Soviet Union), Tomas Jonsson (Sweden), Alexei Gusarov (Soviet Union), Peter Forsberg (Sweden), Alexander Mogilny (Soviet Union), Vladislav Malakov (Soviet Union), Hakan Loob (Sweden), Mats Naslund (Sweden), and Valeri Kamensky (Soviet Union). Then, at Salt Lake City, Canada won its first gold medal in hockey since 1952. On the Canadian team were Joe Sakic, Rob Blake, and Brendan Shanahan, all of whom had previously won Stanley Cups and World Championships. Now they, too, are part of the rarefied, so-called Triple Gold Club.

What object was buried at centre ice in 2002 at the Salt Lake City Winter Olympics?

A Canadian named Trent Evans from Edmonton, Alberta, took care of the ice at Salt Lake City's E Center during the Winter Olympics in 2002. When he noticed there was no dot to indicate where to drop the puck for faceoffs, he buried a Canadian dollar coin, a loonie, under the ice at the centre ice faceoff circle and obscured it with some yellow paint. Both the Canadian women's and men's hockey teams were told about the good-luck charm but were asked not to breathe a word about it. Canada went on to win gold in both men's and women's hockey. After the medals were won, Wayne Gretzky, executive director of the Canadian men's team, held a press conference and pulled the loonie out of his jacket pocket, telling the assembled, "We took it out of the ice tonight and we're going to present it to the Hall of Fame. We got two gold medals out of it. That's pretty special." Strangely enough, at the 2006 Winter Olympics a loonie wasn't buried at centre ice. In those Games, Canada's men's hockey team failed to get any medal, though the women's team did strike gold. Loonies were buried in the ice at the Olympic curling competition that year, and the Canadian men's team grabbed gold.

What family played in the 1956, 1960, and 1980 Winter Olympic for the U.S. hockey team?

The patriarch of the Christian family, Ed, was instrumental in building the Warroad Lakers' arena in Minnesota. Ed had three children — Bill, Roger, and Gordon — all of whom grew to prominence in U.S. hockey. Gordon, the eldest, played on the 1955 World Championship team for the United States and the following year helped the American national team win a silver medal at the Olympics in Italy. Middle brother Roger and the younger Bill played on the 1960 Olympic gold-medal team at Squaw Valley, California. The three brothers all travelled with the U.S. national team to the Soviet Union in 1957–58 for a series of exhibition games, the first time the two superpowers squared off in such a tournament. In all, Roger played 18 years with the Warroad Lakers senior amateur club and Bill played 23 years. In 1964 Bill established Christian Brothers Inc., the most successful makers of hockey sticks and equipment in the United States. Perhaps most famous of all, however, was Bill's son, Dave, who played on the 1980 Miracle on Ice Olympic team, which took gold for the Americans exactly 20 years after their first Olympic victory. Dave played 15 seasons (1979–80 to 1993–94) in the NHL, competing in Canada Cup tournaments in 1981, 1984, and 1991, the year the United States went all the way to the final before losing to Canada. Bill and Roger were inducted into the U.S. Hockey Hall of Fame; in 1998 Bill also made it into the International Ice Hockey Federation's Hall of Fame.

What two actors played U.S. coach Herb Brooks in the movies?

Although best known as the coach of America's gold-medal-winning Miracle on Ice team at the Winter Olympics at Lake Placid, New York, in 1980, the St. Paul, Minnesota-born Herbert "Herb" Brooks began his hockey career in 1955 as a player at the University of Minnesota. He nearly made the gold-medal-winning U.S. team at the 1960 Winter Olympics at Squaw Valley, California, won a bronze medal with the American club at the 1962 World Championship, and played for his country in both the 1964 and 1968 Winter Olympics. After retiring as a player, he became the head coach of the University of Minnesota's men's hockey team and won three national championships there, a success that helped make him coach of the national team. After the stunning gold medal victory in 1980, in which U.S. goaltender Jim Craig allowed only 15 goals in seven games, Brooks coached in Switzerland for a year and then began a middling career as an NHL coach with the New York Rangers. He later coached the Minnesota North Stars and the New Jersey Devils and was France's coach at the Nagano Winter Olympics in 1998. Midway through the 1999–2000 NHL season, he was made interim coach of the Pittsburgh Penguins until season's end. Later he served as a scout for the Penguins. At the Salt Lake City Winter Olympics in 2002, Brooks was back again as the head coach of the U.S. national team, winning a silver medal this time. On August 11, 2003, the man often described as the greatest hockey coach in U.S. history, was killed in a car accident in Minnesota. The two actors who played him in movies were Karl Malden (*Miracle on Ice*, 1981) and Kurt Russell (*Miracle*, 2004).

What was the first Olympic hockey team to win a medal on home ice?

At the 1928 Olympic Winter Games in St. Moritz, Switzerland, ice hockey was utterly dominated by the Canadian team. The ten other teams in the tournament were Great Britain, France, Belgium, Hungary, Sweden, Czechoslovakia, Poland, Switzerland, Austria, and Germany. The Canucks received a bye into the medal round because of their gold win at the 1924 games and, in a three-game round-robin, took gold again by defeating Sweden 11–0, Great Britain 4–0, and the home team of Switzerland 13–0. For their part, the Swiss hosts defeated Germany 1–0 and tied Austria 4–4, but in addition to losing to Canada, they were defeated 4–0 by Sweden, who took silver. In the match for the third place, however, the Swiss were able to defeat Great Britain 4–0 to become the first Olympic ice hockey ever team to win a medal on home ice.

Men's Olympic Hockey Medal Winners

Year	Gold	Silver	Bronze
1920	Canada	United States	Czechoslovakia
1924	Canada	United States	Great Britain
1928	Canada	Sweden	Switzerland
1932	Canada	United States	Germany
1936	Great Britain	Canada	United States
1948	Canada	Czechoslovakia	Switzerland
1952	Canada	United States	Sweden
1956	Soviet Union	United States	Canada
1960	United States	Canada	Soviet Union
1964	Soviet Union	Sweden	Czechoslovakia
1968	Soviet Union	Czechoslovakia	Canada
1972	Soviet Union	United States	Czechoslovakia
1976	Soviet Union	Czechoslovakia	West Germany
1980	United States	Soviet Union	Sweden
1984	Soviet Union	Czechoslovakia	Sweden
1988	Soviet Union	Finland	Sweden
1992	Russia	Canada	Czechoslovakia
1994	Sweden	Canada	Finland
1998	Czech Republic	Russia	Finland
2002	Canada	United States	Russia
2006	Sweden	Finland	Czech Republic

When did women's hockey debut at the Winter Olympics?

It took a long time, but finally in 1998 at the Nagano, Japan, Winter Olympics, women's hockey became an event. Although Canada dominated the women's side of the sport at the time, the first Olympic gold medal was snatched from the country by Team USA, led by Cammi Granato, Karen Bye, Sarah Tueting, Colleen Coyne, and Sara Decosta. Canada got its revenge, though, winning gold at the next two Winter Olympics: 2002 in Salt Lake City and 2006 in Turin, Italy.

Have any athletes died while participating in their sports at the Olympics?

The Olympics has seen only four athlete's die while participating in their events. This is perhaps surprising, given the sheer numbers of events held, and perhaps not surprising, because of the fitness and general competence of the athletes. Two were at summer games, two at winter. In 1912 in Stockholm, Portuguese marathon runner Francisco Lazaro, 21, collapsed from sunstroke and

Quickies

Did you know ...

that the top scorer in the 1928 Winter Olympic ice hockey tournament was Dave Trottier who scored 12 goals in three games and also logged three assists? Trottier would go on to have a successful career in the NHL, most notably helping the Montreal Maroons' sweep the Toronto Maple Leafs in the 1934–35 Stanley Cup finals.

heart trouble and died the next day. In 1960 at Rome, Danish cyclist Knut Jensen died during the Olympic road race as a result of ingesting amphetamines and nicotinyl tartrate, supposed performance boosters. Jensen crashed and fractured his skull.

Both winter deaths happened during the 1964 Innsbruck Olympics. Australian downhill racer Ross Milne, 19, was killed when he flew off the course during a training run and slammed into a tree. Polish-born British luge competitor Kazimierz Kay-Skrzypeski was killed during a trial run on the Olympic course two weeks before the Games began.

Women's Olympic Hockey Medal Winners			
Year	Gold	Silver	Bronze
1998	United States	Canada	Finland
2002	Canada	United States	Sweden
2006	Canada	Sweden	United States

What is the correct name for a luge athlete?

Given that the sleds they ride on routinely reach speeds of 120–160 km/hr, one might think luge competitors should be called thrill seekers, or maybe just crazy. While they may indeed require a certain devil-may-care attitude to participate in the sport, the correct technical term for a luge competitor is actually "slider." It is incorrect to call them lugers, as many people do.

Quickies
Did you know ...
that luge is the French word for sled?

Why were three members of the East German women's luge team disqualified from the 1968 Grenoble Olympics?

At the Grenoble Olympics in 1968, three East German women luge sliders were disqualified for heating the runners on their sleds, including Ortrun Enderlein and Anna-Maria Müller who were in first and second place, respectively, after the third run and, as it turned out that day, would certainly have won gold and silver medals. Heating the runners — once common in the sport, but since banned — creates an advantage, as the warm runners melt the ice of the track, resulting in less friction when going downhill. After the disqualifications, the fourth run of the event was cancelled due to the poor

Quickies
Did you know ...
that of the 108 medals awarded in luge since 1964, German teams have won 65 of them?

weather conditions. This meant that Italy's Erika Lechner, who had been in third behind Enderlein and Müller, immediately advanced to the gold podium. Silver and Bronze were taken by Christa Schmuck and Angelika Dünhaupt, both of whom were member of — you guessed it! — the East German team.

What are the origins of the names for figure skating jumps?

The unfamiliar names for figure skating jumps are from the athletes who introduced them.

- *Axel* — The only jump initiated while skating forward, it was named after Norwegian Axel Paulsen who introduced the move in 1883.
- *Salchow* — A jump performed with a backward inside edge takeoff. Ulrich Salchow of Sweden was the first Olympic gold medallist in men's figure skating and World Champion 10 times between 1900 and 1911. A triple Sachow is three complete airborne revolutions.
- *Lutz* — Performed from a backward outside edge. Alois Lutz of Vienna introduced this move in the first decade of the twentieth century.

What athlete took the most medals at the Turin Olympics in 2006?

Canadian Cindy Klassen started out as a ice hockey player, but after missing the squad for the Nagano Olympics, she turned to speed skating. Her international Olympic breakthrough came in 2002 when she took bronze in the 3,000m race at Salt Lake City. It wasn't until 2006, however, that we saw her in her full Olympic glory. That year Klassen brought home five medals — one for every event she had entered. She was the most titled athlete of the 2006 Winter Games.

Men's Olympic Speed Skating Records				
Event	**Result**	**Name**	**Country**	**Games**
500m	34.42	Casey FitzRandolph	U.S.	2002 Salt Lake City
1,000m	1:07.18	Gerard van Velde	Netherlands	2002 Salt Lake City
1,500m	1:43.95	Derek Parra	U.S.	2002 Salt Lake City
5,000m	6:14.66	Jochem Uytdehaage	Netherlands	2002 Salt Lake City
10,000m	12:58.92	Jochem Uytdehaage	Netherlands	2002 Salt Lake City
2x500m	69.23pts	Casey FitzRandolph	U.S.	2002 Salt Lake City
Team pursuit	3:43.64	Matteo Anesi	Italy	2006 Turin
		Enrico Fabris	Italy	2006 Turin
		Ippolito Sanfratello	Italy	2006 Turin

What was the first event in the first Winter Olympics?

The first event ever to be decided in a Winter Olympics was the men's 500m speed skating race. It was held in 1924 in Chamonix, France, at an International Olympic Committee-sanctioned "Winter Sports Week", which was later retroactively christened the first Winter Olympics by the IOC. American Charles Jewtraw won the event.

Women's Olympic Speed Skating Records

Event	Result	Name	Country	Games
500m	37.30	Catriona Le May Doan	Canada	2002 Salt Lake City
1,000m	1:13.83	Chris Witty	U.S.	2002 Salt Lake City
1,500m	1:54.02	Anni Friesinger	Germany	2002 Salt Lake City
3,000m	3:57.70	Claudia Pechstein	Germany	2002 Salt Lake City
5,000m	6:46.91	Claudia Pechstein	Germany	2002 Salt Lake City
2x500m	74.75pts	Catriona Le May Doan	Canada	2002 Salt Lake City
Team pursuit	3:01.24	Kristina Groves	Canada	2006 Turin
		Cindy Klassen	Canada	2006 Turin
		Christine Nesbitt	Canada	2006 Turin

Who are Yang Yang (A) and Yang Yang (S)?

Along with Chunlun Wang and Dandan Sun, Yang Yang (A) and Yang Yang (S) were members of the China's women's Short Track Speed Skating team at the Nagano Games in 1998, and Salt Lake City, 2002. To stem confusion over which Yang was which, the letters of their birth months — August and September — were appended to their names. The written distinction between Yang Yangs (A) and (S) was for the benefit of non-Chinese speakers, because their names were pronounced differently in Chinese.

Men's Short Track Olympic Speed Skating Records

Event	Result	Name	Country	Games
500m	41.802	Marc Gagnon	Canada	2002 Salt Lake City
1000m	1:26.739	Ahn Hyun-Soo	South Korea	2006 Turin
1500m	2:15.942	Kim Dong-Sung	South Korea	2002 Salt Lake City
5000m relay	6:43.376	Ahn Hyun-Soo	South Korea	2006 Turin
		Lee Ho-Suk	South Korea	2006 Turin
		Seo Ho-Jin	South Korea	2006 Turin
		Song Suk-Woo	South Korea	2006 Turin

Women's Short Track Olympic Speed Skating Records

Event	Result	Name	Country	Games
500m	44.118	Yang Yang (A)	China	2002 Salt Lake City
1000m	1:31.235	Yang Yang (A)	China	2002 Salt Lake City
1500m	2:21.069	Choi Eun-Kyung	South Korea	2002 Salt Lake City
3000m relay	4:12.793	Choi Eun-Kyung	South Korea	2002 Salt Lake City
		Min-Kyung Choi	South Korea	2002 Salt Lake City
		Joo Min-Jin	South Korea	2002 Salt Lake City
		Park Hye-Won	South Korea	2002 Salt Lake City

Who is the oldest person to have won a medal in Olympic speed skating?

While almost any given Olympic sport is, quite literally, a young person's game, speed skaters tend to stick with it to a riper age than athletes in other events. Canada's Frank Stack, for example, skated in three Winter Olympics: 1932 Lake Placid (where he took bronze in the 10,000m race), 1948 St. Moritz, and 1952 Oslo. By the time of his final Olympic event, the 500m race at Oslo, in which he placed 12th, Stack was just a month over the age of 46. But while many other speed skaters also over 40 have competed in the Olympics, none have ever won medals. The distinction of oldest speed skater to have won a medal belongs to Finland's Julius Skutnabb. At the first Winter Olympics in Chamonix in 1924, he took part in every speed skating event, earning a silver in the 5,000m race and gold in the 10,000m. The

Cindy Klassen's 2006 Turin Olympic Triumph

Event	Medal
1,500m	Gold
1,000m	Silver
Team Pursuit (6 laps)	Silver
3,000m	Bronze
5,000m	Bronze

Chamonix Games were the only ones at which a combined event was also contested and based on Skutnabb's overall results, he took bronze in that category. Skutnabb returned to the Olympics in 1928, competing only in the 5,000m race. He took silver in the event at age 38 years 245 days, and remains the oldest speed skater — man or woman — to have ever won a medal at the Olympics.

Olympic Medal Wins for Yang Yang (A) vs Yang Yang (S)

Games	500m	1000m	3000m relay
Turin 2006	—	(A) Bronze	—
Salt Lake City 2002	(A) Gold	—	(A) and (S) Silver
Nagano 1998	(S) Silver	(S) Silver	(A) and (S) Silver

Why did Anders Haugen receive a bronze medal in ski jumping at age 83?

Norwegian-born Anders Haugen was the captain of the American ski team at the Winter Olympics in both Chamonix (1924) and St. Moritz (1928). At Chamonix he was listed as the fourth-place finisher in the ski jump event, but 50 years later, in 1974, a Norwegian ski historian discovered a mathematical scoring error from the Chamonix ski jumping event that showed Haugen had actually placed third. At age 83, Haugen was presented with his bronze medal.

Why was there no skiing at the 1940 Winter Olympic Games?

Alpine skiing events were included for the first time at the Winter Olympic in 1936, when the twin Bavarian towns of Garmisch and Partenkirchen playing hosts. Before anyone could hit the slopes, however, a major controversy erupted, as the IOC, overruling the International Ski Federation, declared that ski instructors could not take part in the Olympics because they were paid professionals. Incensed, the Austrian and Swiss skiers boycotted the events with the exception of a few Austrians who decided to become Germans and take part. The dispute carried on after the Games and it was decided that skiing would not be included in the 1940 Olympics.

Oldest and Youngest Ever Olympic Speed Skaters				
Olympics	Athlete	Team	Age	Medals Won
1924 Chamonix	Albert Tebbit	United Kingdom	51 years 30 days	none
1972 Sapporo	Lee Gyeong-Hui	South Korea	13 years 338 days	none

Why did Henri Oreiller almost not ski in the Oslo Games of 1952?

A member of the French underground during World War II, Henri Oreiller was known as "The Acrobat" because he was able to negotiate the slopes of Val d'Isère on one ski. When the 1948 St. Moritz Winter Games began, Oreiller was full of confidence. Although there were 112 skiers entered in the downhill event, he boasted that the others were wasting their time because he would win easily. But when he awoke on the morning of the competition, he faced an unexpected setback: he could not find his famous red skis. Finally they were discovered on the roof of the car of an American who had taken them by mistake. Once he'd found his skis, Oreiller lived up to his boasts and took two skiing golds and one bronze for France.

Quickies
Did you know ...
that at the first Winter Olympics in Chamonix, France in 1924, the last ranked competitor in the 50km cross country skiing event finished 2:30 hours after Norway's Thorleif Haug, who won the event in 3:44 hours? The grueling race was held in a violent and icy cold wind storm.

Quickies
Did you know ...
that three months before the Albertville Olympics in 1992, Norwegian downhill skier Kjetil André Aamodt became so ill with mononucleosis that he lost 11kg while in hospital where he had to be drip-fed? He recovered splendidly and took gold in the super-G and bronze in the giant slalom at Albertville.

Has any women's ski team ever won a triple — gold, silver, and bronze — all in one event?

This has only ever been done once, in 1964 at Innsbruck, where the Austrian women's team made the first and only triple in the history of Alpine skiing at the Olympic Winter Games: in the downhill, on the Axamer Lizum run, Christl Haas took gold ahead of Edith Zimmermann (silver) and Traudl Hecher (bronze).

What did ski jumper Simon Ammann do at the Salt Lake City 2006 Winter Olympics to surprise the world?

Quickies
Did you know ...
that after his skiing career, Frenchman Henri Oreiller turned to auto racing? He died in 1962 behind the wheel of his Ferrari in a crash at the Linas-Montlhéry autodrome.

Quickies
Did you know ...
that on February 1, 1964, 18-year-old French skier Marielle Goitschel finished second in the slalom, just 76 one-hundredths of a second behind her older sister, Christine? Two days later, it was Christine's turn to take silver, as Marielle won gold in the giant slalom.

Quite simply, Ammann won two gold medals. This was a surprise to everyone because prior to those Games the best the Swiss skier seemed capable of at the Olympics was his 35th place finish in the Normal Hill event and his 39th finish in the Large Hill event at the 1998 Nagano Games. Going into Salt Lake, his best non-Olympic result ever on the Normal Hill was 26th place and he had not once won a World Cup event. Nonetheless, Ammann shocked everyone by jumping to gold on both the Normal and Large hills, defeating top-tier jumpers such as Germany's Sven Hannawald and Poland's Adam Małysz, each of whom came into those Games with multiple World Championships.

tennis

How did tennis get its name?

In the eleventh century, French monks started playing a game by batting a crude handball around the monastery. It was a kind of handball with a rope strung across a courtyard. The game progressed and became popular with royalty before catching on in England in the thirteenth century. When returning a ball over the net, the French players shouted, "*Tenez*," meaning "Here it comes" or "Take it."

How did tennis get the terms *seeded* and *love*?

Tennis was popularized by the French nobility, and because a zero looked like an egg, that's what they called it. *Egg* in French is *l'oeuf*, which became *love* in English. The seeding or placing of the best players within favourable tournament positions required other players to graciously cede — yield or give up — the spots. In time, the word mutated to the spelling of its homonym, *seed*, and so players were said to be *seeded*.

> **Quickies**
> *Did you know ...*
> that there is obscure manuscript evidence suggesting French knights introduced a tennis-like game, called *tenez*, to the Italian city of Florence in the year 1325?

Why are legal issues, basketball games, and tennis tournaments all settled on a "court"?

Like *courtesy*, the word *court* evolved from the Latin words *cum*, meaning "together," and *hortus*, from which we derive *horticulture* — so a court was an enclosed garden where young boys of noble birth learned proper social conduct. In both the judicial and sporting sense, a court is a specified area within which you are expected to practise courtesy while respecting authority.

> **Quickies**
> *Did you know ...*
> that the grass on the tennis courts at Wimbledon is cut to exactly eight millimetres in height?

Where is the world's oldest tennis court?

Falkland Palace in Fife, Scotland, is the site of the oldest tennis court still in use. The court was built in 1539, and is used to play 'real' tennis, a racquet sport played inside a closed room. Unlike most real tennis courts, the Falkland Court is not fully enclosed as it does not have a roof. Another real tennis court was built by Henry VIII in Hampton Court

Palace, near London, England. The original court, built in 1532, was demolished. The one in use today dates from 1625.

There are approximately 45 real tennis courts still in existence around the world. The Royal Tennis Court at Hampton Court Palace is the hub of real tennis activity.

Who invented the game of squash?

Squash is a racquet sport played off the four walls of a room. It started in 1830 at an exclusive boarding school in England called Harrow, when students noticed that a punctured racquetball offered a greater variety of shots and lots of exercise. Two schools of the game developed, the English one using a softball, and a North America version that used a smaller hardball. Both games called for a 32-foot-deep court, but the English court was wider at 21 feet than the 18.5 foot courts of the North American game. The game is now played in almost 150 countries. Championships are held for men and women in many age groups, and the development of glass-walled courts has led to regular television coverage.

Have any husband-and-wife team ever won mixed doubles at Wimbledon?

In January 1926, Britons Kitty McKane and Leslie Godfree married while on a tennis tour of South Africa. Later that year they became the only husband and wife team ever to win the mixed doubles at Wimbledon. McKane also won her second Wimbledon singles title that year and reached the final of the women's doubles for the third time, the first time having been in 1922 when she was partnered by her sister, Margaret Stocks.

What is the Tennis Masters Cup?

The Tennis Masters Cup is the third iteration of a championship tournament that started as The Masters tournament in 1970. In 1990 it became the ATP Tour World Championship when the Association of Tennis Professionals (ATP) took over the tournament from the International Tennis Federation (ITF). At that time the ITF began running a similar championship event known as the Grand Slam Cup. In 1999 the two organizations agreed to discontinue the two competing year-end tournaments and formed a jointly owned event — the Tennis Masters Cup.

Who was the first tennis player to win the Tennis Masters Cup?

The first Tennis Masters Cup tournament was played in 2000. It was won by Gustavo Kuerten of Brazil who defeated American Andre Agassi 6–4, 6–4, 6–4.

What is the Davis Cup and who was the first winner?

The world's premier men's team tennis tournament is the Davis Cup. The competition began in 1900 as a competition between Great Britain and the U.S. It has grown since then to see over 130 countries entered in competition. The first Davis Cup in 1900 was won by the United States. The competition was originally known as the International Lawn Tennis Challenge. Its name was changed to the Davis Cup in 1945 following the death of player Dwight Davis.

> **The Four Annual Grand Slam Tennis Tournaments**
>
> - The Australian Open, held in January. First held in 1905.
> - Tournoi de Roland-Garros, or the French Open, held between mid-May to early June. First held in 1891 and opened to international competition in 1925.
> - Wimbledon, held in England during June and July. First played in 1877.
> - U.S. Open, held in August and September. First held in 1881.

What is the "open era"?

In 1968, commercial pressures in the sport of tennis led to the abandonment of the distinction between professionals and amateurs, inaugurating the "open era," in which all players could compete in all tournaments. The open era in tennis began that year, when Grand Slam tournaments abandoned the longstanding rules of amateurism and allowed professionals to compete.

What female tennis player holds the record for the most consecutive U.S. Open singles championships?

The U.S. Open tennis tournament is one of the oldest tennis championships in the world, first contested in 1881. Records for most consecutive championships can be divided into two eras. In the open era (1968 on), Chris Evert had four wins from 1975–78. In the pre-open era (prior to 1968), it is a tie, as Molla Bjurstedt Mallory had four wins from 1915–18, and Helen Jacobs had four from 1932–35.

> **Quickies**
>
> **Did you know ...**
> that the first Grand Slam tournament to go "open" was the French Open?

Men with the Most Consecutive U.S. Open Singles Wins		
Player	**Consecutive Wins**	**Years**
Richard D. Sears	7	1881, 82, 83, 84, 85, 86, 87
Bill Tilden	6	1920, 21, 22, 23, 24, 25
William Larned	5	1907, 08, 09, 10, 11
Roger Federer	5	2004, 05, 06, 07 08

What men have the most U.S. Open singles championships?

Richard D. Sears, Bill Tilden, and William Larned all won seven U.S. Open men's singles championships prior to 1968. Jimmy Connors, Pete Sampras, and Roger Federer are tied at five for the most open-era men's singles championship

What women have the most U.S. Open singles championships?

Chris Evert has the most open-era singles championships in the U.S. Open, with six, while Molla Bjurstedt Mallory holds the record for the most pre-1968 U.S. Open singles titles, with eight.

The First Singles Tennis Champions of the Open Era

- 1968 men's singles champion: Arthur Ashe
- 1968 women's singles champion: Virginia Wade

Who were the first American tennis players to win the French Open?

The first American man to win the French Open was Don Budge, in 1938. The first American woman to win the French Open was Helen Wills, in 1928.

Has anyone won a tennis grand slam within one calendar year twice?

Australian Rod Laver won all four grand slam tennis events in 1962 and then did it again in 1969. In the years between he only won a single grand slam event, Wimbledon in 1968. He never won another grand slam event after 1969.

Who was Roland Garros?

The French Open is known as Les Internationaux de France de Roland Garros or Tournoi de Roland-Garros. Garros was a pioneering French aviator. In 1913 he became the first aviator to fly across the Mediterranean Sea (from France to Tunisia). He was also a pilot during World War I and was shot down and killed on October 5, 1918, a little more than a month before the end of the war. In the 1920s a tennis center in Paris that Roland-Garros attended was renamed in his honour as the Stade de Roland Garros. The French Open derives its name from the aviator and stadium.

When was the last time a British tennis player won the singles event at Wimbledon?

The last time the male singles event at Wimbledon was won by a British tennis player was in 1936, when it was won by Fred Perry. The last time the female singles event was won by a British tennis player was in 1977, when it was won by Virginia Wade.

What female and male tennis players have the most consecutive singles wins at Wimbledon?

The woman with the most consecutive singles wins in the history of Wimbledon is Martina Navratilova, who triumphed six times in a row from 1982–1987. For the men, William Renshaw holds the record with six consecutive Wimbledon wins from 1891–1896.

What is the weight of a tennis ball?

The International Tennis Federation (ITF), which is the world governing body for tennis, indicates that a regulation tennis ball at sea level should weigh between 1.975 and 2.095 ounces. Furthermore, regulation tennis balls at sea level must measure between 2.575 and 2.700 inches in diametre. Balls must also be either white or yellow in colour.

Who was the first unseeded tennis player to win Wimbledon?

The first unseeded tennis player to become a Wimbledon champion was Boris Becker, in 1985, at the age of 17. Becker defeated eigth seed Kevin Curren 6–3, 6–7, 7–6, 6–4 to take Wimbledon. He was also the first German to win Wimbledon.

Who was the first tennis player to win the WTA Tour Championships?

The WTA Tour Championships is an annual women's tennis tournament held at the end of the season for the top-ranked players on the Women's Tennis Association tour. The WTA Tour Championships were first played as the Virginia Slims Championships in 1971. The first winner was American Billie Jean King.

What is the Kremlin Cup and who were the first winners?

The Kremlin Cup is a tennis tournament held annually in the autumn at Moscow's Olympic Stadium. The tournament was first held in 1990 for men. A women's competition was added in 1996. The first male winners were Andrei Cherkasov (Soviet Union), in singles, and Hendrik Jan Davids (Netherlands) and Paul Haarhuis (Netherlands), in doubles. The first female winner was Spain's Conchita Martínez, in singles.

What team won the first Fed Cup?

The Fed Cup is the women's premier team-tennis championship, similar to the men's Davis Cup. It was founded as the Federation Cup in 1963 to commemorate the 50th anniversary of the International Tennis Federation (ITF). The name was changed to the Fed Cup in 1995. The inaugural event attracted 16 countries and was won by the United States.

When was the first tennis tournament held at Wimbledon?

The All England Lawn Tennis and Croquet Club, which stages the annual Wimbledon tennis tournament, is a private club founded in 1868, originally as The All England Croquet Club. Its first grounds were off Worple Road, in Wimbledon, a suburb of London, England. In 1875 lawn tennis was added to the activities of the club and two years later, in spring 1877, the club was renamed The All England Croquet and Lawn Tennis Club. The first Wimbledon tennis tournament was held that year with the only event being the men's singles, which was won by Spencer Gore, from a field of 22. The club moved to its current site on Church Road in 1922.

What was *sphairistike*?

Sphairistike was an ancient Greek ball game the name of which one Major Walter Wingfield borrowed for a new sport he patented in England in 1874. Sphairistike combined the net from badminton, the ball from fives, and the scoring from racquets. Sound familiar? That's because the nearly unpronounceable sphairistike eventually came to be called "lawn tennis," since Major Wingfield used that term in his patent application to distinguish the new sport from a much older indoor game often called court tennis.

Court Surfaces at the Four Grand Slam Tennis Events		
Event	**Venue**	**Court surface**
Australian Open	Melbourne Park	Plexicushion (acrylic over polymers)
French Open	Stade de Roland Garros (Paris)	Clay
Wimbledon	All England Lawn Tennis and Croquet Club (London)	Rye grass
U.S. Open	Arthur Ashe Stadium (Queens, NY	DecoTurf (asphalt over polymers)

What male tennis player won the most consecutive men's singles titles at Wimbledon?

Ernest Renshaw won six consecutive Wimbledon men's singles titles from 1882 to 1889. In the modern era (since the club moved to Church Rd in 1922), two players have won five consecutive Wimbledon men's singles titles, Bjorn Borg, from 1976 to 1980, and Roger Federer, from 2003 to 2007.

What female tennis player has the most French Open singles wins?

The woman who has the most singles wins at the Tournoi de Roland Garros is Chris Evert who won the French Open seven times (1974, 1975, 1979, 1980, 1983, 1985, and 1986). Steffi Graf is second with six wins (1987, 1988, 1993, 1995, 1996, and 1999).

Who holds the record for being cumulatively ranked the number one tennis player in the world for the most amount of time?

Steffi Graff was ranked the number one tennis player in the world for 377 weeks throughout her career. This is a record for both men's and women's tennis.

What male tennis star has the fastest serve ever recorded?

In 2004 at the Davis Cup, American tennis star Andy Roddick delivered a serve clocked at an astonishing 249.45 kilometres per hour.

What female tennis player has the fastest serve ever recorded?

Brenda Schultz-McCarthy delivered the fastest serve ever recorded for a female tennis player. One of her serves was clocked at 209.21 kilometres per hour during a 2006 WTA Tour qualifying match in Cincinnati.

Who was the youngest player to ever win a Wimbledon championship?

Martina Hingis became the youngest ever Wimbledon champion when she teamed with Helena Suková to win the women's doubles title in 1996, at the age of 15 years, 282 days. The previous holder of the record was Lottie Dodd, who won the first of her five Wimbledon Ladies singles championships in 1887 at the age of 15 years, 285 days.

Quickies
Did you know ...
that Martina Navratilova has the most Wimbledon women's singles championships, with nine wins?

Who was the first unseeded player to win the Wimbledon men's singles championship?

Boris Becker became the first unseeded player to win the Wimbledon singles title when he did it in 1985 at the age of 17, defeating Kevin Curren in four sets. This victory also made Becker the youngest male to ever win the Wimbledon title. Becker defended his title the following year, defeating Ivan Lendl in straight sets. The only other unseeded player to win the Wimbledon men's singles championship was Goran Ivanievic, who did so in 2001.

What male and female tennis players have won the most Australian Open Championship titles?

Roy Emerson holds the record for the most Men's Australian Open Championships with six wins (1961, 1963, 1964, 1965, 1966, and 1967). Margaret Smith holds the record for the most Women's Australian Open Championships with seven wins (1960, 1961, 1962, 1963, 1964, 1965, and 1966).

golf

Who gave golf its hole?

The precise origin of the game of golf is not known. It is generally agreed among historians that games involving pebbles or small balls being struck with sticks across open ground towards elevated targets have existed worldwide for eons. But the first recorded reference to such a game, in which the goal was to sink the ball into a hole in the ground, is from 943 A.D. China. The *Dongxuan Records,* written by Wei Tai of the Song Dynasty, describe the Chinese game of *chuiwan*, which was played in a circuit on a lawn with many holes. Popular with royalty and commoners alike, *chuiwan* was often depicted in Chinese poetry, opera, and painting until the middle of the Ming Dynasty, in the fifteenth century, when it disappeared. While it is commonly contended that the Scottish introduced the hole to golf, Chinese historians hold that trade between East and West during the Middle Ages might have easily introduced *chuiwan*-like games to Europe, although no records show early European versions of the game employing a hole.

Who first brought golf to Scotland?

As early as 1262, the Flemish played *chole*, a game in which a ball is struck by a club across a field towards a goal post. In 1421, during the Hundred Years' War, Hugh Kennedy, Robert Stewart, and John Smale, three Scottish soldiers, first played *chole* while their regiment was in western France to help French forces fight the English at the Battle of Baugé. The English were defeated, and the trio brought *chole* back to Scotland, where the game eventually evolved into modern golf.

What is the origin of the word *golf*?

The word *golf* first appeared in a Scottish statute issued in 1457 by James II, King of Scots, banning the game. In Scotland, from the Middle Ages until the mid-1800s, the printed word saw many variations in spelling, including *gouff, goiff, goff, gowff,* and *golph.* The exact etymology is not known, though it is possible that the word derived from the names of the similar Dutch games *colf* or *kolf* — terms which themselves derive from the Old Norse word *kolfr*, meaning *club*. Yet, interestingly, there are no recorded instances of the Scottish term being spelled with the initial letters *c* or *k*, so it is equally — or perhaps more — likely that the word evolved from the old Scottish word *gouf*, meaning to strike.

> **Quickies**
> ***Did you know …***
> that early golf club makers in Scotland were also bow makers for archery?

Why did James II, King of Scots, ban golf in 1457?

By the mid-fifteenth century, golf was extremely popular in Scotland. So popular, in fact, that the Parliament of James II felt it was necessary to issue a decree banning the game. At the time, 1457, Scotland was preparing to defend itself against possible invasion by the English, and golf was distracting soldiers from archery practice. In both 1470 and 1491 the ban was extended, but it was by then ignored by the Scottish people. In 1502, with the Treaty of Glasgow between Henry VII of England and James IV of Scotland, the ban on golf was finally lifted. James IV almost immediately took up the sport himself.

Why do we refer to golf courses as "links"?

The word *link* is derived from the Old English word *hlinc*, meaning "to lean," and was once used to describe a rising bank or ridge of "leaning" ground. In Scotland, the word came to be used for the coastal strips of semi-barren land found between the ocean and inland farming areas. Links land was too sandy for crops, so it was used for golfing and other leisure activities. There were no trees close to the beach and the sand traps were natural, with tall, reedy grass as the only vegetation. Otherwise worthless, these narrow strips of public land would eventually become extremely valuable as golf courses.

Five Rarely Recorded "Royal and Ancient" Moments in Scots Golf

- **1502, at Perth** — James IV, King of Scots, lifts a ban on golf, then purchases clubs himself
- **1562, at Montrose** — The 4th Earl of Montrose, James Graham, records in his diary that he played golf the day before his wedding
- **1567, at Seton House** — Mary, Queen of Scots, plays golf within days of her husband's assassination
- **1619, at Dornoch** — The 14th Earl of Sutherland, John Gordon, age 16, receives his first set of clubs, purchased for £10
- **1641, at Leith Links** — King Charles I receives news of the Irish Rebellion while playing golf

Where was the first golf clubhouse built?

In 1768, the Honourable Company of Edinburgh Golfers built the first clubhouse dedicated to golf at Leith Links, north of Edinburgh. Called the "Golf House," the building, which stood at the location of today's Queen Margaret University College, serviced a golf course of only five holes.

Who played in the first international golf match?

We know only half the story. The first international golf match was played in 1682 between Scotland and England. James II, Duke of York — after whom New York would later be named — played for Scotland with George Patterson, hosting two English noblemen at Leith. The Scots won, and apparently no one felt it important enough to note the names of the losers. We don't know who they were.

Who was the first caddie?

The word *caddie* is thought to have been introduced to English from the French word *cadet*, meaning younger brother or junior. It is believed that in the early 1500s, Mary, Queen of Scots, first encountered the practice of using a caddie in France, where junior soldiers were assigned to carry the clubs of royalty. The word *cadet* first appeared in English in 1610 and the word *caddie* in 1634. The first known Scottish caddie was Andrew Dickson, who carried the clubs of the Duke of York during the first international match in 1682.

How did St. Andrews invent the 18-hole course when the Old Course had 11 fairways?

In 1744, the St. Andrews Society of Golfers was formed. Golf was by then very popular in Scotland, but there was no standardized course. The St. Andrews course consisted of 11 fairways. For a full round, golfers played all 11 in one direction, then turned around and played them back in the opposite direction, making a total of 22 holes. On October 4, 1764, the members of St. Andrews made one of the most important decisions in golf history. They decided that the first four holes were too short, so they voted to combine them into two holes. Thus was born the 18-hole golf course.

The 12 Oldest Golf Clubs Outside the Island of Great Britain

- Royal Calcutta Golf Club, Kolkata, India (1829)
- Pau Golf Club, Billère, France (1856)
- Royal Montreal Golf Club, Montreal, Quebec, Canada (1873)
- Bangalore Golf Club, Bengaluru, India (1876)
- Royal Belfast, Belfast, Northern Ireland (1881)
- Curragh Golf Club, County Kildare, Ireland (1883)
- Oakhurst Links, White Sulphur Springs, West Virginia, U.S. (1884)
- Royal Cape Golf Club, Wynberg, Cape Town, South Africa (1885)
- St. Andrew's Golf Club, Yonkers, New York, U.S. (1888)
- Hong Kong Golf Club, Hong Kong, China (1889)
- Shinnecock Hills Golf Club, Southampton, New York, U.S. (1891)
- Royal Adelaide Golf Club, Adelaide, Australia (1892)

Why is it incorrect to think the 18-hole course corresponds to the number of shots in a fifth of whisky?

In 1764, when the St. Andrews members created the 18-hole course, there was no standard bottle size being used in Scotland for whisky, nor was there such a thing as an ounce measure. In the seventeenth and eighteenth centuries, bottles were hand blown and irregular, but the common goal was the equivalent of a 30-ounce bottle. Since there were no other sizes available, to have consumed a full bottle of whiskey at that time would have left all but the most robust players barely able to stand, let alone accurately swing a golf club.

Which was the first "Royal" golf course?

In 1833, the Perth Golfing Society in Scotland received a patronage from King William IV to become the Royal Perth Golfing Society. It was the first golf club to hold the distinction, a year prior to St. Andrews. The Royal Perth's present-day patron is Prince Andrew, Duke of York.

Who was Allan Robertson?

Born in 1815, Allan Robertson was the world's first golf professional and the first player to break 80 on the Old Course at St. Andrews, shooting 79 in 1858. He made his living playing for wagers and was also one of Scotland's top ball and club makers, with a shop on St. Andrews links where he made feathery balls (leather balls hard-packed with feathers). He was mentor to Old Tom Morris, who would go on to become one of the world's best players. The duo parted ways in 1849 after Robertson discovered Morris playing golf with a gutty, a less expensive ball made of gutta-percha that would soon make the feathery obsolete. Robertson died from jaundice in 1859.

Who was Old Tom Morris?

Old Tom Morris was born at St. Andrews, Scotland, in 1821, and was an apprentice ball maker to Allan Robertson. The two men often played together in matches, and it is said that they were never beaten. After leaving Robertson's shop when the two men had a falling out over Morris's use of a gutta-percha ball, Morris served as "keeper of the greens" at Prestwick Golf Club, where he also competed in the first Open Championship (predecessor to the British Open) in 1860, finishing second. He was the greenkeeper at St. Andrews from 1865 to 1904, where he mentored future course designer Donald Ross. "Old Tom" won the British Open in 1861, 1862, 1864, and 1867, and still holds the record for oldest champion (age 46, in 1867) and largest margin of victory (13 strokes, in 1862). He died in 1908, outliving his son Young Tom Morris by 32 years.

Who was Young Tom Morris?

Born in 1851 at St. Andrews, Scotland, Young Tom Morris was golf's first known prodigy and the son of famed greenkeeper Old Tom Morris. At the age of 13 he won his first contest, an exhibition match in Perth, and at 16, he took his first pro match, at Carnoustie. The next year, he won his first of four British Opens, and also scored the first hole-in-one on record. In 1869, he won the Open again, with his father coming in second. He also won in 1870 and 1872 (there was no Open in 1871). Young Tom died on Christmas Day 1875, at age 24, four months after his wife and child died during childbirth. It is said he perished of heartbreak.

Who were the "Great Triumvirate"?

Long before Palmer, Nicklaus, and Player there was J.H. Taylor, Harry Vardon, and James Braid. The trio dominated pro golf from 1894 to 1914, winning the British Open (then called simply "The Open") an astounding 16 times between them. It is unlikely that any group will hold such sway over the game again.

Who was Donald Ross?

Born in 1872, Donald Ross served an apprenticeship under the legendary greenkeeper Old Tom Morris at St. Andrews before moving to the United States in 1899 to become one of America's most notable golf course designers. He had a hand in more than 600 course designs or redesigns. His masterpieces are considered to be Pinehurst No. 2, Seminole, Oak Hill, and Oakland Hills. As a golfer, Ross won the North and South Open in 1903, 1905, and 1906, the Massachusetts Open in 1905 and 1911, finished fifth in the 1903 U.S. Open, and eighth in the 1910 British Open. In 1947, Ross helped found the American Society of Golf Course Architects, at Pinehurst, and was the organization's first president. He died in 1948.

Who were the Apple Tree Gang?

In 1887 a Scotsman named Robert Lockhart, who was living in New York, returned from a trip to Scotland with a set of a dozen or so golf clubs and as many golf balls. On February 22, 1888, during a winter thaw, he and his friend John Reid set up a six-hole course in a local cow pasture. Asking their friend — and the owner of the pasture — Henry O. Tallmadge to join them, Lockhart showed the men how golf was played. The game caught on so quickly amongst their peers that Lockhart soon sent to Scotland for five more sets of clubs and, on November 14, 1888, the course was moved to a 30-acre location in Yonkers, on the banks of the Hudson River. Famously, the new course was home to many apple trees, so with Reid appointed the first president, Lockhart, Tallmadge, and their friends became the "Apple Tree Gang," founding the St. Andrew's Golf Club, which is today the longest continuously operating golf club in the United States, though it moved to Hastings-on-Hudson in 1897.

Why was the USGA founded?

The USGA, or the Amateur Golf Association of the United States, as it was first known, was founded in December 1894 after a player named Charles Blair Macdonald lost tournaments at St. Andrew's and Newport and protested that the winner of those tournaments could not be called the national champion since golf was not governed by a single body in the United States. Members of five clubs — St. Andrew's, Newport, the Country Club (in Brookline, Massachusetts), Chicago Golf Club, and Shinnecock Hills (on Long Island) — joined together to form the new regulating body for golf in the United States.

What is the oldest operating golf club in North America?

It is the Royal Montreal Golf Club, founded in 1873, that holds the title of the oldest operating golf course in North America. Eleven years after its creation, the club received a patronage from Queen Victoria. Originally a nine-hole course in Fletcher's Field, part of Mount Royal Park, the club moved in 1896 to Dixie, in the parish of Dorval, and then to its current location on Île-Bizard in 1959, where 45 holes were constructed.

Who set down the first rules of golf?

On March 7, 1744, the city of Edinburgh presented a silver cup to the Gentlemen Golfers of Leith to be used in the first annual open championship. The club, which would eventually become the Honourable Company of Edinburgh Golfers, set down the first official golfing rules to govern the competition. It was played on a five-hole course at Leith Links, and John Rattray was its first champion. The Leith rules were later formally adopted by St. Andrews and became the foundation of the modern game.

Why do golfers yell "fore"?

There are two possible sources for the word *fore* as it is used in golf — one from the UK, the other American. In the UK, where *fore* has been used since the 1800s to warn people of errant shots, the belief is that the word originated as a contraction of the word *before* and was adopted for use in golf from the military. In those ages, cannons used in battle were not particularly accurate, and sometimes artillery volleys meant to fly over the heads of advancing forces would veer into the backs of the troops. The warning "Beware before!" would be shouted to warn of the impending danger. In the United States, it is believed that the term *fore* evolved from the word *forecaddie*. Early golf in America was not played on courses but on village greens — public parklands also used for picnics, horseback riding, and other leisure activities. Slaves were engaged as forecaddies sent out in advance of golf-ing parties to warn people of the impending danger. Golf balls may be smaller than cannon balls, but they still smart! At some point, it is believed, *forecaddie* was short-ened to *fore* as party members shouted out to their caddies.

What is the origin of the term "shotgun start"?

In May 1956, Jim Russell, the pro at Walla Walla Country Club in Washington state, devised a tournament format in which play-ers were assigned starting tees throughout the course. At the sound of a shotgun blast, the tournament began, and each player went around the full 18 holes, ending at the one prior to the one at which he started. It was a clever way to reduce the time it took to run a tournament. Today, the shotgun blast has been replaced by a siren on many courses, or by a synchronized start time.

The 10 Most Egregious Breaches of Golfing Etiquette

- Making sounds or movements while your opponent is taking a shot, especially on the tee or green.
- Not repairing fairway divots and pitch marks on the green.
- Not raking a bunker after a shot.
- Stepping on your opponent's putting and through-line.
- Taking carts or bags onto the green.
- Playing too slowly and not yielding.
- Throwing clubs in anger.
- Not yelling "Fore!" to warn others of your approaching shot.
- Gabbing on a cell phone while on the links.
- Men urinating on the course.

Was the Nassau bet invented in the Bahamas?

No. The Nassau bet was invented in 1900 by John B. Coles Tappan, captain of Nassau Country Club in Glen Cove, New York, on Long Island. The Nassau is actually three bets: one for the front nine holes, one for the back nine, and one for all 18. A payout is made to the winner of each. The Nassau is also a popular tournament format, which substitutes prizes for money. Nassau Country Club, once a private course on the estate of J. P. Morgan, was named for the county in which it is situated, which in turn was named, like the Bahamian city, after the first Dutch king, William of Orange-Nassau.

What is a *barkie*?

Have you ever accidentally hit a tree with a shot? Of course you have. Next time, place a barkie bet with your fellow players. A barkie is a side bet won when a golfer, after hitting a tree, still makes par on a hole. But you have to actually hit tree bark — a mere brush through the leaves doesn't count. So aim well.

What is a *whiff*?

A whiff is a stroke named after the sound it makes, but it might as well be so named because it stinks so badly. Every golfer has done it. You line up the shot, raise the club, and then take your swing, completely missing the ball. It's an embarrassing moment, as that club *whiff*s through the air, and it is also costly: according to the rules, as soon as the clubface passes through the plane where it would have hit the ball (if only you'd kept your head down), it costs you one stroke. Intent, as they say, is everything.

> **Quickies**
> *Did you know ...*
> that after a putt, if your ball hangs on the lip of the hole for longer than 10 seconds, and then drops in, that drop is to be counted as a stroke?

What is the difference between a pitch and a chip?

While there's no hard and fast rule, a pitch is generally thought of as having a high, soft arc and landing with little roll, while a chip is usually lower in trajectory and rolls more.

What is the doughnut effect?

Golf etiquette dictates that a player not step within one foot of the cup. Golf instructor Dave Pelz observed that, as golfers retrieve their sunk balls, their footsteps compress the grass in a circle bordering that one-foot radius. This creates a doughnut-like area immediately around the cup that is slightly higher than the compressed area. The resulting variations in turf conditions can affect the course of a putt. Pelz coined the term *doughnut effect* to describe the appearance of the compressed turf.

What is an *archaeopteryx*?

Archaeopteryx is the name given to a score of 15 or more over par on a single hole. Two such scores exist on the professional record books: Tommy Armour shot a 23 on a par-5 at the 1927 Shawnee Open, and Philippe Porquier shot a 20 on a par-5 in the 1978 French Open. The archaeopteryx was a real bird that lived in the late Jurassic period around 155–150 million years ago.

What is the difference between a pro golfer and a golf pro?

A pro golfer, such as Tiger Woods or Annika Sorenstam, plays competitive golf for money on one of the many tours overseen by a governing body such as the Professional Golfers' Association of America (PGA) or Ladies Professional Golf Association (LPGA). Pro golfers also often make money from product endorsements. A golf

The Ten Most Troublesome Shots

- **Topping** (a.k.a. dink) — The bottom edge of the clubface strikes the top of the ball.
- **Skull** — The leading edge of clubface hits the middle of the ball.
- **Skyball** (a.k.a. Alice) — The top edge of the clubface hits the bottom of the ball.
- **Fat** (a.k.a. chunk) — The club strikes the ground before hitting the ball.
- **Thin** — The clubface strikes the ball too high.
- **Hook** — The clubface is slightly closed at impact, causing the ball's trajectory to curve from left to right (the opposite for lefties).
- **Duck hook** (a.k.a. snap hook, quacker) — A severe hook.
- **Slice** (a.k.a. banana ball) — The clubface is slightly open at impact, causing the ball's trajectory to curve right to left (the opposite for lefties).
- **Whiff** — The stroke misses the ball completely.
- **Shank** — The club hosel hits the ball, sending it on a trajectory almost parallel with the clubface.

Names of Golf Hole Scores

- **Condor** — four under par
- **Albatross** (a.k.a. double-eagle) — three under par
- **Eagle** — two under par
- **Birdie** — one under par
- **Scratch** — par
- **Bogey** — one over par
- **Hawk** — two over par
- **Grouse** — three over par
- **Turkey** — four over par
- **Goose** — five over par
- **Snipe** — six over par
- **Quail** — seven over par
- **Partridge** — eight over par
- **Vulture** — nine over par
- **Dodo** — 10 over par
- **Great auk** — 11 over par
- **Moa** — 12 over par
- **Roc** — 13 over par
- **Phoenix** — 14 over par
- **Archaeopteryx** — 15 or more over par

pro is a "club professional" who works at a specific golf course, overseeing golf operations, teaching golf, and selling equipment. Golf pros typically work their way up through the industry, often receiving certification from the PGA or other golf organization. At large clubs there may be many golf pros reporting to the club's senior pro, or director of golf.

Why was J.C. Snead penalized for wearing a hat?

Actually, it was for *not* wearing a hat. The rules of golf state that only authorized golf equipment may be used for putting. In 1977, J.C. Snead found this out the hard way when wind lifted his hat from his head during play on the fourth hole of The Players Championship. The hat blew across the green and hit his ball, moving it, and Snead was penalized two points for illegally putting with his hat.

> **Quickies**
> *Did you know ...*
> that in one of the strangest penalties for breach of etiquette on the pro circuit, Tommy Bolt was fined $250 during the 1959 Memphis Open for noisily passing wind while another player was putting?

What was the worst lightning incident in pro golf?

At the 1975 Western Open in Chicago, Lee Trevino and Jerry Heard were sitting together near the thirteenth green during a rain stoppage when they were struck by lightning. The bolt hit Trevino first, then jumped to Heard. Both men suffered spinal damage. Both went on to win future championships. During the same storm, elsewhere on the course, Bobby Nichols and Tony Jacklin were also each hit by separate bolts.

What kind of club did Alan Shepard use to shoot golf balls on the moon?

Alan Shepard, who commanded the Apollo 14 mission from January 31 to February 9, 1971, was the fifth astronaut to walk on the moon. One of the last things he did on the moon before returning to Earth was to strike two golf balls with a club that had been fashioned by attaching a Wilson 6-iron head to the telescoping handle of a contingency sample tool, normally used for scooping up moon dirt. Shepard had clearance from his superiors to perform the shots, though only if the mission was going well. While the famous golf club is on display at the USGA Museum in New Jersey, the balls are still up there.

Who hit the longest drive with a feathery ball?

The feathery ball, which succeeded wooden golf balls, first appeared sometime between the fourteenth and sixteenth centuries, and were themselves eventually supplanted by the rubber-like gutta-percha ball, which appeared in the 1850s. The feathery was made of a sewn leather skin, stuffed until it was rock hard with feathers, and painted white. In 1836, Samuel Messieux, a modern languages master at Madras College, recorded the longest drive ever with a feathery ball, hitting one 361 yards from the Hole O' Cross green to the Hell Bunker at Elysian Fields, St. Andrews.

What's the longest drive ever hit on the pro circuit?

On September 25, 1974, 64-year-old Mike Austin hit the longest recorded drive by a professional golfer on tour, while playing in the U.S. National Seniors Open Championship in Las Vegas. Using a steel-shafted persimmon driver, Austin blasted a ball 515 yards from the fifth teeing ground at Winterwood Golf Course, landing his shot 65 yards beyond the flagstick on the par-4 hole!

What are the odds of making a hole-in-one?

In 2000, Dr. Francis Schied, a mathematics professor at Boston University, was commissioned by *Golf Digest* magazine to calculate the odds. Using all available data, Dr. Scheid placed the odds of hitting an ace at 5,000 to 1 for a "low-handicapper," and 12,000 to 1 for an "average player." A low-handicapper will have a 20-percent chance of making an ace within 1,000 rounds. At 5,000 rounds, the odds become 1 to 1. And it must be remembered that, while the golf world strives to keep accurate records, not all aces are reported each year, and of course, not all reported aces were actually made!

Quickies
Did you know ...
that the odds of getting struck by lightning in your life are one in 5,000? The odds of getting struck twice, one in nine million. Lee Trevino has been struck twice on the golf course.

Why do Japanese golfers buy hole-in-one insurance?

In Japan, it is a custom that any golfer who scores an ace throws a huge party and showers everyone he knows with gifts to share the luck. The tab can easily run over $10,000, so golfers routinely take out hole-in-one insurance to cover the potential cost of their good fortune.

What's the highest score ever posted by a pro on a single hole?

At the Shawnee Open in 1927, Tommy Armour shot what is called an archaeopteryx, which is the name given to a single-hole score of 15 or more over par, when he shot a 23 on a par-5. One week earlier, he had won the U.S. Open.

Who was the youngest golfer to shoot his age?

Bob Hamilton shot a 59 at the Hamilton Golf Club in Evansville, Indiana, in 1975, becoming the youngest player on record to shoot his age.

Who was the youngest pro golfer to shoot his age?

Sam Snead shot a 67 at the 1979 Quad Cities Open, matching his age and nabbing the record for youngest pro to shoot his age.

Who was the youngest pro golfer to beat his age?

Walter Morgan shot a 60 in the 2002 AT&T Canada Senior Open Championship, beating his age by one stroke.

Who was the oldest golfer to shoot his age?

Arthur Thompson shot a 103 at the Uplands Golf Club in Victoria, British Columbia, in 1972, becoming the oldest golfer to shoot his age.

Who holds the record for beating his age by the most strokes?

Ed Ervasti shot a 72 at Sunningdale Golf & Country Club in London, Ontario, in 2007, beating his age of 93 by 21 strokes.

Which pro holds the record for beating his age by the most strokes?

Joe Jimenez shot a 62 at the 1995 Ameritech Senior Open when he was 69 years old.

The Worst Single-Hole Scores on Record

- **161**: Mrs. J.F. Meechan took 40 strokes to escape a water hazard at the 1913 Shawnee Invitational.
- **20**: Philippe Porquier on the par-5 13th hole at the 1978 French Open.
- **18**: Willie Chisholm took 13 strokes to get out of the rocks at the 1919 U.S. Open
- **15**: Hermann Tissies was stuck in a bunker at the 1950 British Open
- **15**: Brian Barnes took 11 putts on one hole at the 1968 French Open
- **12**: Arnold Palmer hit four balls out of bounds on one hole at the 1961 Los Angeles Open
- **9**: Al Chandler took three whiffs on one hole in the 1986 Senior Tournament Players Championship

What is "revetting"?

Revetting is the process used on links courses of building up the wall of a bunker by stacking layers of sod on top of each other. This gives the walls of the bunker a steep, almost vertical aspect that protects the sand from wind and drives many golfers to the brink of tears.

What is the difference between a links course and other courses?

The term *links land* was used in Scotland to describe the unused stretches of land that run between the seashore and inland farms. Sandy, yet green, the lands were not useful for farming, so they became public land, used for leisure activities like horseback riding and picnics. As golf's popularity grew, the links lands in Scotland became, to an increasing extent, designated solely for golf use. Links courses tend to have a slightly more natural, or wild, aspect to them. It is not clear whether that is because it is simply the nature of the lands or because most are steeped in tradition, and thus no one wants to tamper with them. They are not typically extremely hilly, but will rather have rolling and undulating terrains with few, if any, trees. While some inland courses have been built to resemble links courses, if a golf course is not on such a piece of geography, there will always be a dispute as whether it is a true links course. There are fewer than 250 true links courses in the world, most of them in the British Isles.

Quickies
Did you know ...
that the world's longest golf course is the par-77 International Golf Club in Bolton, Massachusetts, at 8,325 yards?

Why are the first nine holes on a course called "out" and the last nine called "in"?

This tradition comes from the Old Course at St. Andrews, which is laid out on a narrow stretch of links land. At St. Andrews, golfers play "out" from the clubhouse, from the first teeing ground to the 10th green, then turn around and play "in" to the clubhouse, going back over the same land but shooting for different holes.

Why is it called the "green" when the whole golf course is green?

In the 1800s and earlier, an area of public grassy land near a village or town was called a "green," as in "the village green." Early golf was not always played on a course. In addition to links lands in Scotland, which were public land in golf's early days, golf was played in England, Ireland, and America on such "greens," all of which were commonly used for other activities as well, such as picnics, strolling, and cricket. Golfers shot for holes dug at intervals on the village green — a frequent cause for concern amongst innocent bystanders — and it is thought that from this the modern golf term *green* emerged.

Quickies

Did you know …

that the world's highest golf course is the Tactu Golf Club in Morococha, Peru, which sits 14,335 feet above sea level?

Have there always been teeing grounds?

Not only were there no tees prior to the late nineteenth century, there were also no teeing grounds. It is not known precisely when, but sometime after Old Tom Morris became greenkeeper at St. Andrews in 1864, he introduced separate teeing grounds for each hole on the Old Course. Prior to this, players simply teed off from within two club lengths of the previous hole.

Is the proper terminology "green committee" or "greens committee"?

The USGA indicates that in most cases where the word *green* is used in golf terminology, it should be singular: green fee, greenkeeper, green section, green committee. Thus, "greens committee" is incorrect.

What were early golf balls made of?

The first golf balls in Scotland were made from hardwoods such as beech and box-wood. Made by hand, they were irregular in shape and size. Written records are all that remain about wooden balls, which were in use between the fourteenth and seventeenth centuries. It is believed that such balls were made by bowmakers, who also made early golf clubs.

Who Typically Tees Up Where? The Meanings of Markers on a Teeing Ground

- **Black** — championship players in tournaments
- **Blue** — men with low handicaps
- **White** — men with middle or high handicaps
- **Yellow** — when behind the white markers; championship players; in front of the white markers, senior men
- **Red** — ladies' markers
- **Green** — juniors and beginners hit from here

What is a gutty ball?

In 1848, after returning to Scotland from a trip to Malaysia, the Rev. James Patterson, of Dundee, realized that some rubber-like material in which he had packed a statue for the trip would be ideal for making golf balls. The material was the hardened sap of the gutta-percha tree. Within a very short period, manufacturers were producing gutty balls by injecting the sap into metal moulds.

What is a bramble ball?

The bramble ball, in use during the last two decades of the 1800s, was named after the bramble, otherwise known as the blackberry. It was the first gutty ball manufactured with a raised pimple pattern on its surface.

What is *balata*?

Balata, sometimes called natural latex, is the sap of the tree of the same name which grows in South America, Central America, the Caribbean, and Guyana. When dried, it achieves a hard, rubber-like consistency similar to that of gutta-percha. Spalding, in 1903, was the first company to manufacture balata-covered golf balls.

Quickies
Did you know ...
that the world's largest bunker is called Hell's Half Acre, and it is on the seventh hole of the Pine Valley Golf Club in Pine Valley, New Jersey?

Quickies
Did you know ...
that enough goose feathers went into a feathery ball to fill a top hat?

Why do dimples make a golf ball fly farther?

Think of a truck driving fast down a dirt road. As air passes over the truck, it separates from the back of the truck, and dust and dirt are pulled up from the road into a swirling cloud. That's because the air is working to fill up the space the truck had occupied just a moment before. As the truck moves forward, it leaves a constant bubble of low air pressure behind it. The force created by this bubble is called pressure drag, and it not only pulls up dust, but also exerts a small force on the truck itself, trying to pull it backwards, and that drag consumes some of the truck's energy. The same thing happens to a golf ball flying through the air. As the ball moves through the air, pressure drag behind it slows it down, consuming some of the energy you gave the ball with your swing. So, what if you could make the area of pressure drag behind the ball smaller?

That's what dimples do. Flying golf balls push air in front of them. As soon as that air can get around the ball to where it is not being pushed any longer, it floats away — it separates from the surface of the ball. On a smooth ball, this separation happens at the sides of the ball. But dimples disturb the air enough to create a very thin layer of swirling air, called a turbulent boundary layer, just on the surface of the ball that pulls the surrounding air farther around behind the ball. As a result, the air separates from the ball later and the area of pressure drag is reduced. Ironically, the dimples actually increase friction against the air slightly, but the payoff in reduced pressure drag far outweighs that loss.

How many dimples are on a golf ball?

The number of dimples on a golf ball varies from model to model, but most models will have 300 to 500 dimples. The most common quantity is 336, while the record is held by the Dimplit, which has 1070 dimples — 656 small ones and 414 large. Once over 300, the quantity of dimples on a ball does not greatly affect flight or distance; it is the dimensions of the dimples and their symmetrical layout that is important.

Who was Coburn Haskell?

Anyone who cracked open a golf ball before about 1995 will be familiar with the Haskell design. In 1899, Coburn Haskell and Bertram G. Work, an employee of the B.F. Goodrich Company in Akron, Ohio, patented a ball made with a rubber core wound tightly with a long strand of rubber and covered with gutta-percha. The ball revolutionized the game with its long-range performance,

Quickies

Did you know …

that there are over two billion golf tees used in the United States annually?

becoming the standard for decades to come. The next year, Goodrich went into mass production on the ball.

What do the numbers on a golf ball mean?

Single-digit numbers on golf balls are there simply for identification purposes, so that if you and another member of your party are each using, say, the same model of Top-Flite ball, you can play different numbers, like a 3 and a 4, to tell your balls apart. Double-digit numbers indicate the ball's compression rating. Triple-digit numbers tell you how many dimples are on the ball.

What does a ball's compression rating indicate?

Before the advent of the modern solid-core golf ball in the late 1990s, it was felt essential for golfers to know the compression rating of their balls. In simple terms, this is how much a Haskell-style golf ball will compress when hit by a club. The more the ball compresses, the more energy it absorbs from your swing and the less power it will have. Consider the difference between hitting a sponge and a stone. The sponge travels less distance because so much of the energy of your swing is absorbed by the sponge's compression. Of course, that's an extreme comparison. A low compression rating was between 70 and 80, while a high one was 110. But those higher-rated, extremely hard balls were difficult to control, because, well, they were like rocks and you had to hit them very hard to transfer energy. Most modern golf balls do not indicate a compression rating.

Why do clubs have horizontal grooves on their faces?

First introduced in 1902 by a Mr. E. Burr, grooves on the face of a club perform two functions. First, they create a textured surface for the ball to "climb" as it rolls up the clubface upon impact. The effect is like having multiple tiny chopping impacts on the ball's surface, and that traction creates spin. Secondly, in wet conditions, the grooves channel water away from the ball's surface upon impact, reducing slippage, much like a car tire's tread on a wet road.

What is a *cleekmaker*?

After the invention of the gutty ball in the mid-1800s, demand for harder clubs increased, since the gutty itself was very hard and could damage wooden clubs. Metal golf clubs became popular. Blacksmiths who specialized in this trade were called cleekmakers.

What is a "cavity-back" iron?

When a ball is struck, the force of the blow causes the clubhead to rotate slightly on its centre of gravity, and this in turn can cause the ball to leave the clubface at an undesired angle. The greater the rotation, the worse the shot, especially when the ball is hit with the club's toe or heel. The more that rotation can be reduced, the more forgiving the clubhead will be. The backs of the heads of cavity-back irons have been bored out to allow for greater weight, and thus strength, around the perimetre of the clubhead. When a ball is accidentally hit with the toe or heel of the clubface, such perimetre weighting, as it is called, inhibits rotation of the club. Irons that have not been bored out are called musslebacks.

What is a "ring mashie"?

In the late 1870s, no "free drop" provision existed in the rules of golf governing casual water. If a ball landed in such water, it had to be played. The ring mashie was an iron designed for such an occasion. Also called a "president's iron" because it was clear headed, the ring mashie was an iron with a hole cut through the clubhead large enough that water and muck could pass through, but not the ball. Needless to say, the idea did not take off, and the ring mashie is today a rare collector's item.

Who was "Little Ben"?

The Wilson 8802 putter is one of the most famous models in the world. Favoured by such masters as Arnold Palmer and Phil Mickelson, the 8802 was popularized by Ben Crenshaw, whose father bought him one for $20 when Crenshaw was a teenager. He used it his entire career and it came to be known as "Little Ben." Many people consider Crenshaw to have been the greatest putter ever.

Who was Calamity Jane?

To most of history, Calamity Jane was the famous companion of Wild Bill Hickok, but for golfing historians, Calamity Jane was not a *who*, she was a *what*. In 1923, when taking in a round at Nassau Country Club with pro Jim Maiden, legendary player Bobby Jones complained that he was off his putting game. On the 18th green, Maiden loaned him his own putter to try out. It was a simple forged putter with an offset blade and hickory shaft, made by Condie, which Maiden had nicknamed Calamity Jane. Jones immediately fell in love with the putter and, six days later, won his first U.S. Open with it. Calamity Jane remained in his bag until he retired in 1930.

Why do golfers wear only one glove?

The purpose of the golf glove is to decrease the amount of pressure applied by the top hand during the backswing, while allowing you to maintain your grip. By putting a layer between the club grip and the palm of your hand, the glove dampens the amount of force with which the top hand grips the club at the height of the backswing. This desired looseness sets up the downswing, when the grip is tightened for power.

Why are old-fashioned golfers' trousers called plus-fours?

From the mid-1800s through the early twentieth century, a popular form of trouser was the knickerbocker, which was loosely tailored around the thighs, but came to a taper ending two inches below the knee. Golfers found knickerbockers too constricting during their backswings, so a longer version was invented that added two more inches to the length. The longer knickerbockers were called "plus-fours," because they ended four inches below the knee.

Who is Iron Byron?

Quickies
Did you know ...
that it is wrong to think that golf is an acronym for "Gentlemen Only, Ladies Forbidden"? The word golf dates back to the fifteenth century, and acronyms were rarely used before the twentieth century outside of cabalistic esoterica and acrostic poetry. In fact, the word acronym itself was not coined until 1943.

Iron Byron is a *what*, not a *who*. Iron Byron is a robot used by the USGA to measure golf balls and clubs to make sure they conform to official standards. The machine, which was named after golfer Byron Nelson, replicates a perfect swing that it can repeat hundreds, or thousands, of times in a test situation.

Why do golfers sometimes say "be the number" after hitting the ball?

This expression is typically used after a golfer has hit the ball and feels that it was a good shot. The number being referred to is the number of the club for the shot — 3-wood, 6-iron, etc. What the golfer is saying is, "Be the right club number that I chose for this shot."

Why do some people say there is a "buried elephant" on the course?

This is a cute expression, often used by TV commentators, to describe a small yet noticeable mound in a green. The implication is that an elephant has been buried under the green in that spot, causing the pronounced bump.

What is frog hair?

This term is used to describe the cropped collar of grass around the green, otherwise known as the apron, that separates it from the fairway.

What does *par* mean?

Par is a Latin word meaning "equal." It has been used widely in martial and financial circles since the seventeenth century. By the late 1890s, golf courses were being rated by "par value."

Why do we call holes played one under par a birdie, and two under an eagle?

During the 1800s in America, the word *bird* was used as a slang term for an impressive and exceptional accomplishment. On the golf course, when someone played a hole in one stroke under par, a companion might say, "That was a bird of a shot," in the same way that someone today might say, "That was a cool shot." Out of the word *bird* hatched the word *birdie*, which was in common use in golf to describe a hole played one under par by 1910. By 1922, the term *eagle* appeared on American golf courses to describe a two-under-par hole, presumably because this bird was so admired by Americans.

Why do we call a hole played one over par a bogey?

As early as 1836, there was reference in English literature to "Old Bogey," a name for the devil. This evolved to mean a goblin or evil person, and eventually simply something to be feared. In 1890, a system was adopted at some Scottish golf courses that established the number of shots it should take for a golfer to complete holes. The term *par* was not widely used in relation to golf at the time, but there was a popular dance hall song called "Hush, Hush, Hush Here Comes the Bogey Man," and golfers came to adopt the term *bogey* as slang for the devilishly difficult task of completing a hole in its prescribed number of shots. Thus, what we now call *par* became known as *bogey*. In 1911, the USGA defined *par* as "perfect play without flukes and under ordinary weather conditions, always allowing two strokes on each putting green" and adopted a new national standard that set par at slightly lower numbers than the existing Scottish bogey system. Thus, *bogey* eventually became known as shooting one over par.

Five Nicknames for Not-So-Great Shots

- **Angel Gooser**: a drive that reaches for the heavens
- **Captain Kirk**: a shot that goes "where no man has gone before"
- **Fried Egg**: a ball half-buried in the sand
- **Gopher Killer**: a drive that buzzes along at gopher height
- **Lorena Bobbit**: a very nasty slice

What is a chicken wing?

No, this is not something you eat at the clubhouse after a round. It's a term used by club pros to describe a flaw in a golfer's swing in which the lead elbow bends — just like a chicken wing — at an angle pointed away from the body, usually resulting in a blocked or pushed shot.

What is a golden ferret?

Quickies
Did you know ...
that putt is a word of Scottish origin that, as far back as 1300, referred to the act of throwing stones or heavy weights overhand as in a contest of strength? It eventually came to mean a push or a shove, and is now defined as a gentle tap.

Ferrets have log been used to hunt creatures such as rabbits out of holes, but in golf, the term sometimes has the opposite meaning. Shooting the ball out of the bunker onto the green is called a ferret, but when — like a ferret — a player pokes his head up out of that trap and does not see his ball on the green because he has put it in the hole, that's called a golden ferret.

Historical Scottish Names for Clubs and Their Approximate Modern Equivalents

- **Brassie** — 2-wood
- **Spoon** — 3-wood
- **Cleek** — driving iron
- **Mid mashie** — 3-iron
- **Mashie iron** — 4-iron
- **Mashie** — 5-iron
- **Spade mashie** — 6-iron
- **Mashie niblick** — 7-iron
- **Pitching niblick** — 8-iron
- **Niblick** — 9-iron
- **Jigger** — wedge

What is a "rutter"?

Used prior to 1850, a rutter was a niblick (iron) with a small head used for hitting balls out of ruts created by carts.

What is the origin of the word *duffer*?

The word *duffer*, which in golf describes someone of little ability, made its leap to the golf lexicon out of the slang vocabulary of thieves. In the 1700s, the word *duffer* appeared in Scotland as slang to describe a person who peddles worthless goods as though they are of value — otherwise known as a counterfeiter. Thieves referred to this practice as "doffing." By 1842, *duffer* had evolved to mean a person without practical ability or skill, and one can understand how this lent itself quite readily to the golf course.

How did the word *dormie* originate?

In match play, *dormie* describes a situation wherein one player is leading by the same number of holes left to play. This means that the best the player's opponent can do is tie the match. The precise origin of the word is not known, but the USGA indicates that the word may be derived from the French *dormir*, meaning to sleep. In English, *dormer* was a pre–nineteenth-century term for a sleeping area, such as a bedroom or dormitory, and is still in use when describing a dormer window, which is often a bedroom window in a house. When a golf match is said to have "gone dormie," it means that its competitive aspect has gone to sleep and the leading player can relax.

Why do golfers call a do-over a "mulligan"?

Like so much else in golf, the term *mulligan* is one of those things that evolved without the presence of a secretary to record the minutes of its introduction to the game. In fact, given the nature of the mulligan, it likely never would have evolved at all if an official had been present. The word was part of the golfer's vocabulary by the 1940s, and according to the USGA, it was likely named in honour of a player who was inclined towards taking free do-overs after less-than-perfect shots, such as David Mulligan, a member at

St. Lambert Country Club in Montreal, who would often take what he called "correction shots," or John "Buddy" Mulligan, known for replaying poor shots at Essex Fells Country Club in New Jersey.

What are the yips?

According to the Mayo Clinic, 33 to 48 percent of all serious golfers have experienced the yips, a psychological and neuromuscular condition in which a golfer experiences involuntary movement — twitches, spasms, jitters, and jerks — during a golf stroke, especially during putting. While the idea may sound frivolous, the yips have been the subject of serious study in sports medicine and have affected the careers of a number of athletes, including Tommy Armour, who retired from golf because of the yips and is said to have coined the term.

Who won the most major titles from a single event?

While most people may think this title is held by someone like Jack Nicklaus, Tiger Woods, or Bobby Jones, the actual record holder is an amateur from England. In the late 1800s and early 1900s, the British Amateur championship was considered a major tournament. Between 1888 and 1912, John Ball of Hoylake, England, won the tournament an astounding eight times. He was the first English-born player to win the British Open, and the first player to win both the British Open and the British Amateur in the same year — 1890.

Who is the only player to have won the U.S. Open three years running?

Willie Anderson is reputed to have been one of the greatest golfers ever to have lived. Had he not died at the young age of 30, it is likely his name would have become as synonymous with golf as those of Bobby Jones, Ben Hogan, and Jack Nicklaus — the only players to have equalled his total of Tour championships. What no one has equalled is Anderson's record of three consecutive U.S. Open wins, from 1903 to 1905. Between 1897 and 1910, he won the U.S. Open a total of four times, placed second once, third once, fourth twice, and fifth three times. He also won the Western Open four times.

Quickies
Did you know ...
that Sam Snead won his third straight PGA Seniors Championship in 1967 using a croquet-style putting stance and stroke that the USGA would outlaw within the year?

Why was the 54th president of the USGA so unusual?

For a sport that once banned women from play, golf has come a long way, baby. In 1996, four-time Curtis Cup player Judy Bell was elected the 54th president of the USGA, becoming the first woman to head golf's ruling body in the United States. At the ceremony when she accepted her position, taking the helm from Reg Murphy, she said, "I bet that's the first time the incoming president kissed the outgoing president on the way to the dais."

Why was Sandy Lyle eliminated from the 1980 Kenyan Open?

At the 1980 Kenyan Open, Sandy Lyle was paired with Nick Faldo in one round. On the second hole, he ran a piece of tape along the pop of his putter head to eliminate distracting sun glare. Faldo noticed the tape, but said nothing — until, that is, after nine holes had been played, at which point he mentioned it to tournament officials. The tournament committee determined that Lyle had altered the playing characteristics of the club during a round, a violation of the rules, and they disqualified him.

Who was the first Japanese player to win a PGA Tour event?

His trademark putting style made him stand out no matter which tour he was competing in — the PGA Tour, the Champions Tour, PGA European Tour, Australasian Tour, Japan Golf Tour, or the Japan Senior Tour. Isao Aoki has won tournaments on all those tours, and anyone who has seen him putt, with the toe of his putter raised at an angle off the green, will remember his unique style and formidable skill. It was not with a putter, however, that he sealed a win on the PGA Tour, becoming the first Japanese player to do so. No, on the final hole of the 1983 Hawaiian Open, much to the shock of leader Jack Renner, Aoki sank a 128-yard shot with a pitching wedge. The resulting eagle gave him the one-shot edge he needed to defeat Renner.

Why is Seve Ballesteros called "the car-park champion"?

Perhaps the best European golfer of all time, and certainly one of the best on the world stage, Seve Ballesteros won 94 titles in his career, including five majors, six European Tour Orders of Merit, and four Ryder Cups. Ballesteros won the Harry Vardon Trophy for lowest scoring average on the European PGA Tour six times. But perhaps the moment he is best remembered for was at the 1979 British Open at Royal Lytham, when he hit an errant drive off the sixteenth tee, landing the ball in a temporary parking lot. Using a 3-wood, he recovered, landing his ball on the green and holing out for a birdie. He went on to win the championship, and has been known ever since as "the car-park champion."

Who is Sir Michael Bonallack?

From 1957 to 1973, Michael Bonallack was one of the most notable and successful amateur golfers in Great Britain. Though he could have turned pro, he chose not to, winning the Amateur Championship five times, the English Amateur four times, the English Open Amateur Stroke Play Championship three times (plus one tie), and appearing on the Walker Cup team nine times, twice as captain (once a non-playing captain). In 1972, he was given the Bobby Jones Award by the USGA for distinguished sportsmanship in golf. He sat as secretary of the R&A from 1984 to 1999 and was captain in 2000. In 1998, Bonallack was knighted by Queen Elizabeth for his contributions to golf.

Who was the first woman to earn a modern career Grand Slam?

Nineteen eighty-six was a banner year on the LPGA for Pat Bradley. Not only did she become the first woman to surpass the $2 million mark in career earnings that year, but she also won the Kraft Nabisco Championship and the LPGA Championship to become the first woman to complete a career Grand Slam, having won the U.S. Women's Open in 1981 and the du Maurier Classic (the Canadian Women's Open) — which was at that time a major championship — in 1980.

What is Tiger Woods's real first name?

Although he has legally changed his name to Tiger, Tiger Woods's real first name is Eldrick, a name that was invented by his mother, Kultida, because it began with *E* after Tiger's father Earl, and ended with *K* after herself.

How did Tiger Woods get his feline nickname?

Woods was given the nickname Tiger by his father, Earl, the day after he was born. Earl was a career soldier with the U.S. Army, retiring as a lieutenant colonel, who served two tours in Vietnam. The nickname was given in honour of Vuong Dang Phong, a Vietnamese Army colonel and comrade of Earl's to whom he had given the same nickname years earlier. Tiger Woods never met his nicknamesake; Phong died in a Viet Cong prison after the war.

> **Quickies**
>
> *Did you know ...*
> that Chick Evans was so opposed to the idea of practice swings that he made it a personal rule never to swing a golf club except to hit a golf ball?

Who was the youngest person to play on the women's pro circuit?

In 1967, at her father's insistence, 10-year-old Beverly Klass turned pro, playing in four events that year, including the U.S. Open. As a result, the LPGA passed a rule barring golfers younger than 18 from full-time tour membership. Beverly Klass has since painted a picture of the abuse and violence perpetrated on her and her family by her father in his attempts to drive her career. She eventually rejoined the LPGA, at 18, but was unable to achieve significant success.

> **Quickies**
>
> *Did you know ...*
> that the only LPGA player to have won the Rookie of the Year Award, Player of the Year Award, and Vare Trophy in the same season was Nancy Lopez, in 1978?

How long after turning pro did it take Jack Nicklaus to achieve a career Grand Slam?

In 1962, Jack Nicklaus made his professional debut at the Los Angeles Open, finishing 21 strokes back and earning $33.33. Later that year, he picked up three wins on the PGA Tour: the U.S. Open, the Seattle Open, and the Portland Open. In 1963, he won his first Masters and PGA Championship. It wasn't until 1966 that he won the British Open. Four years into his pro career, Nicklaus had completed his first of three career Grand Slams.

Has any player ever lost all four majors in playoffs?

Yes, and the dubious honour belongs to none other than Greg Norman. In playoffs, the Great White Shark — as Norman is called because of his size and his white-blond hair — lost the 1984 U.S. Open to Fuzzy Zoeller, the 1986 PGA Championship to Bob Tway, the

1987 Masters to Larry Mize, and the 1989 British Open, in a three-way playoff that saw Mark Calcavecchia defeat Norman and Wayne Grady.

Ten Top Golfers Who Started as Caddies

- Harry Vardon
- Walter Hagen
- Ben Hogan
- Byron Nelson
- Gene Sarazen
- Sam Snead
- Seve Ballesteros
- Tony Lema
- Tony Jacklin
- Bernhard Langer

Who was the first player to break 70 in all four rounds of the U.S. Open?

In 1968, Lee Trevino became the first player to break 70 in all four rounds of the U.S. Open. It was Trevino's first win in a major.

What was Arnold Palmer's first professional victory?

In 1955, at only 26 years old, Arnold Palmer stepped onto the pro stage and won the Canadian Open for his first professional victory.

How many Canadians have won major championships?

The tournaments that have been designated majors, in both men's and women's golf, have varied over the years. But since the beginning of all major tournaments, only five Canadians have managed to rise to the champion ranks. In 2003, Mike Weir, of Sarnia, Ontario, delighted his country by dawning the green jacket at the Masters. In 1971 and 1966, Gary Cowan, of Kitchener, Ontario, won the United States Amateur Championship. Ross "Sandy" Somerville, of London, Ontario, also took that tournament in 1932. In the women's field, Canada has produced two winners of the LPGA Championship: Sandra Post, of Oakville, Ontario, in 1968, and Jocelyne Bourassa, of Shawinigan, Quebec, in 1973.

Who holds the longest winning streak in PGA history?

Between February and August 1945, Byron Nelson won 11 straight PGA tournaments, including the PGA Championship and the Canadian Open. It remains the longest winning streak in PGA history. The streak was broken by then-amateur Freddie Haas at the Memphis Invitational.

Ten Animalistic Nicknames of Pro Golfers

- **Golden Bear** — Jack Nicklaus
- **Tiger** — Eldrick Woods
- **Walrus** — Craig Stadler
- **Great White Shark** — Greg Norman
- **Angry Ant** — Gavin Coles
- **Pink Panther** — Jesper Parnevik
- **Bulldog** — Corey Pavin
- **Chicken Hawk** — Fred Funk
- **Rabbit Ears** — Davis Love III
- **Moo** (Thai for "little pig") — Onnarin Sattayabanphot

Who are the youngest golfers to have won major championships?

Young Tom Morris was certainly one of the greatest golfers to have ever lived. If he had not died at the age of 24 — already with four British Open wins to his credit — he would have likely set a multitude of records that would still be standing. One record he did achieve was to be the youngest player ever to win a major tournament, taking his first British Open at the age of 17, in 1868. In the modern era (post-1900), the youngest winner is Johnny McDermott, who took the 1911 U.S. Open at the age of 19. For women, Morgan Pressel is the youngest to have won a major with her victory in the 2007 Kraft Nabisco Championship at the age of 19.

Has any player ever won a Grand Slam?

No one, technically speaking, has won a Grand Slam — not in the modern sense of the term, anyway. A Grand Slam in the modern sense is the winning of all four professional majors — the Masters, the U.S. Open, the British Open, and the PGA Championship — in the space of one tour calendar year. The closest any modern player has come is Tiger Woods, who won the last three of the four in 2000, and then the Masters in early 2001. This is often called the Tiger Slam.

Quickies

Did you know ...

that in 1945, Harold "Jug" McSpaden finished second 13 times on the PGA Tour and in the top ten 31 times — records that stand today?

The term Grand Slam is borrowed from bridge and was first used in golf in 1930 when Bobby Jones won the British Open, the U.S. Open, the United States Men's Amateur Golf Championship, and The (British) Amateur Championship. Since the creation of the Masters in 1934, and the rise of pro golfing, no one has won a true modern Grand Slam.

Why are Masters champions presented with a green jacket?

Augusta National Golf Club in Augusta, Georgia, is one of the world's most exclusive golf clubs, and since 1934 it has annually hosted one of golf's most prestigious professional tournaments, the Masters. Symbolic of that tournament is the green jacket that is passed from one winner to the next each year. The tradition of the green jacket ultimately stems from 1939, when it was decided that Augusta members would wear the distinctive garment at the Masters to distinguish themselves from non-members. In 1949, it was decided that Masters winners should become honorary members of the club and were thus presented with a green jacket. The first such recipient, in 1949, was Sam Snead.

> **While No Player Holds a Modern Grand Slam, the Following Elite Group Holds Career Grand Slams, Having Won All Four Majors in Their Careers**
>
> *Men*
> - Gene Sarazen
> - Ben Hogan
> - Gary Player
> - Jack Nicklaus
> - Tiger Woods
>
> *Women*
> - Pat Bradley
> - Juli Inkster
> - Annika Sörenstam
> - Louise Suggs
> - Karrie Webb
> - Mickey Wright

Has the Masters always been called the Masters?

When the Masters tournament was created, Bobby Jones officially called it the Augusta National Invitational Tournament, even though Augusta's founding chairman, Clifford Roberts, had suggested calling it the Masters. Sportswriter Grantland Rice decided Roberts was right, and he called it the Masters when covering the first tournament. Other writers followed suit, and after five years, Jones relented and changed the name.

How well did Bobby Jones perform in the first Masters?

Not very well at all. Jones came out of a four-year retirement to compete in the inaugural Masters in 1934. His appearance drew a crowd of spectators 10,000 strong. Unfortunately, Jones could only give them a 294 and a tie for 13th place. Horton Smith took the tournament, shooting 284 and winning $1,500.

> **Players with Multiple Masters Wins**
>
> - **6**: Jack Nicklaus
> - **4**: Arnold Palmer, Tiger Woods
> - **3**: Jimmy Demaret, Sam Snead, Gary Player, Nick Faldo
> - **2**: Horton Smith, Byron Nelson, Ben Hogan, Tom Watson, Seve Ballesteros, Bernhard Langer, Ben Crenshaw, José María Olazábal, Phil Mickelson

What do they eat at the Champions' Dinner?

Every year on the Tuesday before the Masters, and ever since Ben Hogan hosted the first one in 1952, all past Masters champions (and a few select guests) are invited to dine at the Champions' Dinner at Augusta. The menu is chosen by none other than the reigning champion. Who pays the bill? None other than the reigning champion.

The Only Players Who Have Won the U.S. Open on Their First Try

- **Horace Rawlins** — 1895 (the first-ever U.S. Open)
- **Fred Herd** — 1898
- **Harry Vardon** — 1900
- **George Sargent** — 1909
- **Francis Ouimet** — 1913

Who was the oldest winner of the U.S. Open?

The oldest winner of the U.S. Open was Hale Irwin, who took his third victory in the national championship at age 45, in 1990, at Medinah Country Club in Medinah, Illinois. It was the 90th U.S. Open and Irwin came in at 280, eight under par. Irwin made a 50-foot birdie putt on the final hole to tie Mike Donald. In the first-ever sudden-death finish in U.S. Open history, Irwin birdied the 19th to take the championship.

Where was the first U.S. Open golf tournament played?

The first U.S. Open was played at the nine-hole Newport Golf and Country Club in Newport, Rhode Island, in 1895. It was won by Horace Rawlins, a 21-year-old Englishman who was the assistant pro at the course. Rawlins took home $150 from a total purse of $335.

Who posted the lowest 18-hole score in the U.S. Open?

There's a four-way tie for this distinction. In 2003, Vijay Singh posted 63 for the second round at Olympia Fields. In 1980, Jack Nicklaus and Tom Weiskopf each carded 63 in the first round at Baltusrol. And in 1973, Johnny Miller shot 63 in the final round at Oakmont. Of the four, only Nicklaus and Miller won the tournament in their respective years.

Players With the Most Wins at the U.S. Open

- **Willie Anderson**: 1901, 1903, 1904, 1905
- **Bobby Jones**: 1923, 1926, 1929, 1930
- **Ben Hogan**: 1948, 1950, 1951, 1953
- **Jack Nicklaus**: 1962, 1967, 1972, 1980

How is the PGA Championship different from other major championships?

When the PGA Championship was established in 1916, golf was largely run by wealthy amateurs, and professional golfers were not held in high esteem. The PGA Championship was formulated as a platform exclusively for professionals, and it is the only major that does not invite leading amateurs to compete. It is the only one that reserves a large number of places — 20 of 156 — for club professionals. Since 1968, the PGA Tour has been independent of the PGA of America. The PGA Tour is an elite organization of tournament professionals, but the PGA Championship is still run by the PGA of America, which is mainly a body for club and teaching professionals. The PGA Championship is the only major that does not explicitly grant entry to the top 50 players in the official world golf rankings.

> **Only Three Left-Handed Players Have Won Major Championships**
>
> - **Bob Charles**: 1963 British Open
> - **Mike Weir**: 2003 Masters
> - **Phil Mickelson**: 2004 and 2006 Masters, 2005 PGA Championship

What benefits come from winning the PGA Championship?

PGA champions are automatically invited to play in the other three majors (the Masters, U.S. Open, and the British Open) for the next five years, and are exempt from qualifying for the PGA Championship for life. They also receive membership on the PGA Tour for the following five seasons and invitations to the Players Championship for five years.

> **Quickies**
>
> *Did you know ...*
> that the British Open has only once been played outside the island of Great Britain: in 1951, at the Royal Portrush Golf Club in County Antrim, Northern Ireland?

What is the origin of the British Open trophy called the Claret Jug?

The real name of the silver trophy awarded to the winner of the British Open is the Championship Cup. It is called the Claret Jug because it looks like the type of jug that wine might have been served from in the nineteenth century. The Jug came into use in 1873, twelve years after the first British Open (called simply "The Open" back then) was played in Scotland. Prior to that, and with the exception of 1871, the tournament trophy was a Challenge Belt, which was passed from winner to winner each year. The rules, however, stated that if anyone should win the tournament three years running, they could keep the belt for life. Young Tom Morris did exactly that, after winning in 1868, 1869, and 1970. He might have also won in 1871, but the tournament was not played that year due to the lack of a trophy. A silver claret jug was eventually commissioned, but it was not ready before the 1872 tournament, which was also won by Young Tom Morris. By the time the Claret Jug was ready, for the 1873 tournament, Morris was dead.

When was prize money first awarded at the British Open?

It wasn't until 1863, the third year of the British Open, that a cash prize was established. A purse of £10 was awarded that year, to be shared between those who finished in second, third, and fourth places. The winner received only the Championship Belt to keep for a year. In 1864, a prize of £6 was established for the winner. Today, the British Open has a total purse of £4.2 million pounds.

Why was the playoff at the 1911 British Open not finished?

In 1911, the great Harry Vardon found himself in a playoff in the British Open against Frenchman Arnaud Massy, the only person from outside Great Britain who'd won the Open, having taken it in 1907. Vardon was then considered one of the premier British golfers, with four previous Open wins to his credit, and by the end of the 35th hole of the 36-hole playoff on Royal St. Georges, his superior skill was evident: Vardon was leading Massy 143 to 148. Apparently realizing he was up against the impossible, Massy picked up his own ball and conceded the title before the final hole.

> **Quickies**
> *Did you know ...*
> that the Ryder Cup has only twice been played on a non-British or non-American course: in 1997, at Valderrama in Sotogrande, Spain, and second in 2006 at the Kildare Hotel and Golf Club (a.k.a. The K Club) in County Kildare, Ireland?

Who was Samuel Ryder?

Samuel Ryder was a wealthy British businessman and keen golfer who lived from 1858 to 1936. He made his fortune through the innovation of packaging plant seeds in paper envelopes. In 1925, Ryder proposed a tournament between teams of British and American professional golfers modelled after the Walker Cup, an amateur version of the same format. The next year, Ryder paid for the trophy, and the first Ryder Cup tournament was played in 1927 at the Worcester Country Club in Worcester, Massachussetts.

How is the European Ryder Cup team selected?

The European Ryder Cup team is made up of the five players with the most points based on world rankings, and the five top money winners in European Tour Order of Merit tournaments. The final two European players are selected by the team captain. The European captain himself is selected by a 14-member European Tour Tournament Committee.

How is the American Ryder Cup team selected?

The American Ryder Cup Team is made up of the players who finish in the top eight based on points awarded for monetary earnings in sponsored events over the two years prior to the tournament. Those events include the Masters Tournament, the U.S. Open, the Open Championship, and PGA Championship, as well as other non-major PGA Tour events. The final four American players are selected by the team captain. The American captain himself is selected by a committee of four PGA of America officers, who consult with the CEO of the PGA and senior staff.

Who is the golfer depicted on top of the Ryder Cup trophy?

The small figure dressed in plus-fours and addressing a ball on top of the Ryder Cup trophy is Abe Mitchell, a British golf pro who was sponsored by Samuel Ryder, founder of the tournament. Mitchell played on three British Ryder Cup teams.

Why did the playoff of the 2003 Presidents Cup result in a tie?

Unlike other cup competitions, which do not resolve ties with playoffs, at the 2003 Presidents Cup it was decided a playoff would be held in the event of a tie. The captains of each team designated one player each to represent their team: U.S. captain Jack Nicklaus chose Tiger Woods, while Ernie Els was the pick of captain Gary Player to represent the international team. The event did result in a tie, so Woods and Els went head to head. After three holes it was still tied and getting dark, so Nicklaus and Player agreed to just call it a tie after all. But Player hadn't banked on the Americans keeping the cup, so he balked. Nicklaus conferred with his team and it was agreed that they should share the cup with the international team. For the first time in cup competition history, a trophy was shared.

Have any fathers and sons competed in the same Champions Tour events?

One event in the Champions Tour (the PGA's senior men's tour) has seen a father and son compete against each other. In the 1993 GTE West Classic, at the Wood Ranch Golf Club in Simi Valley, California, both Jerry Barber and his son Tom were in the field. Jerry, at 76, shot 221, one stroke better than his 50-year-old son.

Why do Kraft Nabisco Championship winners jump in the lake?

It was called the Colgate Dinah Shore Championship from 1972 to 1981, the Nabisco Dinah Shore Championship from 1982 to 1999, the Nabisco Championship from 2000 to 2001, and the Kraft Nabisco Championship from 2001 to the present, but call it what you will, this tournament is one of the most important events on the LPGA Tour. One of the four women's majors, it was founded in 1972 and became a major in 1983. It is played at the Mission Hills Country Club in Rancho Mirage, California, each April and is home to one of golf's most eccentric traditions. Following her second win of this championship in 1988, Amy Alcott, in a spontaneous moment of celebration, leapt into Champion's Lake, which surrounds the 18th hole. She did it again after winning in 1991, this time accompanied by tournament host and founder Dinah Shore. But it wasn't until 1994, after Shore died and winner Donna Andrews leapt to honour her memory, that the tradition took hold. Ever since, every winner has jumped in the lake.

Have any left-handed women players won LPGA tournaments?

In 1974, lefty Bonnie Bryant won the Bill Branch LPGA Classic. She remains the only left-handed woman to have won an LPGA tournament.

Who was the first British golfer to win the U.S. Women's Open?

In 1987, Laura Davies, at the age of 24, became the first British golfer to win the U.S. Women's Open. By then, she had already won the Women's British Open, in 1986, and been awarded two Ladies European Tour Awards of Merit. When she won the U.S. Open, she was not yet a member of the LPGA Tour. Her win, in an 18-hole playoff against Ayako Okamoto and JoAnne Carner, led the LPGA Tour to amend its constitution so that Davies could be granted automatic membership. Davies's U.S. Women's Open victory also made her the first golfer to hold both the British and U.S. women's open titles simultaneously.

Why do some greens at St. Andrews have two holes?

The links of the Old Course at St. Andrews have been in play for centuries — some say as far back as 1400. The Old Course originally consisted of 11 holes, played in one direction going "out" (away from the clubhouse) and then back in the opposite direction "in," for a total round of 22 holes. With the exception of the 11th and 22nd holes, every green did double duty: players would shoot for the same cups going out and in — so, for example, the green and cup for hole 10 going out would serve as the green and cup for hole 12 coming in. Often a group would meet another group on a green coming the other direction, and everyone would have to share the hole. In 1774, the course was reduced to 18 holes. By 1857, things had become so congested that the club had expanded the size of the greens and cut two holes into each one through the middle of the course. Golfers playing out shot for the hole marked with a white flag, while golfers playing in shot for the red flag.

Names of the Holes on the Old Course at St. Andrews

- **No. 1** — Burn
- **No. 2** — Dyke
- **No. 3** — Cargate (out)
- **No. 4** — Ginger Beer
- **No. 5** — Hole o' Cross (out)
- **No. 6** — Heathery (out)
- **No. 7** — High (out)
- **No. 8** — Short
- **No. 9** — End
- **No. 10** — Bobby Jones
- **No. 11** — High (in)
- **No. 12** — Heathery (in)
- **No. 13** — Hole o'Cross (in)
- **No. 14** — Long
- **No. 15** — Cargate (in)
- **No. 16** — Corner of the Dyke
- **No. 17** — Road
- **No. 18** — Tom Morris

What is the difference between the Royal and Ancient Golf Club of St. Andrews and the R&A?

The Royal and Ancient Golf Club of St. Andrews, where golf has been played since as early as the fifteenth century, is not only a private golf course in Scotland, but since its early days it was the governing body for golf worldwide, most importantly administering the game's rules and organizing the British Open. In 1897, three years after the founding of the USGA, St. Andrews established its Rules of Golf Committee to officially oversee the rules of golf in all territories except America and Mexico, which were governed by the USGA. In 2004, the club spun off these official duties to a newly formed group of companies collectively known as the R&A. That body, which maintains close ties with the golf club, now oversees the rules of golf and other administrative functions everywhere except America and Mexico.

Quickies

Did you know …
that opened in 1893, the Royal Worlington & Newmarket Golf Club in Suffolk, England, is the only nine-hole course with Royal designation?

What is the difference between the "left-hand circuit" and the "right-hand circuit" at St. Andrews?

Until the early 1860s, when Old Tom Morris rejigged the Old Course at St. Andrews, introducing a separate green for the first hole, play went around the course in a clockwise direction. The new green permitted play in either a clockwise or anti-clockwise direction, and for many years, the course was played clockwise one week, anti-clockwise the next. Today, play runs anti-clockwise except for a few days each year. The anti-clockwise route is known as the right-hand circuit, while the clockwise route is called the left-hand circuit.

Why is there a plaque showing Arnold Palmer's name on what looks like a grave marker beside the 16th fairway of Royal Birkdale Golf Club in England?

The 1961 British Open, played at Royal Birkdale in Southport, England, was plagued by gales and storms. Despite the bad weather, and despite receiving a penalty stroke when his ball moved in a bunker, Arnold Palmer dominated the second round, shooting a 73. On what was then the 15th hole, Palmer's tee shot landed off the fairway in a sandy depression under a tangle of blackberry bushes. Rather than pitching to the fairway, Palmer slashed an amazing 6-iron through the rough and landed on the green for a two-putt par. The shot so astounded spectators that a plaque was placed on the spot. Palmer went on to win the title, beating Dai Rees by one stroke.

Which was the first golf club to admit women members in North America?

The Royal Montreal, in Quebec, holds many notable records, including being the longest continuously running course in North America and the first course to employ a club professional (Englishman Willie Davis), but perhaps its most notable achievement was to be the first course in North America to admit women members, in 1891.

Why are holes 11, 12, and 13 at Augusta called "Amen Corner"?

On the course itself, the holes are, respectively, called "White Dogwood," "Golden Bell," and "Azalea," but they were given their collective name by writer Herbert Warren Wind in an article for *Sports Illustrated* following the 1958 Masters. Wind named the corner after a jazz song called "Shouting at Amen Corner" because of the seemingly miraculous events surrounding Arnold Palmer's play on those three holes during Sunday's round that year. The course had been soaked by rain the previous night, so a local rule allowed players to take a free drop on balls that were embedded. On the 12th hole, Palmer hit the ball past the green, embedding it in a steep slope. There was confusion about the local rule, so Palmer played out the hole with two balls — his original lie and a drop. Palmer carded five with the original ball and three with the second. It took a while, but on the

15th hole the committee informed Palmer that his drop was legal. The difference led to his first major win.

What is the longest golf course in the world?

In the Himalayas, at more than 10,000 feet above sea level, is the Jade Dragon Snow Mountain Golf Club, which holds the record as the longest golf course in the world. Designed by Neil Haworth and situated at the foot of Jade Dragon Snow Mountain, the 18-hole, par-72 course measures 8,548 yards in length. It boasts a 711-yard par-5 hole and two others longer than 680 yards. Five of its par-4s are longer than 500 yards, and three of its par-3s are more than 260 yards. The bright side of playing this monstrous course is that, at this high altitude, balls carry 20 percent farther than at sea level.

Names of the Holes at Augusta National

- **No. 1** — Tea Olive
- **No. 2** — Pink Dogwood
- **No. 3** — Flowering Peach
- **No. 4** — Flowering Crab Apple
- **No. 5** — Magnolia
- **No. 6** — Juniper
- **No. 7** — Pampas
- **No. 8** — Yellow Jasmine
- **No. 9** — Carolina Cherry
- **No. 10** — Camellia
- **No. 11** — White Dogwood
- **No. 12** — Golden Bell
- **No. 13** — Azalea
- **No. 14** — Chinese Fir
- **No. 15** — Firethorn
- **No. 16** — Redbud
- **No. 17** — Nandina
- **No. 18** — Holly

Where are Clifford Roberts's remains?

If anyone knows exactly where the remains of Augusta National's founding chairman, Clifford Roberts, are, they aren't saying. But one thing is for certain: they are somewhere on the grounds of the famous golf course he helped Bobby Jones build. After serving as Augusta's chairman from 1931 to 1976, Roberts committed suicide by gunshot in 1977 on Augusta's par-3 course and left instructions that his ashes be buried in an unmarked grave on the course grounds. Since Roberts ruled Augusta, especially after Jones's death in 1971, we can be certain his instructions were followed.

Quickies
Did you know ...
that the world's longest golf hole — the seventh at the Satsaki Golf Course in Sano, Japan — is a 964-yard par-7?

Where is the Church Pews Bunker?

The Church Pews Bunker is the name of a specific bunker at Oakmont Country Club in Oakmont, Pennsylvania. The bunker is wedged between the third and fourth fairways and is made up of 12 narrow rows of grass cutting across a wide triangle of sand. The name "Church Pews" comes from the fact that the rows resemble church pews. More than a few players have prayed for help getting out of them.

Quickies
Did you know …
that the Emirates Golf Course in Dubai consumes a million gallons of water per day?

Who had a licence to kill gophers?

That would be none other than Carl Spackler, the deranged assistant greenkeeper from the Bushwood Country Club in the film *Caddyshack*. Spackler, played by Bill Murray, will stop at nothing to kill a gopher that lives on the course and taunts him, even if it means dynamiting the fairways.

Ten Most Outrageous Golf Moments from Non-Golf Films

- *Animal House* — Otter dings Neidermeyer's ROTC chrome helmet and then spooks his horse with a stinging golf drive.
- *M*A*S*H* — Hawkeye and Trapper fire golf balls from the helipad dressed in bathrobes and drinking martinis.
- *Goldfinger* — Bond and Goldfinger are in a "friendly" challenge match. Bond knows Goldfinger is cheating and says to his caddy, "If that's his original ball, I'm Arnold Palmer."
- *The King of Comedy* — At his character's golf course home, a very angry and unfunny Jerry Lewis wields a driver while greeting Robert De Niro.
- *Roger & Me* — Lefty documentary filmmaker Michael Moore ambushes genteel and conservative wealthy ladies on the links.
- *I Am Legend* — The return of Bagger Vance … post apocalypse. A very lonely Will Smith drives golf balls into the Hudson River.
- *Uncle Buck* — John Candy nails his niece Tia's creepy, fleeing boyfriend with a solid drive.
- *Jackass: The Movie* — Johnny Knoxville and pals blast an air horn at golfers trying to tee off.

Who wrote the theme song to the film *Caddyshack*?

The theme song from *Caddyshack*, "I'm Alright," was written and performed by pop star Kenny Loggins, formerly of Loggins & Messina. The song is best remembered as it plays over the closing credits, accompanied by a dancing gopher.

Who wrote the theme song to the Masters tournament?

The rather saccharine theme song that is heard playing during TV broadcasts of the Masters tournament was written by Dave Loggins, the cousin of pop star Kenny Loggins, who coincidentally wrote the theme song for *Caddyshack*. Dave Loggins's song, titled "Augusta," was inspired by a visit to the famous Bucolic golf course. He released it on a 1995 collection of songs about golf called "The New Course Record."

Did Kevin Costner know how to play golf before making *Tin Cup*?

In *Tin Cup*, CBS Sports golf analyst Gary McCord, who had a short pro golf career in the 1970s, plays himself. He spent a lot of time on the set with Kevin Costner, coaching him on how a PGA pro would swing a club. Costner did not know much about playing golf before the film, but McCord has said he was the fastest study he'd ever seen. During filming, the two men attended the Bob Hope Classic Telethon to do some golfing for charity. In attendance were numerous PGA Tour pros. Costner got to the tee box and fumbled around pretending not to know what he was doing, barely able to tee up the ball, then wound up and smacked his drive long and straight down the fairway. Afterwards, he winked at McCord and said, "I fooled 'em for one shot!"

Quickies

Did you know ... that the Hawaiian location of Hurley's makeshift golf course on the island in TV's *Lost* is the Ka'a'awa Valley, the same place where Dr. Alan Grant (Sam Neill) and the two children encounter a ferocious T-Rex in Steven Spielberg's *Jurassic Park*?

What happened to the real Eddie Lowry, Francis Ouimet's caddie, played by Josh Flitter in the film *The Greatest Game Ever Played*?

Eddie Lowry, the 10-year-old caddie depicted in the film *The Greatest Game Ever Played*, was a real person — as, of course, was Francis Ouimet, for whom Lowry carried clubs. Oiumet went on to become a leading figure in international golf after winning the 1913 U.S. Open with Lowry at his side. Lowry grew up to become a wealthy car salesman with a string of dealerships in California. He liked to sponsor amateur golfers, and also employed them in his dealerships. Lowry and Ouimet remained lifelong friends, and when Ouimet died in 1967, Lowry was one of his pallbearers.

Who is the greatest golf novelist ever?

As they say on the links, this one is halved, because it is almost impossible to choose between P.G. Wodehouse's riotous slapstick follies set in the 1920s, and Dan Jenkins's profane and irreverently hilarious contemporary works — especially the masterpiece *Dead Solid Perfect*. In a playoff, the edge goes to Wodehouse only because he was just so darned prolific and everything he wrote was note-perfect.

What was the earliest golf film?

It might have been the earliest instalment of *America's Funniest Home Videos*. The 1896 short film (they were all short back then) *Golfing Extraordinary, Five Gentlemen* is the earliest record we have today of golf on film. Made by American Brit Acres, it was shot with a Kineopticon camera, invented by Acres, and it showed one golfer, among several, taking a whiff shot and then falling down.

bowling

Who invented ten-pin bowling?

American ten-pin bowling has its roots in a similar German game called kegel. Kegel, which is still played today, emerged in the twelfth century as a luck or betting game. Using a round stone, competitors had to knock down nine pins — called *kegels* — that were standing in a diamond formation. Because of the negative influences of gambling, the game was outlawed in Germany in 1335. Soon after, King Edward III outlawed it in England with threat of the death penalty. The French also outlawed it, but not until 1454. By the seventeenth century, however, the aristocracy had picked up the game and it re-emerged a largely innocent pastime played at special occasions. German immigrants eventually brought the game to New York in the eighteenth century, where it once again became associated with gambling. Because of this association it was outlawed by the Governor of New York in 1868. To get around the new law, kegel players simply added another pin to the game and thus American 10-pin bowling was born.

> **Quickies**
> *Did you know …*
> that the first official mention of the game of kegel is found in the chronicle of the German city of Rothenburg in the year 1157?

> **Quickies**
> *Did you know …*
> that in 1265, the citizens of the towns of Xanten and the monks of the monastery St. Victor formed a "kegelorum," the first kegelclub?

Who invented five-pin bowling?

In 1905, a pool hall owner named Thomas F. "Tommy" Ryan decided to install Canada's first "regulation" ten-pin alley in a second storey above a jewelry store in downtown Toronto. The 10-lane establishment, known as the Toronto Bowling Club, resembled a southern plantation, with potted palm trees, ceiling fans, string orchestra, piano and an immense lunch counter. In 1909, responding to customer complaints about the size and weight of the 10-pin balls, Ryan had his father turn down five of the larger pins on a lathe, to approximately three quarters of their original size. He then spaced five of these pins equally on the 36" 10-pin triangle. Ryan took a hand sized hard rubber ball — approximately 5" in diametre and 3.5lbs in weight — and rolled it down the 10-pin lane to invent 5-pin bowling. In 1912 he added rubber rings to the pins.

> **Quickies**
> *Did you know …*
> that in 1940, Tillie Hosken of Toronto became first female bowler ever to roll a perfect "450" 5-pin game?

Regulation Dimensions of a Bowling Lane (10 and 5 pin)

Length of approach	Length past foul line	Width
15ft minimum	62ft 10 3/16in	41–42in

Regulation Measurements of a Bowling Ball

Style	Diametre	Weight
10-pin	8.5 inches	16 lbs max.
5-pin	4–5 inches	3.25–3.62lbs

What is a "Swiss cheese" ball?

In 10-pin bowling, when a bowler purchases a ball, the holes are custom drilled to fit his or her hand. A Swiss cheese ball is a ball with many holes in it, used in the shop to determine the proper fit for a bowler so the holes can be drilled.

What are bowling balls made of?

At the beginning of the twentieth century, bowling balls were made of a hard type of wood called lignum vitae. In 1905 the first rubber bowling ball, named the Evertrue, was introduced. Nine years later the Brunswick Corporation, which had been until then a manufacturer of billiard balls, released their Mineralite Ball, which became a huge success due to its hard rubber compound. Such balls dominated the market until the 1970s, when polyester balls were developed. In the 1980s, urethane bowling balls were introduced. Today's bowling balls, which began being produced in the early 1990s, are made using a core weighted with bismuth graphite or barium — to offset loss of weight from the finger holes — and coated with polyester, urethane, or resin. Such balls, especially resin coated, provide exceptional reaction on the lane surface allowing for greater control.

When was the first automatic pinsetter introduced?

In the first half of the twentieth century, bowling pins were replaced upright at the end of lanes by boys called pinsetters, young lads who would jump down from a ledge and set up the pins for the next bowler. The first automatic pinsetter was debuted to the public by the American Machine and Foundry company at the American Bowling Congress National Championships in Buffalo in 1946. But it wasn't until five years later, in 1951, that one found a permanent home in a bowling ally in Michigan. By 1952, however, the machines were in production and the "pin boys" became some of the first American workers to be replaced by mechanical robots.

Why does a bowling ball sometime appear to slide part way down the lane before it starts to roll?

Wooden bowling lanes are treated with mineral oil daily to protect them from the action of the balls. Typically, the first two-thirds of a lane is oiled rather heavily, while the final third is oiled lightly. As a result, a properly thrown ball will slide straight down the lane until it encounters the less-oiled surface, and then curve toward the pins as it gains better traction.

Quickies

Did you know …

that there is no regulation minimum weight for a 10-pin bowling ball, but the correct weight to use is about one-tenth of your own weight?

Quickies

Did you know …

that a pin that's hidden behind another pin is called a barmaid?

Quickies

Did you know …

that bowling etiquette indicates that you should always let the bowler in the lane to the right of you go first?

The Ten Best Bowlers From Movies and TV

Character	Movie/TV series	Actor
Dude	*The Big Lebowski*	Jeff Bridges
Archie Bunker	*All in the Family*	Carroll O'Connor
Ralph Kramden	*The Honeymooners*	Jackie Gleason
Buck Russell	*Uncle Buck*	John Candy
Fred Flintstone	*The Flintstones*	Alan Reed (voice)
Roy Munson	*Kingpin*	Woody Harrelson
Bobby Dupea	*Five Easy Pieces*	Jack Nicholson
Alice Nelson	*Brady Bunch*	Ann B. Davis
Homer Simpson	*The Simpsons*	Dan Castellaneta
Gaffney	*Scarface (1932)*	Boris Karloff

Why is it called a "buzzard" when a bowler throws three splits in a row?

A split is a spare combination in which the head pin is down and the remaining pins have one or more intermediate pins down immediately ahead of or behind them. The symbol for a split on the score card is a cir-

Quickies

Did you know …

that the popular cartoon character Homer Simpson, from the TV show, *The Simpsons*, once bowled a perfect game? This feat had the town treating him like a celebrity for the majority of the episode.

cle. Throwing three splits in a row is called a buzzard because, like those feathered harbingers of doom, you can see them circling your dying score.

Quickies

Did you know …

that in bowling, throwing three strikes in a row is called a turkey? No one knows why.

Quickies

Did you know …

that in 10-pin bowling there are 459 possible split combinations?

Quickies

Did you know …

that a pin that remains standing after an apparently perfect hit is, for good reason, called a burner? You just got burned.

What is a "Brooklyn"?

A Brooklyn is a strike that makes contact on the left side of the head pin for a right-handed bowler and on the right side of the head pin for a left-handed bowler.

running

What is the longest race held in the world today?

The world's longest running race, held annually in Queens, New York, is the Self-Transcendence 3,100 Mile Race. Created in 1997, the race consists of 5649 laps of a .5488 mile circuit within 51 days. The circuit itself is one city block in Jamaica, Queens — 164th Place to Abigail Adams (84th) Avenue to 168th Street to Grand Central Parkway. The race winner receives a T-shirt and a plastic trophy.

What is the shortest foot race in the world?

Held in La Crosse, Wisconsin, the St. Patty's Day .01k is billed as the "world's shortest run and walk." The 32.8ft race has been held every year on March 17 since 2007 as a charity fundraiser. Its sponsor is — you guessed it — a local pub.

> **Quickies**
> *Did you know ...*
> that the record time for completing the Self-Transcendence 3,100 Mile Race is held by Madhupran Wolfgang Schwerk who broke his own time of 42 days 13:24:03, set in 2002, with a new record of 41 days 08:16:29 in July 2006?

What was pedestrianism?

In the seventeenth and eighteenth centuries, when an English nobleperson went out in a carriage they were accompanied by footmen who walked or ran along beside the carriage to clear obstacles and ensure its smooth transit. It was not uncommon for such aristocrats to make wagers with their peers over whose footmen were the fastest. Such competitions evolved into a sport called pedestrianism in the nineteenth century, which consisted of professional walking races. Out of these competitions evolved the modern sport of Racewalking.

> **Quickies**
> *Did you know ...*
> that the women's record in the Self-Transcendence 3,100 Mile Race is held by Suprabha Beckjord who completed the distances in 49 days 14:30:54 in 1998? Beckjord is the only person to have completed every edition of the race.

What are the World Marathon Majors?

The World Marathon Majors (WMM) is a championship-style competition started in 2006. Men and women compete for separate purses of $500,000 U.S. based on the best results in five annual marathons. Points are awarded to the top 5 finishers in each race, as follows: 1st — 25; 2nd — 15; 3rd — 10; 4th — 5; 5th — 1. The races are Boston, London, Berlin, Chicago, and New York City. In the years they are contested, points are also awarded for the International Association of Athletics Federations (IAAF) World Championships Marathon (in odd-numbered years), and the Olympic Marathon (in years evenly divisible by four).

Winners of the World Marathon Majors

Series	Men (Nation)	Points	Women (Nation)	Points
2006–07	Robert K. Cherulyot (Kenya)	80	Gete Wami (Ethiopia)	80
2007–08	Martin Lel (Kenya)	76	Irina Mikitenko (Germany)	65

Why do the World Marathon Majors have a two-year competition cycle but an annual prize?

Each World Marathon Majors series spans two calendar years, with the second year of one series overlapping the first year of the next. The reason for this is that elite marathon athletes compete in only two or three races per calendar year, thus the two-year cycle provides a larger sample of performance per athlete. However, it also means that, since the prize is handed out annually, each race counts against two cycles. In short, marathoners get to double dip.

What is the oldest non-Olympic marathon still being held?

The annual Boston Marathon was first held in 1897 and is today the world's oldest non-Olympic marathon race. The race, which is run on Patriot's Day (the third Monday of April), was inspired by the success of the marathon held at the first modern Olympics in 1896.

The Last Ten Marathon World Record Times — Men

Time	Athlete (Nation)	Marathon	Date
2:04:26	Haile Gebrselassie (Ethiopia)	Berlin	Sep 30, 2007
2:04:55	Paul Tergat (Kenya)	Berlin	Sep 28, 2003
2:05:38	Khalid Khannouchi (U.S.)*	London	Apr 14, 2002
2:05:42	Khalid Khannouchi (Morroco)	Chicago	Oct 24, 1999
2:06:05	Ronaldo da Costa (Brazil)	Berlin	Sep 20, 1998
2:08:05	Steve Jones (UK)	Chicago	Oct 21, 1984
2:12:12	Abebe Bikila (Ethiopia)	Tokyo Olympics	Oct 21, 1964
2:15:17	Abebe Bikila (Ethiopia)	Rome Olympics	Sep 10, 1960
2:25:39	Yun Bok Suh (South Korea)	Boston	Apr 19, 1947
2:32:36	Hannes Kolehmainen (Finland)	Antwerp Olympics	Aug 22, 1920

*Khannouchi became a U.S. citizen in 2002.

The Last Ten Marathon World Record Times — Women

Time	Athlete (Nation)	Marathon	Date
2:15:25	Paula Radcliffe (UK)	London	Apr 13, 2003
2:17:18	Paula Radcliffe (UK)	Chicago	Oct 13, 2002
2:18:47	Catherine Ndereba (Kenya)	Chicago	Oct 7, 2001
2:19:46	Naoko Takahashi (Japan)	Berlin	Sep 30, 2001
2:20:43	Tegla Loroupe (Kenya)	Berlin	Sep 26, 1999
2:21:06	Ingrid Kristiansen (Norway)	London	Apr 21, 1985
2:22:43	Joan Benoit (U.S.)	Boston	Apr 18, 1983
2:25:29	Grete Waitz (Norwal)	London	Apr 17, 1983
2:25:29	Allison Roe (New Zealand)	New York	Oct 25, 1981
2:25:42	Grete Waitz (Norway)	New York	Oct 26, 1980

Who holds the world record for running the mile backwards?

Backward running is called retrorunning. The record for the 1 mile retrorun is held by German extreme athlete and tower runner Thomas Dold, who ran the mile backward in 5:46.59 on July 18, 2004 at Meßkirch, Germany. Aside from other retrorunning records, Dold has also placed first in numerous runs up skyscraper stairways — called tower runs — such as the annual Empire State Bulding Run Up competition, which he has won four times, and the Taipei 101 Tower Runup. Tower runs are done running forwards.

Quickies
Did you know ...
that the word mile comes from the Latin *mille*, meaning thousand? A mile was 1,000 Roman strides, a stride being two paces.

Thomas Dold's Retrorunning Records

Event	Time	Date	Place
400m	1:09.65 min	June 17, 2005	Utrecht, Netherlands
800m	2:31.30 min	September 20, 2008	Pietrasanta, Italy
1,000m	3:20.09 min	July 13, 2008	Nußloch, Germany
1,500m	5:24 min	May 7, 2006	Gengenbach, Germany
1 mile	5:46.59 min	July 18, 2004	Meßkirch, Germany
2,000m	7:13.00 min	July 18, 2004	Meßkirch, Germany
3,000m	11:25.85 min	September 13, 2006	Düsseldorf, Germany

Who was the first winner of the Boston Marathon?

On April 19, 1897, John J. McDermott of New York won the first Boston Marathon with a time of 2:55:10. At that time, the Boston Marathon was a 24.5 mile race from Ashland to Boston. In 1924 the race moved its start to Hopkinton, where it still starts today. In 1927, to conform with Olympic guidelines, the race was lengthened to its current distance of 26 miles, 385 yards.

Why was Kathrine Switzer expelled from the American Amateur Athletic Union in 1967?

At the encouragement of her Syracuse University coach, long-distance runner Kathrine Switzer entered the 1967 Boston Marathon, but she did so under the name K. V. Switzer and showed up to the race — receiving number 261 from officials — with her hair pushed under a hat and dressed in a baggy sweat suit. Why all the secrecy? Because at that time women were banned from running in the Boston Marathon. Four miles into the race, Switzer took off her sweat suit and let her hair down. A press bus pulled along side and on the bus was race co-director Jock Semple who flew off the bus in a rage, grabbing Switzer and trying to rip off her race number. Little did he know, Switzer's boyfriend, an ex-All-American football player, was close by and he launched a tackle at Semple that sent him flying into the gutter. Switzer took off running and finished the race in just under four hours. Afterwards she was expelled from the American Amateur Athletic Union for violating the following rules: running with men, running without a chaperone, and running more than 1.5 miles (it was believed that doing so would injure a woman).

Quickies

Did you know ...

that women were not permitted to run in the Boston Marathon until 1972?

Who was the first runner to win back-to-back Boston Marathons?

Canadian runner John Caffery was the first person to win back-to-back Boston Marathons. He leading the pack in 1900, with a time of 2:39:44, and in 1901, with a time of 2:29:23. Both times were course records.

Has any person running on foot ever beaten a horse and rider in a marathon?

Twice, almost. That is, almost a marathon. The Man versus Horse Marathon is an annual race in Llanwrtyd Wellsover, Wales, that at 22 miles is is just shy of marathon distance. Nonetheless, it is a workout for competitors which include people running on foot as well as riders on horseback. Since the first race was run in 2000, runners have beaten horse and rider twice.

		Winners and Losers in the Man versus Horse Marathon	
Year	Type	Winner	Opponent
2000	Horse	Heather Evans on Royal Mikado (2:08)	Mark Croasdale (2:10)
2001	Horse	Heather Evans on Royal Mikado (2:08:06)	Martin Cox (2:17:17)
2002	Horse	Robyn Petrie-Ritchie on Druimguiga Shemal (2:02)	James McQueen (2:19)
2003	Horse	Robyn Petrie-Ritchie on Druimguiga Shemal (2:02)	Mark Croasdale (2:17)
2004	Human	Huw Lobb (2:05:19)	Zoe White on Kay Bee Jay (2:07:36)
2005	Horse	Lise Cooke on Gifted Lady (02:19:11)	Martin Shaw (02:26:03)
2006	Horse	Denise Meldrum on Tarran Bay (2:10:29)	Haggai Chepkwony (2:19:06)
2007	Human	Florian Holzinger (2:20:30)	Geoffrey Allen on Lucy (2:31:26)
2008	Horse	Geoffrey Allen on Dukes Touch of Fun (2:18:13)	John Macfarlane (2:18:43)

cycling

Who was James Moore?

James Moore was an English bicycle racer who lived in France from the late nineteenth to mid-twentieth century. He is popularly regarded as the winner of the first official cycling race in the world, a 1200m sprint held in 1868 at St-Cloud, Paris. Moore rode a wooden bicycle with iron tires called a velocipede. The next year he won the world's first road race, Paris-Rouen, covering the 123km in 10 hours and 45 minutes. He was one of the first stars of cycle racing, dominating competition for many years.

> **Quickies**
> *Did you know ...*
> that James Moore's wooden velocipede is on display at the Ely Museum in Cambridgeshire, England, alongside the Penny Farthing that won the World Cycling Championships of 1874?

What is a boneshaker?

Early bicycles, invented in France, were called velocipedes. Stemming from the mid-nineteenth century, such machines were of many different designs. Some had two wheels, some three and even four. Some two-wheelers were propelled by pedals mounted on the front wheel, while three- and four-wheeled designs used treadles and levers to drive the rear wheels. Others had no pedals at all but were propelled by pushing off the ground with the feet in a sort of running motion. The earliest versions were made out of wood, while later models were forged out of iron and steel. Because they didn't have tires (rolling instead on solid steel or wooden rims), the nickname "boneshaker" emerged for the vehicles in reference to the jolting, rough ride one could expect on the cobblestone streets of the day.

> **Quickies**
> *Did you know ...*
> that Scottish blacksmith Kirkpatrick MacMillan gave cycling a boost back in 1839 when he devised the first pedal-and-crank mechanism to power velocipedes?

> **Quickies**
> *Did you know ...*
> that when purchasing a penny farthing, one chooses a front wheel with a radius matching one's inseam length?

> **Quickies**
> *Did you know ...*
> that the word tire is an abbreviation of the word attire, which derives from the Old French *atirier*, meaning to arrange, order, or equip? In the nineteenth century, one would attire a wheel with a tire.

What was the first bicycle?

The first group of two-wheeled, human powered vehicles to be called "bicycles" appeared in the 1870s. They were what people today think of upon hearing the term "penny farthing." Also called "ordinary bicycles" and "high wheelers," they had very tall front wheels and small back wheels.

What is the origin of the phrase "taking a header"?

The rider of the penny farthing sat high above the vehicle's center of gravity. Unlike so-called "bonerattler" velocipedes, which had smaller wheels, the penny farthing's large front wheel provided comfort because of its ability to absorb shocks from small bumps in the road. But in a collision with a slightly larger object, such as a large stone or an unconscious drunken vagabond, the machine's back wheel would lift off the ground and the driver would be pitched forward. With his legs trapped beneath the handlebars, he would be dropped to the pavement head-first in front of the large front wheel. This spectacular stunt was called "taking a header."

> **Quickies**
>
> *Did you know ...*
> that the reason a penny farthing has such a large front wheel is to increase the distance the bicycle will travel in a single pedal stroke, as well as its rate of speed?

Why is it called a penny farthing?

The penny farthing-style bicycle, with the large front wheel and small back, got its nickname because the two wheels reminded people of two British coins, the large penny and smaller farthing.

Why are penny farthings called "ordinary bicycles" when there's nothing ordinary about them at all?

Between about 1870 and 1885, if you said you rode a bicycle, people know what you were talking about: a penny farthing. Because such high wheelers were prone to accidents, however, efforts were being made to devise a new type of bicycle that did not put its driver at so much risk. The challenge was to find a way to reduce the front wheel's size without sacrificing comfort, speed, or the distance a penny farthing could travel in a single pedal stroke (i.e., the circumference of the front wheel). Metallurgical advances in 1885 provided part of the answer in the form of a compact chain that could be used with a system of gears to drive a bicycle's back wheel. This innovation permitted the vehicle to have two wheels of the same size while, through gear ratios, maintaining the speed and distance power of the penny farthing. The comfort issue was resolved a few years later when future John Dunlop invented the pneumatic. The newfangled machines, invented by John Kemp Stanley, were called "safety bicycles," and in order to distinguish between them and penny farthings, the latter came to be called "ordinary bicycles."

> **Quickies**
>
> *Did you know ...*
> that by 1878 Great Britain was home to 20 bicycle manufacturers and 189 cycling clubs?

Who won the first Tour de France?

The annual Tour de France was first held in 1903 and ran 2,478 km in six stages clock- wise around the country from Montgeron

to Lyon, Marseille, Toulouse, Bordeaux, Nantes, and Paris. The race lasted from July 1–19, and offered a prize of twenty-thousand francs. Each of the 60 competitors paid a 10 franc entry fee. Unlike today, there were no teams. Maurice Garin, a 32-year-old chimney sweep with ten-years racing experience, won three of the six stages, taking the overall race by a margin of 2:49.21 over the next rider, Lucien Pothier.

Who won the 1904 Tour de France?

Four months after winning the 1904 Tour de France, Maurice Garin, along with the race's second, third, and fourth-place finishers, were all disqualified for rules infractions by the Union Vélocipédique Française and the yellow jersey was awarded to the race's fifth-place finisher, Switzerland's Michel Frederick. No one knows exactly why the four were dis- qualified. The reasons were not released at the time and records were lost during WWII.

Stage Results of the First Tour de France, 1903

Stage	Date	Route	Length	Winner (nation)	Race leader
1	1 July	Paris–Lyon	467 km (290 mi)	Maurice Garin (France)	Maurice Garin
2	5 July	Lyon–Marseille	374 km (232 mi)	Hippolyte Aucouturier (France)	Maurice Garin
3	8 July	Marseille–Toulouse	423 km (263 mi)	Hippolyte Aucouturier (France)	Maurice Garin
4	12 July	Toulouse–Bordeaux	268 km (167 mi)	Charles Laeser (Switzerland)	Maurice Garin
5	13 July	Bordeaux–Nantes	425 km (264 mi)	Maurice Garin (France)	Maurice Garin
6	18 July	Nantes–Paris	471 km (293 mi)	Maurice Garin (France)	Maurice Garin

Top 10 Finishers of the First Tour de France, 1903

Rank	Rider	Nation	Time
1	Maurice Garin	France	94:33.14
2	Lucien Pothier	France	+2:49.21
3	Fernand Augereau	France	+4:29.24
4	Rodolphe Muller	Italy	+4:39.30
5	Jean Fischer	France	+4:58.44
6	Marcel Kerff	Belgium	+5:52.24
7	Julien Lootens	Belgium	+9:31.08
8	Georges Pasquier	France	+10:24.04
9	François Beaugendre	France	+10:52.14
10	Aloïs Catteau	Belgium	+12:44.57

Who is Mellow Johnny?

Mellow Johnny is not a who, it's a what. Each day in the Tour de France the famous yellow jersey is worn by the overall leader, as of the end of the previous day's racing. If you win the overall race, then it is said you won the yellow jersey. Many other cycling races have adopted yellow jerseys, but the Tour de France began the tradition. The formal introduction of the yellow jersey was in 1919 as a promotion gimmick for the Tour's creator, the French sports newspaper L'Auto, which was printed on yellow paper. Mellow Johnny is the nickname given to the yellow jersey by American cyclist Lance Armstrong — an intentional mispronunciation of the French *maillot jaune*

There are Four Special Jerseys to be Won in the Tour de France

Jersey	Meaning	Prize
Yellow	Overall winner	€ 450,000
Green	Points winner (sprints)	€ 25,000
Polka-dot	Best climber	€ 25,000
White	Best rider under 25 yrs	€ 20,000

Has anyone ever won three jerseys in one Tour de France?

Only one rider has ever taken home the yellow, green, and polka-dot jerseys after a single Tour de France. In 1969, giving perhaps the greatest ever performance in the Tour de France, Belgian rider Eddie Merckx, 24, won yellow for overall, green for points, and polka-dot for mountain climbs. (There was no white Jersey in 1969.)

When did cyclist Lance Armstrong first win the Tour de France?

American cyclist Lance Armstrong first won the Tour de France in 1999. He holds the record for the most Tour de France wins, with seven, and the most consecutive Tour de France wins, also seven. He won his last Tour de France in 2005.

Riders with the Most Days in the Yellow Jersey in the Tour de France

Rank	Rider	Nation	Number of days
1	Eddy Merckx	Belgium	96
2	Lance Armstrong	U.S.	83
3	Bernard Hinault	France	78
4	Miguel Indurain	Spain	60
5	Jacques Anquetil	France	51
6	Antonin Magne	France	39
7	Nicolas Frantz	Luxembourg	37
8	Andre Leducq	France	35
9	Louison Bobet	France	34
10	Ottavio Bottecchia	Italy	33

Riders with Three or More Tour de France Wins

Wins	Name	Nation	Years
7	Lance Armstrong	U.S.	1999, 2000, 2001, 2002, 2003, 2004, and 2005
5	Jacques Anquetil	France	1957, 1961, 1962, 1963, and 1964
5	Eddy Merckx	Belgium	1969, 1970, 1971, 1972, and 1974
5	Bernard Hinault	France	1978, 1979, 1981, 1982, and 1985
5	Miguel Indurain	Spain	1991, 1992, 1993, 1994, and 1995
3	Philippe Thys	Belgium	1913, 1914, and 1920
3	Louison Bobet	France	1953, 1954, and 1955
3	Greg Lemond	U.S.	1986, 1989, and 1990

Has any Canadian ever worn the yellow jersey in the Tour de France?

Two of the three Canadians who have appeared in the Tour de France have worn the yellow jersey. Steve Bauer rode in 11 Tours and pulled on the yellow jersey twice, both times in the 1988 race. That year Bauer led the Tour on day two, and also on days 8–11. The other Canadian to wear yellow was Alex Stieda, who led the Tour on its second day in 1986.

Quickies

Did you know ...
that between 1993 and 2005 Lance Armstrong raced in the Tour de France 11 times and won won 25 individual stages?

Who was the first American to win the Tour de France?

It was not until 1986 that an American, Greg LeMond, first won the yellow jersey. LeMond ended up with a total of three Tour de France victories (1986, 1989, and 1990).

Who was the last Frenchman to win the Tour De France?

The Tour de France was last won by a Frenchman in 1985, by Bernard Hinault. His winning time was 113 hours 24 minutes and 23 seconds. It was the fifth and final Tour win for Hinault, having also won in 1978, 1979, 1981, and 1982.

Quickies

Did you know ...

that between 1969 and 1997 Eddy Merckx raced in the Tour de France seven times and has won 34 individual stages?

Canada's Complete Tour de France Record

Year	Name	Place
1985	Steve Bauer	10th
1986	Steve Bauer	23rd
1986	Alex Stieda	120th
1987	Steve Bauer	74th
1988	Steve Bauer	4th
1989	Steve Bauer	15th
1990	Steve Bauer	27th
1991	Steve Bauer	97th
1992	Steve Bauer	nc
1993	Steve Bauer	101th
1994	Steve Bauer	nc
1995	Steve Bauer	101th
1997	Gordon Fraser	nc

nc = race not completed

Who has the most wins of the Vuelta a España?

The Vuelta a España (Tour of Spain) was first held in 1935 and has been an annual event since 1955. In its history only two cyclists have won the event three times: Switzerland's Tony Rominger, in 1992, 1993, and 1994; and Spain's Roberto Heras, in 2000, 2003, and 2004.

Who has the most wins of the Giro?

The Giro d'Italia (Tour of Italy), or as it is called, "the Giro," started in 1909 in Milan. Along with the Tour de France and the World Cycling Championship, the Giro d'Italia makes up the Triple Crown of Cycling. Along with the Tour de France and the Vuelta a España it is one of the three Grand Tours. Since 1909, three cyclists have tied for the most individual wins, with five each. They are:

- Alfredo Binda from Italy in 1925, 1927, 1928, 1929, and 1933;
- Fausto Coppi from Italy in 1940, 1947, 1949, 1952, and 1953; and
- Eddy Merckx from Belgium in 1968, 1970, 1972, 1973, and 1974.

What is *keirin*?

Have you've seen those track cycling races where riders churn around an oval at extremely slow speeds for most of the event and then suddenly sprint like mad in the final lap or two? That is keirin, a sport invented in Kokura City, Japan, in 1948 that has become extremely popular with Japanese gamblers. A keiran race stars with a pack of six to nine riders following a motorized pace bike at a very slow speed. As the pace bike circles the track, it gradually accelerates and the riders jockey for position behind it. They are not allowed to pass the vehicle. After three laps, the pace bike veers off the track down into the center area. This is the signal for the sprint. With two laps to go, the pack of riders will stand in the pedals and give it their all trying to pass one another. As speeds reach up to 70 kilometres per hour, the riders will aggressively bump each other and attempt to prevent passing by cutting each other off. All within the rules, such tactics often leads to spectacular crashes, and always lead to dramatic photo finishes.

> **Quickies**
> *Did you know ...*
> that no cyclist has ever won all three Grand Tour events — Tour de France, Giro d'Italia, and Vuelta a Espana — in the same year?

> **Five Cyclists Have Won All Three Grand Tours In Their Career**
>
> * **Jacques Anquetil** (France): five Tours (1957, 1961, 1962, 1963, and 1964), two Giros (1960 and 1964), and one Vuelta (1963).
> * **Alberto Contador** (Spain): one Tour (2007), one Giro (2008), and one Vuelta (2008).
> * **Felice Gimondi** (Italy): one Tour (1965), three Giros (1967, 1969, and 1976), and one Vuelta (1968).
> * **Bernard Hinault** (France): five Tours (1978, 1979, 1981, 1982, and 1985), three Giros (1980, 1982, and 1985), and two Vueltas (1978 and 1983).
> * **Eddy Merckx** (Belgium): five Tours (1969, 1970, 1971, 1972, and 1974), five Giros (1968, 1970, 1972, 1973, and 1974), and one Vuelta (1973).

When did helmets become mandatory in road cycle races?

In 1995 Fabio Casartelli was chosen as a member of the Motorola team to ride the Tour de France. In stage 15, Casartelli and several other riders fell on the descent from

> **Quickies**
> *Did you know ...*
> that the bicycle track relay race called a "Madison" is named after the place where it was invented, New York's Madison Square Garden?

the Col de Portet d'Aspet. He struck a concrete block along the road, and was immediately transported to a hospital by helicopter, but was declared dead on arrival. Although it is debatable if a helmet would have saved Casartelli's life, helmets soon became obligatory in professional cycling races.

Who were the BUMS?

In Long Beach, California, in 1970, a 14-year-old kid named Scot Breithaupt organized the first-ever Bicycle Motocross (BMX) race. The race had 35 participants, who paid Breithaupt a quarter each to enter the race. At the next race 150 kids showed up.

Out of this, Breithaupt created the prototype governing body for BMX, called Bicycle United Motocross Society (BUMS). He went on to stage more races, using his own motorcross trophies as awards, issued member cards, created a points system, and wrote a rulebook for the burgeoning sport. He staged the first state championship in 1972, at age 16, and the first professional race in 1975, with a purse of $200 U.S.

When was the first Tour of California race held?

The Tour of California annually starts in San Francisco Bay Area, travels through the California redwoods, wine country and the Pacific Coast, and finishes in Los Angeles County in Southern California. The first Tour of California was held in February of 2006, and was won by Floyd Landis of the United States. The three races held since then have all been won by fellow American Levi Leipheimer.

Why was leader Michel Pollentier booted out of the 1978 Tour de France?

When Belgian rider Michel Pollentier arrived first at the precipitous Alpe d'Huez to take the race leader's yellow jersey in stage 16 of the 1978 Tour de France, he had to first take a drug test. According to one report, officials conducting the post-stage test became suspicious when, "Pollentier began pumping his elbow in and out as if playing a set of bagpipes." Ordered to lift his jersey, the Belgian did so to reveal an elaborate plumbing system running from a rubber, urine-filled bulb under his arm to the test tube. Pollentier served a two-month suspension before he started racing again.

What is LOTOJA?

LOTOJA stands for LOgan TO JAckson. It is a USA Cycling sanctioned road race held annually on the first or second Saturday in September. The race, which starts at Logan, Utah, and finishes in Teton Village, Wyoming (a few miles northwest of Jackson), is one of the longest single-day road cycling races in North America. The course covers 332km and includes three mountain passes with a total climb of nearly 3,000m. The race incorporates men's and women's categories and since 2001 has also included a tandem competition.

LOTOJA Race Tandem Champions			
Year	Riders	From	Time
2001	G. Gardiner and G. Brown	Kaysville, UT	8:54.34
2002	Z. Treasure and K. Crawford	Ogden, UT	7:48.48
2003	Z. Treasure and K. Crawford	Ogden, UT	8:19.57
2004	Z. Treasure and K. Crawford	Ogden, UT	8:58.29
2005	Z. Treasure and K. Crawford	Ogden, UT	10:35.16
2006	Z. Treasure and K. Crawford	Ogden, UT	10:04.30
2007	M. Sheeran and B. Jeppson	St. George, UT	9:25.57
2008	T. Petzold and J. Petzold	Birmingham, MI	9:49.01

What are Alleycat races?

Starting in Toronto, Canada, in 1986, urban bicycle messengers began organizing unsanctioned bicycle races in the downtown cores of major North American cities. They call these events Alleycat Races. These checkpoint-to-checkpoint races have very few rules or regulations. They culminate, in part, each year with the annual Cycle Messengers World Championships, which were held for the 16th time in Toronto in June 2008. In addition to a three hour street race, events included 300m sprints, cargo race carrying heavy packages, bunny-hop over a bar, bike polo, track stand, skids, and the slow race. Over 700 competitors from around the world attended.

Quickies
Did you know ...
that a sanctioned bicycle race held as a single event, not in stages, which consists of multiple laps around a circuit of closed public streets is called a criterium?

What is the Stupor Bowl?

The Stupor Bowl is an unsanctioned series of Alleycat cycling competitions held in Minneapolis, Minnesota, during the Superbowl Weekend each year. Organized by bicycle couriers and held in the dead of winter, the Stupor Bowl has run for nine years and has been known to draw over 200 competitors.

Quickies
Did you know ...
that when track cyclists stop their bikes and balance in one spot, the tactic, which is used to try to force an opponent to take the lead, is called "sur place," meaning "on place"?

skiing and snowboarding

What is the longest ski race in the world?

The Lauberhorn ski race takes place annually near Wengen in the Bernese Oberland, Switzerland, on the longest downhill run in the world. Its enormous length of 4.455 km results in run times of two and a half minutes (about 30–45 seconds longer than regular downhill races) and the achievement of top speeds close to 150 kilometres per hour.

What is the highest altitude at which someone has skied?

The highest altitude ever skied was recorded by Yuichiro Miura of Japan. On May 6, 1970, he skied 1.6 miles down Mt. Everest starting from an elevation of 26,200. He reached a peak speed of 93.6 mph.

The World's Ten Longest Ski Jumps

Rank	Year	Skier (nation)	Nation	Length	Location
1	2005	Bjørn Einar Romøren	Norway	239 metres	Planica, Slovenia
2	2005	Matti Hautamäki	Finland	235,5 metres	Planica, Slovenia
3	2005	Bjørn Einar Romøren	Norway	234,5 metres	Planica, Slovenia
4	2005	Janne Ahonen	Finland	233,5 metres	Planica, Slovenia
4	2008	Gregor Schlierenzauer	Austria	233,5 metres	Planica, Slovenia
6	2008	Gregor Schlierenzauer	Austria	232,5 metres	Planica, Slovenia
6	2008	Anders Bardal	Norway	232,5 metres	Planica, Slovenia
8	2003	Matti Hautamäki	Finland	231 metres	Planica, Slovenia
8	2005	Tommy Ingebrigtsen	Norway	231 metres	Planica, Slovenia
10	2005	Roar Ljøkelsøy	Norway	230,5 metres	Planica, Slovenia

Who was the skier shown crashing in the famous opening sequence of ABC's Wide World of Sports?

Slovenian ski jumper Vinko Bogataj might better be known as Mr. Agony of Defeat, because in the opening credits of the popular 1970s TV show ABC's Wide World of Sports, he was shown in a spectacular ski-jump crash. "The thrill of victory," intoned the announcer over a shot of Muhammad Ali celebrating a win, and then as the shot cut to Bogatai's crash, "and the agony of defeat." On the day of the crash, March 21, 1970, Bogataj was competing at the Ski-flying World Championships in Oberstdorf, West Germany. Midway down the ramp on his third jump, Bogataj realized weather conditions had made the ramp too fast. He attempted to lower his center of gravity and stop his jump, but instead lost his balance completely. He fell and rocketed out of control off the front corner of the ramp, tumbling and flipping wildly, and crashing through a retaining fence near a crowd of stunned spectators before coming to a halt. Despite the ferocity of the crash, Bogataj suffered only a mild concussion.

What is the meaning of "Super G"?

In alpine skiing, you'll often hear references to the "Super G" race. This is the Super Giant Slalom, king of the downhill races. The Super G combines the speed of downhill racing, and the agility required in slalom racing. Unlike regular slalom, skiers are allowed only one run on the Super G course, and they may not take practice runs. It's not unusual for a top athlete in this sport to reach speeds of 88–96 kilometres per hour.

Why do we call a bump on a ski slope a "mogul"?

A mogul on a ski slope is a mound of snow usually caused when another skier makes a turn and carves an indentation into the snow with his skis while simultaneously plowing the snow downhill slightly into a pile.

Sometimes mogul runs are fashioned intentionally with a series of mounds all the way down a slope to test the ability of skiers to navigate without crashing. The word mogul in this usage has nothing at all to do with the Mogal (or Mughal) Empire that, from the fifteenth to the nineteenth centuries, ruled much of the Indian subcontinent — where not a lot of alpine skiing is done! Instead, mogul here is a corruption of the Austrian word "mugel" which means "small hill" or "mound." It came into popular English use in the mid-twentieth century.

What is yo-yo skiing?

On ski hills with tow lifts or gondolas, skiers ride up to the top of the slope on the lift, disembark and then ski down, repeating the process over and over. But what if you want to ski a slope that does not have a lift? To do this, some skiers apply nylon surfaces to the bottoms of their skis — called climbing skins — that create grip and permit them to ski — or skin — uphill. When they get up to the top, they take off the skins and ski back down. This is called yo-yo skiing, because these skiers go in both directions, up and down, just like a yo-yo.

What does "KL" mean?

In 1930 Swiss skier Dr. Walter Amstutz wanted to find out how fast one could ski downhill in the space of a single kilometre, so he created a new competition called the *kilometre lancé* (kilometre spear). The KL, as it is called, consists of a straight one kilometre run down a very steep slope. It is today part the competitive skiing category called speed skiing. Speed skiing records are now maintained in four events: the original KL (also called Classic), which today uses advanced aerodynamic equipment developed specifically for the sport; Production, which uses only commercially produced downhill ski equipment; Monoski, which uses a single, wide ski, like a snowboard, except the skier faces forward; and conventional Snowboard.

World Record Speed Skiers

Event	Skier	Location	Date	Speed
Men's KL	Simone Origone	Les Arcs, France	Apr 19, 2006	251.400 Km/h
Women's KL	Sanna Tidstrand	Les Arcs, France	Apr 19, 2006	242.590 Km/h
Men's Production	Mathieu Sage	Les Arcs, France	Apr 19, 2006	210.770 Km/h
Monoski	Xavier Cousseau	Les Arcs, France	Apr 19, 2006	212.260 Km/h
Snowboard	Daren Powell	Les Arcs, France	May 2, 1999	201.907 Km/h

Who invented the snowboard?

Much of the credit here goes to Tom Sims, though he never officially patented his invention. In 1963, Sims was a grade eight student in Haddonfield Middle School, in Haddonfiled, New Jersey. His shop class project was to make a custom skateboard, but instead, Sims, who was an avid skier and skateboarder, made what he called "a skateboard for the snow." It was made out of plywood, measured 38" x 8", had a carpeted top, and an aluminum bottom. Today it is on display at the Colorado Snowboard and Ski Museum in Vail, Colorado. Sims went on to become a world champion snowboarder — though not on that board!

What was a "snurfer"?

On Christmas Day 1965, a man named Sherman Poppen fastened together two skis, side-by-side, and tied a rope on the front end for steering. The new toy, which he had made for his daughter, became a hit with the neighbourhood kids, who took rides standing on it going down a toboggan hill. Poppen's wife called it the "snurfer," as in snow surfer. Poppen patented the toy and, in partnership with the Brunswick Company, sold over 300,000 snurfers in the late 1960s. It was the first snowboard prototype to go into mass production.

What is "hardbooting"?

Snowboarding styles are split into two major camps: those that evolved from skiing events, and those that evolved from skateboarding events. Skiers who took up the sport adapted ski slope events to snowboarding, such as slalom, giant slalom, Super G, and speed snowboarding. This branch of the sport is called "alpine snowboarding," but it is also sometimes called "hardbooting" because the participants wear boots that are very similar to conventional hard-shelled ski boots. The branch of snowboarding adapted from skateboarding is called "freestyle," and uses a soft-shell boot to allow snowboarders flexibility while performing tricks and stunts. Such snowboarders do not limit themselves to the ski slopes and will use any snow-covered terrain available to enjoy their sport.

What is the difference between a halfpipe used in snowboarding and those used in skateboarding and BMX?

Imagine if you cut a giant length of pipe down the middle to create a long "U" and then set that pipe on the ground with the long opening facing up. That, essentially, is the halfpipe used in snowboarding, skateboarding, and BMX. Riders zip from one side of the pipe to the other, up and down the walls, performing tricks and stunts each time they clear the upper lip of a wall. There are three main differences between the snowboard-

ing halfpipe and those used in skateboarding and BMX. The first, obviously, is the snow. You're not going to have a very pretty run in a snowboard halfpipe without it! The second difference is slope. While skateboard and BMX halfpipes lay flat on the ground, snowboarding halfpipes are higher at one end. Finally, the snowboard halfpipe is closed at the elevated end to create an entry ramp from which snowboarders launch their runs.

What is big air?

Freestyle snowboard events include big air, the half-pipe, and slopestyle. In big air competition, snowboarders launch from a ramp and perform stunts in mid-air. They're judged on height, distance, difficulty, and landing.

The Parts of the Halfpipe

- **Flat**: the floor running down the center of the halfpipe.
- **Trannies**: the curved transition between the flat and the wall of the halfpipe.
- **Verts**: the vertical wall of the halfpipe.
- **Lip**: the top edge of the vertical wall.
- **Deck**: the horizontal flat platform on top of the wall.
- **Entry Ramp**: the curved end of the halfpipe where a run is started.

What is slopestyle?

In slopestyle, snowboarders do their tricks while going down a ski slope navigating around and over obstacles such as boxes, railings, and moguls.

What is snowboardcross?

In snowboardcross four to six snowboarders race together downhill through a winding course that includes moguls, jumps, and steeply banked curves. Competitions involve a series of heats, traditionally with the first two riders in each heat advancing to the next round. The overall winner is the rider that finishes first in the final round.

Quickies

Did you know ...

that in snowboarding, if you ride with your left foot in front of you, you are called "regular," but if you ride with your right foot in front you are called "goofy"? About 30% of snowboarders are goofy.

Who won the first National American Snowboarding Championship?

It was actually called the National Snowsurfing Championship. Organized by snowboarder Paul Graves, it took place in 1982 at Suicide Six Ski Area in Woodstock, Vermont. Downhill and slalom races were featured. Tom Sims won the downhill but fractured his thumb crashing into the hay bales at the finish line. Doug Bouton, riding for the Burton team, won first place overall.

What is "Your Responsibility Code"?

In both skiing and snowboarding a code of conduct rules the slopes. It is the skier's responsibility to follow the code, so it is called "Your Responsibility Code" and its tenets are as follows:

1. Always stay in control and be able to stop or avoid other people or objects.
2. People ahead of you have the right of way. It is your responsibility to avoid them.
3. You must not stop where you obstruct a trail or are not visible from above.
4. Whenever starting downhill or merging onto a trail, look uphill and yield to others.
5. Always use devices to help prevent runaway equipment.
6. Observe all posted signs and warnings. Keep off closed trails and out of closed areas.
7. Prior to using any lift, you must have the knowledge and ability to load, ride, and unload safely.

Quickies

Did you know ...

that the first snowboarding World Cup was held in 1987, with events in both Europe and America?

Quickies

Did you know ...

that in snowboarding, when a person's arms are flailing in the air as he tries to recover lost balance, it's called "rolling down the windows"?

What is an "expression session"?

An expression session is a non-competitive alpine snowboarding rally. The term originated with surfers, who held such events to show off their style.

Six Gastronomically Nicknamed Snowboarding Tricks

- **Canadian bacon air**: The rear hand reaches behind the rear leg to grab the toe edge of the board between the bindings while the rear leg is straightened.
- **Chicken salad air**: The rear hand reaches between the leg and grabs the heel edge of the board between the bindings while the front is straightened.
- **Eggplant**: The front hand is planted on the lip of the halfpipe wall while the snowboarder rises into an inverted position above the lip and rotates 180 degrees in a backside direction and lands going forward.
- **McEgg**: An invert in which the athlete plants the front hand on the wall, rotates 540 degrees in a backside direction and lands riding forward.
- **Pop tart**: An aerial move in which the rider goes up backwards and lands going forward, thus not rotating.
- **Roast beef air**: An aerial manoeuvre in which the rider grabs the heel edge of the board between the bindings with the rear hand and the rear leg is straightened.

auto racing

How many coloured flags are used in auto racing, and what do they mean?

Seven flags are used as signals to drivers in car races: a green flag starts the race; a yellow flag means "don't pass"; a red flag means "stop for an emergency"; a black flag signals a rule infraction; a white flag indicates that the leaders are starting the last lap; a blue flag with a diagonal stripe tells slower cars to move aside; and finally the checkered flag means the race is over.

What is rallying?

Rallying is a form of point-to-point motor racing that takes place on closed public or private roads with modified production or specially built road-legal cars. Drivers race against the clock. The sport began with the 1894 Paris-Rouen Horseless Carriage Competition, although the term "rally" did not become connected with the sport until the racing of the first Monte Carlo Rally in 1907.

Who was the first woman to win a round at the World Rally Championship?

The World Rally Championship (WRC) is an international rally car series culminating with a champion driver and manufacturer. The series consists of 12 three-day events driven on surfaces ranging from gravel and tarmac to snow and ice. Each rally is split into 15–25 stages run against the clock. At the Rallye Internazionale di Sanremo in 1981, Audi Quatro driver Michele Mouton of France became the first, and remains the only, woman to win a round of the WRC. In 1982 she finished second in the World Rally Championship.

What does the acronym "NASCAR" stand for?

NASCAR stands for National Association for Stock Car Auto Racing.

What is a stock car?

In the early years of NASCAR, a stock car was an automobile that has not been

Quickies
Did you know ...
that that the first Rallye Internazionale di Sanremo was held in 1928, with Roemeniĕ Urdareanu driving a Fiat 520?

modified from its original factory configuration. The idea was to race in the exact cars that came off the factory floor, thus testing not only the cars, but also the skills of the drivers who did not receive any advantages from modifications or customization of the vehicles. Later the term stock car came to mean any production-based automobile used in racing. Today, although stock-cars are highly modified versions of what come off the factory floor, they still conform to a strict set of regulations that enforce uniformity in the design of such aspects as chassis, suspension, and engine. The term stock car is used to differentiate such a car from a custom-built car designed only for racing purposes, such as an F1 car.

What does "Win on Sunday, sell on Monday" mean?

Seeing car sales generated by the popularity of NASCAR in the early 1950s, auto dealers coined the phrase "Win on Sunday, sell on Monday." NASCAR races were typically held on Sundays and because the cars used in races were, in very large part, the exact models for sale in auto showrooms, if a car won a NASCAR race on a Sunday, the next day there would be a spike in sales for that vehicle.

What does the white flag mean in a NASCAR race?

In a NASCAR race, the white flag signifies one lap remaining in the race.

What is so unusual about the Infineon Raceway and Watkins Glen International Speedway?

The NASCAR Sprint Cup Series sees a total of 36 races run on over 20 different tracks annually. In all cases except for two, the drivers of these races never encounter right-hand turns on any of the tracks. Which two tracks are the oddballs? The Infineon Raceway, in Sonoma, California, which hosts NASCAR's Toyota/Save Mart 350 race, presents a total of 10 turns to NASCAR drivers, three of which are to the left. Meanwhile, drivers in NASCAR's Centurian Boats race held at Watkins Glen International Speedway, in Watkins Glen, New York, must navigate 11 turns on the course, with four of them veering left.

What does the blue flag with a yellow diagonal stripe mean in a NASCAR race?

In a NASCAR race, a blue flag with a yellow diagonal stripe is shown to warn slow drivers that faster cars are approaching.

What does a yellow strip on the back of a NASCAR race car mean?

A yellow strip on the rear of a NASCAR race car indicates a rookie driver.

Former Names of NASCAR's Sprint Cup Series

- 1949: Strictly Stock Series
- 1950–1971: Grand National Series
- 1972–2003: Winston Cup Series
- 2004–2007: NEXTEL Cup Series
- 2008: Sprint Cup Series

When was the first NASCAR race?

The first NASCAR race was held on June 19, 1949, at the Charlotte Speedway in North Carolina. The winner was Jim Roper.

What is the connection between bootlegging and NASCAR?

During the prohibition period in the United States (1920–1933), bootleggers in the Appalachia regions of the deep south often ran homemade whisky from stills to customers. For this, they would use production model cars that had been modified for increased storage and greater speed to outrun police. In the 1940s, this activity evolved into stock car races on roads and tracks in Tennessee, North Carolina, and Florida, until a driver and promoter named Bill France, Sr., organized the first formal NASCAR race in 1949. France, whose son Brian is today's CEO of NASCAR, went on to built NASCAR's two most famous tracks: Daytona International Speedway, home of the Daytona 500, and the Talladega Superspeedway, in Alabama.

Why do NASCAR courses always run counter-clockwise?

When NASCAR started they didn't have radios in the cars, so the drivers would have to make hand signals with their crews to know when to make pit stops. Since they sit on the left side of the car, they drove with that window closest to the infield to be able to see their crew and so the crew could see them.

> **Quickies**
> *Did you know ...*
> that the annual Daytona Cup race draws over 17 million TV viewers?

Who was the first driver to win back-to-back Daytona 500s?

Richard Petty was the first driver to win back-to-back Daytona 500s in 1973 and 1974. Coincidentally, Richards's dad, Lee Petty, won the first Daytona 500 in 1959.

> **Quickies**
> *Did you know ...*
> that the Indianapolis 500 race is only 200 laps long? That's because the Indianapolis Speedway track is 2.5 miles in length, so 500 refers to the number of miles travelled during the race.

Who was the first European to drive in the Indianapolis 500?

The Indianapolis 500 was first run in 1911, and that race saw four Europeans compete, all of whom lived in the U.S. at the time but held foreign passports. They, along with their final places in the race, were: Italian Ralph DePalma (sixth), Norweigan Gil Anderson (11th), Frenchman Charles Baise (34th), and Swede Arthur Chevrolet (36th).

Who was the first European to win the Indianapolis 500?

When Jules Goux of France won the Indianapolis 500 in 1913, he was not only the first European to do so, but also one of five drivers that year to have travelled from Europe for the race. They were the first Europeans to have done so. The others, and their places in the race, were: Frenchman Albert Guyot (fourth), Belgian Theodore Pilette (fifth), and Italians Vincenzo Trucco (20th) and Paul Zuccarelli (22nd).

> **The Top Three Indy 500 Winners With Four Wins Each**
>
> • **A.J. Foyt**: 1961, 1964, 1967, and 1977
> • **Al Unser, Sr.**: 1970, 1971, 1978, and 1987
> • **Rick Mears**: 1979, 1984, 1988, and 1991

Who is the youngest winner of the Indianapolis 500?

Troy Ruttman was 22 years, 80 days old when he won the 36th Indianapolis 500 on May 30, 1952.

Who is the oldest winner of the Indianapolis 500?

Al Unser was 47 years, 360 days old when he won the 71st Indianapolis 500 on May 24, 1987.

What is the name of the trophy presented to the winner of the Indianapolis 500?

The trophy presented to the winner of the Indianapolis 500 is called the Borg-Warner Trophy. It was commissioned in 1935 by the Borg-Warner Automotive Company. In 1936, Indianapolis 500 winner Louis Meyer was the first driver to receive the trophy.

Why does the winner of the Indianapolis 500 drink milk in Victory Lane?

Rather disgustingly, three-time Indianapolis 500 winner Louis Meyer regularly drank buttermilk to refresh himself on a hot day and just happened to drink some in Victory Lane as a matter of habit after winning the 1936 race. An executive with what was then the Milk Foundation was so elated when he saw the moment captured in a photograph in the sports section of his newspaper the following morning that he vowed to make sure it would be repeated in coming years. There was a period between 1947–55 when milk was apparently no longer offered, but the practice was revived in 1956 and has been a tradition ever since.

Have women ever competed in the Indianapolis 500?

Five women have raced in the Indianapolis 500: Janet Guthrie (1977–79), Lyn St. James (1992–97, 2000), Sarah Fisher (2000–04, 2007), Danica Patrick (2005–07), and Milka Duno (2007). None have won.

Who was the first woman to win an IndyCar race?

Danica Patrick became the first woman to win an IndyCar race when she won the Japan 300 on April 20, 2008.

What is the "Triple Crown" of motorsport?

The Triple Crown of Motorsport is an unofficial motorsport achievement, regarded as winning the three most prestigious auto races in the world in one's career: the Indianapolis 500, the 24 Hours of Le Mans, and the Monaco Grand Prix.

What does "F1" mean?

The name "F1" means Formula 1, and it refers to the highest class of auto racing sanctioned by the Fédération Internationale de l'Automobile (FIA), which is the world governing body for the sport. The formula itself is a complex set of specifications set out by FIA which dictate the requirements and limitations for a car to be eligible to compete in F1 races.

What does *parc fermé* mean?

Prior to qualifying for each F1 race, the cars are inspected by officials and weighed. After weighing, the cars are held in a paddock, sectioned off by the FIA, which is known as *parc fermé* (closed park). Teams may not do work on the cars, other than routine maintenance, until the cars are released from parc fermé for the race the next morning. This measure guarantees that the cars are not modified or enhanced after having been approved for the qualifying run.

Acceleration Rates for F1 Cars

- 0 to 100 km/h: 1.7 seconds
- 0 to 200 km/h: 3.8 seconds
- 0 to 300 km/h: 8.6 seconds

What does an F1 car cost?

You won't find an F1 car at your local auto dealership, so it is difficult to put a final price tag on one of those rockets. Add the fact that teams are notoriously secretive about budgets, and it becomes quite difficult to come up with a final price tag. Still, figures do sometimes leak out. For example, in November 2008, it was reported that the McLaren team sank about $7 million U.S. just into servicing driver Lewis Hamilton's car between the Chinese and Brazilian grand prix. Needless to say, an F1 car's value is based on an accumulation of such expenses incurred over time, which can reach many hundreds of millions of dollars.

F1 Magazine's Estimated F1 Team Budgets for 2003

- **Ferrari**: $443,800,000
- **Williams**: $353,300,000
- **McLaren**: $304,600,000
- **Toyota**: $290,400,000
- **BAR**: $225,100,000
- **Renault**: $206,800,000
- **Sauber**: $119,500,000
- **Jordan**: $79,200,000
- **Jaguar**: $78,800,000
- **Minardi**: $39,600,000

Who was the first person to die in an F1 crash?

Italian F1 driver Luigi Musso was killed in an accident during the 1958 French Grand Prix at Reims, France. Musso's Ferrari hurtled off the course on the 10th lap of the 50 lap race. He was thrown off the Reims' track at the tricky Muizone Curve while holding second place. He became the first driver killed in an F1 crash.

Five Women Have Raced in F1, Only Two have Qualified for Starts

Name	Seasons	Entries	Starts	Points
Maria Teresa de Filippis	1958–1959	5	3	0
Lella Lombardi	1974–1976	17	12	0.5
Divina Galica	1976–1978	3	0	
Desiré Wilson	1979	1	0	
Giovanna Amati	1992	3	0	

Why did Lella Lombardi have just 0.5 points when she retired from F1?

Italian driver Lella Lombardi participated in 17 Formula One World Championship Grands Prix, debuting on July 20, 1974. Her best performance in 12 starts came with a sixth place finish at the 1975 Spanish Grand Prix. At that time, this finish would have normally garnered her 1 point (drivers now receive 3 points for sixth), but the Spanish race was a catastrophe, plagued by technical problems, crashes, and deaths, so the distance was cut short. Only half-points were awarded. This means that Lombardi, who retired from F1 in 1976, is not only the sole female driver to ever score points in Formula One, but she also holds the record for lowest non-zero career points.

Has any F1 race ever seen more than one woman driver compete?

The 1976 British Grand Prix was the only F1 race so far in which multiple female drivers were entered. Italian Lella Lombardi and Briton Divina Galicia both entered, but unfortunately, neither qualified for a starting position.

The All-Time Top Ten F1 Cars

Rank	Constructor	Wins	First win
1	Ferrari	209	1951 British Grand Prix
2	McLaren	162	1968 Belgian Grand Prix
3	Williams	113	1979 British Grand Prix
4	Lotus	79	1960 Monaco Grand Prix
5	Brabham*	35	1964 French Grand Prix
5	Renault*	35	1979 French Grand Prix
6	Benetton	27	1986 Mexican Grand Prix
7	Tyrrell	23	1971 Spanish Grand Prix
8	BRM	17	1959 Dutch Grand Prix
9	Cooper	16	1958 Argentine Grand Prix
10	Alfa Romeo	10	1950 British Grand Prix

*tied for 5th place

The All-Time Top Ten F1 Drivers

Rank	Driver	Wins	Seasons active	First win
1	Michael Schumacher	91	1991–2006	1992 Belgian Grand Prix
2	Alain Prost	51	1980–91, 1993	1981 French Grand Prix
3	Ayrton Senna	41	1984–94	1985 Portuguese Grand Prix
4	Nigel Mansell	31	1980–92, 1994–95	1985 European Grand Prix
5	Jackie Stewart	27	1965–73	1965 Italian Grand Prix
6	Jim Clark*	25	1960–68	1962 Belgian Grand Prix
6	Niki Lauda*	25	1971–79, 1982–85	1974 Spanish Grand Prix
7	Juan Manuel Fangio	24	1950–51, 1953–58	1950 Monaco Grand Prix
8	Nelson Piquet	23	1978–91	1980 United States Grand Prix
9	Damon Hill	22	1992–99	1993 Hungarian Grand Prix
10	Fernando Alonso	21	2001, 2003–	2003 Hungarian Grand Prix

* tied for sixth place

Why was Michael Schumacher stripped of his second-place finish in the F1 Championship for 1997?

Quickies
Did you know ...
that on May 8, 1982, Gilles Villeneuve died from a broken neck after crashing his F1 Ferrari during the final qualifying session for the Belgian Grand Prix at Zolder?

At the 1997 Spanish Grand Prix, Canadian Jacques Villeneuve, driving for the Williams team, went into the race knowing that he could win the 1997 F1 Championship only if he beat Michael Schumacher, the Ferrari driver. In lap 48 of the 69 lap race, Villeneuve attempted to pass Schumacher, but the German turned his Ferrari in on him, colliding with the Williams. Unfortunately for Schumacher the tactic failed and left his car unable to finish the race. While the collision damaged and slowed Villeneuve's Williams, he still went on to finish third and win the Championship title. After the race, F1's governing body stripped Schumacher of his second place in the Championship for the collision, calling it a deliberate attempt to influence the championship.

Top Ten Best Racing Movies

Movie	Starring
Talladega Nights: The Ballad of Ricky Bobby (1980)	Will Ferrell
Grand Prix (1966)	James Garner
Winning (1969)	Paul Newman
The Last American Hero (1973)	Jeff Bridges
Days of Thunder (1990)	Tom Cruise
The Cannonball Run (1981)	Burt Reynolds
The Gumball Rally (1976)	Michael Sarazin
The Great Race (1965)	Tony Curtis
Grease Lightning (1977)	Richard Prior
The Fast and the Furious (2001)	Vin Deisel

boxing
and wrestling

Why do we say a person isn't "up to scratch?"

During the early days of bare-knuckle boxing, a line was scratched across the centre of the ring, dividing it into two halves. This is where the fighters met to start the contest, or where they "toed the line" to begin each round. If, as the fight progressed, one of the boxers was unable to toe the line without help from his seconds, it was said he had failed to come "up to scratch."

Why is a boxing ring square?

In the days of bare-knuckle boxing, before modern rules, a circle was drawn in the dirt and prizefighters were ringed by the fans. When one of the men was knocked out of that circle, he was simply pushed back into the ring by the crowd. In 1867, the Marquess of Queensberry introduced a number of rules to boxing, including three-minute rounds and a roped-off square, which fans continued to call the "boxing ring."

Who was the Marquess of Queensberry?

In 1867, boxing's Marquess of Queensberry rules were drafted by Cambridge athlete John Chambers for an amateur championship held at Lillie Bridge in London for Lightweights, Middleweights, and Heavyweights. The rules were published under the patronage of the ninth Marquess of Queensberry. Known ever since as the Marquess of Queensberry rules, they formed the basis for modern boxing, both professional and amateur. The Marquess of Queensberry himself was named John Sholto Douglas, a Peer of Scotland who lived from 1844 to 1900.

Quickies
Did you know ...
that the ninth Marquess of Queensberry's third son, Lord Alfred Douglas, was the companion and lover of Oscar Wilde?

Why do we call the genuine article "the real McCoy"?

In the 1890s, a great boxer known as Kid McCoy couldn't get the champion to fight him, and so to seem beatable, he began to throw the odd bout, and fans never knew if they'd see the "real McCoy." The plan worked, and he became the welterweight champion of the world. Once, while in a bar, McCoy was challenged by a drunken patron who didn't believe that he was the great boxer, and McCoy flattened him. When the man came around, he declared that the man who had knocked him out was indeed the "real McCoy."

The 1867 Marquess of Queensberry Rules

Rule 1: To be a fair stand-up boxing match in a 24-foot ring, or as near that size as practicable.

Rule 2: No wrestling or hugging allowed.

Rule 3: The rounds to be of three minutes' duration, and one minute's time between rounds.

Rule 4: If either man falls through weakness or otherwise, he must get up unassisted, 10 seconds to be allowed him to do so, the other man meanwhile to return to his corner, and when the fallen man is on his legs the round is to be resumed and continued until the three minutes have expired. If one man fails to come to the scratch in the 10 seconds allowed, it shall be in the power of the referee to give his award in favour of the other man.

Rule 5: A man hanging on the ropes in a helpless state, with his toes off the ground, shall be considered down.

Rule 6: No seconds or any other person to be allowed in the ring during the rounds.

Rule 7: Should the contest be stopped by any unavoidable interference, the referee is to name the time and place as soon as possible for finishing the contest; so that the match must be won and lost, unless the backers of both men agree to draw the stakes.

Rule 8: The gloves to be fair-sized boxing gloves of the best quality and new.

Rule 9: Should a glove burst, or come off, it must be replaced to the referee's satisfaction.

Rule 10: A man on one knee is considered down and if struck is entitled to the stakes.

Rule 11: No shoes or boots with springs allowed.

Rule 12: The contest in all other respects to be governed by revised rules of the London Prize Ring.

Quickies

Did you know ...

that a "rabbit punch," describing an illegal action in boxing, comes from a gamekeeper's method of dispatching an injured rabbit by chopping it on the back of its neck with the side of the hand?

Why is a fistfight called "duking it out"?

"Duking it out" and "Put up your dukes" are both expressions from the early 1800s when bare-knuckle boxing was considered a lower-class activity. When Frederick Augustus, the Duke of York, took up the sport, English high society was shocked. The Duke gained so much admiration from the other boxers, however, that they began referring to their fists as their "dukes of York" and eventually as their "dukes."

What's the origin of the expressions "rough and ready" and "rough and tumble"?

Both "rough and ready" and "rough and tumble" came from the sport of boxing. *Rough* still means "crude," so "rough and ready" meant a semi-pro or amateur who, although unpolished and perhaps not as well trained as he should be, was still considered good enough to enter the ring. If a contest was "rough and tumble," both fighters had agreed to throw away the rules, which led to a lot of tumbling.

Why when asking for a loan might you say you need a "stake" to carry you over?

Asking for a stake means you need to see money to continue with a project. The expression comes from the early days of bare-knuckle boxing, when promoters often stiffed the fighters by absconding with the gate money before the count of ten. To ensure that they'd be paid, boxers insisted that their share of the money be placed in a pouch on a stake near the ring, where they could see it during the bout. This was known as stake money.

Why is a fighter's sweeping blow called a "haymaker"?

A haymaker is a powerful blow from a fist that, if it connects, will flatten a boxer's opponent. Farmers used to cut hay by hand with a scythe which is a long handled instrument with an extended very sharp blade (it's the instrument carried by the "grim reaper"). To use a scythe properly, the farmer used long sweeping motions leaving a flattened swath of hay in his path. This sweeping motion resembled the trajectory of the fighters arm when delivering a punch, or a haymaker, from left field and the recipient of that punch was flattened like the hay.

Why is fist fighting called "fisticuffs"?

Boxing is often referred to as the art of fisticuffs. The word began as *fisty cuffs*. It was first recorded as *fisticuffs* in the early seventeenth century. *Cuff* is from the Scandinavian word *kuffa*, meaning to push or shove, while *fist* in Old English was spelled *fyst* and meant a clenched hand. *Fisticuffs* means "to strike with a clenched hand."

Who is the youngest man to win a heavyweight title belt?

Mike Tyson was given his first title shot on November 22, 1986, in a fight against Trevor Berbick. Tyson won the fight and the title by a second round TKO. He was 20 years and four months old and became the youngest heavyweight champion ever.

What is the Canadian connection between Muhammed Ali and Mike Tyson?

When Mike Tyson won his first heavyweight championship bout in November 1986, he took the title from Jamaican-Canadian fighter Trevor Berbick, who had been WBC heavyweight champion since just March 22, 1986. Five years prior, on December 11, 1981, Berbick had been the last fighter to face Muhammed Ali in the ring before Ali retired. The 26-year-old Berbick defeated Ali, 39, by unanimous decision. Berbick remains the only Canadian to have held a world heavyweight title.

Why does Mike Tyson always wear black trunks in the ring?

Mike Tyson wears black trunks in the ring out of mourning for his late trainer, Constantine "Cus" D'Amato, who passed away on November 4, 1985. D'Amato also handled the careers of champion fighters Floyd Patterson and Jose Torres. D'Amato died shortly before Tyson became the heavyweight title-holder in history.

What is the "Scotch Woop"?

He was born Giuseppe Curreri in Sciacca, Sicily, but in the American boxing ring he changed his name to Johnny Dundee. The incongruous Scottish surname soon saw him nicknamed the "Scotch Wop" and the featherweight fighter developed a hitting strategy to go with it. The technique, called the "Scotch Woop," was simple. Dundee bounced off the ropes, and attacked his opponent with the added power of the recoil. It could be devastating to the opponent, but on one occasion it backfired. In a bout against Willy Jackson, in 1917, Dundee came at his opponent full force off the ropes and Jackson simply straight-armed him in the jaw. Dundee was knocked out in the first round.

Top Ten Best Boxing Movies

Movie	Starring
Body and Soul (1947)	John Garfield
Raging Bull (1980)	Robert De Niro
Rocky (1976)	Sylvester Stallone
Hurricane, The (1999)	Denzel Washington
Harder They Fall, The (1956)	Humphrey Bogart
Requiem for a Heavyweight (1962)	Anthony Quinn
Million Dollar Baby (2004)	Hillary Swank
When We Were Kings (1996)	Muhammad Ali
Cinderella Man (2005)	Russell Crowe
Somebody Up There Likes Me (1956)	Paul Newman

Who is the only undefeated and untied heavyweight champion in pro-boxing history?

Rocky Marciano, born in Brockton, Massachusetts, held the title of World Heavyweight Boxing Champion from September 23, 1952, to November 30, 1956. He had a 49–0 record with 43 KOs and remains the only undefeated and untied heavyweight champion in pro boxing history.

What was billed as "The Fight of the Century"?

On March 8, 1971, Muhammad Ali and then-champion Joe Frazier fought each other for the first time, at Madison Square Garden. Nicknamed "The Fight of the Century," it was one of the most eagerly anticipated bouts of all time and still remains one of the most famous. The fight lived up to the hype with an impressive performance from both sides. Frazier knocked Ali down in the 15th and final round with a hard left hook which lead to him winning the fight and retaining his title with a unanimous decision. It was Ali's first professional loss.

Why was Muhammad Ali stripped of his championship title in 1967?

When Muhammad Ali refused to fight in the Vietnam War after being called up on the draft in 1967, the New York State Athletic Commission suspended his boxing license and stripped him of his WBA title. Ali, who had by then converted to Islam, counted himself as a conscientious objector. He was found guilty of draft evasion, fined $10,000 U.S., and sentenced to five years in prison, but remained free on appeal. The case went all the way to the U.S. Supreme Court where the verdict was overturned.

Former Champion Boxers' Contemporary Pro-Boxing Daughters

Father	Daughter	Class	Record
Muhammad Ali	Laila Ali	Super middleweight	24-0-0
Joe Frazer	Jacqueline Frazier-Lyde	Super middleweight	13-1-0
George Foreman	Freeda Forman	Middleweight	5-1-0
Archie Moore	J'Marie Moore	Light heavyweight	2-0-0
Roberto Duran	Irichelle Duran	Super bantamweight	1-2-0
Ingo Johansson	Maria Johansson	Light heavyweight	0–2–0

Who is the only boxer to have defeated Oscar de la Hoya twice?

In his career Oscar de la Hoya lost six fights, two of those by decision to Shane Mosley, one on June 17th, 2000, in Los Angeles, California, and the other in Las Vegas on Sept 13, 2003. His other losses include a controversial decision to Félix Trinidad and a ninth round KO loss to Bernard Hopkins in 2004.

Did Arnold Schwarzenegger ever compete in professional wresting?

Although it might have been fun given his ready-made nickname of "The Terminator," the former Mr. Olympia and current Governor of California Arnold Schwarzenegger never wrestled on the pro-circuit. That said, he did once make an appearance at a WWF Smackdown event to promote his 1999 movie *End of Days*. At the event, Schwarzenegger received an honorary belt naming him World Box Office Champion, and he sat in as a guest ring-side commentator. The night culminated in an eight-man elimination match, and when things got out of hand, Schwarzenegger got as close as he ever would to being a WWF star when he handed a folding chair into the ring for Stone Cold Steve Austin to use over the head of opponent Triple H. Triple H didn't take kindly to Schwarzenegger's interference and took a swing at him, but the Terminator star ducked his punch and then pummeled Triple H to the floor with his fists.

Why did the WWF change its name to the WWE?

The name WWF was a long-standing acronym for the league's proper name, World Wrestling Federation Entertainment Inc., and the league had been using WWF as it's common name since 1979. Unfortunately, so was the World Wildlife Fund. The two organizations had been quarrelling over the use of the initials "WWF" for quite some time and had at one point come to the agreement that wrestling could use "WWF" in North America as much as they wanted, but they had to limit their use overseas. The World Wildlife Fund sued the World Wrestling Federation in 2000 for violating the terms of their previous agreement. It turns out that wrestling merchandise was selling better than expected in Europe. In a settlement agreement, the World Wrestling Federation Entertainment Inc. changed their official name to World Wrestling Entertainment Inc., hence their new name of WWE. WWE can still use their old name of the World Wrestling Federation Entertainment Inc., but just not in acronym form.

Which wrestler is famous for using a move called the "Pedigree"?

In a move technically called the double underhook facebuster, the wrestler bends an opponent facing himself forward at the waist, then hooks his arms under the opponent's elbows, locking his own arms together over the opponent's back. He then jumps in the air and drops to his knees driving the opponent's face into the mat. The move was popularized by the wrestler Triple H who dubbed it the "Pedigree."

Quickies

Did you know …

that after being forced to change it's name from WWF to WWE that some fans were so angry that the WWE created a new brand called the WWF Generation? Fans of the older generations of WWF wrestlers can still buy merchandise with the old WWF logo on it, but the WWF has to be accompanied by the word "Generation."

What is the "Batista Bomb"?

Technically called a sitout powerbomb, wrestler Dave Batista has made this move his own, calling it the "Batisa Bomb." Batista bends an opponent facing him forward at the waist and then wraps his arms around the opponent's midsection. He then lifts the opponent off the ground as the opponent swings upwards until, rather ungraciously, he is sitting on Batista's shoulder with his crotch in Batista's face. Batista then drops him onto his back in what is usually staged as a match-finishing move.

Ten Top Male Wrestlers' Real Names

Ring name	Real name
Hulk Hogan	Terrance Gene Bollea
The Undertaker	Mark William Calaway
Dino Bravo	Adolfo Bresciano
Junk Yard Dog	Sylvester Ritter
Triple H	Paul Michael Levesque
Gorilla Monsoon	Robert James Marella
British Bulldog	David Boy Smith
Brutus "The Barber" Beefcake	Edward Harrison Leslie
Rowdy Roddy Piper	Roderick George Toombs
The Sheik	Edward George Farhat

Who was Hervina?

In January 2000, champion wrestler The Kat was set to defend her Women's WWF title against a mysterious newcomer named Hervina who, it was said, hailed from the town of Intercourse, Pennsylvania. The match was fought in a ring filled with snow, and the Kat appeared dressed as a snowbunny, wearing a white bikini and rabbit ears. Hervina suspiciously wore a full snowmobiler's suit. Hervina won the match easily and then pulled off a wig to reveal that she was actually wrestler Harvey Wippleman, who became the first male to win the Women's Championship.

Which wrestler also battled aliens?

Rowdy Roddy Piper billed himself as a Scotsman, wearing a kilt in the ring, but he was actually born in Saskatoon, Saskatchewan (albeit to parents of Scottish descent). He began wrestling at the age of 15, in 1969, and rose to international celebrity by the 1980s. In 1988 he joined the handful of pro wrestlers who have made the crossover from the square ring to the big screen. Piper appeared that year in director John Carpenter's sci-fi action film, *They Live*, playing a down-on-his-luck drifter named Nada. With the help of special sunglasses, Nada discovers that society's leaders are actually aliens who are enslaving humanity and decides to go on a hunting spree. Entering a bank armed to the teeth, Piper delivered the famous line, "I have come here to chew bubblegum and kick ass, and I'm all out of bubble gum!", before opening fire on the creatures.

Ten Top Female Wrestlers' Real Names

Ring name	Real name
The Fabulous Moolah	Mary Lillian Ellison
Chyna	Joan Marie Laurer
The Kat	Stacy Carter
Kelly Kelly	Barbara Jean Blank
Molly Holly	Noreen Kristina Greenwald
Lita	Amy Christine Dumas
Luna	Gertrude Vachon
Victoria	Lisa Marie Varon
Jazz	Carlene Denise Moore-Begnaud
Barbara Bush	Katherine Dingman

What mysterious thing happened on Wikipedia.org related to the deaths of wrestler Chris Benoit and his family?

On Monday, June 25, 2007, Canadian pro wrestler Chris Benoit was found dead by police, along with his wife Nancy and their young son Daniel, in their home in Atlanta, Georgia. In the double murder-suicide, police determined that Benoit had strangled his wife the previous Friday, smothered his son on late Friday or early Saturday, and then hanged himself inside his weight room on Sunday or Monday. Fourteen hours before the police entered the Benoit home, two updates were made to Benoit's Wikipedia.org page indicating that his wife was dead. The IP addresses for the computers used in the updates were recorded by Wikipedia and given to police. The computers were traced to Connecticut and Australia, but it is not known who made the updates.

Who is the oldest person to have won a WWF title?

The Fabulous Moolah (Mary Lillian Ellison) had perhaps the longest career of any pro wrestler. She wrestled from the early 1950s right through the 1990s. She was also a successful wrestling trainer for female wrestlers. Ellison became the oldest champion in the history of professional wrestling when she won the WWF Women's Championship at age 76, in 1999. She died at age 84 on November 3, 2007, due to complications from surgery.

Wrestlers Who Died from Drug Overdose

Ring name	Real name
Mike Von Erich	Michael Brett Adkinsson
Bam Bam Bigelow	Scott Charles Bigelow
Bobby Duncum Jr.	Bobby Duncum Jr.
Pitbull #2	Anthony Durante
Mr. Perfect	Curt Hennig
Charles Wolfe	Gino Hernandez
Miss Elizabeth	Elizabeth Hulette
Crash Holly	Mike Lockwood
Sherri Schrull	Sherri Martel
Rad Radford	Louie Spicolli
Chase Tatum	Chase Tatum

winners
and champions

Hockey

Memorial Cup Winners

Year	Winner	Opponent	Score
1919	University of Toronto Schools	Regina Patricias	29–8
1920	Toronto Canoe Club Paddlers	Selkirk Fishermen	15–5
1921	Winnipeg Junior Falcons	Stratford Midgets	11–9
1922	Fort William War Veterans	Regina Patricias	8–7
1923	University of Manitoba Bisons	Kitchener Colts	14–6
1924	Owen Sound Greys	Calgary Canadians	7–5
1925	Regina Pats	Toronto Aura Lee	2–0
1926	Calgary Canadians	Queen's University	2–1
1927	Owen Sound Greys	Port Arthur West End Jrs.	2–0
1928	Regina Monarchs	Ottawa Gunners	2–1
1929	Toronto Marlboros	Elmwood Millionaires	2–0
1930	Regina Pats	West Toronto Nationals	2–0
1931	Elmwood Millionaires	Ottawa Primroses	2–1
1932	Sudbury Cub Wolves	Winnipeg Monarchs	2–1
1933	Newmarket Redmen	Regina Pats	2–0
1934	Toronto St. Michael's Majors	Edmonton Athletics	2–0
1935	Winnipeg Monarchs	Sudbury Cub Wolves	2–1
1936	West Toronto Nationals	Saskatoon Wesleys	2–0
1937	Winnipeg Monarchs	Copper Cliff Redmen	2–1
1938	St. Boniface Seals	Oshawa Generals	3–2
1939	Oshawa Generals	Edmonton Athletic Club	3–1
1940	Oshawa Generals	Kenora Thistles	3–1
1941	Winnipeg Rangers	Montreal Royals	3–2
1942	Portage la Prairie Terriers	Oshawa Generals	3–1
1943	Winnipeg Rangers	Oshawa Generals	4–2
1944	Oshawa Generals	Trail Smoke Eaters	4–0
1945	Toronto St. Michael's Majors	Moose Jaw Canucks	4–1
1946	Winnipeg Monarchs	Toronto St. Michael's Majors	4–3
1947	Toronto St. Michael's Majors	Moose Jaw Canucks	4–0
1948	Port Arthur West End Bruins	Barrie Flyers	4–0
1949	Montreal Royals	Brandon Wheat Kings	4–3–1
1950	Montreal Junior Canadiens	Regina Pats	4–1
1951	Barrie Flyers	Winnipeg Monarchs	4–0
1952	Guelph Biltmore Mad Hatters	Regina Pats	4–0
1953	Barrie Flyers	St. Boniface Canadiens	4–1
1954	St. Catharines Teepees	Edmonton Oil Kings	4–0–1
1955	Toronto Marlboros	Regina Pats	4–1

1956	Toronto Marlboros	Regina Pats	4–0–1
1957	Flin Flon Bombers	Ottawa Junior Canadiens	4–3
1958	Ottawa-Hull Junior Canadiens	Regina Pats	4–2
1959	Winnipeg Braves	Peterborough TPT Petes	4–1
1960	St. Catharines Teepees	Edmonton Oil Kings	4–2
1961	Toronto St. Michael's Majors	Edmonton Oil Kings	4–2
1962	Hamilton Red Wings	Edmonton Oil Kings	4–1
1963	Edmonton Oil Kings	Niagara Falls Flyers	4–2
1964	Toronto Marlboros	Edmonton Oil Kings	4–0
1965	Niagara Falls Flyers	Edmonton Oil Kings	4–1
1966	Edmonton Oil Kings	Oshawa Generals	4–2
1967	Toronto Marlboros	Port Arthur Marrs	4–1
1968	Niagara Falls Flyers	Estevan Bruins	4–1
1969	Montreal Junior Canadiens	Regina Pats	4–0
1970	Montreal Junior Canadiens	Weyburn Red Wings	4–0
1971	Québec Remparts	Edmonton Oil Kings	2–0
1972	Cornwall Royals	Peterborough Petes	2–1
1973	Toronto Marlboros	Québec Remparts	9–1
1974	Regina Pats	Québec Remparts	7–4
1975	Toronto Marlboros	New Westminster Bruins	7–3
1976	Hamilton Fincups	New Westminster Bruins	5–2
1977	New Westminster Bruins	Ottawa 67's	6–5
1978	New Westminster Bruins	Peterborough Petes	7–4
1979	Peterborough Petes	Brandon Wheat Kings	2–1 (OT)
1980	Cornwall Royals	Peterborough Petes	3–2 (OT)
1981	Cornwall Royals	Kitchener Rangers	5–2
1982	Kitchener Rangers	Sherbrooke Castors	7–4
1983	Portland Winter Hawks	Oshawa Generals	8–3
1984	Ottawa 67's	Kitchener Rangers	7–2
1985	Prince Albert Raiders	Shawinigan Cataractes	6–1
1986	Guelph Platers	Hull Olympiques	6–2
1987	Medicine Hat Tigers	Oshawa Generals	6–2
1988	Medicine Hat Tigers	Windsor Spitfires	7–6
1989	Swift Current Broncos	Saskatoon Blades	4–3 (OT)
1990	Oshawa Generals	Kitchener Rangers	4–3 (OT)
1991	Spokane Chiefs	Drummondville Voltigeurs	5–1
1992	Kamloops Blazers	Sault Ste. Marie Greyhounds	5–4
1993	Sault Ste. Marie Greyhounds	Peterborough Petes	4–2
1994	Kamloops Blazers	Laval Titan	5–3
1995	Kamloops Blazers	Detroit Jr. Red Wings	8–2
1996	Granby Prédateurs	Peterborough Petes	4–0
1997	Hull Olympiques	Lethbridge Hurricanes	5–1

1998	Portland Winter Hawks	Guelph Storm	4–3 (OT)
1999	Ottawa 67's	Calgary Hitmen	7–6 (OT)
2000	Rimouski Océanic	Barrie Colts	6–2
2001	Red Deer Rebels	Val-d'Or Foreurs	6–5 (OT)
2002	Kootenay Ice	Victoriaville Tigres	6–3
2003	Kitchener Rangers	Hull Olympiques	6–3
2004	Kelowna Rockets	Gatineau Olympiques	2–1
2005	London Knights	Rimouski Océanic	4–0
2006	Québec Remparts	Moncton Wildcats	6–2
2007	Vancouver Giants	Medicine Hat Tigers	3–1
2008	Spokane Chiefs	Kitchener Rangers	4–1
2009	Windsor Spitfires	Kelowna Rockets	4–1

IIHF Men's World Hockey Championship Medal Winners

Year	Gold	Silver	Bronze
1920	Canada	United States	Czechoslovakia
1924	Canada	United States	Great Britain
1928	Canada	Sweden	Switzerland
1930	Canada	Germany	Switzerland
1931	Canada	United States	Austria
1932	Canada	United States	Germany
1933	United States	Canada	Czechoslovakia
1934	Canada	United States	Germany
1935	Canada	Switzerland	Great Britain
1936	Great Britain	Canada	United States
1937	Canada	Great Britain	Switzerland
1938	Canada	Great Britain	Czechoslovakia
1939	Canada	United States	Switzerland
1947	Czechoslovakia	Sweden	Austria
1948	Canada	Czechoslovakia	Switzerland
1949	Czechoslovakia	Canada	United States
1950	Canada	United States	Switzerland
1951	Canada	Sweden	Switzerland
1952	Canada	United States	Sweden
1953	Sweden	West Germany	Switzerland
1954	Soviet Union	Canada	Sweden
1955	Canada	Soviet Union	Czechoslovakia
1956	Soviet Union	United States	Canada
1957	Sweden	Soviet Union	Czechoslovakia
1958	Canada	Soviet Union	Sweden

1959	Canada	Soviet Union	Czechoslovakia
1960	United States	Canada	Soviet Union
1961	Canada	Czechoslovakia	Soviet Union
1962	Sweden	Canada	United States
1963	Soviet Union	Sweden	Czechoslovakia
1964	Soviet Union	Sweden	Czechoslovakia
1965	Soviet Union	Czechoslovakia	Sweden
1966	Soviet Union	Czechoslovakia	Canada
1967	Soviet Union	Sweden	Canada
1968	Soviet Union	Czechoslovakia	Canada
1969	Soviet Union	Sweden	Czechoslovakia
1970	Soviet Union	Sweden	Czechoslovakia
1971	Soviet Union	Czechoslovakia	Sweden
1972	Czechoslovakia	Soviet Union	Sweden
1973	Soviet Union	Sweden	Czechoslovakia
1974	Soviet Union	Czechoslovakia	Sweden
1975	Soviet Union	Czechoslovakia	Sweden
1976	Czechoslovakia	Soviet Union	Sweden
1977	Czechoslovakia	Sweden	Soviet Union
1978	Soviet Union	Czechoslovakia	Canada
1979	Soviet Union	Czechoslovakia	Sweden
1981	Soviet Union	Sweden	Czechoslovakia
1982	Soviet Union	Czechoslovakia	Canada
1983	Soviet Union	Czechoslovakia	Canada
1985	Czechoslovakia	Canada	Soviet Union
1986	Soviet Union	Sweden	Canada
1987	Sweden	Soviet Union	Czechoslovakia
1989	Soviet Union	Canada	Czechoslovakia
1990	Soviet Union	Sweden	Czechoslovakia
1991	Sweden	Canada	Soviet Union
1992	Sweden	Finland	Czechoslovakia
1993	Russia	Sweden	Czech Republic
1994	Canada	Finland	Sweden
1995	Finland	Sweden	Canada
1996	Czech Republic	Canada	United States
1997	Canada	Sweden	Czech Republic
1998	Sweden	Finland	Czech Republic
1999	Czech Republic	Finland	Sweden
2000	Czech Republic	Slovakia	Finland
2001	Czech Republic	Finland	Sweden
2002	Slovakia	Russia	Sweden
2003	Canada	Sweden	Slovakia

2004	Canada	Sweden	United States
2005	Czech Republic	Canada	Russia
2006	Sweden	Czech Republic	Finland
2007	Canada	Finland	Russia
2008	Russia	Canada	Finland
2009	Russia	Canada	Sweden

Note: All Olympic Ice Hockey Tournaments between 1920 and 1968 also counted as World Championships. There were no World Championships from 1940 to 1946. In the Olympic years 1980, 1984, and 1988, no IIHF World Championships were staged.

IIHF Men's Junior Hockey Championship Medal Winners

Year	Gold	Silver	Bronze
1977	Soviet Union	Canada	Czechoslovakia
1978	Soviet Union	Sweden	Canada
1979	Soviet Union	Czechoslovakia	Sweden
1980	Soviet Union	Finland	Sweden
1981	Sweden	Finland	Soviet Union
1982	Canada	Czechoslovakia	Finland
1983	Soviet Union	Czechoslovakia	Canada
1984	Soviet Union	Finland	Czechoslovakia
1985	Canada	Czechoslovakia	Soviet Union
1986	Soviet Union	Canada	United States
1987	Finland	Czechoslovakia	Sweden
1988	Canada	Soviet Union	Finland
1989	Soviet Union	Sweden	Czechoslovakia
1990	Canada	Soviet Union	Czechoslovakia
1991	Canada	Soviet Union	Czechoslovakia
1992	Soviet Union	Sweden	United States
1993	Canada	Sweden	Czechoslovakia
1994	Canada	Sweden	Russia
1995	Canada	Russia	Sweden
1996	Canada	Sweden	Russia
1997	Canada	United States	Russia
1998	Finland	Russia	Switzerland
1999	Russia	Canada	Slovakia
2000	Czech Republic	Russia	Canada
2001	Czech Republic	Finland	Canada
2002	Russia	Canada	Finland

2003	Russia	Canada	Finland
2004	United States	Canada	Finland
2005	Canada	Russia	Czech Republic
2006	Canada	Russia	Finland
2007	Canada	Russia	United States
2008	Canada	Sweden	Russia
2009	Canada	Sweden	Russia

Stanley Cup Winners

Year	Winners	Opponents	Result
1927	Ottawa Senators	Boston Bruins	2–0–2
1928	New York Rangers	Montreal Maroons	3–2
1929	Boston Bruins	New York Rangers	2–0
1930	Montreal Canadiens	Boston Bruins	2–0
1931	Montreal Canadiens	Chicago Black Hawks	3–2
1932	Toronto Maple Leafs	New York Rangers	3–0
1933	New York Rangers	Toronto Maple Leafs	3–1
1934	Chicago Black Hawks	Detroit Red Wings	3–1
1935	Montreal Maroons	Toronto Maple Leafs	3–0
1936	Detroit Red Wings	Toronto Maple Leafs	3–1
1937	Detroit Red Wings	New York Rangers	3–2
1938	Chicago Blackhawks	Toronto Maple Leafs	3–1
1939	Boston Bruins	Toronto Maple Leafs	4–1
1940	New York Rangers	Toronto Maple Leafs	4–2
1941	Boston Bruins	Detroit Red Wings	4–0
1942	Toronto Maple Leafs	Detroit Red Wings	4–3
1943	Detroit Red Wings	Boston Bruins	4–0
1944	Montreal Canadiens	Chicago Blackhawks	4–0
1945	Toronto Maple Leafs	Detroit Red Wings	4–3
1946	Montreal Canadiens	Boston Bruins	4–1
1947	Toronto Maple Leafs	Montreal Canadiens	4–2
1948	Toronto Maple Leafs	Detroit Red Wings	4–0
1949	Toronto Maple Leafs	Detroit Red Wings	4–0
1950	Detroit Red Wings	New York Rangers	4–3
1951	Toronto Maple Leafs	Montreal Canadiens	4–1
1952	Detroit Red Wings	Montreal Canadiens	4–0
1953	Montreal Canadiens	Boston Bruins	4–1
1954	Detroit Red Wings	Montreal Canadiens	4–3
1955	Detroit Red Wings	Montreal Canadiens	4–3
1956	Montreal Canadiens	Detroit Red Wings	4–1

1957	Montreal Canadiens	Boston Bruins	4–1
1958	Montreal Canadiens	Boston Bruins	4–2
1959	Montreal Canadiens	Toronto Maple Leafs	4–1
1960	Montreal Canadiens	Toronto Maple Leafs	4–0
1961	Chicago Blackhawks	Detroit Red Wings	4–2
1962	Toronto Maple Leafs	Chicago Blackhawks	4–2
1963	Toronto Maple Leafs	Detroit Red Wings	4–1
1964	Toronto Maple Leafs	Detroit Red Wings	4–3
1965	Montreal Canadiens	Chicago Blackhawks	4–3
1966	Montreal Canadiens	Detroit Red Wings	4–2
1967	Toronto Maple Leafs	Montreal Canadiens	4–2
1968	Montreal Canadiens	St. Louis Blues	4–0
1969	Montreal Canadiens	St. Louis Blues	4–0
1970	Boston Bruins	St. Louis Blues	4–0
1971	Montreal Canadiens	Chicago Blackhawks	4–3
1972	Boston Bruins	New York Rangers	4–2
1973	Montreal Canadiens	Chicago Blackhawks	4–2
1974	Philadelphia Flyers	Boston Bruins	4–2
1975	Philadelphia Flyers	Buffalo Sabres	4–2
1976	Montreal Canadiens	Philadelphia Flyers	4–0
1977	Montreal Canadiens	Boston Bruins	4–0
1978	Montreal Canadiens	Boston Bruins	4–2
1979	Montreal Canadiens	New York Rangers	4–1
1980	New York Islanders	Philadelphia Flyers	4–2
1981	New York Islanders	Minnesota North Stars	4–1
1982	New York Islanders	Vancouver Canucks	4–0
1983	New York Islanders	Edmonton Oilers	4–0
1984	Edmonton Oilers	New York Islanders	4–1
1985	Edmonton Oilers	Philadelphia Flyers	4–1
1986	Montreal Canadiens	Calgary Flames	4–1
1987	Edmonton Oilers	Philadelphia Flyers	4–3
1988	Edmonton Oilers	Boston Bruins	4–0
1989	Calgary Flames	Montreal Canadiens	4–2
1990	Edmonton Oilers	Boston Bruins	4–1
1991	Pittsburgh Penguins	Minnesota North Stars	4–2
1992	Pittsburgh Penguins	Chicago Blackhawks	4–0
1993	Montreal Canadiens	Los Angeles Kings	4–1
1994	New York Rangers	Vancouver Canucks	4–3
1995	New Jersey Devils	Detroit Red Wings	4–0
1996	Colorado Avalanche	Florida Panthers	4–0
1997	Detroit Red Wings	Philadelphia Flyers	4–0
1998	Detroit Red Wings	Washington Capitals	4–0

1999	Dallas Stars	Buffalo Sabres	4–2
2000	New Jersey Devils	Dallas Stars	4–2
2001	Colorado Avalanche	New Jersey Devils	4–3
2002	Detroit Red Wings	Carolina Hurricanes	4–1
2003	New Jersey Devils	Mighty Ducks of Anaheim	4–3
2004	Tampa Bay Lightning	Calgary Flames	4–3
2005	No Cup awarded due to player strike		
2006	Carolina Hurricanes	Edmonton Oilers	4–3
2007	Anaheim Mighty Ducks	Ottawa Senators	4–1
2008	Detroit Red Wings	Pittsburgh Penguins	4–2
2009	Pittsburgh Penguins	Detroit Red Wings	4–3

Soccer

Canadian National Challenge Cup Winners

Year	Winner
1913	Norwood Wanderers of Winnipeg
1913	Norwood Wanderers of Winnipeg
1915	Winnipeg Scottish
1916–18	No game held due to WWI
1919	Montreal Grand
1920	Hamilton Westinghouse
1921	Toronto Scottish
1922	Calgary Hillhursts
1923	Naniamo Wanderers
1924	United Weston (Winnipeg)
1925	Toronto Ulster
1926	United Weston (Winnipeg)
1927	Naniamo Wanderers
1928	New Westminister Royals
1929	Montreal CNR
1930	New Westminister Royals
1931	New Westminister Royals
1932	Toronto Scottish Vancouver
1933	Toronto Scottish
1934	Verdun Park (Montreal)
1935	Montreal Aldrods
1936	New Westminister Royals
1937	Johnston Nationals (B.C.)

1938	Vancouver North Shore
1939	Vancouver Radials
1940–45	No game held due to WWII
1946	Toronto Ulster United
1947	Vancouver St. Andrews
1948	Montreal Carsteel
1949	Vancouver North Shore
1950	Vancouver City
1951	Toronto Ulster United
1952	Montreal Stelco
1953	New Westminister Royals
1954	Winnipeg Scottish
1955	New Westminister Royals
1956	Vancouver Halecos
1957	Montreal Ukraina
1958	New Westminister Royals
1959	Montreal Alouettes
1960	New Westminister Royals
1961	Montreal Concordia
1962	Winnipeg Scottish
1963	No competition due to financial problems
1964	Vancouver Columbus
1965	Vancouver Firefighters
1966	British Columbia
1967	Ballymena United (Toronto)
1968	Toronto Royals
1969	Vancouver Columbus
1970	No competition due to changing structure
1971	Vancouver Eintracht
1972	New Westminister Blues
1973	Vancouver Firefighters
1974	Calgary Kickers
1975	London Boxing Club
1976	Victoria West
1977	Vancouver Columbus
1978	Vancouver Columbus
1979	Victoria West
1980	Saint John Drydock
1981	Toronto Ciociaro
1982	Victoria West
1983	Vancouver Firefighters
1984	Victoria West

1985	Vancouver Croatia
1986	Hamilton Steelers
1987	Winnipeg Lucania
1988	St. John's Holy Cross
1989	Scarborough Azzuri
1990	Vancouver Firefighters
1991	Vancouver Norvan ANAF
1992	Vancouver Norvan ANAF
1993	Vancouver Westside Rino
1994	Edmonton Ital-Canadians
1995	Mistral-Estrie
1996	Westside CIBC
1997	Edmonton Ital-Canadians
1998	RDP Condores PQ
1999	Calgary Celtics
2000	Winnipeg Lucania
2001	Halifax King of Donair
2002	Winnipeg Sons of Italy
2003	Calgary Callies
2004	Pegasus FC
2005	Scarborough GS United
2006	Ottawa St. Anthony Italia
2007	Calgary Callies
2008	Calgary Callies

FA Cup Winners

Year	Winner	Opponent	Score
1872	Wanderers	Royal Engineers	1–0
1873	Wanderers	Oxford University	2–0
1874	Oxford University	Royal Engineers	2–0
1875	Royal Engineers	Old Etonians	1–1 aet (2–0 replay)
1876	Wanderers	Old Etonians	1–1 aet (3–0 replay)
1877	Wanderers	Oxford University	2–1 aet
1878	Wanderers	Royal Engineers	3–1
1879	Old Etonians	Clapham Rovers	1–0
1880	Clapham Rovers	Oxford University	1–0
1881	Old Carthusians	Old Etonians	3–0
1882	Old Etonians	Blackburn Rovers	1–0
1883	Blackburn Olympic	Old Etonians	2–1 aet
1884	Blackburn Rovers	Queens Park, Glasgow	2–1

1885	Blackburn Rovers	Queens Park, Glasgow	2–0
1886	Blackburn Rovers	West Bromwich Albion	0–0 aet (2–0 replay)
1887	Aston Villa	West Bromwich Albion	2–0
1888	West BromwichAlbion	Preston North End	2–1
1889	Preston North End	Wolverhampton Wanderers	3–0
1890	Blackburn Rovers	Sheffield Wednesday	6–1
1891	Blackburn Rovers	Notts County	3–1
1892	West Bromwich	Albion Aston Villa	3–0
1893	WolverhamptonWanderers	Everton	1–0
1894	Notts County	Bolton Wanderers	4–1
1895	Aston Villa	West Bromwich Albion	1–0
1896	Sheffield Wednesday	Wolverhampton Wanderers	2–1
1897	Aston Villa	Everton	3–2
1898	Nottingham Forest	Derby County	3–1
1899	Sheffield United	Derby County	4–1
1900	Bury	Southampton	4–0
1901	Tottenham Hotspur	Sheffield United	2–2 aet (3–1 replay)
1902	Sheffield United	Southampton	1–1 aet (2–1 replay)
1903	Bury	Derby County	6–0
1904	Manchester City	Bolton Wanderers	1–0
1905	Aston Villa	Newcastle United	2–0
1906	Everton	Newcastle United	1–0
1907	Sheffield Wednesday	Everton	2–1
1908	Wolverhampton Wanderers	Newcastle United	3–1
1909	Manchester United	Bristol City	1–0
1910	Newcastle United	Barnsley	1–1 aet (2–0 replay)
1911	Bradford City	Newcastle United	0–0 aet (1–0 replay)
1912	Barnsley	WestBromwich Albion	0–0 aet (1–0 replay)
1913	Aston Villa	Sunderland	1–0
1914	Burnley	Liverpool	1–0
1915	Sheffield United	Chelsea	3–0
1916–19	No game held due to WWI		
1920	Aston Villa	Huddersfield Town	1–0 aet
1921	Tottenham Hotspur	Wolverhampton Wanderers	1–0
1922	Huddersfield Town	Preston North End	1–0
1923	Bolton Wanderers	West Ham United	2–0
1924	Newcastle United	Aston Villa	2–0
1925	Sheffield United	Cardiff City	1–0
1926	Bolton Wanderers	Manchester City	1–0
1927	Cardiff City	Arsenal	1–0
1928	Blackburn Rovers	Huddersfield Town	3–1
1929	Bolton Wanderers	Portsmouth	2–0

1930	Arsenal	Huddersfield Town	2–0
1931	West Bromwich Albion	Birmingham City	2–1
1932	Newcastle United	Arsenal	2–1
1933	Everton	Manchester City	3–0
1934	Manchester City	Portsmouth	2–1
1935	Sheffield Wednesday	West Bromwich Albion	4–2
1936	Arsenal	Sheffield United	1–0
1937	Sunderland	Preston North End	3–1
1938	Preston North End	Huddersfield Town	1–0 aet
1939	Portsmouth	Wolverhampton Wanderers	4–1
1940–45	No game held due to WWII		
1946	Derby County	Charlton Athletic	4–1 aet
1947	Charlton Athletic	Burnley	1–0 aet
1948	Manchester United	Blackpool	4–2
1949	Wolverhampton Wanderers	Leicester City	3–1
1950	Arsenal	Liverpool	2–0
1951	Newcastle United	Blackpool	2–0
1952	Newcastle United	Arsenal	1–0
1953	Blackpool	Bolton Wanderers	4–3
1954	West Bromwich Albion	Preston North End	3–2
1955	Newcastle United	Manchester City	3–1
1956	Manchester City	Birmingham City	3–1
1957	Aston Villa	Manchester United	2–1
1958	Bolton Wanderers	Manchester United	2–0
1959	Nottingham Forest	Luton Town	2–1
1960	Wolverhampton Wanderers	Blackburn Rovers	3–0
1961	Tottenham Hotspur	Leicester City	2–0
1962	Tottenham Hotspur	Burnley	3–1
1963	Manchester United	Leicester City	3–1
1964	West Ham United	Preston North End	3–2
1965	Liverpool	Leeds United	2–1 aet
1966	Everton	Sheffield Wednesday	3–2
1967	Tottenham Hotspur	Chelsea	2–1
1968	West BromwichAlbion	Everton	1–0 aet
1969	Manchester City	Leicester City	1–0
1970	Chelsea	Leeds United	2–2 aet (2–1 replay)
1971	Arsenal	Liverpool	2–1 aet
1972	Leeds United	Arsenal	1–0
1973	Sunderland	Leeds United	1–0
1974	Liverpool	Newcastle United	3–0
1975	West Ham United	Fulham	2–0
1976	Southampton	Manchester United	1–0

1977	Manchester United	Liverpool	2–1
1978	Ipswich Town	Arsenal	1–0
1979	Arsenal	Manchester United	3–2
1980	West Ham United	Arsenal	1–0
1981	Tottenham Hotspur	Manchester City	1–1 aet (3–2 replay)
1982	Tottenham Hotspur	Queens Park Rangers	1–1 aet (1–0 replay)
1983	Manchester United	Brighton and Hove Albion	2–2 aet (4–0 replay)
1984	Everton	Watford	2–0
1985	Manchester United	Everton	1–0 aet
1986	Liverpool	Everton	3–1
1987	Coventry City	Tottenham Hotspur	3–2 aet
1988	Wimbledon	Liverpool	1–0
1989	Liverpool	Everton	3–2 aet
1990	Manchester United	Crystal Palace	3–3 aet (1–0 replay)
1991	Tottenham Hotspur	Nottingham Forest	2–1 aet
1992	Liverpool	Sunderland	2–0
1993	Arsenal	Sheffield Wednesday	1–1 aet (2–1 replay)
1994	Manchester United	Chelsea	4–0
1995	Everton	Manchester United	1–0
1996	Manchester United	Liverpool	1–0
1997	Chelsea	Middlesbrough	2–0
1998	Arsenal	Newcastle United	2–0
1999	Manchester United	Newcastle United	2–0
2000	Chelsea	Aston Villa	1–0
2001	Liverpool	Arsenal	2–1
2002	Arsenal	Chelsea	2–0
2003	Arsenal	Southampton	1–0
2004	Manchester United	Millwall	3–0
2005	Arsenal	Manchester United	0–0 aet (5–4 penalty shootout)
2006	Liverpool	West Ham United	3–3 aet (3–1 penalty shootout)
2007	Chelsea	Manchester United	1–0
2008	Portsmouth	Cardiff City	1–0
2009	Chelsea	Everton	2–1

World Cup Winners

Year	Winner	Opponent	Score
1930	Uruguay	Argentina	4–2
1934	Italy	Czechoslovakia	2–1

1938	Italy	Hungary	4–2
1950	Uruguay	Brazil	2–1
1954	Germany	Hungary	3–2
1958	Brazil	Sweden	5–2
1962	Brazil	Czechoslovakia	3–1
1966	England	Germany	4–2
1970	Brazil	Italy	4–1
1974	Germany	Netherlands	2–1
1978	Argentina	Netherlands	3–1
1982	Italy	Germany	3–1
1986	Argentina	Germany	3–2
1990	Germany	Argentina	1–0
1994	Brazil	Italy	0–0 aet (3:2 penalty shootout)
1998	France	Brazil	3–0
2002	Brazil	Germany	2–0
2006	Italy	France	1–1 aet (5:3 penalty shootout)

Football

Grey Cup Champions

Year	Winner	Opponent	Score
1909	University of Toronto	Toronto Parkdale	26–6
1910	University of Toronto	Hamilton Tigers	16–7
1911	University of Toronto	Toronto Argonauts	14–7
1912	Hamilton Alerts	Toronto Argonauts	11–4
1913	Hamilton Tigers	Toronto Parkdale	44–2
1914	Toronto Argonauts	University of Toronto	14–2
1915	Hamilton Tigers	Toronto Rowing	13–7
1916–19	No game held due to WWI		
1920	University of Toronto	Toronto Argonauts	16–3
1921	Toronto Argonauts	Edmonton Eskimos	23–0
1922	Queen's University	Edmonton Elks	13–1
1923	Queen's University	Regina Roughriders	54–0
1924	Queen's University	Toronto Balmy Beach	11–3
1925	Ottawa Senators	Winnipeg Tigers	24–1
1926	Ottawa Senators	University of Toronto	10–7
1927	Toronto Balmy Beach	Hamilton Tigers	9–6

1928	Hamilton Tigers	Regina Roughriders	30–0
1929	Hamilton Tigers	Regina Roughriders	14–3
1930	Toronto Balmy Beach	Regina Roughriders	11–6
1931	Montréal AAA	Regina Roughriders	22–0
1932	Hamilton Tigers	Regina Roughriders	25–6
1933	Toronto Argonauts	Sarnia Imperials	4–3
1934	Sarnia Imperials	Regina Roughriders	20–12
1935	Winnipeg Winnipegs	Hamilton Tigers	18–12
1936	Sarnia Imperials	Ottawa Rough Riders	26–20
1937	Toronto Argonauts	Winnipeg Blue Bombers	4–3
1938	Toronto Argonauts	Winnipeg Blue Bombers	30–7
1939	Winnipeg Blue Bombers	Ottawa Rough Riders	8–7
1940	Ottawa Rough Riders	Toronto Balmy Beach	20–7
1941	Winnipeg Blue Bombers	Ottawa Rough Riders	18–16
1942	Toronto RCAF	Winnipeg RCAF	8–5
1943	Hamilton Wildcats	Winnipeg RCAF	23–14
1944	Montreal HMCS Donnacona	Hamilton Wildcats	7–6
1945	Toronto Argonauts	Winnipeg Blue Bombers	35–0
1946	Toronto Argonauts	Winnipeg Blue Bombers	28–6
1947	Toronto Argonauts	Winnipeg Blue Bombers	10–9
1948	Calgary Stampeders	Ottawa Rough Riders	12–7
1949	Montréal Alouettes	Calgary Stampeders	28–15
1950	Toronto Argonauts	Winnipeg Blue Bombers	13–0
1951	Ottawa Rough Riders	Saskatchewan Roughriders	21–14
1952	Toronto Argonauts	Edmonton Eskimos	21–11
1953	Hamilton Tiger-Cats	Winnipeg Blue Bombers	12–6
1954	Edmonton Eskimos	Montréal Alouettes	26–25
1955	Edmonton Eskimos	Montréal Alouettes	34–19
1956	Edmonton Eskimos	Montréal Alouettes	50–27
1957	Hamilton Tiger-Cats	Winnipeg Blue Bombers	32–7
1958	Winnipeg Blue Bombers	Hamilton Tiger-Cats	35–28
1959	Winnipeg Blue Bombers	Hamilton Tiger-Cats	21–7
1960	Ottawa Rough Riders	Edmonton Eskimos	16–6
1961	Winnipeg Blue Bombers	Hamilton Tiger-Cats	21–14
1962	Winnipeg Blue Bombers	Hamilton Tiger-Cats	28–27
1963	Hamilton Tiger-Cats	British Columbia Lions	21–10
1964	British Columbia Lions	Hamilton Tiger-Cats	34–24
1965	Hamilton Tiger-Cats	Winnipeg Blue Bombers	22–16
1966	Saskatchewan Roughriders	Ottawa Rough Riders	29–14
1967	Hamilton Tiger-Cats	Saskatchewan Roughriders	24–1
1968	Ottawa Rough Riders	Calgary Stampeders	24–21
1969	Ottawa Rough Riders	Saskatchewan Roughriders	29–11

1970	Montréal Alouettes	Calgary Stampeders	23–10
1971	Calgary Stampeders	Toronto Argonauts	14–11
1972	Hamilton Tiger-Cats	Saskatchewan Roughriders	13–10
1973	Ottawa Rough Riders	Edmonton Eskimos	22–18
1974	Montréal Alouettes	Edmonton Eskimos	20–7
1975	Edmonton Eskimos	Montréal Alouettes	9–8
1976	Ottawa Rough Riders	Saskatchewan Roughriders	23–20
1977	Montréal Alouettes	Edmonton Eskimos	41–6
1978	Edmonton Eskimos	Montréal Alouettes	20–13
1979	Edmonton Eskimos	Montréal Alouettes	17–9
1980	Edmonton Eskimos	Hamilton Tiger-Cats	48–10
1981	Edmonton Eskimos	Ottawa Rough Riders	26–23
1982	Edmonton Eskimos	Toronto Argonauts	32–16
1983	Toronto Argonauts	British Columbia Lions	18–17
1984	Winnipeg Blue Bombers	Hamilton Tiger-Cats	47–17
1985	British Columbia Lions	Hamilton Tiger-Cats	37–24
1986	Hamilton Tiger-Cats	Edmonton Eskimos	39–15
1987	Edmonton Eskimos	Toronto Argonauts	38–36
1988	Winnipeg Blue Bombers	British Columbia Lions	22–21
1989	Saskatchewan Roughriders	Hamilton Tiger-Cats	43–40
1990	Winnipeg Blue Bombers	Edmonton Eskimos	50–11
1991	Toronto Argonauts	Calgary Stampeders	36–21
1992	Calgary Stampeders	Winnipeg Blue Bombers	24–10
1993	Edmonton Eskimos	Winnipeg Blue Bombers	33–23
1994	British Columbia Lions	Baltimore CFLers	26–23
1995	Baltimore Stallions	Calgary Stampeders	37–20
1996	Toronto Argonauts	Edmonton Eskimos	43–37
1997	Toronto Argonauts	Saskatchewan Roughriders	47–23
1998	Calgary Stampeders	Hamilton Tiger-Cats	26–24
1999	Hamilton Tiger-Cats	Calgary Stampeders	32–21
2000	British Columbia Lions	Montréal Alouettes	28–26
2001	Calgary Stampeders	Winnipeg Blue Bombers	27–19
2002	Montréal Alouettes	Edmonton Eskimos	25–16
2003	Edmonton Eskimos	Montréal Alouettes	34–22
2004	Toronto Argonauts	British Columbia Lions	27–19
2005	Edmonton Eskimos	Montréal Alouettes	38–35
2006	British Columbia Lions	Montréal Alouettes	25–14
2007	Saskatchewan Roughriders	Winnipeg Blue Bombers	23–19
2008	Calgary Stampeders	Montréal Alouettes	22–14

Super Bowl Champions

Game	Year	Winner	Opponent	Score
I	1967	Green Bay Packers	Kansas City Chiefs	35–10
II	1968	Green Bay Packers	Oakland Raiders	33–14
III	1969	New York Jets	Baltimore Colts	16–7
IV	1970	Kansas City Chiefs	Minnesota Vikings	23–7
V	1971	Baltimore Colts	Dallas Cowboys	16–13
VI	1972	Dallas Cowboys	Miami Dolphins	24–3
VII	1973	Miami Dolphins	Washington Redskins	14–7
VIII	1974	Miami Dolphins	Minnesota Vikings	24–7
IX	1975	Pittsburgh Steelers	Minnesota Vikings	16–6
X	1976	Pittsburgh Steelers	Dallas Cowboys	21–17
XI	1977	Oakland Raiders	Minnesota Vikings	32–14
XII	1978	Dallas Cowboys	Denver Broncos	27–10
XIII	1979	Pittsburgh Steelers	Dallas Cowboys	35–31
XIV	1980	Pittsburgh Steelers	Los Angeles Rams	31–19
XV	1981	Oakland Raiders	Philadelphia Eagles	27–10
XVI	1982	San Francisco 49ers	Cincinnati Bengals	26–21
XVII	1983	Washington Redskins	Miami Dolphins	27–17
XVIII	1984	Los Angeles Raiders	Washington Redskins	38–9
XIX	1985	San Francisco 49ers	Miami Dolphins	38–16
XX	1986	Chicago Bears	New England Patriots	46–10
XXI	1987	New York Giants	Denver Broncos	39–20
XXII	1988	Washington Redskins	Denver Broncos	42–10
XXIII	1989	San Francisco 49ers	Cincinnati Bengals	20–16
XXIV	1990	San Francisco 49ers	Denver Broncos	55–10
XXV	1991	New York Giants	Buffalo Bills	20–19
XXVI	1992	Washington Redskins	Buffalo Bills	37–24
XXVII	1993	Dallas Cowboys	Buffalo Bills	52–17
XXVIII	1994	Dallas Cowboys	Buffalo Bills	30–13
XXIX	1995	San Francisco 49ers	San Diego Chargers	49–26
XXX	1996	Dallas Cowboys	Pittsburgh Steelers	27–17
XXXI	1997	Green Bay Packers	New England Patriots	35–21
XXXII	1998	Denver Broncos	Green Bay Packers	31–24
XXXIII	1999	Denver Broncos	Atlanta Falcons	34–19
XXXIV	2000	St. Louis Rams	Tennessee Titans	23–16
XXXV	2001	Baltimore Ravens	New York Giants	34–7
XXXVI	2002	New England Patriots	St. Louis Rams	20–17
XXXVII	2003	Tampa Bay Buccaneers	Oakland Raiders	48–21
XXXVIII	2004	New England Patriots	Carolina Panthers	32–29
XXXIX	2005	New England Patriots	Philadelphia Eagles	24–21

XL	2006	Pittsburgh Steelers	Seattle Seahawks	21–10
XLI	2007	Indianapolis Colts	Chicago Bears	29–17
XLII	2008	New York Giants	New England Patriots	17–14
XLIII	2009	Pittsburgh Steelers	Arizona Cardinals	27–23

Note: The first four Super Bowls were called the "AFL-NFL Championship Game." The name "Super Bowl" and the corresponding Roman numeral were applied to those games retroactively.

Rugby

Rugby League World Cup Winners

Year	Winner	Opponent	Score
1954	Great Britain	France	16–12
1957	Australia	Great Britain	N/A
1960	Great Britain	Australia	N/A
1968	Australia	France	20–2
1970	Australia	Great Britain	12–7
1972	Great Britain	Australia	10–10
1975	Australia	England	25–0
1977	Australia	Great Britain	13–12
1985–88	Australia	New Zealand	25–12
1989–92	Australia	Great Britain	10–6
1995	Australia	England	16–8
2000	Australia	New Zealand	40–12
2008	New Zealand	Australia	34–20

Results of the Rugby World Cup* Since First Contested in 1987

Year	Winner	Opponent	Score
1987	New Zealand	France	29–9
1991	Australia	England	12–6
1995	South Africa	New Zealand	15–12
1999	Australia	France	35–12
2003	England	Australia	20–17
2007	South Africa	England	15–6

*Contested only by rugby union teams. Rugby league teams compete in the Rugby League World Cup.

Baseball

World Series Champions

Year	Winner	Opponent	Result
1903	Boston Red Sox	Pittsburgh Pirates	5–3
1904	No game held due to a boycott		
1905	New York Giants	Philadelphia Athletics	4–1
1906	Chicago White Sox	Chicago Cubs	4–2
1907	Chicago Cubs	Detroit Tigers	4–0
1908	Chicago Cubs	Detroit Tigers	4–1
1909	Pittsburgh Pirates	Detroit Tigers	4–3
1910	Philadelphia Athletics	Chicago Cubs	4–1
1911	Philadelphia Athletics	New York Giants	4–2
1912	Boston Red Sox	New York Giants	4–3
1913	Philadelphia Athletics	New York Giants	4–1
1914	Boston Braves	Philadelphia Athletics	4–0
1915	Boston Red Sox	Philadelphia Phillies	4–1
1916	Boston Red Sox	Brooklyn Dodgers	4–1
1917	Chicago White Sox	New York Giants	4–2
1918	Boston Red Sox	Chicago Cubs	4–2
1919	Cincinnati Reds	Chicago White Sox	5–3
1920	Cleveland Indians	Brooklyn Dodgers	5–2
1921	New York Giants	New York Yankees	5–3
1922	New York Giants	New York Yankees	4–0
1923	New York Yankees	New York Giants	4–2
1924	Washington Senators	New York Giants	4–3
1925	Pittsburgh Pirates	Washington Senators	4–3
1926	St. Louis Cardinals	New York Yankees	4–3
1927	New York Yankees	Pittsburgh Pirates	4–0
1928	New York Yankees	St. Louis Cardinals	4–0
1929	Philadelphia Athletics	Chicago Cubs	4–1
1930	Philadelphia Athletics	St. Louis Cardinals	4–2
1931	St. Louis Cardinals	Philadelphia Athletics	4–3
1932	New York Yankees	Chicago Cubs	4–0
1933	New York Giants	Washington Senators	4–1
1934	St. Louis Cardinals	Detroit Tigers	4–3
1935	Detroit Tigers	Chicago Cubs	4–2
1936	New York Yankees	New York Giants	4–2
1937	New York Yankees	New York Giants	4–1
1938	New York Yankees	Chicago Cubs	4–0
1939	New York Yankees	Cincinnati Reds	4–0

1940	Cincinnati Reds	Detroit Tigers	4–3
1941	New York Yankees	Brooklyn Dodgers	4–1
1942	St. Louis Cardinals	New York Yankees	4–1
1943	New York Yankees	St. Louis Cardinals	4–1
1944	St. Louis Cardinals	St. Louis Browns	4–2
1945	Detroit Tigers	Chicago Cubs	4–3
1946	St. Louis Cardinals	Boston Red Sox	4–3
1947	New York Yankees	Brooklyn Dodgers	4–3
1948	Cleveland Indians	Boston Braves	4–2
1949	New York Yankees	Brooklyn Dodgers	4–1
1950	New York Yankees	Philadelphia Phillies	4–0
1951	New York Yankees	New York Giants	4–2
1952	New York Yankees	Brooklyn Dodgers	4–3
1953	New York Yankees	Brooklyn Dodgers	4–2
1954	New York Giants	Cleveland Indians	4–0
1955	Brooklyn Dodgers	New York Yankees	4–3
1956	New York Yankees	Brooklyn Dodgers	4–3
1957	Milwaukee Braves	New York Yankees	4–3
1958	New York Yankees	Milwaukee Braves	4–3
1959	Los Angeles Dodgers	Chicago White Sox	4–2
1960	Pittsburgh Pirates	New York Yankees	4–3
1961	New York Yankees	Cincinnati Reds	4–1
1962	New York Yankees	San Francisco Giants	4–3
1963	Los Angeles Dodgers	New York Yankees	4–0
1964	St. Louis Cardinals	New York Yankees	4–3
1965	Los Angeles Dodgers	Minnesota Twins	4–3
1966	Baltimore Orioles	Los Angeles Dodgers	4–0
1967	St. Louis Cardinals	Boston Red Sox	4–3
1968	Detroit Tigers	St. Louis Cardinals	4–3
1969	New York Mets	Baltimore Orioles	4–1
1970	Baltimore Orioles	Cincinnati Reds	4–1
1971	Pittsburgh Pirates	Baltimore Orioles	4–3
1972	Oakland Athletics	Cincinnati Reds	4–3
1973	Oakland Athletics	New York Mets	4–3
1974	Oakland Athletics	Los Angeles Dodgers	4–1
1975	Cincinnati Reds	Boston Red Sox	4–3
1976	Cincinnati Reds	New York Yankees	4–0
1977	New York Yankees	Los Angeles Dodgers	4–2
1978	New York Yankees	Los Angeles Dodgers	4–2
1979	Pittsburgh Pirates	Baltimore Orioles	4–3
1980	Philadelphia Phillies	Kansas City Royals	4–2
1981	Los Angeles Dodgers	New York Yankees	4–2

1982	St. Louis Cardinals	Milwaukee Brewers	4–3
1983	Baltimore Orioles	Philadelphia Phillies	4–1
1984	Detroit Tigers	San Diego Padres	4–1
1985	Kansas City Royals	St. Louis Cardinals	4–3
1986	New York Mets	Boston Red Sox	4–3
1987	Minnesota Twins	St. Louis Cardinals	4–3
1988	Los Angeles Dodgers	Oakland Athletics	4–1
1989	Oakland Athletics	San Francisco Giants	4–0
1990	Cincinnati Reds	Oakland Athletics	4–0
1991	Minnesota Twins	Atlanta Braves	4–3
1992	Toronto Blue Jays	Atlanta Braves	4–2
1993	Toronto Blue Jays	Philadelphia Phillies	4–2
1994	No game held due to strike		
1995	Atlanta Braves	Cleveland Indians	4–2
1996	New York Yankees	Atlanta Braves	4–2
1997	Florida Marlins	Cleveland Indians	4–3
1998	New York Yankees	San Diego Padres	4–0
1999	New York Yankees	Atlanta Braves	4–0
2000	New York Yankees	New York Mets	4–1
2001	Arizona Diamondbacks	New York Yankees	4–3
2002	Anaheim Angels	San Francisco Giants	4–3
2003	Florida Marlins	New York Yankees	4–2
2004	Boston Red Sox	St. Louis Cardinals	4–0
2005	Chicago White Sox	Houston Astros	4–0
2006	St. Louis Cardinals	Detroit Tigers	4–1
2007	Boston Red Sox	Colorado Rockies	4–0
2008	Philadelphia Phillies	Tampa Bay Rays	4–1

NCAA Baseball College World Champions by Division

Year	Division I	Division II	Division III
1947	California		
1948	Southern California		
1949	Texas		
1950	Texas		
1951	Oklahoma		
1952	Holy Cross		
1953	Michigan		
1954	Missouri		
1955	Wake Forest		
1956	Minnesota		

1957	California		
1958	Southern California		
1959	Oklahoma St.		
1960	Minnesota		
1961	Southern California		
1962	Michigan		
1963	Southern California		
1964	Minnesota		
1965	Arizona St.		
1966	Ohio St.		
1967	Arizona St.		
1968	Southern California	Chapman	
1969	Arizona St.	Illinois St.	
1970	Southern California	Cal St. Northridge	
1971	Southern California	Fla. Southern	
1972	Southern California	Fla. Southern	
1973	Southern California	UC Irvine	
1974	Southern California	UC Irvine	
1975	Texas	Fla. Southern	
1976	Arizona	Cal Poly Pomona	Cal St. Stanislaus
1977	Arizona St.	UC Riverside	Cal St. Stanislaus
1978	Southern California	Fla. Southern	Rowan
1979	Cal St. Fullerton	Valdosta St.	Rowan
1980	Arizona	Cal Poly Pomona	Ithaca
1981	Arizona St.	Fla. Southern	Marietta
1982	Miami (Fla.)	UC Riverside	Eastern Conn. St.
1983	Texas	Cal Poly Pomona	Marietta
1984	Cal St. Fullerton	Cal St. Northridge	Ramapo
1985	Miami (Fla.)	Fla. Southern	Wis.-Oshkosh
1986	Arizona	Troy	Marietta
1987	Stanford	Troy	Montclair St.
1988	Stanford	Fla. Southern	Ithaca
1989	Wichita St.	Cal Poly	N.C. Wesleyan
1990	Georgia	Jacksonville St.	Eastern Conn. St.
1991	LSU	Jacksonville St.	Southern Me.
1992	Pepperdine	Tampa	Wm. Paterson
1993	LSU	Tampa	Montclair St.
1994	Oklahoma	Central Mo. St.	Wis.-Oshkosh
1995	Cal St. Fullerton	Fla. Southern	La Verne
1996	LSU	Kennesaw St.	Wm. Paterson
1997	LSU	Cal St. Chico	Southern Me.
1998	Southern California	Tampa	Eastern Conn. St.

1999	Miami (Fla.)	Cal St. Chico	N.C. Wesleyan
2000	LSU	Southeastern Okla.	Montclair St.
2001	Miami (Fla.)	St. Mary's	St. Thomas (Minn.)
2002	Texas	Columbus St.	Eastern Conn. St.
2003	Rice	Central Mo. St.	Chapman
2004	Cal St. Fullerton	Delta St.	George Fox
2005	Texas	Florida Southern	Wis.-Whitewater
2006	Oregon State	Tampa	Marietta
2007	Oregon State	Tampa	Kean
2008	Fresno State	Mount Olive	Trinity (Conn.)
2009	LSU	Lynn	St. Thomas (Minn.)

Basketball

NBA Finals Winners

Year	Winner	Opponent	Result
1947	Philadelphia Warriors	Chicago Stags	4–1
1948	Baltimore Bullets	Philadelphia Warriors	4–2
1949	Minneapolis Lakers	Washington Capitols	4–2
1950	Minneapolis Lakers	Syracuse Nationals	4–2
1951	Rochester Royals	New York Knicks	4–3
1952	Minneapolis Lakers	New York Knicks	4–3
1953	Minneapolis Lakers	New York Knicks	4–1
1954	Minneapolis Lakers	Syracuse Nationals	4–3
1955	Syracuse Nationals	Fort Wayne Pistons	4–3
1956	Philadelphia Warriors	Fort Wayne Pistons	4–1
1957	Boston Celtics	St. Louis Hawks	4–3
1958	St. Louis Hawks	Boston Celtics	4–2
1959	Boston Celtics	Minneapolis Lakers	4–0
1960	Boston Celtics	St. Louis Hawks	4–3
1961	Boston Celtics	St. Louis Hawks	4–1
1962	Boston Celtics	Los Angeles Lakers	4–3
1963	Boston Celtics	Los Angeles Lakers	4–2
1964	Boston Celtics	San Francisco Warriors	4–1
1965	Boston Celtics	Los Angeles Lakers	4–1
1966	Boston Celtics	Los Angeles Lakers	4–3
1967	Philadelphia 76ers	San Francisco Warriors	4–2
1968	Boston Celtics	Los Angeles Lakers	4–2
1969	Boston Celtics	Los Angeles Lakers	4–3

1970	New York Knicks	Los Angeles Lakers	4–3
1971	Milwaukee Bucks	Baltimore Bullets	4–0
1972	Los Angeles Lakers	New York Knicks	4–1
1973	New York Knicks	Los Angeles Lakers	4–1
1974	Boston Celtics	Milwaukee Bucks	4–3
1975	Golden State Warriors	Washington Bullets	4–0
1976	Boston Celtics	Phoenix Suns	4–2
1977	Portland Trail Blazers	Philadelphia 76ers	4–2
1978	Washington Bullets	Seattle SuperSonics	4–3
1979	Seattle SuperSonics	Washington Bullets	4–1
1980	Los Angeles Lakers	Philadelphia 76ers	4–2
1981	Boston Celtics	Houston Rockets	4–2
1982	Los Angeles Lakers	Philadelphia 76ers	4–2
1983	Philadelphia 76ers	Los Angeles Lakers	4–0
1984	Boston Celtics	Los Angeles Lakers	4–3
1985	Los Angeles Lakers	Boston Celtics	4–2
1986	Boston Celtics	Houston Rockets	4–2
1987	Los Angeles Lakers	Boston Celtics	4–2
1988	Los Angeles Lakers	Detroit Pistons	4–3
1989	Detroit Pistons	Los Angeles Lakers	4–0
1990	Detroit Pistons	Portland Trail Blazers	4–1
1991	Chicago Bulls	Los Angeles Lakers	4–1
1992	Chicago Bulls	Portland Trail Blazers	4–2
1993	Chicago Bulls	Phoenix Suns	4–2
1994	Houston Rockets	New York Knicks	4–3
1995	Houston Rockets	Orlando Magic	4–0
1996	Chicago Bulls	Seattle SuperSonics	4–2
1997	Chicago Bulls	Utah Jazz	4–2
1998	Chicago Bulls	Utah Jazz	4–2
1999	San Antonio Spurs	New York Knicks	4–1
2000	Los Angeles Lakers	Indiana Pacers	4–2
2001	Los Angeles Lakers	Philadelphia 76ers	4–1
2002	Los Angeles Lakers	New Jersey Nets	4–0
2003	San Antonio Spurs	New Jersey Nets	4–2
2004	Detroit Pistons	Los Angeles Lakers	4–1
2005	San Antonio Spurs	Detroit Pistons	4–3
2006	Miami Heat	Dallas Mavericks	4–2
2007	San Antonio Spurs	Cleveland Cavaliers	4–0
2008	Boston Celtics	Los Angeles Lakers	4–2
2009	Los Angeles Lakers	Orlando Magic	4–1

NCAA Basketball Division I Champions

Year	Winner	Opponent	Score
1939	Oregon	Ohio State	46–33
1940	Indiana	Kansas	60–42
1941	Wisconsin	Washington State	39–34
1942	Stanford	Dartmouth	53–38
1943	Wyoming	Georgetown	46–34
1944	Utah	Dartmouth	42–40 (OT)
1945	Oklahoma A&M	NYU	49–45
1946	Oklahoma A&M	North Carolina	43–40
1947	Holy Cross	Oklahoma	58–47
1948	Kentucky	Baylor	58–42
1949	Kentucky	Oklahoma State	46–36
1950	CCNY	Bradley	71–68
1951	Kentucky	Kansas State	68–58
1952	Kansas	St. John's (NY)	80–63
1953	Indiana	Kansas	69–68
1954	La Salle	Bradley	92–76
1955	San Francisco	La Salle	77–63
1956	San Francisco	Iowa	83–71
1957	North Carolina	Kansas	54–53 (OT)
1958	Kentucky	Seattle	84–72
1959	California	West Virginia	71–70
1960	Ohio State	California	75–55
1961	Cincinnati	Ohio State	70–65 (OT)
1962	Cincinnati	Ohio State	71–59
1963	Loyola (IL)	Cincinnati	60–58 (OT)
1964	UCLA	Duke	98–83
1965	UCLA	Michigan	91–80
1966	Texas	WesternKentucky	72–65
1967	UCLA	Dayton	79–64
1968	UCLA	North Carolina	78–55
1969	UCLA	Purdue	92–72
1970	UCLA	Jacksonville	80–69
1971	UCLA	Villanova*	68–62
1972	UCLA	Florida State	81–76
1973	UCLA	Memphis State	87–66
1974	North Carolina State	Marquette	76–64
1975	UCLA	Kentucky	92–85
1976	Indiana	Michigan	86–68
1977	Marquette	North Carolina	67–59

1978	Kentucky	Duke	94–88
1979	Michigan State	Indiana St.	75–64
1980	Louisville	UCLA*	59–54
1981	Indiana	North Carolina	63–50
1982	North Carolina	Georgetown	63–62
1983	North Carolina State	Houston	54–52
1984	Georgetown	Houston	84–75
1985	Villanova	Georgetown	66–64
1986	Louisville	Duke	72–69
1987	Indiana	Syracuse	74–73
1988	Kansas	Oklahoma	83–79
1989	Michigan	Seton Hall	80–79 (OT)
1990	Nevada-Las Vegas	Duke	103–73
1991	Duke	Kansas	72–65
1992	Duke	Michigan	71–51
1993	North Carolina	Michigan	77–71
1994	Arkansas	Duke	76–72
1995	UCLA	Arkansas	89–78
1996	Kentucky	Syracuse	76–67
1997	Arizona	Kentucky	84–79 (OT)
1998	Kentucky	Utah	78–69
1999	Connecticut	Duke	77–74
2000	Michigan State	Florida	89–76
2001	Duke	Arizona	82–72
2002	Maryland	Indiana	64–52
2003	Syracuse	Kansas	81–78
2004	Connecticut	Georgia Tech	82–73
2005	North Carolina	Illinois	75–70
2006	Florida	UCLA	73–57
2007	Florida	Ohio State	84–75
2008	Kansas	Memphis	75–68 (OT)
2009	North Carolina	Michigan State	89–72

* Standing vacated because team included ineligible players

Lacrosse

Minto Cup Champions

Year	Team	Most Valuable Player
1937	Orillia Terriers	
1938	Mimico Mountaineers	
1939	Orillia Terriers	
1940	Orillia Terriers	
1941–46	No competition due to WWII	
1947	St. Catharines Athletics	
1948	Vancouver Burrards	
1949	Vancouver Norburn Eagletime	
1950	St. Catharines Athletics	
1951	Mimico Mountaineers	
1952	Brampton Excelsiors	
1953	New Westminster Salmonacs	
1954	Vancouver PNE Indians	
1955	Long Branch Monarchs	
1956	Vancouver Legionnaires	
1957	Brampton ABC's	
1958	Brampton ABC's	
1959	Brampton ABC's	
1960	New Westminster Salmonbellies	
1961	Hastings Legionnaires	
1962	Victoria Shamrocks	
1963	Oshawa Green Gaels	Merv Marshall
1964	Oshawa Green Gaels	Gaylord Powless
1965	Oshawa Green Gaels	Jim Higgs
1966	Oshawa Green Gaels	Ken Winzoski
1967	Oshawa Green Gaels	Gaylord Powless
1968	Oshawa Green Gaels	Jim Higgs
1969	Oshawa Green Gaels	Jim Higgs
1970	Lakeshore Maple Leafs	Brian McCutcheon
1971	Richmond Roadrunners	Ted Gernaey
1972	Peterborough PCO's	John Grant
1973	Peterborough PCO's	Paul Evans
1974	Peterborough PCO's	Tim Barrie
1975	Peterborough Gray Munros	Bob Wasson
1976	Victoria Macdonalds	Kevin Alexander
1977	Burnaby Cablevision	Rod Bannister
1978	Burnaby Cablevision	Lloyd Symons

1979	Burnaby Cablevision	John Swan
1980	Whitby Builders	John Jordan
1981	Peterborough James Gang	Larry Floyd
1982	Peterborough James Gang	Larry Floyd
1983	Peterborough James Gang	Doug Evans
1984	Whitby Warriors	Joe Nieuwendyk
1985	Whitby Warriors	Paul Gait
1986	Peterborough Maulers	Gary Gait
1987	Peterborough Maulers	Paul Gait
1988	Esquimalt Legion	Bob Heyes
1989	Peterborough Maulers	Craig Stevenson
1990	St. Catharines Athletics	Randy Mearns
1991	St. Catharines Athletics	Tom Hawke
1992	Six Nations Arrows	Cam Bomberry
1993	Orangeville Northmen	Jason Campbell
1994	New Westminster Salmonbellies	Curtis Palidwor
1995	Orangeville Northmen	Rusty Krueger
1996	Orangeville Northmen	Jim Rankin
1997	Whitby Warriors	Mike Wye
1998	Burnaby Lakers	Cam Sedgwick
1999	Whitby Warriors	Gee Nash
2000	Burnaby Lakers	Matt Roik
2001	St. Catharines Athletics	Matt Vinc
2002	Burnaby Lakers	Nick Patterson
2003	St. Catharines Athletics	Luke Wiles
2004	Burnaby Lakers	Nenad Gajic
2005	Burnaby Lakers	Ilija Gajic
2006	Peterborough Lakers	Shawn Evans
2007	Six Nations Arrows Express	Cody Jamieson
2008	Orangeville Northmen	Stephen Keogh

World Lacrosse Championship Winners

Year	Winner	Opponent	Score
1967	United States	Australia	N/A
1974	United States	3-way tie	N/A
1978	Canada	United States	17–16 (OT)
1982	United States	Australia	22–14
1986	United States	Canada	18–9
1990	United States	Canada	19–15
1994	United States	Australia	21–7

1998	United States	Canada	15–14 (2OT)
2002	United States	Canada	18–15
2006	Canada	United States	15–10

Major League Lacrosse (MLL) Steinfeld Cup Winners

Year	Winner	Opponent	Score
2001	Long Island Lizards	Baltimore Bayhawks	15–11
2002	Baltimore Bayhawks	Long Island Lizards	21–13
2003	Long Island Lizards	Baltimore Bayhawks	15–14 (OT)
2004	Philadelphia Barrage	Boston Cannons	13–11
2005	Baltimore Bayhawks	Long Island Lizards	15–9
2006	Philadelphia Barrage	Denver Outlaws	23–12
2007	Philadelphia Barrage	Los Angeles Riptide	16–13
2008	Rochester Rattlers	Denver Outlaws	16–6

CUFLA Baggataway Cup Champions

Year	Winner
1985	University of Western Ontario
1986	Brock University
1987	McMaster University
1988	University of Western Ontario
1989	Brock University
1990	Brock University
1991	Brock University
1992	Brock University
1993	Brock University
1994	Brock University
1995	University of Guelph
1996	Brock University
1997	Brock University
1998	Brock University
1999	Brock University
2000	University of Guelph
2001	University of Western Ontario
2002	Brock University
2003	Brock University
2004	Brock University
2005	Brock University

2006	Brock University
2007	Brock University
2008	University of Guelph

NCAA Lacrosse Men's Division I Champions

Year	Winner	Opponent	Score
1971	Cornell	Maryland	12–6
1972	Virginia	Johns Hopkins	13–12
1973	Maryland	Johns Hopkins	10–9 (2 OT)
1974	Johns Hopkins	Maryland	17–12
1975	Maryland	Navy	20–13
1976	Cornell	Maryland	16–13 (OT)
1977	Cornell	Johns Hopkins	16–8
1978	Johns Hopkins	Cornell	13–8
1979	Johns Hopkins	Maryland	15–9
1980	Johns Hopkins	Virginia	9–8 (2 OT)
1981	North Carolina	Johns Hopkins	14–13
1982	North Carolina	Johns Hopkins	7–5
1983	Syracuse	Johns Hopkins	17–16
1984	Johns Hopkins	Syracuse	13–10
1985	Johns Hopkins	Syracuse	11–4
1986	North Carolina	Virginia	10–9 (OT)
1987	Johns Hopkins	Cornell	11–10
1988	Syracuse	Cornell	13–8
1989	Syracuse	Johns Hopkins	13–12
1990	Syracuse (vacated)*	Loyola (MD)	21–9
1991	North Carolina	Towson	18–13
1992	Princeton	Syracuse	10–9 OT
1993	Syracuse	North Carolina	13–12
1994	Princeton	Virginia	9–8 (OT)
1995	Syracuse	Maryland	13–9
1996	Princeton	Virginia	13–12 (OT)
1997	Princeton	Maryland	19–7
1998	Princeton	Maryland	15–5
1999	Virginia	Syracuse	12–10
2000	Syracuse	Princeton	13–7
2001	Princeton	Syracuse	10–9 (OT)
2002	Syracuse	Princeton	13–12
2003	Virginia	Johns Hopkins	9–7
2004	Syracuse	Navy	14–13

2005	Johns Hopkins	Duke	9–8
2006	Virginia	Massachusetts	15–7
2007	Johns Hopkins	Duke	11–10
2008	Syracuse	Johns Hopkins	13–10
2009	Syracuse	Cornell	10–9 (OT)

*Syracuse's participation in the 1990 tournament was vacated by the NCAA Committee due to infractions. The NCAA Committee on Infractions determined that Paul Gait had played in the 1990 championship while ineligible. Under NCAA rules, Syracuse and Paul Gait's records for that championship were vacated

Curling

The Tournament of Hearts Winners

Year	Winners	Team Members (Skip, Second, Third, Lead)
1961	Saskatchewan	Joyce McKee, Barbara MacNevin, Sylvia Fedoruk, Rose McFee
1962	British Columbia	Ina Hansen, Isabel Leith, Ada Callas, May Shaw
1963	New Brunswick	Mabel DeWare, Forbis Stevenson, Harriet Stratton, Marjorie Fraser
1964	British Columbia	Ina Hansen, Isabel Leith, Ada Callas, May Shaw
1965	Manitoba	Peggy Casselman, Pat MacDonald, Val Taylor, Pat Scott
1966	Alberta	Gail Lee, Sharon Harrington, Hazel Jamieson, June Coyle
1967	Manitoba	Betty Duguid, Laurie Bradawaski, Joan Ingram, Dot Rose
1968	Alberta	Hazel Jamieson, Jackie Spencer, Gail Lee, June Coyle
1969	Saskatchewan	Joyce McKee, Lenore Morrison, Vera Pezer, Jennifer Falk
1970	Saskatchewan	Dorenda Schoenhals, Linda Burnham, Cheryl Stirton, Joan Anderson
1971	Saskatchewan	Vera Pezer, Joyce McKee, Sheila Rowan, Lenore Morrison
1972	Saskatchewan	Vera Pezer, Joyce McKee, Sheila Rowan, Lenore Morrison
1973	Saskatchewan	Vera Pezer, Joyce McKee, Sheila Rowan, Lenore Morrison
1974	Saskatchewan	Emily Farnham, Pat McBeth, Linda Saunders, Donna Collins
1975	Quebec	Lee Tobin, Michelle Garneau, Marilyn McNeil, Laurie Ross
1976	British Columbia	Lindsay Davie, Robin Klasen, Dawn Knowles, Lorraine Bowles
1977	Alberta	Mryna McQuarrie, Barb Davis, Rita Tarnava, Jane Rempel
1978	Manitoba	Cathy Pidzarko, Iris Armstrong, Chris Pidzarko, Patty Vande
1979	British Columbia	Lindsay Sparkes, Robin Wilson, Dawn Knowles, Lorraine Bowles
1980	Saskatchewan	Marj Mitchell, Shirley McKendry, Nancy Kerr, Wendy Leach
1981	Alberta	Susan Seitz, Myna McKay, Judy Erickson, Betty McCracken
1982	Nova Scotia	Colleen Jones, Monica Jones, Kay Smith, Barbara Jones-Gordon

1983	Nova Scotia	Penny LaRocque, Cathy Caudle, Sharon Horne, Pam Samford
1984	Manitoba	Connie Laliberte, Corinne Peters, Chris More, Janet Arnott
1985	British Columbia	Linda Moore, Debbie Jones, Lindsay Sparkes, Laurie Carney
1986	Ontario	Marilyn Darte, Chris Jurgenson, Kathy McEdwards, Jan Augustyn
1987	British Columbia	Pat Saunders, Louise Herlinveaux, Georgina Hawkes, Deb Massullo
1988	Ontario	Heather Houston, Diane Adams, Lorraine Lang, Tracy Kennedy
1989	Team Canada	Heather Houston, Diane Adams, Lorraine Lang, Tracy Kennedy
1990	Ontario	Alison Goring, Andrea Lawes, Kristin Turcotte, Cheryl McPherson
1991	British Columbia	Julie Sutton, Melissa Soligo, Jodie Sutton, Karri Wilms
1992	Manitoba	Connie Laliberte, Cathy Gauthier, Laurie Allen, Janet Arnott
1993	Saskatchewan	Sandra Peterson, Joan McCusker, Jan Betker, Marcia Gudereit
1994	Team Canada	Sandra Peterson, Joan McCusker, Jan Betker, Marcia Gudereit
1995	Manitoba	Connie Laliberte, Cathy Gauthier, Cathy Clapham, Janet Arnott
1996	Ontario	Marilyn Bodogh, Corie Beveridge, Kim Gellard, Jane Hooper Perroud
1997	Saskatchewan	Sandra Schmirler, Joan McCusker, Jan Betker, Marcia Gudereit
1998	Alberta	Cathy Borst, Brenda Bohmer, Heather Godberson, Kate Horne
1999	Nova Scotia	Colleen Jones, Mary-Anne Waye, Kim Kelly, Nancy Delahunt
2000	British Columbia	Kelley Law, Georgina Wheatcroft, Julie Skinner, Diane Nelson
2001	Nova Scotia	Colleen Jones, Mary-Anne Waye, Kim Kelly, Nancy Delahunt
2002	Team Canada	Colleen Jones, Mary-Anne Waye, Kim Kelly, Nancy Delahunt
2003	Team Canada	Colleen Jones, Mary-Anne Waye, Kim Kelly, Nancy Delahunt
2004	Team Canada	Colleen Jones, Mary-Anne Waye, Kim Kelly, Nancy Delahunt
2005	Manitoba	Jennifer Jones, Jill Officer, Cathy Overton-Clapham, Cathy Gauthier
2006	British Columbia	Kelly Scott, Sasha Carter, Jeanna Schraeder, Renee Simons
2007	Team Canada	Kelly Scott, Sasha Carter, Jeanna Schraeder, Renee Simons
2008	Manitoba	Jennifer Jones, Jill Officer, Cathy Overton-Clapham, Dawn Askin
2009	Team Canada	Jennifer Jones, Jill Officer, Cathy Overton-Clapham, Dawn Askin

The Brier Champions

Year	Winners	Team Members (Skip, Second, Third, Lead)
1927	Nova Scotia	Murray Macneill, Cliff Torey, Al MacInnes, Jim Donahoe
1928	Manitoba	Gordon Hudson, Ron Singbusch, Sam Penwarden, Bill Grant
1929	Manitoba	Gordon Hudson, Don Rolo, Sam Penwarden, Bill Grant
1930	Manitoba	Howard Wood, Victor Wood, Jimmy Congalton, Lionel Wood
1931	Manitoba	Bob Gourlay, Arnold Lockerbie, Ernie Pllard, Ray Stewart

1932	Manitoba	Jimmy Congalton, Bill Noble, Howard Wood, Harry Mawhinney
1933	Alberta	Cliff Manahan, Harold Wolfe, Harold Deeton, Bert Ross
1934	Manitoba	Leo Johnson, Linc Johnson, Lorne Stewart, Marno Frederickson
1935	Ontario	Gordon Campbell, Gord Coates, Don Campbell, Duncan Campbell
1936	Manitoba	Ken Watson, Marvin McIntyre, Grant Watson, Charles Kerr
1937	Alberta	Cliff Manahan, Ross Manahan, Wes Robinson, Lloyd McIntyre
1938	Manitoba	Ab Gowanlock, Bill McKnight, Bung Cartmell, Tom Knight
1939	Ontario	Bert Hall, Erniue Parkes, Perry Hall, Cam Seagram
1940	Manitoba	Howard Wood, Howard Wood Jr., Ernie Pollard, Roy Enman
1941	Alberta	Howard Palmer, Art Gooder, Jack Lebeau, Clare Webb
1942	Manitoba	Ken Watson, Charlie Scrymgeour, Grant Watson, Jim Grant
1943–45		No championship played due to WWII
1946	Alberta	Bill Rose, Austin Smith, Bart Swelin, George Crooks
1947	Manitoba	Jimmy Welsh, Jack Reid, Alex Welsh, Harry Monk
1948	British Columbia	Frenchy D'Amour, Fred Wendell, Bob McGhie, Jim Mark
1949	Manitoba	Ken Watson, Lyle Dyker, Grant Watson, Charles Read
1950	Northern Ontario	Tim Ramsay, Bill Weston, Len Williamson, Billy Kenny
1951	Nova Scotia	Don Oyler, Fred Dyke, George Hanson, Wally Knock
1952	Manitoba	Billy Walsh, Andy McWilliams, Al Langois, John Watson
1953	Manitoba	Ab Gowanlock, Art Pollon, Russ Jackman, Jim Williams
1954	Alberta	Matt Baldwin, Pete Ferry, Glenn Gray, Jim Collins
1955	Saskatchewan	Garnet Campbell, Glen Campbell, Don Campbell, Lloyd Campbell
1956	Manitoba	Billy Walsh, Cy White, Al Langlois, Andy McWilliams
1957	Alberta	Matt Baldwin, Art Kleinmeyer, Gordon Haynes, Bill Price
1958	Alberta	Matt Baldwin, Gordon Haynes, Jack Geddes, Bill Price
1959	Saskatchewan	Ernie Richardson, Sam Richardson, Arnold Richardson, Wes Richardson
1960	Saskatchewan	Ernie Richardson, Sam Richardson, Arnold Richardson, Wes Richardson
1961	Alberta	Hec Gerais, Ray Werner, Ron Anton, Wally Ursuliak
1962	Saskatchewan	Ernie Richardson, Sam Richardson, Arnold Richardson, Wes Richardson
1963	Saskatchewan	Ernie Richardson, Sam Richardson, Arnold Richardson, Mel Perry
1964	British Columbia	Lyall Dagg, Fred Britton, Leo Herbert, Barry Naimark
1965	Manitoba	Terry Braunstein, Ron Braunstein, Don Duguid, Ray Turnbull
1966	Alberta	Ron Northcott, Bernie Sparkes, George Fink, Fred Storey
1967	Ontario	Alf Phillips Jr., Ron Manning, John Ross, Keith Reilly
1968	Alberta	Ron Northcott, Bernie Sparkes, Jim Shields, Fred Storey
1969	Alberta	Ron Northcott, Bernie Sparkes, Dave Gerlach, Fred Storey

1970	Manitoba	Don Duguid, Jim Pettapiece, Rod Hunter, Bryan Wood
1971	Manitoba	Don Duguid, Jim Pettapiece, Rod Hunter, Bryan Wood
1972	Manitoba	Orest Meleschuk, John Hanesiak, Dave Romano, Pat Hailley
1973	Saskatchewan	Harvey Mazinke, George Achtymichuk, Bill Martin, Dan Klippenstein
1974	Alberta	Hec Gervais, Warren Hanson, Ron Anton, Darrel Sutton
1975	Northern Ontario	Bill Tetley, Bill Hodgson, Rick Lang, Peter Hnatiew
1976	Newfoundland	Jack McDuff, Doug Hudson, Toby McDonald, Ken Templeton
1977	Quebec	Jim Ursel, Don Aitken, Art Lobel, Brian Ross
1978	Alberta	Ed Lukowich, Dale Johnston, Mike Chernoff, Ron Schindle
1979	Manitoba	Barry Fry, Gord Sparkes, Bill Carey, Bryan Wood
1980	Saskatchewan	Rick Folk, Tom Wilson, Ron Mills, Jim Wilson
1981	Manitoba	Kerry Burtnyk, Jim Spencer, Mark Olson, Ron Kammerlock
1982	Northern Ontario	Al Hackner, Bob Nicol, Rick Lang, Bruce Kennedy
1983	Ontario	Ed Werenich, John Kawaja, Paul Savage, Neil Harrison
1984	Manitoba	Mike Riley, John Helston, Brian Toews, Russ Wookey
1985	Northern Ontario	Al Hackner, Ian Tetley, Rick Lang, Pat Perroud
1986	Alberta	Ed Lukowich, Neil Houston, John Ferguson, Brent Syme
1987	Ontario	Russ Howard, Tim Belcourt, Glenn Howard, Kent Carstairs
1988	Alberta	Pat Ryan, Don Walchuk, Randy Ferbey, Don McKenzie
1989	Alberta	Pat Ryan, Don Walchuk, Randy Ferbey, Don McKenzie
1990	Ontario	Ed Werenich, Ian Tetley, John Kawaja, Pat Perroud
1991	Alberta	Kevin Martin, Dan Petryk, Kevin Park, Don Bartlett
1992	Manitoba	Vic Peters, Chris Neufeld, Dan Carey, Don Rudd
1993	Onario	Russ Howard, Wayne Middaugh, Glenn Howard, Peter Corner
1994	British Columbia	Rick Folk, Bert Gretzinger, Pat Ryan, Gerry Richard
1995	Manitoba	Kerry Burtnyk, Rob Mekin, Jeff Ryan, Keith Fenton
1996	Manitoba	Jeff Stoughton, Garry Van Den Berghe, Ken Tresoor, Steve Gould
1997	Alberta	Kevin Martin, Rudy Ramcharan, Don Walchuk, Don Bartlett
1998	Ontario	Wayne Middaugh, Ian Tetley, Graeme McCarrel, Scott Bailey
1999	Manitoba	Jeff Stoughton, Garry Van Den Berghe, Jonathan Mead, Doug Armstrong
2000	British Columbia	Greg McAulay, Bryan Miki, Brent Pierce, Jody Sveistrup
2001	Alberta	Randy Ferbey, Scott Pfeifer, David Nedohin, Marcel Rocque
2002	Alberta	Randy Ferbey, Scott Pfeifer, David Nedohin, Marcel Rocque
2003	Alberta	Randy Ferbey, Scott Pfeifer, David Nedohin, Marcel Rocque
2004	Nova Scotia	Mark Darcey, Rob Harris, Bruce Lohnes, Andrew Gibson
2005	Alberta	Randy Ferbey, Scott Pfeifer, David Nedohin, Marcel Rocque
2006	Quebec	Jean-Michel Ménard, Eric Sylvain, François, Maxime Elmaleh
2007	Ontario	Glenn Howard, Brent Laing, Richard Hart, Craig Savill
2008	Alberta	Kevin Martin, Marc Kennedy, John Morris, Ben Hebert
2009	Alberta	Kevin Martin, Marc Kennedy, John Morris, Ben Hebert

Note: The Brier was called the MacDonald Brier from 1927–1979, the Labatt Brier from 1980–2000, the Nokia Brier from 2001–2004, and is currently called the Tim Hortons Brier.

Olympics

Summer Olympics by the Numbers

Year	Location	Countries	Participants	Men	Women	Sports	Events
1896	Athens, Greece	12	176	176	0	9	43
1900	Paris, France	28	1,215	1,193	22	20	95
1904	St. Louis, United States	14	649	643	6	18	94
1906	Athens, Greece	21	840	834	6	13	74
1908	London, Great Britain	22	2,024	1,980	44	24	109
1912	Stockholm, Sweden	28	2,405	2,351	54	17	107
1920	Antwerpen, Belgium	29	2,675	2,597	78	25	161
1924	Paris, France	45	3,254	3,104	150	20	130
1928	Amsterdam, Netherlands	46	3,231	2,921	310	17	120
1932	Los Angeles, United States	39	1,821	1,636	185	18	126
1936	Berlin, Germany	49	4,464	4,106	357	24	143
1940 and 1944	No games held due to WWII						
1948	London, Great Britain	59	4,367	3,933	434	20	149
1952	Helsinki, Finland	69	4,931	4,410	521	19	149
1956	Melbourne, Australia	67	3,187	2,817	370	18	145
1960	Rome, Italy	83	5,346	4,734	612	19	150
1964	Tokyo, Japan	93	5,136	4,456	680	21	163
1968	Mexico City, Mexico	112	5,554	4,771	783	20	172
1972	Munich, West Germany	121	7,113	6,053	1,060	23	195
1976	Montréal, Canada	92	6,071	4,810	1,261	23	198
1980	Moscow, Soviet Union	80	5,253	4,133	1,120	23	203
1984	Los Angeles, United States	140	6,795	5,225	1,570	25	221
1988	Seoul, South Korea	159	8,453	6,251	2,202	27	237
1992	Barcelona, Spain	169	9,385	6,662	2,723	29	257
1996	Atlanta, United States	197	10,329	6,817	3,512	31	271
2000	Sydney, Australia	200	10,647	6,579	4,068	34	300
2004	Athens, Greece	201	10,558	6,257	4,301	34	301
2008	Beijing, China	204	10,904	6,295	4,609	34	302

Top All-Time Summer Olympic Medallists

Athlete	Country	Sport	Gold	Silver	Bronze	Total
Larisa Latynina	USSR	Gymnastics	9	5	4	18
Michael Phelps	USA	Swimming	14	0	2	16
Nikolay Andrianov	USSR	Gymnastics	7	5	3	15
Boris Shakhlin	USSR	Gymnastics	7	4	2	13
Edoardo Mangiarotti	Italy	Fencing	6	5	2	13
Takashi Ono	Japan	Gymnastics	5	4	4	13
Paavo Nurmi	Finland	Running	9	3	0	12
Birgit Fischer-Schmidt	Germany	Canoeing	8	4	0	12
Sawao Kato	Japan	Gymnastics	8	3	1	12
Jenny Thompson	USA	Swimming	8	3	1	12
Dara Torres	USA	Swimming	4	4	4	12
Aleksey Nemov	Russia	Gymnastics	4	2	6	12

Top Summer Olympic Medal-Winning Countries

Country	Gold	Silver	Bronze	Total
United States	942	736	641	2319
Soviet Union	395	319	296	1010
Great Britain	218	272	256	746
France	212	226	257	695
Germany	202	229	250	681
Italy	203	170	179	552
Sweden	143	165	182	490
Hungary	162	148	162	472
Australia	131	140	168	439
East Germany	153	129	127	409

Winter Olympics by the Numbers

Year	Location	Countries	Participants	Men	Women	Sports	Events
1924	Chamonix, France	19	312	299	13	10	17
1928	St Moritz, Switzerland	25	464	436	28	8	13
1932	Lake Placid, United States	17	252	231	21	7	14
1936	Garmisch-Partenkirchen, Germany	28	668	588	80	8	17
1940 and 1944		No games held due to WWII					
1948	St Moritz, Switzerland	28	669	591	77	9	22

1952	Oslo, Norway	30	693	584	109	8	22
1956	Cortina d'Ampezzo, Italy	32	821	689	132	8	24
1960	Squaw Valley, United States	30	665	521	144	8	27
1964	Innsbruck, Austria	36	1,094	895	199	10	34
1968	Grenoble, France	37	1,158	947	211	10	35
1972	Sapporo, Japan	35	1,008	802	206	10	35
1976	Innsbruck, Austria	37	1,129	898	231	10	37
1980	Lake Placid, United States	37	1,072	837	235	10	38
1984	Sarajevo, Yugoslavia	50	1,273	996	277	10	39
1988	Calgary, Canada	57	1,425	1,110	315	10	46
1992	Albertville, France	64	1,801	1,313	488	12	57
1994	Lillehammer, Norway	67	1,738	1,216	522	12	61
1998	Nagano, Japan	72	2,180	1,391	789	14	68
2002	Salt Lake City, United States	77	2,399	1,513	886	15	78
2006	Torino, Italy	79	2,494	1,539	955	15	84

Top All-Time Winter Olympic Medallists

Athlete	Country	Sport	Gold	Silver	Bronze	Total
Bjørn Dæhlie	Norway	Cross-country skiing	8	4	0	12
Raisa Smetanina	Soviet/Russian	Nordic Skiing	4	5	1	10
Stefania Belmondo	Italy	Cross-country skiing	2	3	5	10
Lyubov Yegorova	Russian	Cross-country skiing	6	3	0	9
Ole Einar Bjørndalen	Norway	Biathlon	5	3	1	9
Claudia Pechstein	Germany	Speed Skating	5	2	2	9
Sixten Jernberg	Sweden	Cross-country skiing	4	3	2	9
Uschi Disl (GER)	Germany	Biathlon	2	4	3	9
Ricco Groß	Germany	Biathlon	4	3	1	8
Kjetil André Aamodt	Norway	Alpine Ski Racing	4	2	2	8
Sven Fischer	Germany	Biathlon	4	2	2	8
Galina Kulakova	Soviet	Cross-country skiing	4	2	2	8
Gunda Niemann-Stirnemann	Germany	Speed Skating	3	4	1	8
Karin Kania-Enke	East Germany	Speed Skating	3	4	1	8

Top Winter Olympic Medal-Winning Countries

Country	Gold	Silver	Bronze	Total
Norway	98	98	84	280
United States	78	80	59	217

Soviet Union	78	57	59	194
Austria	51	64	70	185
Germany	68	65	46	179
Finland	41	58	52	151
Canada	38	39	42	119
Sweden	43	31	44	118
Switzerland	38	37	43	118
East Germany	39	36	35	110

Tennis

Wimbledon Open Era Champions

Singles

Year	Men	Women
1968	Rod Laver	Billie Jean King
1969	Rod Laver	Ann Haydon
1970	John Newcombe	Margaret Court
1971	John Newcombe	Evonne Goolagong
1972	Stan Smith	Billie Jean King
1973	Jan Kodes	Billie Jean King
1974	Jimmy Connors	Chris Evert
1975	Arthur Ashe	Billie Jean King
1976	Björn Borg	Chris Evert
1977	Björn Borg	Virginia Wade
1978	Björn Borg	Martina Navrátilová
1979	Björn Borg	Martina Navrátilová
1980	Björn Borg	Evonne Goolagong
1981	John McEnroe	Chris Evert
1982	Jimmy Connors	Martina Navrátilová
1983	John McEnroe	Martina Navrátilová
1984	John McEnroe	Martina Navrátilová
1985	Boris Becker	Martina Navrátilová
1986	Boris Becker	Martina Navrátilová
1987	Pat Cash	Martina Navrátilová
1988	Stefan Edberg	Steffi Graf
1989	Boris Becker	Steffi Graf
1990	Stefan Edberg	Martina Navrátilová
1991	Michael Stich	Steffi Graf
1992	Andre Agassi	Steffi Graf

1993	Pete Sampras	Steffi Graf
1994	Pete Sampras	Conchita Martínez
1995	Pete Sampras	Steffi Graf
1996	Richard Krajicek	Steffi Graf
1997	Pete Sampras	Martina Hingis
1998	Pete Sampras	Jana Novotná
1999	Pete Sampras	Lindsay Davenport
2000	Pete Sampras	Venus Williams
2001	Goran Ivanisevic	Venus Williams
2002	Lleyton Hewitt	Serena Williams
2003	Roger Federer	Serena Williams
2004	Roger Federer	Maria Sharapova
2005	Roger Federer	Venus Williams
2006	Roger Federer	Amélie Mauresmo
2007	Roger Federer	Venus Williams
2008	Rafael Nadal	Venus Williams
2009	Roger Federer	Serena Williams

Doubles

Year	Men	Women
1968	John Newcombe and Tony Roche	Rosie Casals and Billie Jean King
1969	John Newcombe and Tony Roche	Margaret Court and Judy Tegart
1970	John Newcombe and Tony Roche	Rosie Casals and Billie Jean King
1971	Roy Emerson and Rod Laver	Rosie Casals and Billie Jean King
1972	Bob Hewitt and Frew McMillan	Billie Jean King and Betty Stöve
1973	Jimmy Connors and Ilie Nastase	Rosie Casals and Billie Jean King
1974	John Newcombe and Tony Roche	Evonne Goolagong and Peggy Michel
1975	Vitas Gerulaitis and Sandy Mayer	Ann Kiyomura and Kazuko Sawamatsu
1976	Brian Gottfriied and Raúl Ramírez	Chris Evert and Martina Navrátilová
1977	Ross Case and Geoff Masters	Helen Gourlay and JoAnne Russell
1978	Bob Hewitt and Frew McMillan	Kerry Melville Reid and Wendy Turnbull
1979	Peter Fleming and John McEnroe	Billie Jean King and Martina Navrátilová
1980	Peter McNamara and Paul McNamee	Kathy Jordan and Anne Smith
1981	Peter Fleming and John McEnroe	Martina Navrátilová and Pam Shriver
1982	Peter McNamara and Paul McNamee	Martina Navrátilová and Pam Shriver
1983	Peter Fleming and John McEnroe	Martina Navrátilová and Pam Shriver
1984	Peter Fleming and John McEnroe	Martina Navrátilová and Pam Shriver
1985	Heinz Günthardt and Balázs Taróczy	Kathy Jordan and Elizabeth Smylie
1986	Joakim Nyström and Mats Wilander	Martina Navrátilová and Pam Shriver
1987	Ken Flach and Robert Seguso	Claudia Kohde and Helena Suková
1988	Ken Flach and Robert Seguso	Steffi Graf and Gabriela Sabatini
1989	John Fitzgerald and Anders Järryd	Jana Novotná and Helena Suková

1990	Rick Leach and Jim Pugh	Jana Novotná and Helena Suková
1991	John Fitzgerald and Anders Järryd	Larisa Savchenko and Natasha Zvereva
1992	John McEnroe and Michael Stich	Gigi Fernández and Natasha Zvereva
1993	Todd Woodbridge and Mark Woodforde	Gigi Fernández and Natasha Zvereva
1994	Todd Woodbridge and Mark Woodforde	Gigi Fernández and Natasha Zvereva
1995	Todd Woodbridge and Mark Woodforde	Jana Novtoná and Arantxa Sánchez
1996	Todd Woodbridge and Mark Woodforde	Martina Hingis and Helena Suková
1997	Todd Woodbridge and Mark Woodforde	Gigi Fernández and Natasha Zvereva
1998	Jacco Eltngh and Paul Haarhuis	Martina Hingis and Jana Novtoná
1999	Mahesh Bhupathi and Leander Paes	Lindsay Davenport and Corina Morariu
2000	Todd Woodbridge and Mark Woodforde	Serena Williams and Venus Williams
2001	Donald Johnson and Jared Palmer	Lisa Raymond and Rennae Stubbs
2002	Jonas Björkman and Todd Woodbridge	Serena Williams and Venus Williams
2003	Jonas Björkman and Todd Woodbridge	Kim Clijsters and Ai Sugiyama
2004	Jonas Björkman and Todd Woodbridge	Cara Black and Rennae Stubbs
2005	Stephen Huss and Wesley Moodie	Cara Black and Liezel Huber
2006	Bob Bryan and Mike Bryan	Zi Yuan and Jie Zheng
2007	Arnaud Clement and Michaël Llodra	Cara Black and Liezel Huber
2008	Daniel Nestor and Nenad Zimonjié	Serena Williams and Venus Williams
2009	Daniel Nestor and Nenad Zimonjié	Serena Williams and Venus Williams

Mixed

Year	Winners
1968	Margaret Court and Ken Fletcher
1969	Ann Haydon and Fred Stolle
1970	Rosie Casals and Ilie Na
1971	Billie Jean King and Owen Davidson
1972	Rosie Casals and Ilie Nastase
1973	Billie Jean King and Owen Davidson
1974	Billie Jean King and Owen Davidson
1975	Margaret Court and Marty Riessen
1976	Françoise Durr and Tony Roche
1977	Greer Stevens and Bob Hewitt
1978	Betty Stöve and Frew McMillan
1979	Grreet Stevens and Bob Hewitt
1980	Tracy Austin and John Austin
1981	Betty Stöve and Frew McMillan
1982	Anne Smith and Kevin Curren
1983	Wendy Turnbull and John Lloyd
1984	Wendy Turnbull and John Lloyd
1985	Martina Navrátilová and Paul McNamee
1986	Kathy Jordan and Ken Flach

1987	Jo Durie and Jeremy Bates
1988	Zina Garrison and Sherwood Stewart
1989	Jana Novtoná and Jim Pugh
1990	Rich Leach and Zina Garrison
1991	Elizabeth Smylie and John Fitzgerald
1992	Larisa Savchenko and Cyril Suk
1993	Martina Navrátilová and Mark Woodforde
1994	Helena Suková and Cyril Suk
1995	Martina Navrátilová and Jonathan Stark
1996	Helena Suková and Cyril Suk
1997	Helena Suková and Cyril Suk
1998	Serena Williams and Max Mirnyi
1999	Lisa Raymond and Leander Paes
2000	Kimberly Po and Don Johnson
2001	Daniela Hantuchová and Lukas Friedl
2002	Elena Likhovteva and Mahesh Bhupathi
2003	Martina Navrátilová and Leander Paes
2004	Cara Black and Wayne Black
2005	Mar Pierce and Mahesh Bhupathi
2006	Vera Zvonareva and Andy Ram
2007	Jelena Jankovic and Jamie Murray
2008	Samantha Stosur and Bob Bryan
2009	Anna-Lena Grönefeld and Mark Knowles

U.S. Open Seniors Open Era Champions

Singles

Year	Men	Women
1968	Arthur Ashe	Virginia Wade
1969	Rod Laver	Margaret Smith
1970	Ken Rosewall	Margaret Smith
1971	Stan Smith	Billie Jean King
1972	Ilie Nastase	Billie Jean King
1973	John Newcombe	Margaret Smith
1974	Jimmy Connors	Billie Jean King
1975	Manuel Orantes	Chris Evert
1976	Jimmy Connors	Chris Evert
1977	Guillermo Vilas	Chris Evert
1978	Jimmy Connors	Chris Evert
1979	John McEnroe	Tracy Austin
1980	John McEnroe	Chris Evert

1981	John McEnroe	Tracy Austin
1982	Jimmy Connors	Chris Evert
1983	Jimmy Connors	Martina Navrátilová
1984	John McEnroe	Martina Navrátilová
1985	Ivan Lendl	Hana Madlíková
1986	Ivan Lendl	Martina Navrátilová
1987	Ivan Lendl	Martina Navrátilová
1988	Mats Wilander	Steffi Graf
1989	Boris Becker	Steffi Graf
1990	Pete Sampras	Gabriela Sabatini
1991	Stefan Edberg	Monica Seles
1992	Stefan Edberg	Monica Seles
1993	Pete Sampras	Steffi Graf
1994	Andre Agassi	Arantxa Sánchez
1995	Pete Sampras	Steffi Graf
1996	Pete Sampras	Steffi Graf
1997	Patrick Rafter	Martina Hingis
1998	Patrick Rafter	Lindsay Davenport
1999	Andre Agassi	Serena Williams
2000	Marat Safin	Venus Williams
2001	Lleyton Hewitt	Venus Williams
2002	Pete Sampras	Serena Williams
2003	Andy Roddick	Justine Henin
2004	Roger Federer	Svetlana Kuznetsova
2005	Roger Federer	Kim Clijsters
2006	Roger Federer	Maria Sharapova
2007	Roger Federer	Justine Henin
2008	Roger Federer	Serena Williams

Doubles

Year	Men	Women
1968	Robert Lutz and Stan Smith	Maria Bueno and Margaret Smith
1969	Ken Rosewall and Fred Stolle	Françoise Durr and Darlene Hard
1970	Pierre Barthes and Nikola Pillé	Margaret Smith and Judy Tegart
1971	John Newcombe and Roger Taylor	Rosemary Casals and Judy Tegart
1972	Cliff Drysdale and Roger Taylor	Françoise Durr and Betty Stöve
1973	Owen Davidson and John Newcombe	Margaret Smith and Virginia Wade
1974	Robert Lutz and Stan Smith	Rosemary Casals and Billie Jean King
1975	Jimmy Connors and Ilie Nastase	Margaret Smith and Virginia Wade
1976	Tom Okker and Marty Riessen	Delina Boshoff and Ilana Kloss
1977	Bob Hewitt and Frew McMillan	Martina Navrátilová and Betty Stöve
1978	Robert Lutz and Stan Smith	Billie Jean King and Martina Navrátilová

1979	Peter Fleming and John McEnroe	Betty Stöve and Wendy Turnbull
1980	Robert Lutz and Stan Smith	Billie Jean King and Martina Navrátilová
1981	Peter Fleming and John McEnroe	Anne Smith and Kathy Jordan
1982	Kevin Curren and Steve Denton	Rosemary Casals and Wendy Turnbull
1983	Peter Fleming and John McEnroe	Martina Navrátilová and Pam Shriver
1984	John Fitzgerald and Tomás Smíd	Martina Navrátilová and Pam Shriver
1985	Ken Flach and Robert Seguso	Claudia Khode and Helena Suková
1986	Andrés Gómez and Slobodan Zivojinovic	Martina Navrátilová and Pam Shriver
1987	Stefan Edberg and Anders Järryd	Martina Navrátilová and Pam Shriver
1988	Sergio Casal and Emilio Sánchez	Gigi Fernández and Robin White
1989	John McEnroe and Mark Woodforde	Hana Mandlíková and Martina Navrátilová
1990	Pieter Aldrich and Danie Visser	Gigi Fernández and Martina Navrátilová
1991	John Fitzgerald and Anders Järryd	Pam Shriver and Natalia Zvereva
1992	Jim Grabb and Richey Reneberg	Gigi Fernández and Natalia Zvereva
1993	Ken Flach and Rich Leach	Arantxa Sánchez and Helena Suková
1994	Jacco Eltingh and Paul Haarhuis	Jana Novtoná and Arantxa Sánchez
1995	Todd Woodbridge and Mark Woodforde	Gigi Fernández and Natalia Zvereva
1996	Todd Woodbridge and Mark Woodforde	Gigi Fernández and Natalia Zvereva
1997	Yevgeny Kafelnikov and Daniel Vacek	Lindsay Davenport and Jana Novtoná
1998	Sandon Stolle and Cyril Suk	Martina Hingis and Jana Novtoná
1999	Sébastien Lareau and Alex O'Brien	Serena Willams and Venus Williams
2000	Lleyton Hewitt and Max Mirnyi	Julie Halard and Ai Sugiyama
2001	Wayne Black and Kevin Ullyett	Lisa Raymond and Rennae Stubbs
2002	Mahesh Bhupathi and Max Mirnyi	Virginia Ruano and Paola Suárez
2003	Jonas Björkman and Todd Woodbridge	Virginia Ruano and Paola Suárez
2004	Mark Knowles and Daniel Nestor	Virginia Ruano and Paola Suárez
2005	Bob Bryan and Mike Bryan	Lisa Raymond and Samantha Stosur
2006	Martin Damm and Leander Paes	Nathalie Dechy and Vera Zvonareva
2007	Simon Aspelin and Julian Knowle	Nathalie Dechy and Dinara Safina
2008	Bob Bryan and Mike Bryan	Cara Black and Liezel Huber

Mixed

Year	Winners
1968	Mary-Ann Eisel and Peter Curtis
1969	Margaret Smith and Marty Riessen
1970	Margaret Smith and Marty Riessen
1971	Billie Jean King and Owen Davidson
1972	Margaret Smith and Marty Riessen
1973	Billie Jean King and Owen Davidson
1974	Pam Teeguarden and Geoff Masters
1975	Rosemary Casals and Dick Stockton
1976	Billie Jean King and Phil Dent

1977	Betty Stöve and Frew McMillan
1978	Betty Stöve and Frew McMillan
1979	Greer Stevens and Bob Hewitt
1980	Wendy Turnbull and Marty Riessen
1981	Anne Smith and Kevin Curren
1982	Anne Smith and Kevin Curren
1983	Elizabeth Sayers and John Fitzgerald
1984	Manuela Maleeva and Tom Gullikson
1985	Martina Navrátilová and Heinz Günthardt
1986	Raffaella Reggi and Sergio Casal
1987	Martina Navrátilová and Emilio Sánchez
1988	Jana Novtoná and Jim Pugh
1989	Robin White and Shelby Cannon
1990	Elizabeth Sayers and Todd Woodbridge
1991	Manon Bollegraf and Tom Nijssen
1992	Nicole Provis and Mark Woodforde
1993	Helena Suková and Todd Woodbridge
1994	Elna Reinach and Patrick Galbraith
1995	Meredith McGrath and Matt Lucena
1996	Lisa Raymond and Patrick Galbraith
1997	Manon Bollegraf and Rick Leach
1998	Serena Williams and Max Mirnyi
1999	Ai Sugiyama and Mahesh Bhupathi
2000	Arantxa Sánchez and Jared Palmer
2001	Rennae Stubbs and Todd Woodbridge
2002	Lisa Raymond and Mike Bryan
2003	Katarina Srebotnik and Bob Bryan
2004	Vera Zvonareva and Bob Bryan
2005	Daniela Hantuchová and Mahesh Bhupathi
2006	Martina Navrátilová and Bob Bryan
2007	Victoria Azarenka and Max Mirnyi
2008	Cara Black and Leander Paes

Golf

The Open/British Open Winners

Year	Winner
1860	Willie Park Sr.
1861	Tom Morris Sr.

1862	Tom Morris Sr.
1863	Willie Park Sr.
1864	Tom Morris Sr.
1865	Andrew Strath
1866	Willie Park Sr.
1867	Tom Morris Sr.
1868	Tom Morris Jr.
1869	Tom Morris Jr.
1870	Tom Morris Jr.
1871	No Championship
1872	Tom Morris Jr.
1873	Tom Kidd
1874	Mungo Park
1875	Willie Park Sr.
1876	Bob Martin (Martin finished tied with Davie Strath; Strath refused to take part in the playoff, and Martin was awarded the championship.)
1877	Jamie Anderson
1878	Jamie Anderson
1879	Jamie Anderson
1880	Bob Ferguson
1881	Bob Ferguson
1882	Bob Ferguson
1883	Willie Fernie
1884	Jack Simpson
1885	Bob Martin
1886	David Brown
1887	Willie Park Jr.
1888	Jack Burns
1889	Willie Park Jr.
1890	John Ball Jr.
1891	Hugh Kirkaldy
1892	Harold Hilton
1893	Willie Auchterlonie
1894	J.H. Taylor
1895	J.H. Taylor
1896	Harry Vardon
1897	Harold Hilton
1898	Harry Vardon
1899	Harry Vardon
1900	J.H. Taylor

1901	James Braid
1902	Alexander Herd
1903	Harry Vardon
1904	Jack White
1905	James Braid
1906	James Braid
1907	Arnaud Massy
1908	James Braid
1909	John H. Taylor
1910	James Braid
1911	Harry Vardon
1912	Ted Ray
1913	John H. Taylor
1914	Harry Vardon
1915–19	No championship due to WWI
1920	George Duncan
1921	Jock Hutchison
1922	Walter Hagen
1923	Arthur G. Havers
1924	Walter Hagen
1925	Jim Barnes
1926	Bobby Jones
1927	Bobby Jones
1928	Walter Hagen
1929	Walter Hagen
1930	Bobby Jones
1931	Tommy Armour
1932	Gene Sarazen
1933	Denny Shute
1934	Henry Cotton
1935	Alfred Perry
1936	Alfred Padgham
1937	Henry Cotton
1938	Reginald A. Whitcombe
1939	Richard Burton
1940–45	No championship due to WWII
1946	Sam Snead
1947	Fred Daly
1948	Henry Cotton
1949	Bobby Locke
1950	Bobby Locke
1951	Max Faulkner

1952	Bobby Locke
1953	Ben Hogan
1954	Peter Thomson
1955	Peter Thomson
1956	Peter Thomson
1957	Bobby Locke
1958	Peter Thomson
1959	Gary Player
1960	Kel Nagle
1961	Arnold Palmer
1962	Arnold Palmer
1963	Bob Charles
1964	Tony Lema
1965	Peter Thomson
1966	Jack Nicklaus
1967	Robert DeVicenzo
1968	Gary Player
1969	Tony Jacklin
1970	Jack Nicklaus
1971	Lee Trevino
1972	Lee Trevino
1973	Tom Weiskopf
1974	Gary Player
1975	Tom Watson
1976	Johnny Miller
1977	Tom Watson
1978	Jack Nicklaus
1979	Steve Ballesteros
1980	Tom Watson
1981	Bill Rogers
1982	Tom Watson
1983	Tom Watson
1984	Steve Ballesteros
1985	Sandy Lyle
1986	Greg Norman
1987	Nick Faldo
1988	Steve Ballesteros
1989	Mark Calcavecchia
1990	Nick Faldo
1991	Ian Baker-Finch
1992	Nick Faldo
1993	Greg Norman

1994	Nick Price
1995	John Daly
1996	Tom Lehman
1997	Justin Leonard
1998	Mark O'Meara
1999	Paul Lawrie
2000	Tiger Woods
2001	David Duval
2002	Ernie Els
2003	Ben Curtis
2004	Todd Hamilton
2005	Tiger Woods
2006	Tiger Woods
2007	Pádraig Harrington
2008	Pádraig Harrington
2009	Stewart Cink

U.S. Open Winners

Year	Winner
1895	Horace Rawlins
1896	James Foulis
1897	Joe Lloyd
1898	Fred Herd
1899	Willie Smith
1900	Harry Vardon
1901	Willie Anderson
1902	Laurie Auchterlonie
1903	Willie Anderson
1904	Willie Anderson
1905	Willie Anderson
1906	Alex Smith
1907	Alec Ross
1908	Fred McLeod
1909	George Sargent
1910	Alex Smith
1911	John McDermott
1912	John McDermott
1913	Francis Ouimet
1914	Walter Hagen
1915	Jerome Travers

1916	Chick Evans
1917–18	No championship due to WWI
1919	Walter Hagen
1920	Ted Ray
1921	Jim Barnes
1922	Gene Sarazen
1923	Bobby Jones
1924	Cyril Walker
1925	Willie Macfarlane
1926	Bobby Jones
1927	Tommy Armour
1928	Johnny Farrell
1929	Bobby Jones
1930	Bobby Jones
1931	Billy Burke
1932	Gene Sarazen
1933	Johnny Goodman
1934	Olin Dutra
1935	Sam Parks Jr.
1936	Tony Manero
1937	Ralph Guldahl
1938	Ralph Guldahl
1939	Byron Nelson
1940	Lawson Little
1941	Craig Wood
1942–45	No championship due to WWII
1946	Lloyd Mangrum
1947	Lew Worsham
1948	Ben Hogan
1949	Cary Middlecoff
1950	Ben Hogan
1951	Ben Hogan
1952	Julius Boros
1953	Ben Hogan
1954	Ed Furgol
1955	Jack Fleck
1956	Cary Middlecoff
1957	Dick Mayer
1958	Tommy Bolt
1959	Billy Casper
1960	Arnold Palmer
1961	Gene Littler

1962	Jack Nicklaus
1963	Julius Boros
1964	Ken Venturi
1965	Gary Player
1966	Billy Casper
1967	Jack Nicklaus
1968	Lee Trevino
1969	Orville Moody
1970	Tony Jacklin
1971	Lee Trevino
1972	Jack Nicklaus
1973	Johnny Miller
1974	Hale Irwin
1975	Lou Graham
1976	Jerry Pate
1977	Hubert Green
1978	Andy North
1979	Hale Irwin
1980	Jack Nicklaus
1981	David Graham
1982	Tom Watson
1983	Larry Nelson
1984	Fuzzy Zoeller
1985	Andy North
1986	Ray Floyd
1987	Scott Simpson
1988	Curtis Strange
1989	Curtis Strange
1990	Hale Irwin
1991	Payne Stewart
1992	Tom Kite
1993	Lee Janzen
1994	Ernie Els
1995	Corey Pavin
1996	Steve Jones
1997	Ernie Els
1998	Lee Janzen
1999	Payne Stewart
2000	Tiger Woods
2001	Retief Goosen
2002	Tiger Woods
2003	Jim Furyk

2004	Retief Goosen
2005	Michael Campbell
2006	Geoff Ogilvy
2007	Angel Cabrera
2008	Tiger Woods
2009	Lucas Glover

PGA Championship Winners

Year	Winner
1916	James M. Barnes
1917–18	No championship due to WWI
1919	James M. Barnes
1920	Jock Hutchison
1921	Walter Hagen
1922	Gene Sarazen
1923	Gene Sarazen
1924	Walter Hagen
1925	Walter Hagen
1926	Walter Hagen
1927	Walter Hagen
1928	Leo Diegel
1929	Leo Diegel
1930	Tommy Armour
1931	Tom Creavy
1932	Olin Dutra
1933	Gene Sarazen
1934	Paul Runyan
1935	Johnny Revolta
1936	Denny Shute
1937	Denny Shute
1938	Paul Runyan
1939	Henry Picard
1940	Byron Nelson
1941	Vic Ghezzi
1942	Sam Snead
1943	No championship due to WWII
1944	Bob Hamilton
1945	Byron Nelson
1946	Ben Hogan
1947	Jim Ferrier

1948	Ben Hogan
1949	Sam Snead
1950	Chandler Harper
1951	Sam Snead
1952	Jim Turnesa
1953	Walter Burkemo
1954	Chick Harbert
1955	Doug Ford
1956	Jack Burke Jr.
1957	Lionel Hebert
1958	Dow Finsterwald
1959	Bob Rosburg
1960	Jay Hebert
1961	Jerry Barber
1962	Gary Player
1963	Jack Nicklaus
1964	Bobby Nichols
1965	Dave Marr
1966	Al Geiberger
1967	Don January
1968	Julius Boros
1969	Ray Floyd
1970	Dave Stockton
1971	Jack Nicklaus
1972	Gary Player
1973	Jack Nicklaus
1974	Lee Trevino
1975	Jack Nicklaus
1976	Dave Stockton
1977	Lanny Wadkins
1978	John Mahaffey
1979	David Graham
1980	Jack Nicklaus
1981	Larry Nelson
1982	Raymond Floyd
1983	Hal Sutton
1984	Lee Trevino
1985	Hubert Green
1986	Bob Tway
1987	Larry Nelson
1988	Jeff Sluman
1989	Payne Stewart

1990	Wayne Grady
1991	John Daly
1992	Nick Price
1993	Paul Azinger
1994	Nick Price
1995	Steve Elkington
1996	Mark Brooks
1997	Davis Love III
1998	Vijay Singh
1999	Tiger Woods
2000	Tiger Woods
2001	David Toms
2002	Rich Beem
2003	Shaun Micheel
2004	Vijay Singh
2005	Phil Mickelson
2006	Tiger Woods
2007	Tiger Woods
2008	Pádraig Harrington

The Masters Winners

Year	Winner
1934	Horton Smith
1935	Gene Sarazen
1936	Horton Smith
1937	Byron Nelson
1938	Henry Picard
1939	Ralph Guldahl
1940	Jimmy Demaret
1941	Craig Wood
1942	Byron Nelson
1943–45	No championship due to WWII
1946	Herman Keiser
1947	Jimmy Demaret
1948	Claude Harmon
1949	Sam Snead
1950	Jimmy Demaret
1951	Ben Hogan
1952	Sam Snead
1953	Ben Hogan

1954	Sam Snead
1955	Cary Middlecoff
1956	Jack Burke Jr.
1957	Doug Ford
1958	Arnold Palmer
1959	Art Wall Jr.
1960	Arnold Palmer
1961	Gary Player
1962	Arnold Palmer
1963	Jack Nicklaus
1964	Arnold Palmer
1965	Jack Nicklaus
1966	Jack Nicklaus
1967	Gay Brewer
1968	Bob Goalby
1969	George Archer
1970	Billy Casper
1971	Charles Coody
1972	Jack Nicklaus
1973	Tommy Aaron
1974	Gary Player
1975	Jack Nicklaus
1976	Raymond Floyd
1977	Tom Watson
1978	Gary Player
1979	Fuzzy Zoeller
1980	Steve Ballesteros
1981	Tom Watson
1982	Craig Stadler
1983	Steve Ballesteros
1984	Ben Crenshaw
1985	Bernhard Langer
1986	Jack Nicklaus
1987	Larry Mize
1988	Sandy Lyle
1989	Nick Faldo
1990	Nick Faldo
1991	Ian Woosnam
1992	Fred Couples
1993	Bernhard Langer
1994	José María Olazábal
1995	Ben Crenshaw

1996	Nick Faldo
1997	Tiger Woods
1998	Mark O'Meara
1999	José María Olazábal
2000	Vijay Singh
2001	Tiger Woods
2002	Tiger Woods
2003	Mike Weir
2004	Phil Mickelson
2005	Tiger Woods
2006	Phil Mickelson
2007	Zach Johnson
2008	Trevor Immelman
2009	Angel Cabrera

Bowling

Weber Cup Champions

Year	Winners	Opponents	Score
2000	USA	Europe	18–11
2001	USA	Europe	18–12
2002	USA	Europe	18–13
2003	Europe	USA	18–14
2004	Europe	USA	18–11
2005	Europe	USA	18–16
2006	USA	Europe	18–17
2007	USA	Europe	17–15
2008	USA	Europe	17–13

Bowling World Cup Winners

Men

Year	Winning Country	Canada's Position	Canadian Champion
1966	U.S.	5th	Paul Yoshimasu, Winnipeg, MB
1967	U.S.	7th	Gerry Hill, New Westminister, B.C.
1968	West Germany	2nd	Jim Kramer Sr., Sault Ste. Marie, ON
1969	Canada	1st	Graydon Robinson, Toronto, ON
1970	West Germany	13th	Frank Boehm, Regina, SK

1971	U.S.	7th	Ed Labelle, Winnipeg, MB
1972	Canada	1st	Ray Mitchell, Scarborough, ON
1973	England	2nd	Glen Watson, Toronto, ON
1974	Colombia	9th	Bob Moore, Toronto, ON
1975	Italy	21st	Dan Russo, London, ON
1976	Philippines	11th	Gerard Duranceau, Montreal, QC
1977	Norway	16th	Gerard Duranceau, Montreal, QC
1978	Thailand	21st	Graydon Robinson, Toronto, ON
1979	France	5th	Bob Puttick, Calgary, AB
1980	Philippines	26th	Glen Watson, Toronto, ON
1981	U.S.	6th	Randy Kostenuk, Winnipeg, MB
1982	Norway	10th	Chuck Faas, Calgary, AB
1983	Taiwan	22nd	Norm Kowalchuk, Saskatoon, SK
1984	U.S.	38th	Sid Allen, Winnipeg, MB
1985	Mexico	28th	Jim Kramer Jr., Sault Ste. Marie, ON
1986	Sweden	36th	Mal Campbell, Calgary, AB
1987	Italy	11th	Kit Miller, London, ON
1988	United Arab Emirates	7th	Rod Hull, Burnaby, B.C.
1989	Qatar	33rd	Serge Beaulieu, Chomedey, QC
1990	Finland	5th	Jack Brace, Pickering, ON
1991	U.S.	11th	Bob Woolley, Sault Ste. Marie, ON
1992	Philippines	18th	Clem Perreault, Winnipeg, MB
1993	Germany	4th	Jack Guay, Calgary, AB
1994	Norway	9th	Jack Guay, Calgary, AB
1995	U.S.	4th	Jack Guay, Calgary, AB
1996	Philippines	30th	Rod Hull, Abbotsford, B.C.
1997	Germany	19th	Alan Tone, Grimsby, ON
1998	Taiwan	5th	Jack Guay, Calgary, AB
1999	Germany	37th	Daryl Dutchak, Winnipeg, MB
2000	Sweden	18th	Todd Squire, St. Catharines, ON
2001	Norway	31st	Bob Woolley, Sault Ste. Marie, ON
2002	Finland	35th	Merlin Bunnage, Kelowna, B.C.
2003	Philippines	42nd	Merlin Bunnage, Kelowna, B.C.
2004	Philippines	5th	Jack Guay, Calgary, AB
2005	Canada	1st	Michael Schmidt, Calgary, AB
2006	Finland	3rd	Michael Schmidt, Calgary, AB
2007	U.S.	4th	Michael Schmidt, Calgary, AB
2008	U.S.	4th	Jack Guay, Calgary, AB

Women

Year	Winning Country	Canada's Position	Canadian Champion
1974	Denmark	19th	Terry Quinn, Winnipeg, MB

1975	Canada	1st	Cathy Townsend, St-Therese, QC
1976	U.S.	9th	Diane Semchuk, Calgary, AB
1977	Canada	1st	Rea Rennox, Scarborough, ON
1978	Philippines	24th	Miriam Reid, Calgary, AB
1979	Philippines	6th	Louise Gendron, Chateauguay, QC
1980	Canada	1st	Jean Gordon, Langley, B.C.
1981	England	8th	Judy Peterson, Sault Ste. Marie, ON
1982	Australia	17th	Gloria Collura, Toronto, ON
1983	Australia	Canada did not compete	
1984	Italy	18th	Irene Joyal, Winipeg, MB
1985	Ireland	30th	Celine Pelletier, Montreal, QC
1986	Sweden	13th	Sandra Chadwick (Shott), North Vancouver, B.C.
1987	Netherlands	24th	Diana Long, Spruce Grove, AB
1988	U.S.	17th	Linda Thompson, Hamilton, ON
1989	U.S.	15th	Connie Gonsalves, LaSalle, QC
1990	U.S.	3rd	Sandra Shott, North Vancouver, B.C.
1991	Sweden	23rd	Anne Saasto, Thunder Bay, ON
1992	Germany	15th	Anne Saasto, Thunder Bay, ON
1993	Great Britain	29th	Karen Collura, Etobicoke, ON
1994	South Africa	21st	Karen Collura, Etobicoke, ON
1995	Great Britain	12th	Karen Collura, Etobicoke, ON
1996	Australia	25th	Karen Collura, Etobicoke, ON
1997	Taiwan	17th	Susan Vanderaa, Regina, SK
1998	Australia	16th	Kellie Hindebrandt, Saskatoon, SK
1999	Asutralia	12th	Jill Friis, London, ON
2000	Wales	3rd	Diane Buchanan, Brossard, QC
2001	Japan	12th	Diane Buchanan, Brossard, QC
2002	U.S.	13th	Diane Buchanan, Brossard, QC
2003	Canada	1st	Kerrie Ryan-Ciach, Mississauga, ON
2004	U.S.	2nd	Kerrie Ryan-Ciach, Mississauga, ON
2005	U.S.	31st	Veronica Lalande-Lapointe, Ile-Perrot, QC
2006	U.S.	21st	Veronica Lalande-Lapointe, Ile-Perrot, QC
2007	Australia	41st	Monique Belanger, Estevan, SK
2008	Singapore	8th	Jennifer Park, Nanaimo, B.C.

Running

Boston Marathon Winners

Men

Year	Name	Country	Time
1897	John J. McDermott	United States	2:55:10
1898	Ronald J. McDonald	Canada	2:42:00
1899	Lawrence Brignolia	United States	2:54:38
1900	John Caffrey	Canada	2:39:44
1901	John Caffrey	Canada	2:29:23
1902	Sammy Mellor	United States	2:43:12
1903	John Lorden	United States	2:41:29
1904	Michael Spring	United States	2:38:04
1905	Frederick Lorz	United States	2:38:25
1906	Tim Ford	United States	2:45:45
1907	Thomas Longboat	Canada	2:24:24
1908	Thomas Morrisey	United States	2:25:43
1909	Henri Renaud	United States	2:53:36
1910	Fred Cameron	Canada	2:28:52
1911	Clarence DeMar	United States	2:21:39
1912	Michael Ryan	United States	2:21:18
1913	Fritz Carlson	United States	2:25:14
1914	James Duffy	Canada	2:25:01
1915	Edouard Fabre	Canada	2:31:41
1916	Arthur Roth	United States	2:27:16
1917	Bill Kennedy	United States	2:28:37
1918	Special Military Relay	Camp Devens	2:29:53
1919	Carl Linder	United States	2:29:13
1920	Peter Trivoulides	United States	2:29:31
1921	Frank Zuna	United States	2:18:57
1922	Clarence DeMar	United States	2:18:10
1923	Clarence DeMar	United States	2:23:47
1924	Clarence DeMar	United States	2:29:40
1925	Charles Mellor	United States	2:33:00
1926	John C. Miles	Canada	2:25:40
1927	Clarence DeMar	United States	2:40:22
1928	Clarence DeMar	United States	2:37:07
1929	John C. Miles	Canada	2:33:08
1930	Clarence DeMar	United States	2:34:48
1931	James P. Henigan	United States	2:46:45
1932	Paul DeBruyn	Germany	2:33:36

1933	Leslie S. Pawson	United States	2:31:01
1934	Dave Komonen	Canada	2:32:53
1935	John A. Kelley	United States	2:32:07
1936	Ellison M. Brown	United States	2:33:40
1937	Walter Young	Canada	2:33:20
1938	Leslie S. Pawson	United States	2:35:34
1939	Ellison M. Brown	United States	2:28:51
1940	Gerard Cote	Canada	2:28:28
1941	Leslie S. Pawson	United States	2:30:38
1942	Joe Smith	United States	2:26:51
1943	Gerard Cote	Canada	2:28:25
1944	Gerard Cote	Canada	2:31:50
1945	John A. Kelley	United States	2:30:40
1946	Stylianos Kyriakides	Greece	2:29:27
1947	Yun Bok Suh	Korea	2:25:39
1948	Gerard Cote	Canada	2:31:02
1949	Karl Leandersson	Sweden	2:31:50
1950	Kee Yong Ham	Korea	2:32:39
1951	Shigeki Tanaka	Japan	2:27:45
1952	Doroteo Flores	Guatamela	2:31:53
1953	Keizo Yamada	Japan	2:18:51
1954	Veikko Karvonen	Finland	2:20:39
1955	Hideo Hamamura	Japan	2:18:22
1956	Antti Viskari	Finland	2:14:14
1957	John J. Kelley	United States	2:20:05
1958	Franjo Mihalic	Yugoslavia	2:25:54
1959	Eino Oksanen	Finland	2:22:42
1960	Paavo Kotila	Finland	2:20:54
1961	Eino Oksanen	Finland	2:23:29
1962	Eino Oksanen	Finland	2:23:48
1963	Aurele Vandendriessche	Belgium	2:18:58
1964	Aurele Vandendriessche	Belgium	2:19:59
1965	Morio Shigematsu	Japan	2:16:33
1966	Kenji Kemihara	Japan	2:17:11
1967	David McKenzie	New Zealand	2:15:45
1968	Amby Burfoot	United States	2:22:17
1969	Yoshiaki Unetani	Japan	2:13:49
1970	Ron Hill	Great Britain	2:10:30
1971	Alvaro Mejia	Colombia	2:18:45
1972	Olavi Suomalainen	Finland	2:15:39
1973	Jon Anderson	United States	2:16:03
1974	Neal Cusack	Ireland	2:13:39

1975	Bill Rodgers	United States	2:09:55
1976	Jack Fultz	Virginia	2:20:19
1977	Jerome Drayton	Canada	2:14:46
1978	Bill Rodgers	United States	2:10:13
1979	Bill Rodgers	United States	2:09:27
1980	Bill Rodgers	United States	2:12:11
1981	Toshihiko Seko	Japan	2:09:26
1982	Alberto Salazar	United States	2:08:52
1983	Greg Meyer	United States	2:09:00
1984	Geoff Smith	Great Britain	2:10:34
1985	Geoff Smith	Great Britain	2:14:05
1986	Robert de Castella	Australia	2:07:51
1987	Toshihiko Seko	Japan	2:11:50
1988	Ibrahim Hussein	Kenya	2:08:43
1989	Abebe Mekonnen	Ethiopia	2:09:06
1990	Gelindo Bordin	Italy	2:08:19
1991	Ibrahim Hussein	Kenya	2:11:06
1992	Ibrahim Hussein	Kenya	2:08:14
1993	Cosmas Ndeti	Kenya	2:09:33
1994	Cosmas Ndeti	Kenya	2:07:15
1995	Cosmas Ndeti	Kenya	2:09:22
1996	Moses Tanui	Kenya	2:09:15
1997	Lameck Aguta	Kenya	2:10:34
1998	Moses Tanui	Kenya	2:07:34
1999	Joseph Chebet	Kenya	2:09:52
2000	Elijah Lagat	Kenya	2:09:47
2001	Lee Bong-Ju	South Korea	2:09:43
2002	Rodgers Rop	Kenya	2:09:02
2003	Robert Kipkoech Cheruiyot	Kenya	2:10:11
2004	Timothy Cherigat	Kenya	2:10:37
2005	Hailu Negussie	Ethiopia	2:11:45
2006	Robert Kipkoech Cheruiyot	Kenya	2:07:14
2007	Robert Kipkoech Cheruiyot	Kenya	2:14:13
2008	Robert Kipkoech Cheruiyot	Kenya	2:07:46
2009	Deriba Merga	Ethiopia	2:08:42

Women

Year	Name	Country	Time
1966	Roberta Gibb	United States	3:21:40
1967	Roberta Gibb	United States	3:27:17
1968	Roberta Gibb	United States	3:30:00
1969	Sara Mae Berman	United States	3:22:46

1970	Sara Mae Berman	United States	3:05:07
1971	Sara Mae Berman	United States	3:08:30
1972	Nina Kuscsik	United States	3:10:26
1973	Jacqueline Hansen	United States	3:05:59
1974	Michiko Gorman	United States	2:47:11
1975	Liane Winter	West Germany	2:42:24
1976	Kim Merritt	United States	2:47:10
1977	Michiko Gorman	United States	2:48:33
1978	Gayle S. Barron	United States	2:44:52
1979	Joan Benoit	United States	2:35:15
1980	Jacqueline Gareau	Canada	2:34:28
1981	Allison Roe	New Zealand	2:26:46
1982	Charlotte Teske	West Germany	2:29:33
1983	Joan Benoit	United States	2:22:43
1984	Lorraine Moller	New Zealand	2:29.28
1985	Lisa Larsen Weidenbach	United States	2:34.06
1986	Ingrid Kristiansen	Norway	2:24:55
1987	Rosa Mota	Portugal	2:25:21
1988	Rosa Mota	Portugal	2:24:30
1989	Ingrid Kristiansen	Norway	2:24:33
1990	Rosa Mota	Portugal	2:25:24
1991	Wanda Panfil	Poland	2:24:18
1992	Olga Markova	Russia	2:23:43
1993	Olga Markova	Russia	2:25:27
1994	Uta Pippig	Germany	2:21:45
1995	Uta Pippig	Germany	2:25:11
1996	Uta Pippig	Germany	2:27:12
1997	Fatuma Roba	Ethiopia	2:26:23
1998	Fatuma Roba	Ethiopia	2:23:21
1999	Fatuma Roba	Ethiopia	2:23:25
2000	Catherine Ndereba	Kenya	2:26:11
2001	Catherine Ndereba	Kenya	2:23:53
2002	Margaret Okayo	Kenya	2:20:43
2003	Svetlana Zakharova	Russia	2:25:20
2004	Catherine Ndereba	Kenya	2:24:27
2005	Catherine Ndereba	Kenya	2:25:13
2006	Rita Jeptoo	Kenya	2:23:38
2007	Lidiya Grigoryeva	Russia	2:29:18
2008	Dire Tune	Ethiopia	2:25:25
2009	Salina Kosgei	Kenya	2:32:16

New York City Marathon Winners

Men

Year	Name	Country	Time
1970	Gary Muhrcke	United States	2:31:38
1971	Norman Higgins	United States	2:22:54
1972	Sheldon Karlin	United States	2:27:52
1973	Tom Fleming	United States	2:21:54
1974	Norbert Sander	United States	2:26:30
1975	Tom Fleming	United States	2:19:27
1976	Bill Rodgers	United States	2:10:10
1977	Bill Rodgers	United States	2:11:28
1978	Bill Rodgers	United States	2:12:12
1979	Bill Rodgers	United States	2:11:42
1980	Alberto Salazar	United States	2:09:41
1981	Alberto Salazar	United States	2:08:13
1982	Alberto Salazar	United States	2:09:29
1983	Rod Dixon	New Zealand	2:08:59
1984	Orlando Pizzolato	Italy	2:14:53
1985	Orlando Pizzolato	Italy	2:11:34
1986	Gianni Poli	Italy	2:11:06
1987	Ibrahim Hussein	Kenya	2:11:01
1988	Steve Jones	United Kingdom	2:08:20
1989	Juma Ikangaa	Tanzania	2:08:01
1990	Douglas Wakiihuri	Kenya	2:12:39
1991	Salvador Garcia	Mexico	2:09:28
1992	Willie Mtolo	South Africa	2:09:29
1993	Andres Espinosa	Mexico	2:10:04
1994	German Silva	Mexico	2:11:21
1995	German Silva	Mexico	2:11:00
1996	Giacomo Leone	Italy	2:09:54
1997	John Kagwe	Kenya	2:08:12
1998	John Kagwe	Kenya	2:08:45
1999	Joseph Chebet	Kenya	2:09:14
2000	Abdelkhader El Mouaziz	Morocco	2:10:08
2001	Tesfaye Jifar	Ethiopia	2:07:43
2002	Rodgers Rop	Kenya	2:08:07
2003	Martin Lel	Kenya	2:10:30
2004	Hendrik Ramaala	South Africa	2:09:28
2005	Paul Tergat	Kenya	2:09:30
2006	Marilson Gomes dos Santos	Brazil	2:09:58
2007	Martin Lel	Kenya	2:09:04
2008	Marilson Gomes dos Santos	Brazil	2:08:43

Women

Year	Name	Country	Time
1970	(no finisher)		
1971	Beth Booner	United States	2:55:22
1972	Nina Kuscsik	United States	3:08:41
1973	Nina Kuscsik	United States	2:57:07
1974	Kathrine Switzer	United States	3:07:29
1975	Kim Merritt	United States	2:46:14
1976	Miki Gorman	United States	2:39:11
1977	Miki Gorman	United States	2:43:10
1978	Grete Waitz	Norway	2:32:30
1979	Grete Waitz	Norway	2:27:33
1980	Grete Waitz	Norway	2:25:41
1981	Allison Roe	New Zealand	2:25:29
1982	Grete Waitz	Norway	2:27:14
1983	Grete Waitz	Norway	2:27:00
1984	Grete Waitz	Norway	2:29:30
1985	Grete Waitz	Norway	2:28:34
1986	Grete Waitz	Norway	2:28:06
1987	Priscilla Welch	United Kingdom	2:30:17
1988	Grete Waitz	Norway	2:28:07
1989	Ingrid Kristiansen	Norway	2:25:30
1990	Wanda Panfil	Poland	2:30:45
1991	Liz McColgan	United Kingdom	2:27:23
1992	Lisa Ondieki	Australia	2:24:40
1993	Uta Pippig	Germany	2:26:24
1994	Tegla Loroupe	Kenya	2:27:37
1995	Tegla Loroupe	Kenya	2:28.06
1996	Anuta Catuna	Romania	2:28:18
1997	Franziska Rochat-Moser	Switzerland	2:28:43
1998	Franca Fiacconi	Italy	2:25:17
1999	Adriana Fernandez	Mexico	2:25:06
2000	Ludmila Petrova	Russia	2:25:45
2001	Margaret Okayo	Kenya	2:24:21
2002	Joyce Chepchumba	Kenya	2:25:56
2003	Margaret Okayo	Kenya	2:22:31
2004	Paula Radcliffe	United Kingdom	2:23:10
2005	Jelena Prokopcuka	Latvia	2:24:41
2006	Jelena Prokopcuka	Latvia	2:25:05
2007	Paula Radcliffe	United Kingdom	2:23:09
2008	Paula Radcliffe	United Kingdom	2:23:56

Cycling

Tour de France Winners

Year	Winner	Country
1903	Maurice Garin	France
1904	Henri Cornet	France
1905	Louis Trousselier	France
1906	René Pottier	France
1907	Lucien Petit-Breton	France
1908	Lucien Petit-Breton	France
1909	François Faber	Luxembourg
1910	Octave Lapize	France
1911	Gustave Garrigou	France
1912	Odile Defraye	Belgium
1913	Philippe Thys	Belgium
1914	Philippe Thys	Belgium
1915–18	No race held due to WWI	
1919	Firmin Lambot	Belgium
1920	Philippe Thys	Belgium
1921	Léon Scieur	Belgium
1922	Firmin Lambot	Belgium
1923	Henri Pélissier	France
1924	Ottavio Bottecchia	Italy
1925	Ottavio Bottecchia	Italy
1926	Lucien Buysse	Belgium
1927	Nicolas Frantz	Luxembourg
1928	Nicolas Frantz	Luxembourg
1929	Maurice De Waele	Belgium
1930	André Leducq	France
1931	Antonin Magne	France
1932	André Leducq	France
1933	Georges Speicher	France
1934	Antonin Magne	France
1935	Romain Maes	Belgium
1936	Sylvère Maes	Belgium
1937	Roger Lapébie	France
1938	Gino Bartali	Italy
1939	Sylvère Maes	Belgium
1940–46	No race held due to WWII	
1947	Jean Robic	France
1948	Gino Bartali	Italy

1949	Fausto Coppi	Italy
1950	Ferdinand Kubler	Switzerland
1951	Hugo Koblet	Switzerland
1952	Fausto Coppi	Italy
1953	Louison Bobet	France
1954	Louison Bobet	France
1955	Louison Bobet	France
1956	Roger Walkowiak	France
1957	Jacques Anquetil	France
1958	Charly Gaul	Luxembourg
1959	Federico Bahamontes	Spain
1960	Gastone Nencini	Italy
1961	Jacques Anquetil	France
1962	Jacques Anquetil	France
1963	Jacques Anquetil	France
1964	Jacques Anquetil	France
1965	Felice Gimondi	Italy
1966	Lucien Aimar	France
1967	Roger Pingeon	France
1968	Jan Janssen	Netherlands
1969	Eddy Merckx	Belgium
1970	Eddy Merckx	Belgium
1971	Eddy Merckx	Belgium
1972	Eddy Merckx	Belgium
1973	Luis Ocaña	Spain
1974	Eddy Merckx	Belgium
1975	Bernard Thévenet	France
1976	Lucien Van Impe	Belgium
1977	Bernard Thévenet	France
1978	Bernard Hinault	France
1979	Bernard Hinault	France
1980	Joop Zoetemelk	Netherlands
1981	Bernard Hinault	France
1982	Bernard Hinault	France
1983	Laurent Fignon	France
1984	Laurent Fignon	France
1985	Bernard Hinault	France
1986	Greg LeMond	United States
1987	Stephen Roche	Ireland
1988	Pedro Delgado	Spain
1989	Greg LeMond	United States
1990	Greg LeMond	United States

1991	Miguel Induráin	Spain
1992	Miguel Induráin	Spain
1993	Miguel Induráin	Spain
1994	Miguel Induráin	Spain
1995	Miguel Induráin	Spain
1996	Bjarne Riis	Denmark
1997	Jan Ullrich	Germany
1998	Marco Pantani	Italy
1999	Lance Armstrong	United States
2000	Lance Armstrong	United States
2001	Lance Armstrong	United States
2002	Lance Armstrong	United States
2003	Lance Armstrong	United States
2004	Lance Armstrong	United States
2005	Lance Armstrong	United States
2006	Floyd Landis	United States
2007	Alberto Contador	Spain
2008	Carlos Sastre	Spain

Vuelta a España Winners

Year	Winner	Country
1935	Gustave Deloor	Belgium
1936	Gustave Deloor	Belgium
1937–40	Not held*	
1941	Julian Berrendero	Spain
1942	Julian Berrendero	Spain
1943–44	Not held*	
1945	Delio Rodriguez	Spain
1946	Dalmacio Langarica	Spain
1947	Edouard Van Dyck	Belgium
1948	Bernardo Ruiz	Spain
1949	Not held*	
1950	Emilio Rodriguez	Spain
1951–54	Not held*	
1955	Jean Dotto	France
1956	Angelo Conterno	Italy
1957	Jesus Loroño	Spain
1958	Jean Stablinski	France
1959	Antonio Suarez	Spain
1960	Franz De Mulder	Belgium

1961	Angelino Soler	Spain
1962	Rudi Altig	Germany
1963	Jacques Anquetil	France
1964	Raymond Poulidor	France
1965	Rolf Wolfshohl	Germany
1966	Francisco Gabicagogescoa	Spain
1967	Jan Janssen	Netherlands
1968	Felice Gimondi	Italy
1969	Roger Pingeon	France
1970	Luis Ocaña	Spain
1971	Ferdinand Bracke	Belgium
1972	José Manuel Fuente	Spain
1973	Eddy Merckx	Belgium
1974	José Manuel Fuente	Spain
1975	Augustin Tamames	Spain
1976	José Pesarrodona	Spain
1977	Freddy Maertens	Belgium
1978	Bernard Hinault	France
1979	Joop Zoetemelk	Netherlands
1980	Faustino Ruperez	Spain
1981	Giovanni Battaglin	Italy
1982	Marino Lejarreta	Spain
1983	Bernard Hinault	France
1984	Eric Caritoux	France
1985	Pedro Delgado	Spain
1986	Alvaro Pino	Spain
1987	Luis Herrera	Colombia
1988	Sean Kelly	Ireland
1989	Pedro Delgado	Spain
1990	Marco Giovanetti	Italy
1991	Melchor Mauri	Spain
1992	Toni Rominger	Switzerland
1993	Toni Rominger	Switzerland
1994	Toni Rominger	Switzerland
1995	Laurent Jalabert	France
1996	Alex Zülle	Switzerland
1997	Alex Zülle	Switzerland
1998	Abraham Olano	Spain
1999	Jan Ullrich	Germany
2000	Roberto Heras	Spain
2001	Angel Luis Casero	Spain
2002	Aitor Gonzalez	Spain

2003	Roberto Heras	Spain
2004	Roberto Heras	Spain
2005	Denis Menchov	Russia
2006	Alexandre Vinokourov	Kazakhstan
2007	Denis Menchov	Russia
2008	Alberto Contador	Spain

Note: While the Vuelta a España first started in 1935, it was not held annually until 1955.

Giro d'Italia Winners

Year	Winner	Country
1909	Luigi Ganna	Italy
1910	Carlo Galetti	Italy
1911	Carlo Galetti	Italy
1912	Team Atala (Specific Winner Unkown)	Italy
1913	Carlo Oriani	Italy
1914	Alfonso Calzolari	Italy
1915–18	No race held due to WWI	
1919	Constante Girardengo	Italy
1920	Gaetano Belloni	Italy
1921	Giovanni Brunero	Italy
1922	Giovanni Brunero	Italy
1923	Constante Girardengo	Italy
1924	Giuseppe Enrici	Italy
1925	Alfredo Binda	Italy
1926	Giovanni Brunero	Italy
1927	Alfredo Binda	Italy
1928	Alfredo Binda	Italy
1929	Alfredo Binda	Italy
1930	Luigi Marchisio	Italy
1931	Francesco Camusso	Italy
1932	Antonio Pesenti	Italy
1933	Alfredo Binda	Italy
1934	Learco Guerra	Italy
1935	Vasco Bergamaschi	Italy
1936	Gino Bartali	Italy
1937	Gino Bartali	Italy
1938	Giovanni Valetti	Italy
1939	Giovanni Valetti	Italy
1940	Fausto Coppi	Italy

1941–45	No race held due to WWII	
1946	Gino Bartali	Italy
1947	Fausto Coppi	Italy
1948	Fiorenzo Magni	Italy
1949	Fausto Coppi	Italy
1950	Hugo Koblet	Switzerland
1951	Fiorenzo Magni	Italy
1952	Fausto Coppi	Italy
1953	Fausto Coppi	Italy
1954	Carlo Clerici	Switzerland
1955	Fiorenzo Magni	Italy
1956	Charly Gaul	Luxembourg
1957	Gastone Nencini	Italy
1958	Ercole Baldini	Italy
1959	Charly Gaul	Luxembourg
1960	Jacques Anquetil	France
1961	Arnaldo Pambianco	Italy
1962	Franco Balmamion	Italy
1963	Franco Balmamion	Italy
1964	Jacques Anquetil	France
1965	Vittorio Adorni	Italy
1966	Gianni Motta	Italy
1967	Felice Gimondi	Italy
1968	Eddy Merckx	Belgium
1969	Felice Gimondi	Italy
1970	Eddy Merckx	Belgium
1971	Gösta Pettersson	Sweden
1972	Eddy Merckx	Belgium
1973	Eddy Merckx	Belgium
1974	Eddy Merckx	Belgium
1975	Fausto Bertoglio	Italy
1976	Felice Gimondi	Italy
1977	Michel Pollentier	Belgium
1978	Johan de Muynck	Belgium
1979	Giuseppe Saronni	Italy
1980	Bernard Hinault	France
1981	Giovanni Battaglin	Italy
1982	Bernard Hinault	France
1983	Giuseppe Saronni	Italy
1984	Francesco Moser	Italy
1985	Bernard Hinault	France
1986	Roberto Visentini	Italy

1987	Stephen Roche	Ireland
1988	Andrew Hampsten	United States
1989	Lauren Fignon	France
1990	Gianni Bugno	Italy
1991	Franco Chioccioli	Italy
1992	Miguel Indurain	Spain
1993	Miguel Indurain	Spain
1994	Eugeni Berzin	Russia
1995	Tony Rominger	Switzerland
1996	Pavel Tonkov	Russia
1997	Ivan Gotti	Italy
1998	Marco Pantani	Italy
1999	Ivan Gotti	Italy
2000	Stefano Garzelli	Italy
2001	Gilberto Simoni	Italy
2002	Paolo Savoldelli	Italy
2003	Gilberto Simoni	Italy
2004	Damiano Cunego	Italy
2005	Paolo Savoldelli	Italy
2006	Ivan Basso	Italy
2007	Danilo Di Luca	Italy
2008	Alberto Contador	Spain
2009	Denis Menchov	Russia

Skiing and Snowboarding

Alpine Skiing World Cup Winners

Year	Men's Champion	Country	Women's Champion	Country
1967	Jean-Claude Killy	France	Nancy Greene	Canada
1968	Jean-Claude Killy	France	Nancy Greene	Canada
1969	Karl Schranz	Austria	Gertrud Gabl	Austria
1970	Karl Schranz	Austria	Michèle Jacot	France
1971	Gustav Thöni	Italy	Annemarie Pröll	Austria
1972	Gustav Thöni	Italy	Annemarie Pröll	Austria
1973	Gustav Thöni	Italy	Annemarie Pröll	Austria
1974	Piero Gros	Italy	Annemarie Pröll	Austria
1975	Gustav Thöni	Italy	Annemarie Moser-Pröll	Austria
1976	Ingemar Stenmark	Sweden	Rosi Mittermaier	West Germany
1977	Ingemar Stenmark	Sweden	Lise-Marie Morerod	Switzerland

1978	Ingemar Stenmark	Sweden	Hanni Wenzel	Liechtenstein
1979	Peter Lüscher	Switzerland	Annemarie Moser-Pröll	Austria
1980	Andreas Wenzel	Liechtenstein	Hanni Wenzel	Liechtenstein
1981	Phil Mahre	United States	Marie-Theres Nadig	Switzerland
1982	Phil Mahre	United States	Erika Hess	Switzerland
1983	Phil Mahre	United States	Tamara McKinney	United States
1984	Pirmin Zurbriggen	Switzerland	Erika Hess	Switzerland
1985	Marc Girardelli	Luxembourg	Michela Figini S	witzerland
1986	Marc Girardelli	Luxembourg	Maria Walliser	Switzerland
1987	Pirmin Zurbriggen	Switzerland	Maria Walliser	Switzerland
1988	Pirmin Zurbriggen	Switzerland	Michela Figini	Switzerland
1989	Marc Girardelli	Luxembourg	Vreni Schneider	Switzerland
1990	Pirmin Zurbriggen	Switzerland	Petra Kronberger	Austria
1991	Marc Girardelli	Luxembourg	Petra Kronberger	Austria
1992	Paul Accola	Switzerland	Petra Kronberger	Austria
1993	Marc Girardelli	Luxembourg	Anita Wachter	Austria
1994	Kjetil André Aamodt	Norway	Vreni Schneider	Switzerland
1995	Alberto Tomba	Italy	Vreni Schneider	Switzerland
1996	Lasse Kjus	Norway	Katja Seizinger	Germany
1997	Luc Alphand	France	Pernilla Wiberg	Sweden
1998	Hermann Maier	Austria	Katja Seizinger	Germany
1999	Lasse Kjus	Norway	Alexandra Meissnitzer	Austria
2000	Hermann Maier	Austria	Renate Götschl	Austria
2001	Hermann Maier	Austria	Janica Kostelić	Croatia
2002	Stephan Eberharter	Austria	Michaela Dorfmeister	Austria
2003	Stephan Eberharter	Austria	Janica Kostelić	Croatia
2004	Hermann Maier	Austria	Anja Pärson	Sweden
2005	Bode Miller	United States	Anja Pärson	Sweden
2006	Benjamin Raich	Austria	Janica Kostelić	Croatia
2007	Aksel Lund Svindal	Norway	Nicole Hosp	Austria
2008	Bode Miller	United States	Lindsey Vonn	United States
2009	Aksel Lund Svindal	Norway	Lindsey Vonn	United States

Auto Racing

F1 World Champions

Year	Driver	Points	Constructor	Points
1950	Nino Farina	30	—	—
1951	Juan Manuel Fangio	31	—	—

1952	Alberto Ascari	36	—	—
1953	Alberto Ascari	34.5	—	—
1954	Juan Manuel Fangio	42	—	—
1955	Juan Manuel Fangio	40	—	—
1956	Juan Manuel Fangio	30	—	—
1957	Juan Manuel Fangio	40	—	—
1958	Mike Hawthorn	42	Vanwall	48
1959	Jack Brabham	31	Cooper/Climax	40
1960	Jack Brabham	43	Cooper/Climax	48
1961	Phil Hill	34	Ferrari	40
1962	Graham Hill	42	BRM	42
1963	Jim Clark	54	Lotus/Climax	54
1964	John Surtees	40	Ferrari	45
1965	Jim Clark	54	Lotus/Climax	54
1966	Jack Brabham	42	Brabham/Repco	42
1967	Denny Hulme	51	Brabham/Repco	63
1968	Graham Hill	48	Lotus/Ford	62
1969	Jackie Stewart	63	Matra/Ford	66
1970	Jochen Rindt	45	Lotus/Ford	59
1971	Jackie Stewart	62	Tyrell/Ford	73
1972	Emerson Fittipaldi	61	Lotus/Ford	61
1973	Jackie Stewart	71	Lotus/Ford	92
1974	Emerson Fittipaldi	55	McLaren/Ford	73
1975	Niki Lauda	64.5	Ferrari	72.5
1976	James Hunt	69	Ferrari	83
1977	Niki Lauda	72	Ferrari	95
1978	Mario Andretti	64	Lotus/Ford	86
1979	Jody Scheckter	51	Ferrari	113
1980	Alan Jones	67	Williams/Ford	120
1981	Nelson Piquet	50	Williams/Ford	95
1982	Keke Rosberg	44	Ferrari	74
1983	Nelson Piquet	59	Ferrari	89
1984	Nikki Lauda	72	McLaren/TAG	143.5
1985	Alain Prost	73	McLaren/TAG	90
1986	Alain Prost	72	Williams/Honda	141
1987	Nelson Piquet	73	Williams/Honda	137
1988	Ayrton Senna	90	McLaren/Honda	199
1989	Alain Prost	76	McLaren/Honda	141
1990	Ayrton Senna	78	McLaren/Honda	121
1991	Ayrton Senna	96	McLaren/Honda	139
1992	Nigel Mansell	108	Williams/Renault	164
1993	Alain Prost	99	Williams/Renault	168

1994	Michael Schumacher	92	Williams/Renault	118
1995	Michael Schumacher	102	Benetton/Renault	137
1996	Damon Hil	l97	Williams/Renault	175
1997	Jacques Villeneuve	81	Williams/Renault	123
1998	Mika Häkkinen	100	McLaren/Mercedes	156
1999	Mika Häkkinen	76	Ferrari	128
2000	Michael Schumacher	108	Ferrari	170
2001	Michael Schumacher	123	Ferrari	179
2002	Michael Schumacher	144	Ferrari	221
2003	Michael Schumacher	93	Ferrari	158
2004	Michael Schumacher	148	Ferrari	262
2005	Fernando Alonso	133	Renault	191
2006	Fernando Alonso	134	Renault	206
2007	Kimi Räikkönen	110	Ferrari	204
2008	Lewis Hamilton	98	Ferrari	172

NASCAR Champions

Year	Driver	Points
1949	Red Byron	842.5
1950	Bill Rexford	1959
1951	Herb Thomas	4208.45
1952	Tim Flock	6858.5
1953	Herb Thomas	8460
1954	Lee Petty	8649
1955	Tim Flock	9596
1956	Buck Baker	9272
1957	Buck Baker	10716
1958	Lee Petty	12232
1959	Lee Petty	11792
1960	Rex White	21164
1961	Ned Jarrett	27272
1962	Joe Weatherly	30836
1963	Joe Weatherly	33398
1964	Richard Petty	40252
1965	Ned Jarrett	38824
1966	David Pearson	35638
1967	Richard Petty	42472
1968	David Pearson	3499
1969	David Pearson	4170
1970	Bobby Isaac	3911

1971	Richard Petty	4435
1972	Richard Petty	8701.4
1973	Benny Parsons	7173.8
1974	Richard Petty	5037.75
1975	Richard Petty	4783
1976	Cale Yarborough	4644
1977	Cale Yarborough	5000
1978	Cale Yarborough	4841
1979	Richard Petty	4830
1980	Dale Earnhardt	4661
1981	Darrell Waltrip	4880
1982	Darrell Waltrip	4489
1983	Bobby Allison	4667
1984	Terry Labonte	4508
1985	Darrell Waltrip	4292
1986	Dale Earnhardt	4468
1987	Dale Earnhardt	4696
1988	Bill Elliott	4488
1989	Rusty Wallace	4176
1990	Dale Earnhardt	4430
1991	Dale Earnhardt	4287
1992	Alan Kulwicki	4078
1993	Dale Earnhardt	4526
1994	Dale Earnhardt	4694
1995	Jeff Gordon	4614
1996	Terry Labonte	4657
1997	Jeff Gordon	4710
1998	Jeff Gordon	5328
1999	Dale Jarrett	5262
2000	Bobby Labonte	5130
2001	Jeff Gordon	5112
2002	Tony Stewart	4800
2003	Matt Kenseth	5022
2004	Kurt Busch	6506
2005	Tony Stewart	6533
2006	Jimmie Johnson	6475
2007	Jimmie Johnson	6723
2008	Jimmie Johnson	6684

Indy 500 Champions

Year	Winner
1911	Ray Harroun
1912	Joe Dawson
1913	Jules Goux
1914	René Thomas
1915	Ralph DePalma
1916	Dario Resta
1917–18	No race held due to WWI
1919	Howdy Wilcox
1920	Gaston Chevrolet
1921	Tommy Milton
1922	Jimmy Murphy
1923	Tommy Milton
1924	L.L. Corum and Joe Boyer
1925	Pete DePaolo
1926	Frank Lockhart
1927	George Souders
1928	Louis Meyer
1929	Ray Keech
1930	Billy Arnold
1931	Louis Schneider
1932	Fred Frame
1933	Louis Meyer
1934	Bill Cummings
1935	Kelly Petillo
1936	Louis Meyer
1937	Wilbur Shaw
1938	Floyd Roberts
1939	Wilbur Shaw
1940	Wilbur Shaw
1941	Floyd Davis and Mauri Rose
1942–45	No race held due to WWII
1946	George Robson
1947	Mauri Rose
1948	Mauri Rose
1949	Bill Holland
1950	Johnnie Parsons
1951	Lee Wallard
1952	Troy Ruttman
1953	Bill Vukovich

1954	Bill Vukovich
1955	Bob Sweikert
1956	Pat Flaherty
1957	Sam Hanks
1958	Jimmy Bryan
1959	Rodger Ward
1960	Jim Rathmann
1961	A.J Foyt
1962	Rodger Ward
1963	Parnelli Jones
1964	A.J Foyt
1965	Jim Clark
1966	Graham Hill
1967	A.J Foyt
1968	Bobby Unser
1969	Mario Andretti
1970	Al Unser
1971	Al Unser
1972	Mark Donohue
1973	Gordon Johncock
1974	Johnny Rutherford
1975	Bobby Unser
1976	Johnny Rutherford
1977	A.J Foyt
1978	Al Unser
1979	Rick Mears
1980	Johnny Rutherford
1981	Bobby Unser
1982	Gordon Johncock
1983	Tom Sneva
1984	Rick Mears
1985	Danny Sullivan
1986	Bobby Rahal
1987	Al Unser
1988	Rick Mears
1989	Emerson Fittipaldi
1990	Arie Luyendyk
1991	Rick Mears
1992	Al Unser Jr.
1993	Emerson Fittipaldi
1994	Al Unser Jr.
1995	Jacques Villeneuve

1996	Buddy Lazier
1997	Arie Luyendyk
1998	Eddie Cheever Jr.
1999	Kenny Brack
2000	Juan Pablo Montoya
2001	Helio Castroneves
2002	Helio Castroneves
2003	Gil de Ferran
2004	Buddy Rice
2005	Dan Wheldon
2006	Sam Hornish Jr.
2007	Dario Franchitti
2008	Scott Dixon
2009	Helio Castroneves

Boxing and Wrestling

Boxing Heavyweight Champions

Reign began	Reign ended	Champion	Recognition
August 29, 1885	September 7, 1892	John L. Sullivan	Universal
September 7, 1892	March 17, 1897	James J. Corbett	Universal
March 17, 1897	June 9, 1899	Bob Fitzsimmons	Universal
June 9, 1899	May 13, 1905	James J. Jeffries	Universal
July 3, 1905	February 23, 1906	Marvin Hart	Universal
February 23, 1906	December 26, 1908	Tommy Burns	Universal
December 26, 1908	April 5, 1915	Jack Johnson	Universal
April 5, 1915	July 4, 1919	Jess Willard	Universal
July 4, 1919	September 23, 1926	Jack Dempsey	Universal
September 23, 1926	July 31, 1928	Gene Tunney	Universal
June 12, 1930	June 21, 1932	Max Schmeling	Universal
June 21, 1932	June 29, 1933	Jack Sharkey	Universal
June 29, 1933	June 14, 1934	Primo Carnera	Universal
June 14, 1934	June 13, 1935	Max Baer	Universal
June 13, 1935	June 22, 1937	James J. Braddock	Universal
June 22, 1937	March 1, 1949	Joe Louis	Universal
June 22, 1949	September 27, 1950	Ezzard Charles	NBA
June 6, 1950	June 16, 1951	Lee Savold	EBU
September 27, 1950	June 16, 1951	Ezzard Charles	NBA & NYSAC
June 16, 1951	July 18, 1951	Ezzard Charles	Universal

July 18, 1951	September 23, 1952	Jersey Joe Walcott	Universal
September 23, 1952	April 27, 1956	Rocky Marciano	Universal
November 30, 1956	June 26, 1959	Floyd Patterson	Universal
June 26, 1959	June 20, 1960	Ingemar Johansson	Universal
June 20, 1960	September 25, 1962	Floyd Patterson	Universal
September 25, 1962	February 25, 1964	Sonny Liston	Universal
February 25, 1964	June 19, 1964	Cassius Clay (Muhammad Ali)	Universal
June 19, 1964	February 6, 1967	Cassius Clay (Muhammad Ali)	WBC
March 5, 1965	February 6, 1967	Ernie Terrell	WBA & NYSAC
February 6, 1967	April 29, 1967	Muhammad Ali	Universal
April 29, 1967	March, 1969	Muhammad Ali	WBC
March 4, 1968	February 16, 1970	Joe Frazier	NYSAC
April 28, 1968	February 16, 1970	Jimmy Ellis	WBA
February 16, 1970	January 22, 1973	Joe Frazier	Universal
January 22, 1973	October 30, 1974	George Foreman	Universal
October 30, 1974	February 15, 1978	Muhammad Ali	Universal
February 15, 1978	March 18, 1978	Leon Spinks	Universal
March 18, 1978	September 15, 1978	Leon Spinks	WBA
March 18, 1978	June 9, 1978	Ken Norton	WBC
June 9, 1978	December 11, 1983	Larry Holmes	WBC
September 15, 1978	April 27, 1979	Muhammad Ali	WBA
October 20, 1979	March 31, 1980	John Tate	WBA
March 31, 1980	December 10, 1982	Mike Weaver	WBA
December 10, 1982	September 23, 1983	Michael Dokes	WBA
September 23, 1983	December 1, 1984	Gerrie Coetzee	WBA
December 11, 1983	September 21, 1985	Larry Holmes	IBF
March 9, 1984	August 31, 1984	Tim Witherspoon	WBC
August 31, 1984	March 22, 1986	Pinklon Thomas	WBC
December 1, 1984	April 29, 1985	Greg Page	WBA
April 29, 1985	January 17, 1986	Tony Tubbs	WBA
September 21, 1985	February 19, 1987	Michael Spinks	IBF
January 17, 1986	December 12, 1986	Tim Witherspoon	WBA
March 22, 1986	November 22, 1986	Trevor Berbick	WBC
November 22, 1986	March 7, 1987	Mike Tyson	WBC
December 12, 1986	March 7, 1987	James "Bonecrusher" Smith	WBA
March 7, 1987	August 1, 1987	Mike Tyson	WBA, WBC
May 30, 1987	August 1, 1987	Tony Tucker	IBF
August 1, 1987	August 13, 1989	Mike Tyson	IBF, WBA & WBC
May 6, 1989	January 11, 1991	Francesco Damiani	WBO
August 13, 1989	February 10, 1990	Mike Tyson	Universal
February 10, 1990	October 25, 1990	James "Buster" Douglas	IBF, WBA & WBC
October 25, 1990	November 13, 1992	Evander Holyfield	IBF, WBA & WBC

January 11, 1991	December 24, 19913	Ray Mercer	WBO
May 15, 1992	February 3, 19933	Michael Moorer	WBO
November 13, 1992	December 14, 19923	Riddick Bowe	IBF, WBA & WBC
December 14, 1992	November 6, 1993	Riddick Bowe	IBF & WBA
December 14, 1992	September 24, 1994	Lennox Lewis	WBC
June 7, 1993	October 29, 1993	Tommy Morrison	WBO
October 29, 1993	March 19, 1994	Michael Bentt	WBO
November 6, 1993	April 22, 1994	Evander Holyfield	IBF & WBA
March 19, 1994	March 11, 1995	Herbie Hide	WBO
April 22, 1994	November 5, 1994	Michael Moorer	IBF & WBA
September 24, 1994	September 2, 1995	Oliver McCall	WBC
November 5, 1994	March 4, 19953	George Foreman	IBF & WBA
March 4, 1995	June 28, 19953	George Foreman	IBF
March 11, 1995	May 1, 19961	Riddick Bowe	WBO
April 8, 1995	September 7, 1996	Bruce Seldon	WBA
September 2, 1995	March 16, 1996	Frank Bruno	WBC
March 16, 1996	September 7, 1996	Mike Tyson	WBC
June 22, 1996	November 8, 1997	Michael Moorer	IBF
June 29, 1996	February 17, 19971	Henry Akinwande	WBO
September 7, 1996	September 24, 19961	Mike Tyson	WBA & WBC
September 24, 1996	November 9, 1996	Mike Tyson	WBA
November 9, 1996	November 8, 1997	Evander Holyfield	WBA
February 7, 1997	November 13, 1999	Lennox Lewis	WBC
June 28, 1997	June 26, 1999	Herbie Hide	WBO
November 8, 1997	November 13, 1999	Evander Holyfield	IBF & WBA
June 26, 1999	April 1, 2000	Vitali Klitschko	WBO
November 13, 1999	April 29, 20003	Lennox Lewis	IBF, WBA & WBC
April 1, 2000	October 14, 2000	Chris Byrd	WBO
April 29, 2000	April 22, 2001	Lennox Lewis	IBF & WBC
August 12, 2000	March 3, 2001	Evander Holyfield	WBA
October 14, 2000	March 8, 2003	Wladimir Klitschko	WBO
March 3, 2001	March 1, 2003	John Ruiz	WBA
April 22, 2001	November 17, 2001	Hasim Rahman	IBF & WBC
November 17, 2001	September 5, 20021	Lennox Lewis	IBF & WBC
September 5, 2002	February 6, 20042	Lennox Lewis	WBC
December 14, 2002	April 22, 2006	Chris Byrd	IBF
March 1, 2003	February 20, 20041	Roy Jones Jr.	WBA
March 8, 2003	October 9, 2003	Corrie Sanders	WBO
February 20, 2004	December 17, 2005	John Ruiz	WBA
April 10, 2004	April 1, 2006	Lamon Brewster	WBO
April 24, 2004	November 9, 2005	Vitali Klitschko	WBC
November 9, 2005	August 13, 2006	Hasim Rahman	WBC

December 17, 2005	April 15, 2007	Nikolay Valuev	WBA
April 1, 2006	November 4, 2006	Sergei Liakhovich	WBO
April 22, 2006	February 23, 2008	Wladimir Klitschko	IBF
August 13, 2006	March 8, 2008	Oleg Maskaev	WBC
April 15, 2007	July 4, 2008	Ruslan Chagaev	WBA
June 2, 2007	February 23, 2008	Sultan Ibragimov	WBO
February 23, 2008	present	Wladimir Klitschko	IBF, WBO & IBO
March 8, 2008	October 11, 2008	Samuel Peter	WBC
July 4, 20084	present	Ruslan Chagaev	WBA
August 30, 2008	present	Nikolay Valuev	WBA
October 11, 2008	present	Vitali Klitschko	WBC

NBA — National Boxing Association (became WBA)
EBU — European Boxing Union
NYSAC — New York State Athletic Commission
WBC — World Boxing Council
WBA — World Boxing Association (formerly NBA)
IBF — International Boxing Federation
WBO — World Boxing Organization

**question
and
feature list**

Hockey

Soccer

Football

Rugby

Baseball

Basketball

Lacrosse

Curling

Olympics

Tennis

Golf

Bowling

Running

Cycling

Skiing and Snowboarding

Auto Racing

Boxing and Wrestling

Winners and Champions